"*Power Grab* exposes the agenda of the Obama administration and its allies, from 'green jobs' to the cap-and-trade energy tax as ways to cram down the Left's long-held wish list of demands, and dream of 'organizing society.' Horner reveals what their rhetoric means, how the schemes work and what it all spells for you if they win. *Power Grab* lays bare the plan to replace your individual liberties with the state, securing the Left's dream of making decisions for you and your family: what you can drive, how you can live, and what sorts of jobs and future they deem acceptable for Americans."

—MARK LEVIN, bestselling author and
nationally syndicated radio host

"Chris Horner raises the red flag about the so-called 'green economy.' *Power Grab* shows the dark gray economic fallacies that lie behind the bright 'green' economic fairy tales, in a way everyone can understand, if while laughing between the tears."

—DR. GABRIEL CALZADA, professor of applied
environmental economics at King Juan Carlos University

"*Power Grab* exposes the incestuous relationships between the Obama administration and the piles of taxpayer money it wants to pipeline to the Big Green juggernaut consisting of Big Business and Big Labor. Horner shows that the green agenda isn't so much about a clean environment as it is about redistributing income from us to them."

—STEPHEN MOORE, member of the *Wall Street Journal*
editorial board and senior economics writer

"Chris Horner was right in his bestselling *The Politically Incorrect Guide™ to Global Warming and Environmentalism*. He was right in his book *Red Hot Lies* that exposed the cover-ups, lies, and intimidation of the global-warming alarmists. And he's right again in his new book *Power Grab*, which exposes what the extremists are really after: power over you, your wallet, and even your right to self-government. *Power Grab* is essential reading for fighting back."

—CONGRESSWOMAN MICHELE BACHMANN

"The jury-rigged 'consensus' propping up the climate change-industrial complex is falling apart in no small part due to the efforts of truth-tellers such as Chris Horner. Years from now, people genuinely concerned with the environment will look back on the hysteria of this time and sadly reflect on just how much the mad rush to subsidize foolish energy choices and distort markets distracted us from genuine environmental and human concerns. Luckily, it looks as if common sense is being brought to bear on these issues and Chris' book is in the vanguard of that development."

—JOHN FUND, Columnist, *Wall Street Journal*

POWER GRAB

POWER GRAB

HOW OBAMA'S GREEN POLICIES WILL STEAL YOUR FREEDOM AND BANKRUPT AMERICA

CHRISTOPHER C. HORNER

Since 1947
REGNERY
PUBLISHING, INC.
An Eagle Publishing Company • Washington, DC

Library of Congress Cataloging-in-Publication Data
Horner, Chris.
  Power grab / by Chris Horner.
     p. cm.
  Includes bibliographical references and index.
  ISBN 978-1-59698-599-5
  1. Environmental policy--United States. 2. Energy policy--United States. 3. Obama, Barack. 4. United States--Politics and government--2009- 5. United States--Economic policy--2009- I. Title.
  GE180.H65 2010
  363.7'05610973--dc22

                                          2010009080

Published in the United States by
Regnery Publishing, Inc.
One Massachusetts Avenue, NW
Washington, DC 20001
www.regnery.com

Manufactured in the United States of America

10 9 8 7 6 5 4 3 2 1

Books are available in quantity for promotional or premium use. Write to Director of Special Sales, Regnery Publishing, Inc., One Massachusetts Avenue NW, Washington, DC 20001, for information on discounts and terms or call (202) 216-0600.

Distributed to the trade by:
Perseus Distribution
387 Park Avenue South
New York, NY 10016

With mange tak to my angel Susanne
who makes all of my work possible.
And to William Christopher, Daddy loves you.

No nation has ever taxed and
regulated its way to greatness.
We won't be the first.

CONTENTS

CHAPTER 1

HOW OBAMA'S GREEN POLICIES WILL STEAL YOUR FREEDOM AND BANKRUPT AMERICA

I t's the year 2015. Just around the corner, really. Barack Obama's various policies imposed in the name of "energy independence," "clean energy," and of course "the environment" are now really being felt. The mere threat of their being imposed has long since scared off investment in needed infrastructure, led to planned projects being shelved, and caused some that were underway to be mothballed. Obama's policies have locked up land and sealed off domestic resources, and enabled his "green" pressure group allies to do even more. Now, some industries can't even perform maintenance for fear of triggering EPA investigation.

These consequences were foreseeable. After all, investors had Europe's experience with these policies to warn them. Those who can have gone elsewhere. There were plenty of countries to choose from. China. India. Just over the border in Mexico, for example. Others, like those workers who lost their jobs or were never hired to begin with, weren't so fortunate.

One Monday you wake up to discover that nothing works. Each time this happens, you're a little less surprised. Still, it's never easy. Though once abundant and accessible with the flip of a switch, electricity supply has failed to keep up with demand and is becoming even more scarce. Electricity, natural gas, and gasoline have all been made less available as a direct, intended result of Obama and his allies' agenda. Energy is unreliable now. You know this means a cold shower: scarce or even no power means that things you took for granted are now luxuries. Those living a little further out who rely on a well and an electronic pump have got no water at all.

This is mostly an inconvenience, like how you now live in a small apartment, just as the anti-energy zealots want you to, though lack of reliable power does cause problems—such as the elevator failing to run. This is somewhat more than inconvenient for your elderly neighbors. But the problems don't stop there. Today, you'll be walking to work, too. After that last episode with the traffic lights out, well, that's no way to start your week. Besides, after Obama administration officials pursued their vow to bring our gasoline prices in line with Europe's—even though our society was designed around certain freedoms and automobility—it simply isn't something you can afford on a daily basis. The sirens in the distance seem to have begun early today.

This reminds you that your sister was scheduled to have surgery tomorrow. Hospitals, like schools, and senior citizen homes, all feel the pain of these policies. More power interruptions mean her surgery will get bumped, and she will have to reschedule—again. Soon, your doctor worries, storing blood and medicines will suffer as it does in Third World countries, whose different form of political corruption has also kept them with insufficient power.

You've learned to buy small quantities of milk and other perishables, far more often, because there's no telling how long the refrigerator will stay cold. Besides, like the merchants, you have been forced into using smaller, more expensive units. The price of food has increased along with the price of energy, as energy is needed every step of the way as food is grown, harvested, transported, kept fresh until purchase, and then prepared.

The impacts of unreliable and otherwise insufficient energy are infinite and, to most Americans today, unimaginable. On this fictitious Monday morning without power, your life considered normal today would be a thing of the past, and nothing that could be recaptured easily. Without power, you can't use the microwave; cooking in any form is more expensive and, of course, it's a different task making your family's breakfast in the early morning dark. Just as the ideologues demanded, you've been coerced into a life more like that of so many others who suffer living under the ideal of state-imposed scarcity.

Of course, just as there's little heat in winter, there's little air conditioning in summer. The power company is now able to withhold some of the energy you think you need, just as the president's "Energy and Climate Czar" promised was the administration's goal.[1] It apparently didn't occur to us to ask why a power company would want to do that. Power companies withold power when they are forced to, either by law or physical shortage. When there's not enough to go around, thanks to that agenda premised in "spreading the wealth around," this is what happens.

It's strange that companies like GE, whose old business model led to such classic advertising as "This is the hand that turned on the light," helped lobby an agenda into place that, in the year 2015, will leave some reading by candlelight.

It is difficult to even imagine life without reliable energy on hand, life so unlike the world promoted in that ad by GE when it seemed to have principles, not just a business plan. But you had better start trying—because if Barack Obama has his way, this scenario will become daily life in America. The goal of Obama's "green" policies is to make the cost of producing today's energy from oil and coal and other politically disfavored sources so high that companies quit doing it, and divert their resources into uneconomic (and unreliable) "green" technologies.

Barack Obama tells us that his "green" policies will create jobs in America. Good jobs. Manufacturing jobs. The kind of jobs our politicians assure us they desire to create and keep. And to a certain extent, his policies have done so. However, we have Europe to thank for adopting Obama-style policies that create United States jobs, not our new president. After all, it is Europe's disastrous "cap-and-trade"[2] and other "green jobs"[3] schemes so adored by Obama that created, for example, 175 steel jobs at North American Stainless in Carroll County, Kentucky.[4] For now.

Those jobs were exported here in 2004 by North American's European parent company, Acerinox, after Chief Executive Officer Victoriano Muñoz announced he could no longer justify long-term, capital- and energy-intensive investments while burdened with the new environmental regulations imposed in Europe. Because the United States has not adopted a "cap-and-trade" system, it was an attractive destination for these manufacturing jobs. Incredibly, though, the American political Left favors adopting the same regulations in America that resulted in job loss in Europe—not despite their detrimental economic effects, which Europe is experiencing, but *because of them*.

As Obama admitted in a moment of candor, "Under my plan of a cap and trade system, electricity rates would necessarily skyrocket.... Regardless of what I say about whether coal is good or bad, because I'm capping greenhouse gases, coal power plants, you know, natural gas, you name it, whatever the plants were, whatever the industry was, they would have to retrofit their operations." Obama also let on that the new regulations "will cost money. [Businesses] will pass that money on to consumers."[5] He also mentioned that "this will also raise billions of dollars." The social agenda will be paid for by the imposition of energy scarcity—another of their ideological demands.

Under Obama's economic and energy plans, conventional energy is punished by government policy in order to force the adoption of new, Obama-favored technologies. These plans will force us into energy poverty, a return to government-inspired uncompetitiveness, and a surrender of individual and economic liberties.

Modern environmentalism in a nutshell sounds something like this: impose energy taxes that serve as a rationing scheme (the "cap"), along with mandates of what sort of energy people can use, and in what amount. Environmentalists seek to use the state to create scarcity in order to further impose their will over our lives.

If the Obama administration has its way, we will knowingly repeat the mistakes of other countries that rushed to adopt crippling energy policies. If only we paid heed to those mistakes, instead of trying to force an ideology on a country that Obama and his team believe must be "fundamentally transformed."[6] Spain's Acerinox made the decision to export its growth to America and South Africa back when it still appeared unlikely either country would ever do anything so stupid as replicating Europe's competitiveness-killing debacle. And they were right, at least about South Africa, which continues to reject such measures. Poverty does sometimes help place certain frivolities in perspective, after all. But with Barack Obama's election, the United States is headed for punitive mandates, higher taxes, and the expenditure of billions of dollars of the taxpayers' hard-earned money to politically design an economy premised on uneconomic but politically favored "investments" (as Obama insists on calling wealth transfers from the taxpayers into environmental boondoggles).

It would be one thing if these measures actually helped alleviate alleged global warming that supposedly threatens our well being. But they don't. As I explained in *Red Hot Lies*,[7] no proposal ever tabled would, according to anyone, detectably impact global temperature— the temperature that computer model projections claim man is escalating, though recent cooling and the return of severe winters would seem to repudiate the computers' claims of warming. And even if emissions reductions could have some impact according to these fatally flawed models, they would be made illusory by the "offset" schemes that reward lobbying constituencies while derailing the agenda's supposed purpose of curtailing emissions (detailed in later chapters).

The real issue Americans should be concerned with is the outcome of these "green" schemes: the transfer of your liberties and wealth to the state, and the transfer of jobs to other countries. For example, when the United Kingdom's largest steelmaker, Corus, announced in late 2009 it would close its massive Redcar operations in Teesside, it moved jobs to India, not the United States, because India is a safer haven from "climate" economic edicts.[8] India has decided to forgo further institutionalization of energy poverty. But its official position is that it will pursue massive new sources of energy production.[9]

Likewise, Acerinox's new CEO confided to a friend of mine in mid 2009 that, if America follows through on Obama's threats, the company will send its growth to Malaysia, employing Malaysians instead of Americans. Here we see one net effect of Barack Obama's policy obsessions: they will send jobs to China, Brazil, Indonesia, South Korea, and Mexico, rather than the United States.

Steel, coal, and other heavy industries do not fit into Obama's vision. At the end of his campaign for president, Barack Obama boasted, "We are five days away from fundamentally transforming the United States of America."[10] He wasn't blowing political smoke for the benefit of his supporters. He was telling us all who he is and his plans for us, as he affirmed even before his inauguration.

Barack Obama's radicalism runs deep. When he crowed in San Francisco, "under my plan of a cap and trade system, electricity prices would necessarily skyrocket,"[11] he meant it. And it's not just electricity prices that he wanted to skyrocket, but the costs of politically disfavored "fossil fuels." As everything has the cost of energy embedded in it, costs will rise across the board. The result of these policies will be to crowd millions more toward energy poverty and dependence upon the state. That, too, is by design.

As the Left sees it, if you do not coerce people out of their wretched levels of energy use, they will not change their lifestyles. In the Left's view, these lifestyles must be changed because they are "unsustainable."

Just as the worldview of Obama and his movement blinds them to the truth about the United States, they fail to see the tremendous and overwhelming good of abundant energy—particularly oil, coal, and gas. Access to energy benefitted billions of people as it spread around the world during the past century. Massive reductions in drudgery, poverty, and disease flowed as wealth was created as a direct result. Richer countries became able and willing to assign economic values to environmental protection, to chasing parts per million and even billion. Yet in the U.S., abundant energy, and of course, (other peoples') wealth are viewed as instruments of havoc and even doom to be curbed, their influence diminished. In the words of *Spiked* magazine's Brendan O'Neill, the Left's version of environmentalism "speak[s] to a view of humans as ultimately destructive and of our breakthroughs as gigantic follies that must be decommissioned."[12]

So we should not be surprised that, once installed, the Obama administration hurried some noted radicals into positions not requiring Senate scrutiny, while delaying filling key senior slots. Some of the most extreme had positions outright created for them. Coercive radicalism is what this administration is all about. As certain individuals tapped to wield real power in this administration could not have gained Senate approval, and would have caused deep and lasting political harm in the process of trying, they were slipped in the back door. The appointment of departed Anthony K. "Van" Jones, for example, did not "[reveal] a lapse in the administration's vetting procedures,"[13] as the *Washington Post* reported. Jones, like others, was selected precisely because of his radicalism, not in spite of it, and was dropped only when that radicalism was exposed. The Obama team is smart enough to know that much of its agenda needs to fly under the radar of public scrutiny. Carol Browner, director of the newly created White House Office of Energy and Climate Change Policy, is another who stood zero chance of surviving public scrutiny. Now she lords over cabinet-level staff and often appears at Obama's elbow, revealing her prominent policy role.[14]

America has the greatest energy reserves in the entire world, and it is these resources that ensure our liberty. Though for public consumption President Obama has claimed, "What I think we need to do is increase our domestic energy production,"[15] and "I believe in the need for increased oil production. We're going to have to explore new ways to get more oil, and that includes offshore drilling,"[16] these statements are followed by qualifications that render them meaningless.

In fact, Obama is ensuring that we can't exploit our own resources by placing so many of them off-limits, citing "environmental" concerns. In addition to imposing a delay on an offshore drilling plan ready to go into effect in his first year, and otherwise sealing off domestic oil production, the Obama administration is working with congressional liberals to slam the door on massive natural gas discoveries.

But we'll always have windmills, they say. Except, as you'll see, when we won't.

While China, Russia, and other countries are quick to invest in resource production in Canada and off our shores, the Obama administration has blocked some of these sources from American use and is working to ban others. When China made a bid for ownership of the California oil company Unocal in 2005, it sent policymakers into paroxysms of fear for our national and energy security.[17] But hardly anyone noticed that China has since gained control of far more important resources in our back yard, all while the Obama administration makes us less safe, less secure, and ever more dependent upon foreign sources of energy.

At the same time, Team Obama is teaming with big business, unions, and green pressure groups in an unholy alliance to advance an agenda relieving you of your wealth and freedoms, to their enrichment, in a collaboration designed to move decisions from individual producers and consumers to the federal government. As part of this perverse game, the Left pulls for "green" energy production and then blocks that very same production on environmental grounds or until it can use such projects to enrich favored unions and companies.

Obama's seizure of "green" issues to impose an unadvertised Statist agenda is by no means new; only the boldness and outrageousness of his radicalism are. Obama is orchestrating the largest-scale corporate-government alliance in our nation's history. Some of America's biggest companies are heavily invested in promoting Obama's agenda. Some companies are clearly just in it for the short-term windfall. Yet some among these allies also don't mind the sort of central planning Obama favors—so long as they are the beneficiaries, and their competitors aren't.

Washington moves at a snail's pace except when it is stealing your freedoms—and that is the danger here: freedoms lost are hard to regain, taxes imposed are hard to repeal and, government programs, offices, and departments are nearly impossible to abolish. It took until 2006 for Congress to get around to repealing the 3 percent telephone excise tax originally imposed (at 1 percent) on "the rich" to pay for the Spanish-American War—a 4-month conflict in 1898.[18] Unlike a telephone tax slowly sponging off an ever-expanding universe of "the rich" for 108 years, it's far from clear that the United States can survive a prolonged case of energy socialism.

That's why this book, while about energy, is ultimately about power—its acquisition and abuse, how it is attained, and how Obama's agenda is about stripping you of yours.

America is blessed with vast energy resources. Energy is the engine of our economy and the guarantor of our freedom and safety. But Team Obama believes that the days of abundant energy, which distinguishes us from societies that are less free, must come to an end.

When Republicans seized control of the House of Representatives in the 1994 election, it was in part because of the unpopular energy policies of Vice President Al Gore, including his failed 1993 "BTU"

(British Thermal Unit) tax that would have taxed energy consumption based on the sort of government-favored technology that the Obama administration favors. Gore himself admitted it helped the Republicans.[19] One thing the Left learned from this is the need for subterfuge and to cut deals with pressure groups, labor, and corporate allies.[20]

The "climate" agenda, the culmination of "going green," requires privation that no free society would willingly accept. It is anti-freedom and anti-wealth creation. It is not about environmental protection and most certainly not about the climate. It is about taking your power and your wealth and giving it to the government—and its accomplices. And it's not just about endorsing the federal government; it is about empowering a global bureaucracy. It is one manifestation of what columnist Mark Steyn calls "the hollowness of the modern multicultural West and the search for alternative, globalized identities."[21]

Give the Left time, and it will inflict more damage on our economy and the power of the United States (and our industrialized West) than our enemies could hope to inflict through years of asymmetrical physical warfare.

REALLY BIG GOVERNMENT OBAMA

The Left's agenda is grounded in the idea that we either accept its "global governance" or risk environmental apocalypse. "Global governance" is not to be confused with *a global government*, though clearly the proponents of using "global warming" as an excuse for abdicating liberty and sovereignty would not object to that, either. Both result in the curtailing of democracy, democracy being something that the "global governance" crowd thinks we can do without, too. In

2000, then-French president Jacques Chirac boasted that the Kyoto Protocol on "climate change" would bring with it more beneficial "global governance."[22] Former U.S. vice president Al Gore repeated this desire as recently as the summer of 2009, demanding we recognize the peril of our failure to confront promised, if elusive, global warming with the imposition of supranational governance. But if you scare them, Gore assured us, it will come: "[I]t is the awareness [of environmental catastrophe] itself that will drive the change and one of the ways it will drive the change is through global governance and global agreements."[23]

Meeting the challenge of "global warming" became the emergency reason for European member state governments to approve the European "Constitution" when it began lagging in popular support. Furthermore, in the autumn of 2009, Europe's newly minted High Representative Herman Van Rompuy announced, "the climate conference in Copenhagen is another step towards the global management of our planet."[24]

So either individual nation states cannot be trusted with certain issues because they might actually consider their own national interests, or certain issues must be reshaped or even invented so as to set up that creepiest of all calls, one for "global management of our planet." International bureaucrats need only consult their own ideological predilection that they know best. In *Red Hot Lies*, I cited numerous luminaries of the eco-left and its affiliated industries laying plain their commitment to impose their will upon us all, regardless of the sacrifices to individual liberties that may be required. In fact, they acknowledge that stripping you of your freedoms is so important that suspending democratic decision-making might be the only way to bring the larger "green" agenda about.[25] As one green recently blurted out, in an interview on the BBC, "there is a very strong green fascism in much of the environmental world. I've heard it said at meetings I've been at—that climate change is so important—democracy has to be sacrificed."[26] P 311

A colleague of mine passed along a "tweet" from a former classmate of his in England, Rupert Read, who is now a leading light in the UK Green Party. In it, Read declared, "The great political task of our times: *Not* raising the 'living standards' of the poorest, but rather: narrowing the rich-poor gap."[27] Think about that one. It isn't poverty, the condition in which too many live, which is the problem, it's that some live too well, and it should all be evened out a bit. The rich world—principally meaning the United States—needs somehow to be brought to heel.

Among American elites, *New York Times* columnist Thomas Friedman pined for some form of China's enlightened despotism in the United States. Indeed, this is wistfully dreamt of by green activists and other liberal ideologues because they, like Friedman, are just certain that the world is flat, hot, and crowded. The problem continues to be all of us other people, and our reckless exploitation of freedom. As if to remove all doubt, it was a series of anti-capitalist rants at the December 2009 Copenhagen talks to strike a "Kyoto II" treaty that generated the most enthusiasm.[28] Out in the streets of Copenhagen, among the activists, the hammer-and-sickle banners were prominent. I experienced the same phenomenon when attending another related confab, the Johannesburg Summit 2002 (officially, the World Summit on Sustainable Development), where thugs like Robert Mugabe of Zimbabwe and Fidel Castro of Cuba were the biggest hits among the self-styled green movement.

And Barack Obama has openly placed himself at their service.

CONTROL FREAK

The purpose of the entire "green" enterprise is obvious and, if it were not, we need only look to the comments of Rajendra Pachauri, head of the UN's Intergovernmental Panel on Climate Change, who told the UK's left-wing *Observer* newspaper that prosperous lifestyles of people in the West simply had to be curtailed. To bring this about, he advocated imposition of what even the *Observer* called "radical" taxes, stipulating as well that automobile use must be "curbed" by the state—or some other authority (like the UN).[29]

When pondering the advice of this sage so influential with our president, also consider the welcome he received from a member of the European Parliament, Roger Helmer, when Pachauri joined noted expert Paul McCartney in a special session to hector the European Parliament about eating meat. Meat, as you must know, comes from dangerously flatulent cows who threaten the climate. As Helmer facetiously noted,

> Dr. Pachauri is especially well qualified to advise on climate issues. He commenced his tertiary education at The Indian Railways Institute of Mechanical and Electrical Engineering in Jamalpur, Bihar. He began his career at the Diesel Locomotive Works in Varanasi. He later went to America where he took a Master's degree in Industrial Engineering, and a joint PhD in Industrial Engineering and Economics from the North Carolina State University. Critics may carp that his education bears little relation to climate issues, to Climatology or Atmospheric Physics, but he is nonetheless well placed to offer improbable solutions to highly speculative problems, and of course Paul McCartney is equally well-qualified in climate science.[30]

Then again, this agenda has never actually been about climate. It is about ideology and control—as in controlling others to conform to your ideology.

As columnist George Will noted, "[L]ong before climate change became another excuse for disparaging America's 'automobile culture,' many liberal intellectuals were bothered by the automobile. It subverted their agenda of expanding government—meaning their supervision of other peoples' lives."[31] The American Enterprise Institute's Nick Schulz spotted a spasm of candor from a scientist sympathetic to Pachauri's cause, one who has long played a leading role in promoting this agenda. Ken Caldeira blustered to *Yale Environment 360*, "I believe that we should be outlawing the production of devices that emit carbon dioxide."[32]

These measures are clearly just an excuse to seize your rights in the name of a planetary crisis that, in itself, was designed with the same end in mind.

As a halfway measure, Obama's Environmental Protection Agency chief put in context the federal government's takeover of American car companies (a takeover which, by chance, was announced with "climate Czar" Carol Browner standing prominently next to the president). Administrator Lisa Jackson revealed how this step was the natural response to free enterprise—not misbegotten government policies, of course—having gotten us all into this problems. Besides, "what this country needs is a single national road map that tells auto makers who are trying to become solvent again what kind of car it is they need to be designing and building for the American people."[33] This caused even an NPR reporter to ask whether that's really how Team Obama views the government and its role, prompting Jackson's insistence that individual actors and the market created the problems, so government direction was needed to get us out of them.[34]

Our current governing class tells us the state really had no hand in orchestrating the situation, after all.

Team Obama's efforts to "fundamentally transform the United States of America"[35] were immediate, widespread, and sweeping. The *National Journal* featured a debate about "livability" after someone there noticed that "the Obama administration and leading congressional Democrats appear to be making the creation of 'livable communities'... a central transportation policy goal."[36] However, the "livability" and "happiness" indexes fetishized by the Left are code for coerced inconvenience, discomfort, or merely sameness, trading off individuals' liberties to remove distinctions brought about by unfair quirks such as differences in ingenuity or hard work. But our superiors know that these differences are really only the product of a world in which the successful have won life's lottery, so the spoils need to be spread around a bit.

Livability and the like serve as the rationale for all manner of intrusions. *Innovation NewsBriefs* in October 2009 noted that it was "the Administration's intent to increase the federal role in shaping local development patterns and influencing travel behavior. 'Smart growth' planning and shifting more automobile travel to public transportation have been long-standing goals of progressive planners and assorted anti-sprawl activists, but these goals may now become a matter of federal policy under the Administration's 'livability' initiative."[37]

Secretary of Transportation Ray LaHood did Obama no favors by candidly defending against inquiries about this, stressing that it's no big deal. In fact, he pointed out, "about everything we do around here is government intrusion in peoples' lives."[38] (House Majority Whip James Clyburn helpfully added soon thereafter, "There's nothing in the Constitution that says that the federal government has anything to do with most of the stuff we do."[39] What a team.) In response to the serial intrusions of the federal government into land-use and other local decisions, George Will labeled LaHood the administration's Secretary of Behavior Modification.[40] On this front, there are also a couple of czars LaHood will have to answer to, as we shall see.

The scheming is easy to spot. The Manhattan Institute's Max Schulz pointed out that the House-passed cap-and-trade bill included the Left's catnip word "planning" sixty-nine times.[41]

Buy or sell a home? The global warming agenda has a few things to talk to you about first, inducing costly improvements you have to make before you can hand over the keys, all set forth in the House-passed global warming bill.[42] After the Obama administration bragged about its plans for more expensive, energy-efficient appliance models in new homes, an embarrassing EPA audit emerged "casting doubt on the greenhouse gas emissions reductions claimed by U.S. EPA's most significant climate program," according to trade-press outlet *Climate Wire*.[43] It seems that cheaper off-brand appliances met or exceeded the "EnergyStar"-labeled appliances favored by the Environmental Protection Agency.

Obama and his allies are unlikely to admit with any regularity that their real objectives are social engineering and curtailing your freedom. But that is the agenda, and it is discernable in many of their statements and most of their actions. And it's an agenda that will first require brainwashing the young, it seems, made necessary because, as the IPCC's Rajenda Pachauri told the *Observer*, the rest of us have been "corrupted" by prosperity and comfort.[44] Sadly, our own president agrees.

CHAPTER 2

RENEWABLE FOOLS

We are told by President Obama that we need to mandate politically correct energy sources just like Europe. Indeed, American liberals are infatuated with the idea of Europe's green mandates and other market socialism—viewed from the ivory tower or through the lens of the tourist. This is particularly true when it affords lefties the opportunity to despair of their own country. As we will address the Spanish and German mythologies promoted by Obama in some detail later, let us consider *New York Times* columnist, global warming alarmist, energy scold, and 11,400 square-foot, 7.5 bathroom mansion-dweller Thomas Friedman, who continues to write silly green things like this screed coinciding with the Kyoto II talks in Copenhagen:

As I listened to Denmark's minister of economic and business affairs describe how her country used higher energy taxes to stimulate innovation in green power and then recycled the tax revenues back to Danish industry to consumers to make it easier for them to make and buy the new clean technologies, it all sounded so, well, intelligent. . . . So I asked the Danish minister: "Tell me, what planet are you people from?" [Lene] Espersen laughed. But I didn't. How long are we Americans going to go on thinking that we can thrive in the 21st century when doing the optimal things—whether for energy, health care, education or the deficit—are "off the table."

Let us pause for a moment and remind ourselves that Friedman is crushed by our refusal to charge forward into the twenty-first century by going back to wind power. Think about it.

Friedman continued:

Sorry, but there are no good ideas proven to work in other democratic/capitalist societies that we can afford to shove off our table—not when we need to build a knowledge economy with good jobs and everyone else is trying to do the same.

"Already the green taxes here are quite high," said Espersen. "And even though we know this is not popular with business and industry, it has made all the difference for us. It forced our businesses to become more energy efficient and innovative, and this meant that, suddenly, we were inventing things nobody else was inventing because our businesses needed to be competitive."[1]

Espersen's math, which is straight from a leftist think tank white paper, is as follows: make electricity from disfavored sources really expensive, and spectacularly subsidized, politically favored electricity will in relative terms be made cost-competitive, which pain will in turn make you invent stuff and figure out how to be even more competitive. Notice the paucity of details (in the original, as well) about precisely what it is that high taxes forced the Danes to invent, or why we can't now use their miracle inventions, too. There's a reason for that.

First, the implication of much of what Espersen says is absurd when it isn't misleading, assuming Friedman excerpted it true to her arguments. Friedman's anti-anti-tax rant that followed indicates he fully understands the basic, academic theory of raising taxes to make people behave and calling it success. A theory which he liked, as people generally do who incessantly write in petulant disgust about how Americans don't pay enough for energy. But the part the credulous Friedman really gulped down was that bit about how Denmark "innovated" thanks to tax hikes, then gave some of the money back to allow people to afford the miracle energy innovations (like windmills), which—you should recall even if left unsaid by Espersen and her interlocutor—were so miraculous and innovative that they had to be mandated.

Had Friedman walked into the interview either with a better understanding of Denmark's system, or at least not having checked every journalistic instinct at Customs, he might also have drilled down a little—like the Danes who, thanks to drilling all over the North Sea, Greenland, and elsewhere in the Arctic, have tremendous oil and gas wealth to help underwrite their social experimentation. One Danish think-tanker I know says that the real lesson to take from

his country's experience is "drill, baby, drill!" (Someone bring Friedman the smelling salts.) So, shall we do that, too? This underwriting
from oil and gas revenue is in addition to taxes making Denmark's
household electricity rates (that President Obama might praise as
"skyrocketing") the highest in Europe,[2] four times what they are here
in the United States (and nearly three times what we pay for petrol).[3]
Not that they've reduced their carbon dioxide emissions, supposedly
the point of the whole, expensive affair. They haven't.[4]

Reading Friedman on Espersen, you may have mused, *Why, just
imagine how competitive* we *could be if we simply adopted whatever
miracle technologies Espersen hints are used by Danish industry, but
without the crushing energy tax burden* (which, Espersen implied, was
piled on to force industry to do what the state just knew they were
capable of doing, but were too stubborn to pursue). After all, if Denmark has now done the hard part for us, we can just grab their
competitiveness-enhancing tricks and trinkets and avoid the pain.

But her implication is false, and Friedman either did not know or
chose not to share with his readers that this burden is not, in fact,
placed on Danish industry, even if he teams with the minister to
imply that their shouldering it is proof of the ability of industry to be
competitive despite huge energy price hikes. In truth, Danish businesses are spared that electricity taxation burden—precisely because
it would be competitiveness-killing—by heaping it ever more puni-
tively on their customers: Danish families.[5] As Danish energy experts
have written, "In contrast and in order to keep Danish industry competitive, power to industry is hardly taxed at all."[6]

Clearly, either the Danish minister was embellishing because the
truth hurts, or Friedman was too busy to ask for details, engrossed in
pouting about the unpopularity among his countrymen of punitive

household energy taxes—which force the Danish masses into little, un-Friedman-like homes.

And of course, there are those other, staggering taxes Espersen did obliquely allude to, like a "value added tax" which, combined with other targeted "special duties" on automobiles, leave the Danes joking that it's a good thing they don't get all of the cars they pay for, because where would they put them?

It does not seem to have occurred to Friedman that the Danes are not jealously guarding their miracle inventions that could make us competitive and clean and blonde and morally superior, too. We certainly could elect to buy the windmills and whatever other "green" innovations the minister was too modest to cite. It would be cheaper for us to do so than for the Danes, because we learn from Thomas Friedman that they are having only some portion of their confiscated wealth returned to them, while we are not yet to the point of having that remaining portion of our wealth confiscated in the first place.

So, I suppose I join Mr. Friedman in puzzlement about why we don't just do this, too. Because, although it's clear he wants a mandate, voluntarism by the committed would be a start. Some of us can afford it—people who live in mansions, for example. Next time you see him, ask Tom Friedman how much he paid for his windmills on his Bethesda compound. Just to see how insanely cost-effective these things really are, or how cheap his virtue really is.

BLOWING SUNSHINE ABOUT WIND POWER

We hear how "The wind and sun provide a free source of energy!", which might just be the most disingenuous rallying cry in the energy debate (putting aside the dishonesty of alarmist global warming rhetoric, which is in a category of its own). While it is true that the wind and sun are free, wind power and solar power are bloody expensive. Furthermore, the claim is fairly irrelevant. Coal on your land is as free as the wind that blows across it. It costs money to transform the coal, just like the wind and sun, into useable form. But unlike the wind and sun, coal is a cost-effective energy source. Coal is concentrated energy; sunlight and wind are not. They are diffuse. According to William Tucker, author of the book *Terrestrial Energy*, "Sunlight and wind and so-called 'renewables' are even more diluted than wood, by a factor of about 10 to 50."[7]

So these greenie talking points are aimed at distraction. If you fail to be distracted, you confront the apples-and-oranges comparison: intermittent wind, like solar, cannot replace coal because it cannot provide that which we are really in search of, which is baseload power. Baseload power is the threshold level of power generation that allows us to run public schools, hospitals, the institutions of government, and—horrors—private enterprise during normal business hours.

It is only the serious blowhard who touts windmills as acceptable replacements for reliable energy sources like coal and nuclear. But we now have some serious blowhards, indeed, on the public pad.

For example, in April 2009, Jon Wellinghoff, Obama's appointee to chair the Federal Energy Regulatory Commission (FERC), declared that the United States had no need of new nuclear or coal baseload electricity generation, and that wind was going to be the "cheapest thing to do."[8]

No, that is not a typo. This is the mindset which is guiding our nation's energy planning.

Mr. Wellinghoff's official biography states he attended the now-defunct Antioch Law School in Washington, D.C., founded as somewhat of an experiment in creating activist members of the bar by social militants also instrumental in establishing the taxpayer-funded, and therefore scandalously left-wing Legal Services Corporation.[9] Wellinghoff apparently graduated in Antioch's inaugural class (1975, the school having been established in 1972). Antioch did progress eventually to gain provisional accreditation by the American Bar Association in 1991.

This bio also notes that, as a private lawyer, Wellinghoff authored Nevada's renewables-quota law which, it boasts, was one of only two across the country to receive the seal of approval by the far-left Union of Concerned Scientists.[10]

These facts reveal and help explain the troubling worldview of the chairman of a regulatory body with significant decision-making authority over critical energy decisions. Wellinghoff's claim that the wind will set us free violates common sense (assuming he actually believes it), and is the sort generally made only by the most dogmatic anti-development activist.

By coincidence, the statement came just two weeks after an equally ludicrous claim was made by Interior Secretary Ken Salazar. He was part of the administration's effort to reverse public sentiment, which, on the heels of a gas price spike in 2008, was in favor of increased domestic energy production. Salazar told an audience in Atlantic City that windmills off the East Coast could generate enough electricity to replace most and possibly even all of the coal-fired power plants in the United States.[11]

Politics aside, Dr. Robert Peltier, editor in chief of *Power* magazine, didn't take kindly to such sophomoric rhetoric, calling it "fantasy" and "pure bluster." What got Dr. Peltier's ire was Salazar's absurd claim that it was feasible to develop over 1,000 gigawatts of power, "the equivalent of energy produced from 3,000 medium-sized coal-fired power plants."[12] Wrote Peltier, "If we were to accept Salazar's vision of the potential for offshore wind, the entire 1,800-mile length of the Atlantic coast would be filled with wind turbines to replace our 1,470 coal plants and more than 15,000 other power plants. Ignoring the obvious transmission and distribution difficulties, the cost of these installations, and the price of the power produced, a little elementary school math reveals Salazar's vision as a fantasy."[13]

The reason, as Peltier details, is that even if wealthy elites like the Kennedys and Kerrys, who demand that the nation rely on wind power located near *other* people,[14] suddenly dropped opposition to putting wind where it makes the most sense—in very windy places closest to its customers, where it also pollutes their scenic views—the contraptions still require wide spacing and, therefore, hundreds of square miles simply to supplant one decent sized coal-fired power plant (in theory, but impossible in practice due to wind's intermittent nature).

"If we assume the entire eastern coastline were open to development, then there is room for 3,600 wind turbines, one row deep. Also, if the rating of all these new turbines were the same as for Cape Wind"—that's the project stalled by the Kennedys and Kerrys of the world for threatening their views—"then to replace the entire nation's installed capacity with a like amount of offshore capacity requires 334,462 wind turbines. In other words, the entire east coast would have wind turbines...located every half-mile and 93 turbines deep (over 30 miles) out to sea,"[15] Peltier wrote.

And you thought your power bills were tough to meet now. Peltier referenced a study by the Ocean Energy Institute seeking an enormous 5,000-MW offshore wind farm in the Gulf of Maine.[16] You see, all wind power is expensive, spotty, and requires duplicate investment in conventional backup electricity, because it only works when it feels like it. It's sort of like having to make payments for two cars because one is always breaking down. With greens aggressively blocking wind-mills just about anywhere they're proposed onshore, wind mavens looked offshore, where the gadgets still require backup. Problemati-cally, far from being out in the dusty plains far away from most anyone, the view offshore generally belongs to rich people…who know other people, like judges, lawyers, zoning chairmen, and politi-cians. Further, because of the intricacies of tethering the things and special transmission requirements all related to their being out in the ocean, offshore windmills cost between 2.5 and 3 times as much to build and operate as new conventional energy plants, even despite conventional plants having to pay for their fuel.[17]

So, Peltier wrote, "Extrapolating that estimate to 334,462 wind tur-bines I calculated above produces an estimate with so many zeroes my calculator gives me a zero overflow error."

It also gives our enemies and trade competitors goose bumps of excitement.

Now recall how these enormous windmill displays around the world have not yet resulted in the retirement of any of those coal-fired—or gas—power plants, because those reliable plants remain necessary, 24/7, to back up turbines driven solely by the intermittent wind. Sadly, the wind blows not during summer days when it is hot and the system needs the extra juice, but generally in the wintertime at night. That's true in Denmark, too, incidentally.

In Ohio, an anti-windmill activist named Tom Stacy dared con-tradict the president—who actually calls windmills a "new technology," sigh—by noting, with slightly greater historical accuracy than Obama, that "Wind is an ancient and largely discarded technol-ogy that can only provide volatile, sporadic energy, not the modern power performance and effective capacity we rely upon for afford-able, secure electricity." He also noted that widespread installation of windmills "will not close one coal plant."[18] *Audit this man's taxes and sign him up for a death panel consultation!*

Gas-fired electricity can be dialed up and down with wind activity, though coal cannot jerk its electricity production up and down quite so easily. Of course, hydroelectric power (considered a no-no because it's mean to fish) can readily supply the need of any wind-heavy system for backup, easily shot into the system's veins when the wind chooses not to cooperate. Whatever the "backup"—an odd choice of words given that windmills only work something less than one-third of the time and the sun is equally fickle—renewable energy's requirement of near-100 percent back-stopping capacity that can be dialed up and down in practice means that wind (or solar) cannot really be "substitutes."

Were we to replicate the relative production of Obama's model Denmark (an absurd choice given its population is half the size of Manhattan's), we would need those nice Canadians to build an enormous number of dams as well as nukes just to be ready for when we need the power. That's how Denmark has done it, but with Norway, Sweden, and Germany providing the "easy" backup from those sources. In return, Denmark sends much of its—to the Danes, often useless—wind energy to its neighbors for prices that drop the more the wind blows . . . all the way down to the can't miss price of zero cents per kilowatt hour.[19]

For the Swedes and Norwegians, this odd case of Danish conscience-soothing wastage is essentially without direct cost—indirectly, of course, they did build all of that excess hydro storage and nuke capacity, enabling this game. But it is subsidized by the Danes paying the highest residential electricity rates in Europe. Gestures aren't always cheap, particularly green ones.

Given that we haven't built nukes here in three decades and new dams are unlikely, you will see in more detail later why the gas industry is pushing the windmill and solar mandates. They mean more gas plants, not fewer, and a whole lot of additional expense and waste. And, yes, paying to build roughly twice the capacity you are using does impact your electricity rates, just as would two car payments.

It is inescapable that the wind power that Obama administration officials recklessly insist we can rely on to replace coal and nuclear is variable, not just by the particular month due to seasonal variations, and an individual day due to weather patterns, but by the hour (if the wind blows, it prefers certain times of day), and by the minute (in other words, gusts). In short, its availability has no relationship to demand. Other than that, sure, you can replace traditional sources of energy.

So, the energy ideas spouted by Obama's senior policy officials are bluster and fantasy. Even Obama was caught telling a renewable energy activist on a "rope line" haranguing the president to follow through on making such foolish rhetoric into policy, that, "They can't do it. The technology's not there."[20] By this time he had been in office for a year and possibly some sort of reality had set in. Yet the only result of Obama's supposed newfound knowledge is pro-nuclear rhetoric, along with a promised loan guarantee for one or two nuclear projects. These promises, though, represent merely *one-fiftieth* of the nuclear capacity that Obama's own economic assessments include in order to produce their phony "cap-and-trade" cost estimates, aspects of which are discussed later. However, almost as a rebuke to Obama's support for one new nuke, in 2010 liberal Vermont voted to force its only reactor to close down by 2012. This is the biggest anti-nuke win since the 1970s hysteria put a stop to building new reactors and was taken as a sign that no "renaissance" is actually in the offing.[21]

At precisely his one-year mark Obama's Energy Department issued a report[22] making a far more qualified, less fantastic (though still unbelievable)[23] claim that wind could replace coal and natural gas for 20 to 30 percent of the electricity used in the eastern two-thirds of the United States by 2024. This came from the National Renewable Energy Laboratory, a beehive of ideological activists. My Freedom of Information Act requests to this government agency revealed that their smear of a "green jobs" study and its authors was coordinated with none other than the wind energy's Washington, D.C., lobby, as discussed later. Just so you know how independent such claims are.

Team Obama's green fantasizing represents bluster of a very dangerous sort, because it is bluster that, whether or not its speakers believe it, underlies all of their environmental and economic policies, as well. Which is to say, they are recklessly destining you to an energy and economic debacle.

THE REPLACEMENTS

Given how the greens are wedded to this notion that we can replace traditional energy sources with renewables, let's examine a little more closely the idea that little or no construction of coal or nuclear plants need be allowed thanks to the promise of windmills and solar panels.

In assailing the Obama administration perspective, *Power* magazine's Dr. Robert Peltier did offer ritual fealty to the not unreasonable strategy calling simply for "all of the above," including wind, but concluded: "[T]o represent offshore wind as capable of supplying the nation's entire electricity needs is just pure bluster."[24] Wherever you try this, on land or sea, it takes an enormous amount of space, approximately 100 times as much space as coal or nuclear.[25] And if you consider the entire plant's life-cycle energy requirements, this can even use more energy than it produces. Further, as newly wind-crazy West Texas learned the hard way with rolling blackouts in February 2008, sometimes the wind just stops blowing (when you need it most, during hot summer days), putting the entire operating system in peril.[26]

Consider an August 2009 Bloomberg story, "Wind Promises Blackouts as Obama Strains Grid With Renewables," which opened by daring to note that "President Barack Obama's push for wind and solar energy to wean the U.S. from foreign oil carries a hidden cost: overburdening the nation's electrical grid and increasing the threat of blackouts."[27] Surely you've heard this?

Just how unreasonable Team Obama's assertions are was detailed by Art Robinson, a scientist, former colleague of Linus Pauling, and someone who knows the absurdity of government intervention in energy production. Robinson dissected an early Obama speech touting a government-created solar electricity array at Nellis Air Force Base in Nevada, which Obama called the technology's crowning achievement, to illustrate the insanity of favoring such boondoggles at the expense of allowing proven, reliable performers to perform.

Although Obama was at Nellis to brag on solar, he repeated the spectacular fib about Denmark getting one-fifth of its electricity from windmills. Denmark, a tiny country which openly admits it has "carpeted" the lesser populated areas of its country with the sometimes-deadly eyesores, uses wind to produce from 4.7 percent of the electricity it uses (2006) to 12 percent (2007), depending on how good the wind is in any given year.[28] Again, why make things up if the truth is compelling? The root of the fib is the fact that Denmark produces the equivalent of 20 percent of the quantity of electricity that it uses, but as already noted, much of that is offloaded to the Germans, Norwegians, and Swedes, which countries sell the Danes nuclear and hydroelectric power[29] (not give), and which Danes have been led to believe was produced by their own windmills they pay so dearly for. Incidentally, that also bursts the bubble of the other popular mythology of the Danes being not only wind-happy but nuke-free.

Robinson, in a piece for *Environment & Climate News*,[30] began his analysis of the audacious claims by offering some perspective, noting that not too far away from where Obama spoke there sits what was, in 1988, state-of-the-art nuclear technology, which we stopped building even as the world continued to implement further technological innovations. This is the three-reactor Palo Verde nuclear plant in Arizona, producing six times the electricity of the Hoover Dam.[31] That makes Hoover as productive as half of one of Palo Verde's reactors. Palo Verde was intended to have ten reactors, but green alarmist campaigning stopped the other seven from being built.

Replacing our nuclear fleet's production with solar arrays like those at Nellis would, by Robinson's calculations, require 3.75 million acres or 5,862 square miles of solar cells.[32] Now you see why even Denmark's modest (particularly relative to its claims) windmill contribution is called its "wind carpet." To take green rhetoric to its logical conclusion, Robinson figures that for the astronomical sum of $30 trillion (about 38 "stimulus" bills) and a waiver of environmentalist legal obstruction, you could produce the equivalent of our energy needs—say, to also provide the juice for the plug-in cars we are to drive—by laying down 70,000 square miles of solar panels covering an area the size of Maryland, Hawaii, Massachusetts, Vermont, New Hampshire, New Jersey, Connecticut, Delaware, Rhode Island, and Washington, D.C.[33] Robinson calculates that to replace Palo Verde now would cost an estimated $6 billion (in capital costs, excluding the regulatory hurdles thrown in the way).

Clearly, there is no "replacing" reliable energy with renewables.

Our future as represented by the Nellis installation—constructed at a cost of $100 million and occupying 140 acres of what is typically called by the greens "critical habitat"—is surely a less productive one.[34] According to Robinson's figures, in optimal conditions, this poster-child produces 14 megawatts of electricity, for a reported 30.1 gigawatt hours per year.[35] Palo Verde's cost, adjusted for inflation, was $4.35 billion per reactor (or $13 billion for all three).[36] So each reactor cost forty-one times the cost of Nellis's array in today's dollars, to produce 297 times the electricity, 24/7, on a far smaller footprint.[37]

Robinson makes some other interesting calculations in his article, including one revealing the woeful rate of return on capital invested in renewables. It explains how, given the cost to produce, the Nellis solar installation will only become a net energy producer in somewhere between 50 to 100 years (depending on which rate of return you believe). But since solar will only produce electricity for a fraction of that time, and solar panels just don't last very long, "net producer" status will never occur. By Robinson's calculations, Palo Verde became a net producer of energy after six years.[38]

You see why the greens had to stop what they deem financially (and otherwise) "unsustainable"[39] nuclear power, and how we will all get rich by requiring the economy to run on such "new" sources of electricity as windmills and solar panels instead? No? Missed that? Possibly this is because you detected how these niche sources can *only* survive with mandates, subsidies, and taxes to pay for them. Nuclear power is hardly without its subsidies, but the greens' ritual claim against nuclear—that it could not operate without what's known as the "Price-Anderson" government insurance guarantee (providing a fund to cover what's considered nuclear power's excessive liability) is speculation, particularly given nuclear's success elsewhere in the world, under a variety of different regulatory (and subsidy) structures.

Government bureaucrats—especially those overseeing "stimulus" funds—are unconcerned that their decisions seeking to encourage certain energy sources over others are driven by political and ideological concerns, rather than economics and technology. As senior advisor Matt Rogers, overseeing stimulus funding at the Department of Energy, said, "We are not in the business of picking winners. We're creating competition among innovative approaches in the marketplace."[40] He's half right. They don't pick winners. But they have a terrific record of picking losers. In fact, when the government steps in to support unproven ideas, it is generally because private parties taking risks with their own money cannot be rounded up.

Still, what a beautiful euphemism, matched in its insight in the same article by an Elizabeth Salerno, described as director of data and analysis at the wind industry lobby. She counseled that, when it comes to making renewables, specifically windmills, profitable, "Demand is the trigger. But it has to be long-term, stable demand." Ah. That would be an issue. But she is speaking of demand for something that people don't want, so it's the kind of demand that she is acknowledging has to be required by the government.

From Europe we hear a similar plaintive wail from the Euphemism Hall of Fame. As Ed Crooks of *Financial Times* noted, "Ultimately, however, the only way that the [wind energy] industry will stand any chance at all of attracting the capital it needs is if governments make commitments to guarantee investors' returns."[41] (This is also the nuclear industry's argument, though unlike like wind and solar it finds itself in that position not because it cannot provide energy and pay for itself without mandates, but because it has become demonized as the result of decades-long campaigns.)

FADE FROM GREEN TO BLACKOUT

The more one understands the technologies in play, the harder it becomes to imagine that this taxpayer-funded "renewables" boondoggle is being used as an excuse to block actual productive economic activity. Proven energy sources are slow-walked and confronted with excruciating government hurdles while unreliable sources are promised as what will meet demand. All the while, demand-side management is being imposed to coerce us off energy use. Harder still to conceive is that it gets even more foolish thanks to the behavior of Interior Secretary Ken Salazar's allies inside and out of government.

We know that, because of cost and intermittent supplies, even massive deployment of wind (or solar) is not an actual "alternative" energy supply. As Fred Barnes has written, "To think that wind and solar or other alternative fuels can fill the energy gap requires a belief in what Adriel Bettelheim of *Congressional Quarterly* has called the 'Tinkerbell effect,' as in *Peter Pan*. It consists of believing something will happen just because you wish it would."[42]

But, as we've seen, to even try to make it so would require staggering numbers of the inefficient devices. Of these hypothetical hundreds of thousands of windmills we might install, onshore the greatest concentrations would have to stretch from Texas to Oregon. The Lone Star State notwithstanding, the state and federal government owns the lion's share of the land in that neighborhood. And then there's the issue of how it can take up to $2 million per mile to string special transmission wires to hook windmills up to the system.[43]

That adds up, given that the wind mostly blows, in occasionally useful quantities, way out where no one lives, or in areas populated with people who don't want to have to look at windmills every day. When it blows in places where people do live, the residents paid a lot of money for those views and aren't giving them up without a fight.

Douglas Johnson, a research statistician and senior scientist at the U.S. Geological Survey's Northern Prairie Wildlife Research Center, therefore despairs about these eyesores that "they're going to be all over the place."[44] Don't worry, Doug. No, they aren't. The greens and their pals in the courts won't let "renewables" go up.

A *Wall Street Journal* review of the book *Cape Wind* detailed the elites' battle to make sure only rubes in flyover country will suffer under the noise or remotest view of wind turbines. The reviewer called the conflict "a ripe subject, populated with the sort of people who would be among the first to count themselves as friends of the Earth but the last to accept an environmentally friendly energy source if it meant the slightest cloud on their ocean views."[45]

Windmills aren't going up in any quantity that matters, and trying to force an economy onto the things, or onto solar and other "renewables," is treacherous policy for many reasons, not least of which is the excuse it gives the rationers to block new, and even stop existing, reliable electricity production from continuing.

As soon as Salazar uttered his plan to clear out the bureaucratic clutter to accelerate projects despoiling public lands with renewable energy production, the U.S. Fish & Wildlife Service promised to oppose any wind farms within Wyoming's core sage grouse population areas.[46] It turns out those areas cover a quarter of the state. Needing a few thousand acres of Bureau of Land Management land, the planned China Mountain wind farm in Idaho and Nevada is, at this writing, in trouble due to the fact that it runs through wildlife habitat. The greens' party line is that animals can't cope with such intrusions, even though the project is considered necessary for Nevada to meet its windmill quota law, drafted by none other than the man who is now Obama's pick to chair the Federal Energy Regulatory Commission.[47]

So, really, there's only so much the greens will allow in the name of the Obama administration's erstwhile commitment to put these eyesores up everywhere they can, supposedly to "replace" reliable energy generation, and satisfy both present and future demand.

And what about the $11 billion in windmills sought for the Texas Panhandle corridor, since that's where the wind blows? It turns out that a chicken lives there that merits a high priority listing pending under the Endangered Species Act, and the greens have their priorities: not "green energy," but no energy.

As reported by Bloomberg, "Federal protection for the chickens will hamper Texas's plan to add 5,500 megawatts of wind power in the region by 2013, a 60 percent increase for the state.... 'The windiest parts of some of these states seem to be the areas that still have bigger concentrations of prairie chickens,' [German utility] E.ON chief development officer Patrick Woodson said."[48] Quite the conundrum. Really breaks one's heart to see companies that have helped advance this silly agenda—like E.ON—finding themselves so frustrated.

California Senator Dianne Feinstein worried aloud about how a Mojave ground squirrel would cope, and similar concerns over critters had already prompted über-green poseur Arnold Schwarzenegger to shock the polite folks at a Yale University gathering by blurting out, "If we cannot put solar power plants in the Mojave desert, I don't know where the hell we can put it"[49] (sic). It turns out that many liberals frantic over "global warming" were even more concerned that tortoises, too, could get depressed if forced to live next to expensive, intermittent energy sources. Also relevant are those nagging realities of the massive quantities of water required to cool them in places that receive very little rainfall, and that they take up vastly more space in those untouchable wilds—to produce a fraction of the electricity.[50] When the sun shines. With few clouds.

What about water! for nuclear plants ??

An amusing twist to this story is that the Governator's cousin by marriage, the shrill green activist, and accomplished if generally incoherent ranter, Robert F. Kennedy Jr., was also working to make sure that the relevant parts of the Mojave were not designated as a national monument. And here, at least for a while, the greens appeared to have successfully kept the area off-limits from producing solar energy,[51] following the somewhat more dangerous model of Bill Clinton locking up the world's largest reserve of low-sulfur coal by designating 1.7 million acres of land in southwest Utah as the Grand Staircase-Escalante National Monument (to the apparent delight of his Lippo Group pal James Riady, who had ties to the next largest coal reserve).[52] Kennedy dismissed the greens' "local" concerns, saying, "[T]hey're putting the democratic process and sound scientific judgment on hold to jeopardize the energy future of our country."[53]

Would it surprise you to learn that Kennedy has a stake in Bright-Source Energy Inc., the company the greens discovered "getting a pass," in their words, to slap these solar contraptions up all over federal lands? It turned out as well that, by chance, he is a senior advisor at VantagePoint Venture Partners, which raised $160 million for the enterprise.[54] So, there's environmentalism and then there's, you know, *environmentalism*.

Still, it's nice to have RFK Jr., of all people, assert there's no constitutional basis for the federal Endangered Species Act—those tortoises are merely a "local concern," hallelujah—but I recall something about Kennedys also opposing windmills off Hyannisport for what even RFK Jr. must admit are far more legitimately called "local concerns"—the vistas of the super-wealthy.

Naturally, the greens also want to block the transmission lines needed for the project, which in their own right "would destroy the entire Mojave Desert ecosystem," according to David Myers, who runs a green group opposing putting solar catchers out in such unlikely places as the desert.[55]

The *Los Angeles Times* reports that "the presence of sensitive habitat, rare plants and imperiled creatures such as desert tortoises, bighorn sheep and flat-tailed horned lizards threatens to stall or derail some of the [wind and solar] projects closest to securing permits." Peter Galvin of the hysterically anti-oil, anti-coal "global warming" litigation group the Center for Biological Diversity, somehow managed to say through his grin that "We are not going to just roll over when critical wild lands and last habitats of endangered species are in the mix."[56]

Then there's the "Green Path North," a proposed power line 80-plus miles long to bring solar and wind power from eastern California deserts to the beautiful people in Los Angeles. LA's Department of Water and Power (DWP) (a big "global warming" agitator, incidentally, so yet more heartbreaking irony) ran into the buzz-saw of its beloved green groups and now has decided to abandon its plans, which had already cost it millions of dollars.[57] DWP also halted plans for a 970-acre solar farm near the Salton Sea.[58] Wash, rinse, and repeat, all around the country.

More than a dozen green groups have also asked the federal government—meaning the compliant Obama administration—to block more than 6,000 miles of electricity transmission corridors on Western public lands, because they would carry coal-fired power instead of electricity from windmills. Not that a proposed windmill transmission line would be acceptable. The greens would just change their excuse. According to *E&E News*, "Katie Renshaw, an Earthjustice attorney who helped lead the suit, said the groups are hoping the Obama administration will decide not to defend the corridors and to instead sit down and discuss a possible settlement."[59] She said the

administration's and the groups' goals are in sync. This is one cooperative way to repeal administrative decisions advanced under the
Bush administration while keeping Obama's fingerprints light.

No windmills are to go up in Oregon's Blue Mountain foothills,
either, according to other green groups. "It is a critical wintering range
for deer and elk," says spokesman Richard Jolly.[60] Apparently deer and
elk don't favor the flavor of all that free bird and bat carcass the windmills would provide. Proposed Southern California wind farms have
a history of running into greens protecting a buzzard labeled far more
gracefully than its appearance warrants, the California Condor, which
doesn't fare well against the blades.[61]

But by demanding millions of these Cuisinarts of the air, the
greens, in theory, also demand massive mortality of things that fly. It
seems that the same currents on which the animals migrate are the
ones that would (occasionally) spin the turbines. To meet the president's request that 20 percent of the nation's energy comes from
renewable sources by 2030, the number of turbines would have to
increase 30-fold. "At current mortality rates, the wind industry would
be killing between 900,000 and 1.8 million birds per year," according
to George Wallace of the American Bird Conservancy.[62] That's a lot
of birds. Imagine if those windmill rotors actually turned more often.

While oil companies pay huge fines for bird kills, it's also more than
a little strange that our government, in the name of "the environment,"
demands policies ensuring the death of a minimum 300,000 feathered
friends, according to *Energy Tribune* editor Robert Bryce's calculations
in the *Wall Street Journal*.[63] But the contraptions are also known to
make lots of noise and, yes, even kill people (since 2002, sixty-six people have died in freak windmill accidents, according to the UK's
Caithness Windfarm Information Forum, which claims forty-seven
worker fatalities, plus nineteen among the general public).[64]

Turbines in the West Virginia and Virginia mountains have been held up by greenie lawsuits including under the Endangered Species Act on behalf of the local bats, an animal of horror-genre fame now standing in the way of numerous planned wind farms.[65] Which gives me an idea about a good logo for the greens, seeking to suck the life out of the economy.

In fact, in December 2009 a federal district court judge in Maryland stopped the large, planned, and indeed half-completed Greenbrier industrial wind facility in West Virginia. The ruling could also serve to block wind projects around the country, because the court ruled that construction of the wind turbines, putting (occasionally) turning rotors in the path of things that fly, would violate the Endangered Species Act. This halted completion of the project, which had already constructed 40 of 119 turbines, while also limiting those completed turbines to run just from November to April. The two groups that had filed this suit, after losing every step of the way up to the West Virginia Supreme Court, found a friend in the feds by changing their argument to one on behalf of endangered Indiana Bats.[66]

The judge who ordered the industrial wind facility halted did provide a remedy—one which reveals how great are these hurdles to constructing energy sources, erected by greens who have also claimed for years with feeble sincerity to desire these energy sources instead of the things that actually support our economy and lives. The judge ruled that the developer's only recourse is to apply for an incidental take permit (ITP) from the U.S. Fish & Wildlife Service (FWS), which means there is a fairly reasonable chance for extraordinary bureaucratic delays by the FWS, frustrating Congress' intent to encourage responsible wind turbine development.[67] Of course, even an expedited permit application process could entail one to three years and several million dollars to obtain a take permit.[68] All of which is to say that the court was not delusional, but recognized how it was, in practice, likely just blocking the production of electricity.

This routine is being repeated coast-to-coast, with similar excuses. The First Wind Cascade Wind Farm[69] and the Biomass Gas and Electric Tallahassee Renewable Energy Center[70] were killed in Oregon and Florida, respectively, as were smaller projects like Akeena Solar's, which sought to place solar panels on its own roof.[71] Need I mention this was in California? So here we affirm for all to see that the talking point that "global warming is the greatest threat" is just that: a talking point.

The truth is that the greens have fought "renewable" plants as aggressively as they have conventional sources that work. The U.S. Chamber has located more than 380 such projects blocked or stalled over the last approximately five years which, combined, total over $560 billion and approximately 250,000 direct jobs.[72] Of these blocked projects, 167 were "renewables," bigger by a third than the next closest target, coal projects. (As of January 2010, the breakdown was 167 renewable projects, 129 coal, 41 natural gas, 24 transmission, and 20 nuclear.)[73]

The Chamber also believe they've identified $7 million in taxpayer dollars paid these groups by the U.S. Treasury specifically for the greens' troubles of blocking new energy production.[74] So let's please put to rest the notion that greens and Team Obama support "green energy" in anything but theory. Instead, focus on the fact that, again, the taxpayer pays twice—once from the impacts of the assault on our energy supply, and again to fund green groups waging the war. In fact, if one of those jobs lost was yours, you've paid three times.

Finally, despite the utter absurdity of this soap opera, we really must take this whole tortoise, bat, and squirrel thing seriously. After all, not only were the U.S. Marines tasked with conducting a "green" audit in Afghanistan, but the U.S. Army is already engaged in relocating tortoises here at home so as to not unnerve them with the spectacle of Basic Training.[75] Of course, out of the 600 creatures schlepped elsewhere in 2008, 90 were found to have been eaten by wolves after being shown their new home. It seems the tortoises knew something in taking their chances against raw, "green" recruits, indicating yet again how even the slowest creature is quicker on the uptake than an environmentalist.[76]

In conclusion, you can't put these "new" technologies, rolled out hundreds of years ago and unable to meaningfully contribute to modern needs, anywhere that turtles crawl, birds fly, or Kennedys live. Other than that, hey, it's a land rush to put 'em up.

Terrific harm can be caused on the way to failure. In Europe, for example, "renewables" mandates are, like the cap-and-trade and green jobs schemes detailed in subsequent pages, reaping economic and human impacts. "Ofgem, the UK energy regulator, has estimated that by 2016 the average annual bill in Britain could have risen 60 per cent to £2,000 [about $3,100]. That increase would represent more than 10 per cent of household disposable income once essentials such as housing, food and clothing are taken care of."[77]

At least the UK is waking up to what they have done to themselves, with one industry sage hitting the politicians where they might pay attention: "You will lose a lot more votes if the lights go out than if you are not quite as green as you said you were going to be."[78] Meanwhile, Spain was forced to curb its solar power subsidy in 2008, and the industry there collapsed the next year.[79] Germany, too, was forced to slash its own solar "feed-in tariff," a model for some Democrat lawmakers in the United States pushing solar mandates (these require power providers to buy solar power at terrific rates, passing the cost to the consumer, of course).

The Spanish and German debacles are examined in detail later, as the president has repeatedly told us to "think of what's happening in countries like Spain [and] Germany"[80] (the latter whose lobby for solar power producers said in a statement, "The proposed cut threatens the foundations of the German solar industry").[81]

And in the face of this idiocy, the administration remains determined to push ahead, unconcerned about what, you will see, is its own ignorance of how energy is produced and apparently how it impacts American lives and security, mandating non-performers out of an ideological belief that the demonized energy sources that work must be driven out.

What all of this recklessness ensures is that, in the foreseeable future, we face disaster, and it isn't the sort that can be quickly corrected by simply acknowledging, or being forced to reverse, a mistake. It will take a public demand for massive reform of a bureaucratic and ideological behemoth dependent upon, yet desperate to smother, the productive sectors of the economy, before we can right this ship.

CHAPTER 3

VAN JONES WAS NO ACCIDENT: THE OBAMA ADMINISTRATION'S RADICAL "GREEN" ACTIVISTS

The United States Constitution plainly requires Senate examination and approval of senior officials advising the president on policy and executing the laws of the land. Sure, nominees at this level do tend to get rather full of their role, claiming that it is they, and not the productive sectors supporting them, who run the country. But the truth remains that these people are only in place to implement laws and formulate policy within those laws, working for us—even if that's not always how they view themselves.

Sometimes, political appointees tapped to execute the laws of the land go so far as to believe they are there to, say, *fundamentally transform America*. Elections surely have consequences, but whatever their outcome, we also just as surely still have the Constitution. While opposition to political appointees is, on occasion, grounded in politics as much as is their nomination, such is the right of an individual senator or political party under our system, even if the operating presumption is generally that the president should be granted his desire to appoint whom he chooses—within certain, often elusive boundaries.

Sometimes the Constitution's approval mechanism presents a (seemingly) insurmountable obstacle, through which senators not only oppose but block senior appointees on grounds of temperament or a nominee's troubling record. Convicted criminals, radicals, and others who have little regard for our Constitution, laws, or system generally are not well-suited for providing sober counsel on operating within our laws or system.

When Senate opposition becomes clear, it is common practice for an administration to make its case for the nominee publicly, or move on to another choice. Sometimes, a temporary "recess" appointment places a controversial nominee in office for a limited period.

That is how most administrations have followed the rules developed over our history. The current administration, however, isn't most administrations.

In fact, President Obama set a record for delaying the appointment of nearly 200 top officials for a full year after he was elected (as well as appointing a record low percentage of senior officials with private-sector experience). These slots included, incredibly, the job of running Medicare and Medicaid, even as Obama keened over the necessity of drastically extending and reforming those programs as part of his push for radical overhaul of the health delivery and payment systems.[1]

Yet Obama did rush to bring extremists into positions of influence to advise him, even into phony jobs made up simply to get them in place, ASAP. He did this to the constitutionally offensive point of ensconcing high-ranking advisors to lord over Senate-confirmed Cabinet officials in newly created positions simply to avoid the scrutiny and disclosure that come with a Senate confirmation process. Advice of a certain sort simply had to be had, right away, in order to immediately begin the assigned revolutions. So this approach on the whole had less to do with actual governance than with that "fundamental transformation" thing.

Obama did this generally, though not exclusively, through the creation of many "Czars," who quite often came in through the back door, having new positions conjured for them, thereby evading Senate scrutiny and confirmation. This path was chosen for certain radicals due to obvious fear of providing fodder to those lawmakers who would stand in the way of his transformative plans by exposing his choices (unlike a surprisingly disinterested media).

When it came to some existing, recognized positions that do require confirmation, Obama still did not shy away from radicals with extreme, bizarre, and even supremely embarrassing records that screamed out for delay, reconsideration, and even a senatorial "hold" blocking the nomination. Such was the case of "chief science advisor" John Holdren. No "hold" was placed or blocking campaign conducted on his nomination, though he is a close presidential advisor who sees nothing objectionable about the government sterilizing the public through the drinking water supply to confront ecological catastrophes including Holdren's long-held fever dream of a "population crisis," which is behind many of his fellow greens' fears.[2]

Sadly, such leading radicals placed in the president's inner circle, with histories of bombastic pronouncements and curious constitutional theories, faced no opposition. On those rare occasions that the radical appointee was subjected to Senate scrutiny, staff and senators paid little heed to the warning signs available to any who looked. As detailed later, our Secretary of Energy as well as our already-noted chairman of the Federal Energy Regulatory Commission are fervent anti-fossil fuel crusaders. We now have a "regulatory Czar" (which actually is a long-existing position) who believes that trees and animals should be granted standing to sue their human aggressors.

All of which leaves one bewildered that the chattering class's first reaction was to mutter in confusion over how a former convict and self-described radical Communist named Anthony K. "Van" Jones could slip through the screening process. Jones didn't actually slip through. His radical beliefs and revolutionary fervor were well known to administration officials who brought him in. Obama confidante Valerie Jarrett said they'd been watching him for years and aggressively recruited him.[3] One photo made the rounds, to no media attention, of a younger Barack Obama with Jones. It was a strange image, in which Jones is clearly the Alpha, the star up against whom the apparently admiring Obama mugged.[4]

Van Jones was not hired in spite of his extreme views on policy, race, the economy, government power, community organizing, and the appropriate use of taxpayer funds. He was hired because of them. It took mere moments for opponents of his elevation—to be, as he put it, "a community organizer inside the federal family"[5]—to spread the lurid details. But we were expected to find comfort in the idea that the federal government's incompetence is so great that it somehow found nothing of concern in his background, despite his alarming record being readily available online.

Jones fit right in, until the embarrassment that would have come for any number of such radicals, had they been exposed to a confirmation process, became too much and Obama threw Jones under the bus, with Reverend Jeremiah Wright and his own grandmother. Jones resigned in September 2009.

Also instructive was how, despite the lack of interest in naming a Medicare chief—with supposed billions in readily dealt-with waste, fraud, and abuse ready to be saved, though apparently *later*—Obama quickly brought in numerous early hires from green activist groups with histories of advocacy on behalf of a movement committed to limiting your freedoms. For example, the CEO of Al Gore's "global warming" advocacy foundation, Cathy Zoi, was promptly installed as a senior official in the Department of Energy. As TreeHugger.com gushed, placing things in a perspective I appreciate: "First President Obama snatched up Van Jones from Green for All to be Special Advisor for Green Jobs, Enterprise and Innovation at the Council for Environmental Quality. And now he's hired Alliance for Climate Protection CEO Cathy Zoi to serve as Assistant Secretary for Energy Efficiency & Renewable Energy in the Department of Energy, pending her confirmation."[6] This is the office managing billions of the "green jobs" loot that Van Jones, et al, were so excited about, of which Jones apparently boasted that $500 million was "smuggled" into the stimulus bill,[7] money the Apollo Alliance and another Jones group had "been trying to get for years."[8] Oh, and the kind going to an industry her old boss is so heavily invested in. Huh.

And it wasn't long before Zoi's office in the Department of Energy was implicated in a chain of events culminating in United States taxpayer-funded agencies assailing Spanish academics for publishing research about their own country that discomfited Team Obama and threatened their plans.[9] This Spanish paper, with research led by Dr. Gabriel Calzada, revealed that Spain's energy policies were unsustainable without government subsidies, caused electricity rates to go up, and had cost more than two jobs that would have been created by the private sector for every one the state created.

These revelations embarrassed Obama, who often used Spain as an example of a "green jobs" economy—a successful model of his brand of energy reform. (He then switched to Denmark, whose equally unimpressive experience which we have touched on and is detailed later).[10] Subsequently, someone in the administration actually dispatched a taxpayer-funded agency, the Department of Energy through its National Renewable Energy Laboratory (NREL), to produce a white paper slamming the study. Outrageously, as I learned using the Freedom of Information Act (FOIA), they sent their draft for comment and assistance to the wind energy's Washington, D.C., lobby, the American Wind Energy Association, and the left-wing Center for American Progress. Before this revelation, as I explained in my article for biggovernment.com, instead of disproving Dr. Calzada's research, "two young activists who wrote the paper merely further embarrassed the administration with their flailing complaints: the Spanish team failed to speculate in the absence of official data, and eschewed an economic model designed some time ago far to our east for central planners in favor of a real-world 'opportunity cost' model used by people who invest *their own* money. Thus, spaketh our government, the study employs 'non-traditional methodology' and is unworthy of consideration."[11]

In tracking down how assailing research by a foreign academic assessing his own nation's domestic policies became a priority for taxpayer-funded agency, I filed a request under FOIA with the Department of Energy's National Renewable Energy Laboratory in Golden, Colorado. They provided 663 pages of documents in response, one of which revealed that a "rebuttal" was first emailed by an Avi Gopstein, the Science Policy Fellow for the American Association for the Advancement of Science (which has become increasingly a global warming activist group)—in Cathy Zoi's DOE Office of Energy Efficiency and Renewable Energy (EERE). In it he said that the need for a rapid response was a priority. Copied were EERE's chief operating officer, deputy assistant secretary, and director of strategic planning and analysis.[12] Another email flatly said Zoi requested it.

More than this remains unknown. Zoi's office, after stonewalling my request for months, delivered a huge file to me just as this book was going to press.[13] An administration must have its priorities. Hit-jobs on inconvenient people who challenge unsupportable claims are, it seems, high up on the list for the current administration.

Conversely, read what you will into the Administration showing no interest in filling certain other slots. For example, the Obama administration sniffed at bipartisan pressure to nominate someone to fill the position of top watchdog at the Environmental Protection Agency,[14] despite (or perhaps because of?) the EPA's authorization of the quick transfer of huge sums to community organizing groups and the like. The "watchdog" would be an independent officer charged with preventing fraud, waste, and abuse in other green funding streams through audits and investigations.

And Team Obama had already had to fire Gerald Walpin, that bothersome inspector general over at the group overseeing AmeriCorps, for having stumbled onto some inconvenient truths of the same sort in the very first weeks of the administration. After being reminded of the sort of troublemaking that independent investigators can cause—like Walpin looking into curious expenditures involving political allies, which only led to turning up more unsavory dealings, like AmeriCorps money being put to unauthorized and highly questionable uses—why create headaches?[15]

Little attention was paid to Lisa Jackson, head of New Jersey's Department of Environmental Protection, when she was named to head Obama's EPA. After all, Obama had already brought in Carol Browner, in circumvention of the approval process, to actually run things as "Energy and Climate Czar"—a breathtaking and illustrative move detailed below. Still, *Rolling Stone* beamed, headlining a profile "The Eco-Warrior: President Obama has appointed the most progressive EPA chief in history."[16]

And then there were the rare, non-alarming picks not cleared by the green movement. Take, for example, the choice to head the Office of Surface Mining, which caused a furor—but not merely because the greens didn't pick him. Most enraging, it appears they feared he might actually allow surface mining to occur. Not to worry. The newly appointed head of the Office of Surface Mining dutifully came out with anti-mining regulations, arguably even skirting a court order in doing so.[17] Under Obama, there's little chance that much new mining will be allowed any time soon, and as you will read, the war to bring it to a halt rapidly escalated.

THE PROGRESSIVE MIND: WHY OBAMA'S GREEN RUSH AND BACKDOOR MOVES?

Before examining two key radicals rushed into the Obama administration to execute his plans, consider why he sought to fill the executive branch with such ideological warriors in the crusade to "fundamentally transform" your freedoms.

The short answer is that this is merely an extension of how the Left operates. It has long been their game plan to try to reinvent America using existing authorities and levers of power once one of their very own was in place. Doing so without being transparent in their revolutionary measures offers better hopes for imposing their agenda. Besides, pushing the legal envelope by bringing about policy changes from within the executive branch is a great insurance policy in case their congressional henchmen fail, and even possibly get voted out of office, as appears increasingly possible despite huge congressional majorities at the beginning of Obama's term.

In the inaugural edition of *National Affairs*, William Schambra explained the leftists' philosophy behind aggressive, sneaky, and even possibly unconstitutional governance by activists in the executive branch:

> Progressivism's solution was to shift the administration of public affairs out of the hands of citizens and politicians still in the thrall of fragmented (and therefore dysfunctional) views of social reality, and into the hands of a new professional class steeped in the social sciences. They alone could formulate coherent intellectual maps of an interrelated world, and interventions sophisticated enough to bend the causal chains in the desired direction....
>
> Progressive reformers throughout the 20th century came to denigrate the wisdom and relevance of the American Constitution, which frustrated centralization and coordination by dispersing governing power across the states and over the branches of government. Once thought essential to American freedom, these institutions now came to be seen as impediments to coherent national governance.... [18]

The combination of Obama's admitted objectives with the apparent "by whatever means necessary" philosophy of the radical movement that staffs his administration reveals how precarious a position the nation is now in as the administration executes his notions of governance.

It should come as no surprise when Obama administration officials boast about their close and cooperative working arrangement with green groups on major and contentious policy matters, even to the point of collaborating on a patently illegal regulatory maneuver. Assistant Administrator of the Environmental Protection Agency Gina McCarthy did just that during her Senate confirmation hearing, suggesting close working relationships with the litigious greens as the insurance for the administration to get away with doing what it wants, even if the law says otherwise.[19]

In short, and as explained in further detail in chapter 4, Obama's EPA chose to regulate carbon dioxide emissions in the name of global warming, after the Supreme Court ruled that the Agency could do so but did not have to. Doing so would, as a matter of statutory necessity due to arcane details in the Clean Air Act, trigger a cavalcade of EPA regulation down to the level even of Washington, D.C., issuing permits for small retail store activity. The host of statutory implications of EPA's move would be disastrously costly so, in order to avoid what even EPA admitted in a regulatory finding would be "absurd results,"[20] the Agency decided it would read the number 250 tons of CO_2 emissions (written in the Clean Air Act as the level of emissions triggering regulation) to mean 25,000 tons (so as to not regulate very small emitters of something that this effort inherently admits the law was never intended to regulate).

As the Senate Environment Committee Republicans noted: "As it turns out, regulating greenhouse gases under the Clean Air Act isn't so easy. This is not the fault of Justice Kennedy and the liberal bloc of the Supreme Court. EPA has chosen its path. Now EPA is looking for a way out. Its solution is to evade the law."[21] So when asked about the prospect of the administration's green allies forcing regulations, Ms. McCarthy informed the Committee that she would just reach out to them, implying that some accommodation was in the offing to let this administration do something clearly in contravention of the law, but setting up regulatory and political blackmail available for use the moment a president ran afoul of the greens.

THAT WHOLE CZAR BUSINESS

John Podesta is a former White House Chief of Staff to Bill Clinton. He is currently the president of George Soros's pet project, the Obama-cheerleading Center for American Progress. Podesta gave a June 2009 speech—in Europe, naturally—bearing the creepy but revealing conference title, "The Great Transformation: Climate Change as Cultural Change" (as in fundamental transformation and all that). In reassuring Obama's European base that the American president was fully on board with European left-wingers' agenda for America, Podesta said, in part:

> Since his inauguration, the urgency and complexity of creating a low-carbon economy have driven President Obama to make energy transformation not only the centerpiece of his environmental policy, but also his economic program to produce broad based growth and produce jobs. He began by appointing a team that shared his priorities and possessed the expertise to turn his campaign ideas into sound policy. Dr. Steven Chu—a Nobel Prize winner and Secretary of Energy, Carol Browner—to run the White House office on energy and climate change, John Holdren, the President's Science Advisor. All deeply committed to emissions reduction. On

the diplomatic front, Secretary Hillary Clinton's first trip abroad as Secretary of State was to China, where climate change held top billing on her agenda, in league with the global economic crisis. The Secretary was accompanied by Todd Stern, who holds the newly created position of Special Envoy for Climate Change, is responsible for forging international cooperation ahead of the Copenhagen meeting, and is my former colleague at the Center for American Progress.[22]

Of the five officials named here as being so critical to imposing the "global warming" (and otherwise the anti-energy, anti-population, and anti-liberty) agenda on America, two are Senate-confirmed, constitutional cabinet officers. Three of them are so-called "Czars." (Stern is the "Climate Change Envoy," while Browner has the larger portfolio of energy and "climate"; Holdren underwent a *pro forma* Senate confirmation which, aside from the standard fear of non-scientist lawmakers of engaging a scientist on his issues, was incomprehensible for reasons described below.)

By this, therefore, Podesta tells us quite a lot, and the message was clear early on. *National Review Online*'s Ed Craig pointed out the dichotomy between what was presented to the public and the real centers of influence in the Obama White House. He noted that "President-Elect Obama has assembled an ostentatiously moderate cabinet on most policy fronts—but on energy and the environment, his staff is genuinely radical: from card-carrying Socialist Carol Browner[23] to academic attack-dog John Holdren."[24] Obama selected a moderate if private sector-free Cabinet to cover up rabid backdoor-men. It just might be radical enough to work.

So Obama refused to subject key administration advisors to standard processes and scrutiny—never mind his endless campaign

promises to be oh-so-transparent—despite their managing important areas of national policy and controlling massive sums in taxpayer
money. Disconcertingly, this structure may make these most controversial, and sometimes trouble-prone, agents of the president actually
immune from congressional questioning or any meaningful oversight.[25]

Presidents before Obama have classified aides as czars. Obama,
however, takes this practice to new lengths. That he did so is far less
the point than why he did so. As Rich Galen expresses it in his blog,
"Mullings":

> President Obama has moved an extraordinary amount of
> power into the White House. There, assistants to the Presi-
> dent can be hired without that pesky "advise and consent"
> business which allows the Senate vote on the suitability of
> nominees for many senior administration posts. Second,
> because the Senate didn't judge them in the first place, under
> the highly developed concept of "executive privilege," it is
> nearly impossible for the Congress—House or Senate,
> Republican or Democrat—to demand, even under sub-
> poena—that an assistant to the President come to the Hill
> and testify.[26]

Galen raises a good question: how, precisely, does the Freedom of
Information Act apply to these offices that exist nowhere in the Executive Branch structure described in statute? I suppose it will take
expensive and time-consuming litigation to sort that out. But in the
meantime, why would the administration decide to allow the public
to see the proceedings of offices which are removed even from the
gaze of congressional oversight? Quite simply, it won't.

In his capacity as president pro tempore of the Senate, West Virginia Democrat Senator Robert Byrd, the self-appointed guardian of congressional prerogatives, sent an official protest to Obama, stating that this end run around the Constitution and shirking of traditional levels of transparency amounted to an attempt to subvert the authority of the U.S. Congress, which threatens the constitutional system of checks and balances.[27]

So, given the president's reticence to have his closest advisors examined, let's take a closer look at some of these radicals he found so important to rush into place, and what they're up to.

THE OBAMA RADICALS

Carol Browner

Carol Browner has returned to federal service as a senior advisor, with Oval Office access and stature so great that she appears prominently at the president's side for all manner of critical announcements—including, terrifyingly, on his plans for fundamentally transforming America's automobile companies, or at least the two he got his meat hooks into. The intolerably independent Ford will surely come along later under duress. As we'll see, Browner occasionally steps into the light to acknowledge her influence.

Well before he was inaugurated, Obama plucked Browner from her lucrative activities on the boards of several green groups, as well as Soros's Center for American Progress. It seems that after deleting records which were the subject of litigation seeking forced disclosure of Browner's and her agency's close working relationship with green pressure groups, Browner revolved through the Environmental Protection Agency's door to slots on the possibly grateful boards of the Audubon Society, the highly partisan League of Conservation Voters, and Al Gore's Alliance for Climate Protection. (Remember, Gore bragged of having received $300 million to re-brand "global warming" as the "climate crisis," and is steeped in the practice of shrilly arguing that wherever anyone gets their funding dictates their opinions.[28])

The Internet at first proved embarrassing, posting rumors of Browner's pending appointment as Climate Czarina, telling all who were interested that she was active and high-ranking—a "Commissioner," actually—with a project of the Socialist International, Commission for a Sustainable World Society.[29] This Commission for a Sustainable World Society is a "global warming" advocacy group quite taken with the idea of global governance, if not so much with capitalism. This is surely one more reason why Browner was never nominated to a cabinet position, although she now sits in a position with just the same—or possibly more—influence. So then the airbrushers got busy, in classic socialist form, and the matter was quietly glossed over.

As Kathy Shaidle wrote in FrontPageMagazine.com when Browner's likely role in the Obama administration was emerging:

> The Socialist International's "organizing document" blames capitalism for "devastating crises and mass unemployment" alongside "imperialist expansion and colonial exploitation." Similarly, Socialist International's Commission for a Sustainable World Society, the organization's action arm on climate change Browner worked on, "says the developed world must reduce consumption and commit to binding and punitive

limits on greenhouse gas emissions." What makes Browner's association with the Socialist International noteworthy is that, after the worldwide failure of socialism, she continues to share many of its anti-capitalist views—and if confirmed as climate czar, she promises to translate them into policy.[30]

Humorously, about the same time these truths were unfolding, the trade website *Climate Wire* reported that Danish Socialist MEP Dan Jørgensen, vice-chairman of the European Parliament's Committee on the Environment, called for Europe's cap-and-trade scheme to be more like—wait for it—Barack Obama's.[31] Obama, you see, wanted to sell all of the ration coupons to industry, while Europe (and, soon, the U.S. Congress) chose to give them away to buddies in industry at least for the first decade or so. To Obama's credit, while his revenue-raising scheme is more Statist than the market-socialist version favored by Europe and congressional liberals, at least it is more efficient in that it cuts out the private companies from wetting their beaks too much, leaving that to the state.

But such praise is of the sort that Obama would likely prefer not be too widely circulated. Americans on the whole don't take to socialism or its adherents quite so well as Browner and her friends. One would think even Republican senators might have found Browner's troubling connections and ideas worth causing a stir, demanding some answers, if not their constitutional role of approving her before funding the position concocted to get around such scrutiny. "No Pasarán!" they might have cried in the language of international socialism, which Ms. Browner would surely appreciate. Alas, no. But at least House Republican Leader John Boehner's office hinted at what ought to be asked. As Boehner's spokeswoman proffered:

Does she agree with the [the Commission for a Sustainable World Society]'s positions on global governance—that the United States should abdicate its international leadership to international organizations? Does she support its position that the international community should be the ultimate arbiter of climate change policy? These are questions that merit answers—especially when you consider this group's deep skepticism about America's ability to be a force for positive change in the world.[32]

These are also questions that might trigger an inquiry about Browner's erstwhile business partner and Clinton administration Doppelgänger, Madeleine Albright, who, according to *Pravda*, went to Russia while she and Browner were partners to say she didn't want the United States to be the leading state in the world any longer.[33] It's just too hard, and frankly we don't deserve it. The Kyoto agenda is, by coincidence, aimed at making such wishes come true. But it was Albright with whom Browner teamed up to provide consulting services through the "Albright Group" (described by lefty-favorite SourceWatch as "secretive about their clients,"[34] which doesn't mix well with the confirmation process). Given Browner's background and the Obama White House's description of her as "a founder and principal of The Albright Group LLC, a global strategy firm and of Albright Capital Management, an investment advisory firm that focuses on emerging markets,"[35] it is fair to presume this means she was a high-priced navigator of how to get one's hands on those "environmental"—and specifically "global warming"—billions she helped ensure were a new and booming outflow from the government.

Carol Browner was therefore not only too close for comfort with Big Green (especially given her troubling legal history, detailed below), but also a highly paid advisor to companies she won't—and, this way, never had to—tell the public about. Such are the discussions one gets around by creating phony jobs for radicals.

Senator Byrd admonished Obama that, among other things, Browner and her fellow czars are "not accountable for their actions to the Congress, to Cabinet officials, and to virtually anyone but the President."[36] Browner can plead that she has no legal authority, although she does not shy away from leaving the impression that she's in control, as in an interview with the *Washington Post*, in which she described the "rather long" list of the Bush administration regulations she was going to "roll back."[37] Because of, you know, all of that environmental devastation—and global cooling, incidentally—that occurred on Bush's watch.

Aware of the true nature of Browner's role with Obama, Senator James Inhofe of Oklahoma noted during the confirmation hearing of Obama's nominee to be Deputy Director of the White House's Council on Environmental Quality that the would-be employee was accepting an inherently emasculated position. "CEQ serves a critical role in shaping environmental policy within the executive branch. . . . [But] I must say that you have a difficult job ahead of you, not least because Carol Browner, the White House Energy and Climate Change Czar, appears to be coordinating environmental policy out of her office. Of course, we in the Senate have little idea as to how her office functions or what contributions it makes to the interagency policy process."[38]

There are reasons to be suspicious of Carol Browner being anywhere near the levers of power ever again, a prospect she had seemingly made impossible during her last tour, even before the radical associations. As Max Schulz of the Manhattan Institute writes, she "served eight ferocious years as Bill Clinton's EPA chief, after having been Senator Al Gore's legislative director. . . . Fortunately, many of the Browner EPA's more aggressive actions were reversed in the legislature or through the courts—in fact, some of her employees wound up facing criminal charges for falsifying evidence and manipulating lab results."[39] Indeed, Browner's history of accepting the restraints that come with being a public servant is an unhappy one. She is the embodiment of the classic liberal mindset of being in government to impose radical change from within by getting around laws—not following the Constitution in simply executing and upholding them.

For example, consider the way she departed the Clinton-Gore administration. Browner's EPA admitted culpability and accepted a fine of $600,000 (of your money) in settling a racial case involving an African-American EPA employee, one of at least one hundred fifty such employee complaints filed during her tenure.[40] Even *Time* magazine took note just as Browner had left office, apparently believing that she was highly unlikely to be in a position again requiring that they cover for her. A February 2001 story described festering racial problems during her reign. *Time* quoted at length the career official whose lawsuit resulted in that settlement, Anita Nickens, who claimed discrimination under Browner in disturbing detail. Nickens vowed that she had been passed over for promotions for being too "uppity" and said that "we [African-American employees] were treated like Negroes, to use a polite term. We were put in our place."[41] In settlement, the Environmental Protection Agency acknowledged it had engaged in discrimination and retaliation against whistleblowers. The actions of Browner's EPA led to Congress passing a law, the "NoFear" government whistleblower protection act.[42]

It was clear from this episode, among many others, that a confirmation hearing would have been an embarrassment and possibly a disaster.

On the very final day of her tenure with the Clinton administration, as George W. Bush prepared to take the reins after defeating Browner's old boss Al Gore, Browner ordered EPA information technicians to delete all of her computer files. According to testimony, her specific order, which if you knew nothing about her would surely be inexplicable, was: "I would like my files deleted. I want you to delete my files."[43] She later swore up and down that she kept just personal information on the computer and only wanted it to be completely purged as a courtesy. Oh, and the computers of three other senior officials, too. Courteous to a fault, this lady.

The problem is that, by coincidence, she had just been enjoined by a federal court to do the very opposite, and preserve her records. She claimed cluelessness as a defense. Apparently Browner the lawyer also didn't know about the litigation culminating in this on-yer-way-out order, seeking to have her completely and publicly air the details of which green pressure groups she had been working with to rush out regulations before she left, leaving political landmines for the Bush administration. She also must have had no idea that her lawyers, mere days before and on her behalf, sought to block the motion seeking the order, which therefore was clearly pending. And, as it later came out, somehow her staff knew better than to try to comply with the court's order to search her office for documents.[44]

That's an awful lot of ignorance and coincidences. With Browner we are dealing either with a breathtakingly unaware yet sober public servant—as it seems her supporters dismissing this history as somehow not disqualifying would have us believe—or with someone who sneers at the law in an apparent belief that it doesn't apply to her, one of the most cynical, least honest senior government employees since and maybe even before the Nixon administration. Your call.

Judge Royce Lamberth ordered the sanctions because he said Browner's EPA had shown "contumacious conduct"—which the Associated Press helpfully informed readers meant "obstinate resistance to authority."[45] As a result of Browner's document destruction, the Environmental Protection Agency was held in contempt. The refusal to heed the court's order to preserve the records led the judge to also order her—through the EPA, so once again using your dollars—to pay the plaintiff's fees and costs. At least this time your money went to pay the Landmark Legal Foundation, kudos to Mark Levin.[46]

Did I mention that Browner speaks of her time as Clinton-Gore's EPA head with statements like, "One of the things I'm the proudest of at EPA is the work we've done to expand the public's right to know"?[47] Of course you are, dear.

So it is in keeping with character that Browner was subsequently revealed to have instructed her Obama administration colleagues and the auto industry executives she was muscling to accept a California-style global warming regime on vehicles, "to put nothing in writing, ever" regarding secret negotiations she was orchestrating on the matter. In a letter of protest after learning of this, Republican Rep. James Sensenbrenner wrote that Browner "intended to leave little or no documentation of the deliberations."[48] After all, documentation can cause so much extra work when it comes time to destroy it.

However, as the *Washington Examiner*'s Mark Tapscott reported, federal law requires that officials preserve documents concerning significant policy decisions, so if this instruction were reasonably taken to be to destroy any notes taken, then it is a criminal act.[49] Notwithstanding any legal implications, the import of her instruction and the law's intent quite obviously run contrary to each other.

It seems somehow fitting that the most transparent administration in history should bring on board someone with such a curious relationship with the concept of transparency. But then again, in his inauguration speech Obama vowed to "restore science to its rightful place,"[50] which both he and Browner seem to believe is wherever it can't get in the way of their politics.

Browner has a long track record of politicizing science. While running EPA for Clinton-Gore, she was actually quite well-known for it. NPR's Bob Edwards must have choked on his *Morning Edition* script when reporting in 2000 that "a federal court earlier this year overturned an Environmental Protection Agency rule regarding a chemical in drinking water. The decision was made after EPA administrator Carol Browner declined to follow the findings of the agency's own scientists as to what was safe."[51]

In 1997, Browner's EPA tenure was described by Michigan state regulator Russell Harding in *Forbes* magazine as "by far the most politicized EPA I've seen in my three decades of working in state governments.... It is an agency driven more by sound bites than by sound science."[52] The theme of that piece was Browner's *modus operandi* of mission creep, and nothing could better describe the series of incremental "green" regimes she initiated, which continued later in the Bush Interregnum (and to this day) with the assistance of those green groups and surely those unnamed others paying her for advice and, we must assume, intercession.

No one who witnessed the smear campaign of 30-year career EPA scientist Alan Carlin—who internally exposed, then publicly blew the whistle on, the collapsed scientific case for "global warming" (Obama's excuse to regulate every aspect of the economy)—should be surprised to learn that Browner's EPA had a history of also mistreating scientists who refused to play along with her politics.

Under Browner in 1998, six EPA scientists were canned after writing a letter to the editor of a newspaper, expressing their opinion that certain overzealous, and what proved to be scientifically unsupportable, Browner regulations "stand to harm rather than protect public health and the environment."[53] You may also have heard about two EPA lawyers being forced, under Obama-Browner, to take down a YouTube video critical of the dismal performance of carbon cap-and-trade in the real world until they removed a reference to their thirty years assessing such programs for EPA. "This is another example of the EPA playing dirty to get green,"[54] said Rep. Sensenbrenner, the ranking Republican on the House Select Committee on Energy Independence and Global Warming.

As Kimberley Strassel wrote in the *Wall Street Journal*, this and the Carlin episodes were indicative of "the Obama EPA, and its new suppressing, paranoid style."[55] Which is vintage Browner.

To illustrate the hypocrisy, scientists in Browner's EPA had complained about being enlisted for politics, with one even testifying in a deposition: "We were being asked to [advocate against legislation] during government business hours, and the purpose was to protect EPA funding levels."[56]

Jonathan Adler, now a professor of law at Case Western Reserve University, wrote way back in 1996 about Browner's aggressive politicization of EPA, and in a way that may ring alarm bells when recalling her document destruction and subsequent career working with green pressure groups.

Adler revealed how:

[Browner's] EPA has also benefited from giving taxpayer dollars to ostensibly apolitical organizations. Earlier this year it was disclosed that the EPA funded the National Parent

Teachers Association (PTA) in order to develop support for EPA regulatory programs. According to an internal Agency memo obtained by the newsletter "EPA Watch," EPA "would fund a 'cooperative agreement' with the association. For its part, the PTA will produce 'an environmental awareness newsletter that will potentially reach millions of PTA members nationwide.' This would benefit the EPA because, according to the memo, 'the newsletter will include environmental buzz words, terms and definitions, hotlines, and news items.' The memo concluded that 'the PTA could become a major ally for the agency in preventing Congress from slashing our budget, but their voices need to be heard.'"[57]

For her particularly improper work with green groups and campaigning against the opposition-controlled Congress, Browner received a letter of rebuke from a House subcommittee, which made strong claims, including that "the concerted EPA actions appear to fit the definition of prohibited grass-roots lobbying. . . . The prima facie case is strong that some EPA officials may have violated the criminal law."[58]

Liberal bureaucrats generally don't get the rough treatment by media types because, after all, their hearts are in the right place (like science, it would seem, this means out of the way where they can't cause problems). But by the end of Browner's EPA term, it was just too much for some. The *Cincinnati Enquirer* editorialized, "Regulatory zealot Carol Browner has established environmental rules that were opposed in some cases even by EPA's own scientists. We've had enough of the Browner gang's capricious rule-making, politicized 'science' and lack of accountability."[59] Of one thing we can be sure. No Republican who had been subjected to such a piece titled "EPA—Clean It Up," would ever be snuck back in later.

The trade press, which owes its existence to an aggressive and intriguing regulatory environment, also weighed in around the same time and in equally firm terms. *The Electricity Daily* wrote that "EPA's abuse and misuse of science is no surprise and well known to those who follow the agency closely." The publication wrote that, far from meriting an elevation to cabinet status for the Environmental Protection Agency, as Browner long demanded, "From the abysmal performance of the agency under Administrator Carol Browner, one wonders whether the question today shouldn't be: why not abolish the EPA?"[60]

Things always seem to come back to Browner's relationship with the truth. You may recall how she oversaw the most expensive regulation in our nation's history. Clean Air Act regulations were sprung on the day before Thanksgiving in 2006 in order to bury it, so you know it was big. These regulations were so shoddy in their underlying scientific support that something called the Information Quality Act was passed in response.[61] What's more, Browner engaged in some of what we by now see as rather familiar behavior in order to marginalize critics of the move, with something less than honesty. Science writer Michael Fumento detailed how "the standards are 'not about outdoor barbecues and lawn mowers,' she testified [to Congress in 1997], smearing such assertions as 'junk science' and 'scare tactics.' Said Browner: 'They are fake. They are wrong. They are manipulative.' Frank O'Donnell, then-executive director of the Clean Air Trust, called talk of regulating lawn mowers 'crazed propaganda.'"[62]

The critics, of course, turned out to have been telling the truth, as regulations of precisely the sort Browner swore were not thereby authorized soon followed.[63]

Browner also seems to have a bit of a power thing going on. Consider this peach of an interview with *US News & World Report* in

March 2009, in which she blurted out that, in her mind, "We need to make sure that we're really moving electricity in the smartest way and using the most cost-effective electricity at the right time of day. Eventually, we can get to a system where *an electric company will be able* [sic] *to hold back some of the power so that maybe your air conditioner won't operate at its peak, you'll still be able to cool your house, but that'll be a savings to the consumer*"[64] (emphasis added). Ah, yes. The "we" who can get to this position, who presumably would set the standard for how cool your house should be able to get, refers to the state. And you might consider a thank-you note for their having saved you money by figuring out how to turn your thermostat up and down, to where they know you really want it—since this assumes that you stupid people can't figure that out on your own.

The interview may have taken place in 2009, but it sure seems to leap right out of the script for "2001: A Space Odyssey." You know, Climate Czar HAL is afraid she can't open those vents for you. This mission is too important to allow you to jeopardize it.

All of these anecdotes, of course, bear no relation to the fact that Ms. Browner had a position created for her, ensuring she would not experience disclosure requirements or Senate scrutiny.

Everyone's got a few critics. But the smoke and even blazing fires surrounding Carol Browner's history generally, and specifically her tenure at the Environmental Protection Agency, should have been a career-ender so far as senior government service is concerned. Instead, an equally brazen scofflaw named Barack Obama promoted her to continue performing her committed environmental advocacy, but this time from inside the White House.

Hard as it is to imagine, it is actually possible for someone to make Browner appear somewhat measured, if in a nasty, partisan kind of way.

John Holdren

Obama's chief science advisor John Holdren did not have Carol Browner's record of seemingly going out of his way as a public servant to generate enmity, if only because he spent most of his time working for an environmentalist advocacy group. As such he also didn't have Browner's troubling history with the courts, but Holdren did say things about how he views the law and government and to what ends they ought to be put that are at least as disturbing. Remember, he is the man to whom our president turns for science advice, chosen after a selection process that surely involved looking into the man's background, writings, and philosophy.

Enough of what you are about to read was aired before Holdren's confirmation hearing that further inquiry should have been demanded, which would have quickly turned up the rest. Anyone working in environmental policy surely knew about him, and right away my colleague at the Competitive Enterprise Institute, William Yeatman, raised detailed alarm about Holdren's "40-year record of outlandish scientific assertions, consistently wrong predictions, and dangerous public policy choices" making him "unfit to serve as White House Science Adviser."[65] Instead, it seemed, the Republicans did not want to cause a stir over such seemingly small fry as the president's science advisor. But no one rising to the level of requiring "advice and consent" should ever be the subject of such abdication of responsibility, particularly when, as in Holdren's case, Obama had not even deprived them of it.

Not even one senator voted to reject Holdren's appointment.

Fortunately, enough of Holdren's record ultimately found its way to daylight, thanks to private citizens doing their own work, that the influence of Holdren and his pronouncements will be muted. His extremism now trails him like toilet paper stuck to his shoe. His views are so cringe-worthy as to demand scrutiny of any decision-making he contributes to or participates in.

A longtime leading global warming alarmist (after being a global cooling alarmist), Holdren makes several appearances in my book *Red Hot Lies*.[66] His name also pops up throughout the history of gaining massive taxpayer funding of the global warming industry. Most shamefully, Holdren was also enlisted by *Scientific American* in that magazine's effort to smear and otherwise discredit Bjørn Lomborg, the "Skeptical Environmentalist" in what might be the global warming establishment's most disgraceful moment (explored in detail in *Red Hot Lies*).[67]

We see Holdren's name in the context of a "temporary nominating group" established in the National Academy of Sciences a couple of decades ago as a back door to bring in more environmentalist activists.[68] That is to say, it enabled the election of apparently otherwise unlikely members, who then formed blocking minorities keeping inconvenient scholars out. I wrote (citations omitted), "Vocal alarmists Stephen Schneider and John Holdren, a professor at Harvard who is primarily employed by the Woods Hole Research Center (an environmental advocacy group…) were also elected from the temporary nominating group, so we see the cadre of global warming alarmists elected to the National Academy of Sciences actually came in through other than the regular channels. And the process self-perpetuates."[69]

With this past of Holdren's as prologue, the following focuses just on Holdren's views relevant to policies the Obama administration is working on, to date, stealing your economic freedoms.

For instance, despite his posture as a man of science, Holdren appears to be driven in great part by a mission to redistribute wealth. Drape that with as many buntings proclaiming a "population crisis" as you wish, but that is a political or ideological stance. Consider a statement illustrative of an attitude Holdren has often espoused: "The rate of growth of material consumption is going to have to come down, and there's going to have to be a degree of redistribution of how much we consume, in terms of energy and material resources, in order to leave room for people who are poor to become more prosperous."[70] It's tough for an anti-population nut to strike the ritual, "for the children!" rhetorical pose, so Holdren says it's about the poor. But the record is clear that to him it's mostly about control, and ultimately for the purpose of managing population to whatever levels he and his kind think are acceptable at any given time.

As Holdren's confirmation neared, writer Mark Hemingway noted in the *Washington Examiner* how:

> Over the weekend, a blogger at Zombietime.com unearthed a book written over 30 years ago by John Holdren, President Obama's "science czar." The book, *Ecoscience*, was co-written with neo-Malthusian prophet of doom and scientific laughingstock Paul Ehrlich. In it, Holdren advocates a series of bizarre and horrifying measures to deal with an overpopulation threat that never materialized. Among the suggestions in the book: Laws requiring the abortion or adoption of illegitimate children; sterilizing women after having two children; legally requiring "reproductive responsibility" to those deemed by pointy-headed eugenicists to "contribute to general social deterioration"; and incredibly, putting sterilizing agents *in the drinking water.* [71] (emphasis in original)

These were indeed passages in a textbook co-authored by Holdren, conveyed as solutions being bandied about by population zealots—

he would view them instead as contemporaries, I suppose—and as such, you might say he and his co-authors endorsed. Regardless, the arguments were hardly condemned. Indeed, the *Washington Examiner*'s David Freddoso had already quoted passages from the book revealing how Holdren "argues repeatedly that [populated control] is sometimes necessary, and necessity trumps all ethical objections."[72] Further, quoting Holdren:

> "Several coercive proposals deserve discussion, mainly because some countries may ultimately have to resort to them unless current trends in birth rates are rapidly reversed by other means. Some involuntary measures could be less repressive or discriminatory, in fact, than some of the socio-economic measures suggested." Holdren refers approvingly, for example, to Indira Gandhi's government for its then-recent attempt at a compulsory sterilization program.[73]

Holdren was quite clear that some of these proposals "deserve[d] discussion," rationalizing why that was so, and he most certainly did not raise the notions to condemn them but to air them and explain their possible utility.

So, after the circulation of this highly damning laundry list from the Holdren/Ehrlich book, one Holdren defender, a writer/activist named Chris Mooney (who is also a fervent supporter of all things left-wing and alarmist) claimed that "Only at the end of an article insinuating that these were Holdren's positions did the [*Washington*] *Times* actually quote the staff of the Office of Science and Technology Policy, which then refuted all the claims."[74]

Wrong. Holdren's office, however implausibly, merely *disavowed that he supported them.* He had to say that, regardless of whether that was heartfelt (a little difficult to believe given his own words) or spin—or else he need not have bothered unpacking his boxes; he'd have found himself tossed under the bus like Van Jones was, and just as rightly.

Besides, how would Holdren refute the claims? He can't say he perpetuated them in his book only to decry them—clearly, he considered them proposed response measures deserving discussion. Maybe we just misread those passages. In fact, here's that statement by Holdren's office that the *Washington Times* item supposedly with great unfairness saved for last which supposedly "refuted" the statements: "When asked whether Mr. Holdren's thoughts on population control have changed over the years, his staff gave the *Washington Times* a statement that said, 'This material is from a three-decade-old, three-author college textbook. Dr. Holdren addressed this issue during his confirmation when he said he does not believe that determining optimal population is a proper role of government. Dr. Holdren is not and never has been an advocate for policies of forced sterilization.'"[75] This is a slightly less sophisticated twist on "that's old news."

It is, however, less sophisticated in its clumsiness. *It's old news. Two other people thought it, too. Besides, I never really thought so.* Or, as David Harsanyi wrote in the *Denver Post*, "If that is so, I wondered, why is his name on a textbook that brought up such policy? Did he not write that part? Did he change his mind? Was it theoretical? No straightforward answer was forthcoming."[76]

I'm not sure what it is about these radical "Czars," who are generally so boastful of their views, yet have such curious relationships with candor.

These views about a constantly escalating population crisis (a crisis that never actually materialized except in the subjective and possibly opportunistic imaginations of Statists), which were perpetuated by Holdren, are extremely dangerous to be so closely associated with a man who now rants about a worsening warming crisis in the face of no warming. Crises are in the eye of the beholder, and Holdren beholds them at all turns.

The *New York Times*'s John Tierney wrote of Holdren (who also predicted an impending ice age in 1971):

> What interests me are not the disaster specifics but rather Dr. Holdren's tendency to foresee worst-case situations that require new public policies. (In the 1970s, he and Dr. Ehrlich discussed controlling population by giving sweeping powers to a new "Planetary Regime.") I've previously written about criticism[77] that a climate-change report from the White House and federal agencies exaggerates the threat of natural disasters. Does Dr. Holdren have a worst-case bias in his interpretation of data?[78]

Yes, yes, he does, as does his entire band, because those scenarios are the means that they use to frame each issue they seek to ride as the excuse for their agenda of organizing society.

Holdren's defenders—and all defenders of warming alarmists who previously ran around warning about cooling—claim that those predictions of cooling were never actually uttered. Sort of like the population stuff. The inconvenient truth about such claims is that they run contrary to what Holdren wrote with the Ehrlichs. For example, again in *Ecoscience*, "Many observers have speculated that the cooling could be the beginning of a long and persistent trend in that direction—that is, an inevitable departure from an abnormally warm period in climatic history."[79] Again, their text did not elevate these many observers to dismiss them, but to broadcast their stance, seemingly with endorsement.

As if such haggling is necessary after reading about Holdren's ideal for a "planetary regime"—the polite term we know now is "global governance." Let's just stipulate up front that he is a hard-core leftist of the 1960s variety. If nothing else, this is evidenced by his leading role in the Pugwash Conference, a largely anti-American, Soviet-apologist organ of intellectuals.[80]

Creeped out yet? Michelle Malkin also uncovered that Holdren's intellectual mentor is Harrison Brown, a "distinguished member" of the International Eugenics Society[81] with whom Holdren later worked on a book about his own hobbyhorse of overpopulation. "In *The Challenge to Man's Future,* Brown envisioned a regime in which the 'number of abortions and artificial inseminations permitted in a given year would be determined completely by the difference between the number of deaths and the number of births in the year previous.'" Otherwise, "we faced a planet 'with a writhing mass of human beings.' He likened the global population to a 'pulsating mass of maggots.'"[82]

One could dwell for pages on Holdren's obsession with using coercive, central government to curtail (other) people, though, again, it is no secret that that is the "green" agenda's ultimate goal. Holdren has long associated with the leading population doomsayers (who have been proved more and more spectacularly wrong each decade), like his notorious *Ecoscience* co-authors Paul and Anne Ehrlich of *Population Bomb* and *Population Explosion,* who gained fame, fortune, and academic prestige by being spectacularly wrong but at least horribly pessimistic (and Statist) for decades. As is typical of their shared doomsaying, Holdren and the Ehrlichs collaborated to hold a "Cassandra Conference" in 1988 (called "Cassandra" after the Greek lass from mythology whose prophecies were always true and always ignored), writing yet another book about the horrors brought on the planet by (again, other) people—horrors which, they said, were sure to get worse.[83] And these are Holdren's chosen collaborators.

Obama said we should judge him by the people he surrounds himself with. Okay. During the process of Holdren's elevation to the White House, only one Republican ventured into these waters with any specificity, and just as with stimulus funding of green groups, that Republican was Louisiana Senator David Vitter. At Holdren's confirmation, Vitter asked whether Holdren believed that "determining optimal population is a proper role of the government."[84] Holdren said he did not. Case closed. Except that John Holdren was obviously brought in to the Obama White House for the very specific purpose of advancing the radical Left environmentalist—and specifically global warming—agenda. Or cooling, should that continue as is now predicted.

As regards his relationship with the increasingly absurd global climate industry, recall how the always-vocal Holdren predicted in the mid-1980s that climate-related catastrophes might kill as many as one billion people before the year 2020.[85] He now brushes away such failed catastrophism as not requiring explanation.

To fully understand Holdren, and the man who selected him to be his scientific brain, you must understand that Holdren's fashionable if overwrought rhetoric—civilization being threatened by "ecocide"[86] and "ecocastrophe"[87]—describes visions that each have an equally disturbing remedy. In fact, it almost seems like the desired remedy drives the crackpot (and worse) theories.

The Competitive Enterprise Institute's Yeatman found that Holdren has, quite simply, made a career out of being a professional catastrophist.[88] However, Holdren sells his seemingly ideologically driven catastrophism as science. Science it is not, though whatever it is, it is apparently one of those fields that you can succeed at by never being right. Sort of like being my broker. Or the president of CBS News.

Like fellow Obama appointee Cass Sunstein, Holdren apparently also endorsed giving trees legal standing in court to sue.[89] He wrote that this evolution in our legal tradition would have a "most salubrious" environmental impact.[90] He agreed that trees are no different for those purposes than corporations, and corporations can sue. And Batman's a scientist.

Possibly those trees could sue Holdren for trying to deprive them of carbon dioxide, otherwise known as "plant food." In his circles it is a dangerous "pollutant" to be controlled, because it turns out that, while trees breathe it in to produce oxygen, apparently industrial Man also produces it. So, otherwise salubrious or not, that makes it a bad, bad thing.

As Yeatman concludes,

> Holdren's priorities are out of whack. In any definition of development, humans should take precedence over plants and animals. Economists have demonstrated that beyond a certain low level of per-capita GDP (such as China is now overcoming), a society's environment improves. That's why the wealthiest countries have the highest environmental quality. Economic development is the key to human well-being. De-development" [that would be de-population and abandoning today's technology favored by Holdren, and the central premise of the global warming agenda] "would cause just the sort of human suffering that Holdren has—incorrectly—ascribed to unabated population growth and global warming.[91]

It was Barack Obama who asked to be judged by the company he keeps. Doing so, and also judging his company by theirs, is very informative and very worrying.

CHAPTER 4

OBAMA'S "GLOBAL WARMING" POWER GRAB: TAXING AND STEALING YOUR LIBERTIES

Her Majesty's Government in Great Britain is busily pushing through its next step in the Statist assault on liberty, which our own president declares to be an urgent and necessary response to the threat of catastrophic Man-made global warming. In England, greens have proposed that each individual be issued a carbon dioxide ration "number," to be used like the rationing cards during World War I and II. After all, this is war. A *London Telegraph* headline announcing the rationing proposal read, "Everyone in Britain should have an annual carbon ration and be penalised if they use too much fuel, the head of the Environment Agency will say."[1]

The UK's ruling class turned their gaze to the reckless masses with this project on the heels of a previous, economically inane political gesture commonly "called cap-and-trade," under which the state allo-cated energy use "allowances" to businesses.[2] That proved such a disaster that it was only fair to keep it in place—and extend it to the little people.

This is a country whose elites have ensured no new power plants are coming on line to meet demand, and where conversation has openly turned to the blackouts that will come should their economy recover soon. It is a country where already one in five households are considered as being in energy poverty, thanks to policies driving elec-tricity prices up 70 percent in one decade, contributing to a similarly dramatic spike in "excess winter deaths" among the elderly.[3] The British citizenry were promised a portion of this cost would be "recy-cled" to them in a yearly check that did them precious little good as they froze in anticipation. The state might as well sniff, "Let them burn carbon credits."

Meanwhile, Prime Minister Gordon Brown, seeing how this chases jobs and investment elsewhere, called for the creation of a "global policeman" to monitor all individual countries' compliance with any future emissions reduction targets, with the EU taking the lead.[4] And Barack Obama gazes jealously at this perversion of priorities, hoping he can soon pull it off here, too.

To get there, Obama plans on frightening timid politicians into seeking "bipartisanship," that catnip for weak-willed Republicans in Washington eager for the approval of the establishment press and Georgetown cocktail set. The UK has seen bipartisanship blossom on environmental ploys in a deadly race to the bottom, having that to thank for their energy quandary. Thus this madness proceeds unhin-dered by any unusual political controversy, aside from some actual conservatives fleeing the Conservative Party for a fledgling, newer model.[5] UK politicians continue to pursue the climate change agenda even amid revelations in late 2009—originating in the UK, colloquially dubbed "ClimateGate" and aired far more aggressively by their media than here—that critical data underlying the premise of temperature rise had been cravenly manipulated. Results were manufactured, and other basic data were destroyed or lost, by the alarmists at the University of East Anglia.[6]

As the ration card measure went to the Brit lawmakers for a vote, Mark Steyn skewered the idea that:

> "every citizen be required to carry a carbon card that must be presented, under penalty of law, when buying gasoline, taking an airplane or using electricity. The card contains your yearly carbon ration to be drawn down with every purchase, every trip, every swipe." ... But don't worry. It'll all be very scientific. Your carbon allowance numbers will be kept in a big database. Maybe in East Anglia?[7]

Indeed, we are increasingly told to just take the word of and implicitly trust our liberties to people who have proven they are among the last on earth to be trusted or allowed the benefit of the doubt.

Europe is once again offering our homegrown statists a trial run, which we are to adopt regardless of how their schemes (fail to) perform. Real world experience notwithstanding, this is inescapably where Obama is headed with his obsessive drive to ration energy through state-imposed price and physical scarcity.

Rationing, taxing, and taking control is what the environmentalists and their movement are all about. And the cost of their dedicated campaign is mounting. *Los Angeles Examiner* "Ecopolitics" columnist Paul Taylor writes how, after thirty years of incessant, squeaky-wheel, and panic-driven enviro-activism, "today, the massive costs of

American environmental protections are embedded in all of our products, services and daily activities, and total about 5 percent of our gross domestic product (GDP)—equal to our national defense and homeland security GDPs combined."[8] And the environmentalists are only just beginning, having advanced the brass ring of their "cap-and-trade" and anti-energy "global warming" agenda to the cusp of success by electing the most radical administration and Congress our country has ever seen.

OBAMA'S PLAN, YOUR PAIN

On top of aggressively locking up land and otherwise suppressing domestic energy production, detailed in chapter 8, Barack Obama instructed his administration to quickly begin implementing the anti-energy agenda using existing authority, pressing the limits of and contorting that authority where necessary. This execution, led by the radicals we saw him hurriedly stuff in newly created, backdoor positions of high influence, was universally tied in some way to "global warming"—though he fell back in his 2010 State of the Union address, on "even if you doubt" what he called, to sustained laughter from nearly half the gallery in attendance, "the overwhelming scientific evidence," well, his environmentalist demands "are the right thing to do."[9]

That is, of course, an admission that the evidence is no such thing, and the laughter signaled an awareness of how the flimsy scientific underpinning was confirmed soon after Obama's inauguration as having been falsified. It winks at the fact that "climate" and "clean energy" are just excuses for the Left's agenda.

In response to "ClimateGate," President Obama panicked and flew to Copenhagen, where he "politically committed"[10] the United States to Kyoto-like promises in order to pressure an obviously reluctant Congress. Of course he agreed, because by attending, he signaled that the nations demanding handouts and shackles on our competitiveness could hold him hostage. Attempting to spin his doubling down on green, the White House scurried to its blog to tout the dog's breakfast of "global warming" programs Obama was busy forcing on taxpayers as virtuous and the stuff of prosperity. These programs included a staggering $80 billion for his buddies invested in uneconomic alternative energy.[11] Also included were "the first ever joint fuel economy/greenhouse gas emissions standards for cars and trucks,"[12] and making basic home conveniences more expensive through more than two dozen "stringent energy efficiency standards for commercial and residential appliances, including microwaves, kitchen ranges, dishwashers, lightbulbs and other common appliances."[13]

To help burnish his Copenhagen appearance, Obama had the Environmental Protection Agency make a Clean Air Act "Endangerment Finding," claiming that man-made carbon dioxide endangers human health and the environment.[14] This declaration of war on the U.S. economy came, naturally, on December 7, 2009, a date that shall live in economic infamy should Congress or litigation fail to stop it. Obama seized the potential authority to regulate absolutely everything in your daily life. Of a similar vein was the cap-and-trade legislation he pushed in Congress which also imposed hundreds of other new mandates, rules, programs, and agencies, discussed in detail later.

The White House also bragged of other actions on the way, like a federal renewable electricity quota, which is yet another way to make you to pay much more for your electricity.[15] They telegraphed a re commitment to new federal building energy efficiency standards. The legislation Obama supported a required an audit and expensive retrofit of individual homes before owners are permitted to sell.[16] And there are also plans for a new federal low carbon transportation fuel standard which, as is described in later pages, aims to keep our most abundant prospective source of oil imported from friendly shores—Canada's oil sands—out of the American market. This particular tenet of the green faith is actually something Obama adopted immediately upon his election to the Senate.[17]

On his blog, the president's team also trumpeted: "For the first time, the U.S. will catalogue greenhouse gas emissions from large emission sources."[18] Such moves requiring reporting, threatening to cover tens of thousands of businesses with massive reporting obligations, is generally sold by the greens in other contexts as "right to know," which is a standard Statist line prefacing most regulatory intrusions and rhetorically buttressed with the rather disingenuous "it's just a list!" To the White House's credit, they broke the greens' mold and offered no such pretention, but instead said right up front that this list was actually assembled for the obvious purpose of being used. The White House calls its move "an important initial step toward measurable and transparent reductions."[19] So, they're coming to get you and don't mind if you know it. What are you gonna do about it, anyway?

As if that were not enough, the White House thumped its chest over their offshore energy boondoggle, by which they seek to keep our own oil and gas out of reach by promising windmills instead. According to a December 2009 Rasmussen Reports survey, 76 percent of the public oppose such tomfoolery when it comes to offshore-energy, while 70 percent of the political class swoon for it, presumably over the opportunity it affords to posture and preen for a shrill and frivolous minority.[20] The scandalous nature of the administration again ignoring public desire, and irresponsibility among the political elites, deepened in February 2010 when the *Wall Street Journal* published an email unearthed from the Department of the Interior. This email showed that pro-drilling comments submitted to the Interior's Minerals Management Service as part of a rulemaking's public comment process surpassed anti-drilling comments by a 2 to 1 margin.[21]

But Team Obama remained obsessed with imposing some "carbon" constraint scheme by whatever means possible—through Congress or, the people unwilling, through the Environmental Protection Agency and a treaty, or, if the Senate proves unwilling, then a "congressional-executive agreement" serving as the equivalent of a treaty, just not requiring two-thirds of the Senate to approve it. Whatever form any such pact would take, it is scheduled to be agreed at November 2010 talks in Mexico, originally scheduled for six days after the election, but pushed back three weeks after Scott Brown's Senate victory put a scare in the entire Statist establishment.[22] Brown had expressly condemned cap-and-trade and the growing scientific scandals, in Massachusetts no less, and faced no discernable blowback.[23] Apparently even the UN-types read newspapers.

Or was it coincidence. Regardless, should the 2010 elections not go as poorly as the Left expects (as of this writing, although politics can be fickle, even with mounting public outrage over Obama and leftism), you will see an emboldened Obama tie us up in a Kyoto II, by "treaty" or otherwise.

THE ISSUE IS NEVER THE ISSUE

Even though the Senate version of the "global warming" legislation Obama demands requires deeper "greenhouse gas" emission cuts than the House bill—to 20 percent below 2005 levels by 2020, compared to 17 percent,[24] both of which are the stuff of fantasy or else a very deep and prolonged recession—this energy rationing measure now apparently is actually all about "clean energy ," "creating 'green jobs,'" and "energy security" (the magic words, according to focus groups).

After a rhetorical transition period based on promises to include some sort of legislative balm to "soften the blow"[25] from the bill's punishing restrictions, Democrat Senator Boxer of California apparently decided that, if you're going to stretch the truth, tell a whopper. By the fall of 2009, she had come out shrilly insisting what could prove to be the biggest tax increase in American history is really a "jobs bill."[26] Implicitly, then, it was just designed as a "global warming" bill because the masses don't take "jobs" seriously, and so the task demanded flying in under the "global warming" flag. But it's a jobs bill. Really.

These politicians were not deterred by the absurdity of claiming that job creation will result from energy rationing. Remember, this is the same crew who also tried Plan C—claiming the scheme was about "national security." It only stands to reason, then, that the rest of that team's related efforts to block electricity transmission lines are in the name of jobs and national security. Like their team's opposition to nuclear power or coal-mining. Just like their efforts to block pipelines of all varieties . . . domestic drilling . . . offshore drilling . . . Navy submarine training[27] . . . bombing exercises[28] . . . and underwater explosives training.[29] The list goes on. That's all jobs and national security stuff, too. It's just what these people are about.

In addition to these implausible "jobs" and "national security" rationales, as the agenda took further water late in Obama's first year, its proponents waved around a Congressional Budget Office (CBO) report to claim that, under the parameters CBO was told to analyze,[30] a Senate "global warming" bill was needed because it was a deficit reduction measure. It would ostensibly create a "net surplus" of $21 billion[31] over its first decade of operation. You see, all you have to do is ignore the real-world economic impact of energy rationing (that's the "static" scoring approach which ignores how variables interact). This was also another way of saying that the plan increased federal revenues by about $854 billion between 2010 and 2019 from selling energy-use ration coupons.[32] But it would also increase direct spending by about $833 billion.[33] Disregard for a moment what must have been a lame joke about dedicating a whopping 2.5 percent of the tax-grab to reducing the deficit[34]—a dollar amount which might have one day been real money; just not in Obama's Washington. Instead, note the spin job at work in claiming that a massive extraction of about $1 trillion in wealth from private economic activity is virtuous.

OBAMA: TAX COLLECTOR FOR THE GREEN STATE

The most high-profile of Obama's "environmental" schemes to steal your freedoms is the Kyoto-inspired "cap-and-trade." It appeared stalled in the Senate this year, but like the health care experience showed, the Left is not simply going to accept resistance to their marquee agenda items like seizing control of key sectors of the economy. It is being molded right now into cynical twists like "cap-and-dividend" (promising to refund a thousand bucks or so to certain households, at last admitting the cost[35]), and a "carbon-linked fee." The latter is just an idea concocted by a few oil companies most of which had previously supported cap-and-trade, to massage what they fear is "inevitable" legislation, by working out how to pass the costs directly to you, not them. Team Obama also might just seek to ram cap-and-trade through if need be.

That would be very harmful, economically. When applied not to an actual pollutant but to the intentional product (CO_2) of combusting "fossil" energy, it is a sneaky, indirect tax on energy. Obama is being honest when he says this government mandate will *necessarily* cause your energy prices to *skyrocket*. It would be the biggest intervention in people's lives and the economy since World War II. It would turn the United States into a second-rate economic power.

After breaking the seal almost immediately on his campaign pledge not to raise "any form" of taxes on those making less than $250,000 per year,[36] Obama set about to increase your energy taxes with this levy on gasoline, heating oil, natural gas, and most electricity (especially the half that is coal-fired). He is thereby also increasing the effective taxation of chemicals, plastics, and fertilizer, all of which require not only large quantities of energy but also natural gas as feedstock. This also translates into increasing the price of food. Indeed, everything, as the cost of energy is embedded in all prices.

Although, on the eve of the House voting on its bill, the Obama administration cooked up some phony figures to downplay the cost of the scheme—like the infamous claim that it would only cost "a postage stamp a day"—even those cost figures amount to tens of billions of dollars per year.[37] That's a lot of money if still a far cry from administration estimates of anywhere from $100 billion to $300 billion per year set forth in documents I obtained from the Treasury Department under the Freedom of Information Act. Or more. Columnist Declan McCullagh noted at the time that, "One Treasury document says climate change-related policies could yield additional 'revenues up to several percentage points of annual GDP (i.e. equal in size to the corporate income tax).' According to IRS figures, corporate income tax revenues totaled $395.5 billion in 2007."[38]

These figures are just revenues to the state from selling the ration coupons—forget the actual cost to the economy and households. The largest tax hike in history to date is a subject of debate, whether one uses inflation-adjusted dollars or size relative to our economy at the time (percentage of gross domestic product), but this $300 billion figure would equal 2 percent of our economy and would therefore be substantially larger than almost all others battling for the mantle in the absence of Obama's energy tax, and almost certainly the largest in terms of inflation-adjusted dollars.[39]

As to specific cost projections, modeling estimates generally fall in a range of $1,700 to $3,100 per year per family of four. In fact, it turned out that the claim made by the administration that the House bill would actually only cost a household of four a "postage stamp a day" was the product of accounting trickery, and when deconstructed actually admits to well over a thousand dollars per year per household of four.[40] Slightly more honest were those candid internal administration assessments in the Treasury Department documents I received through a Freedom of Information Act request which, when distilled, would peg costs at between $1,761 to $3,522 per average household per year.[41] Would you pay a "global warming tax," of any amount in that range, if asked? Of course not, and that's why they're not asking.

The short form of what this legislation means was detailed in a study by government contractor Science Applications International Corporation (SAIC).[42] SAIC said that the House-passed bill, which the Senate version only made more stringent, would reduce America's gross domestic product by $2.2 to $3.1 trillion between 2012 and 2030.[43] Industrial output would immediately decline, by up to 6.5 percent, while substantially reducing net employment (by between 420,000 and 620,000 jobs) even after factoring in the alleged silver bullet of "green" jobs.[44] All of this is logical given that electricity prices, again per SAIC, would rise by 50 percent and gasoline prices by 26 percent. That's what Obama was talking about. Household income would drop by over $1,200, with the deepest hit being the Midwestern agricultural and manufacturing heartland.[45]

This was one of the less critical independent assessments of the bill, and was in line with various assessments by government bureaucrats.

At this point I dare not discuss the MIT professor[46] whom the Democrats trotted out to say that much of the enormous cost of their cap-and-trade bill wasn't really a cost to your family, because the money was going to the government, and after all, the taxpayer receives a dollar in government for every dollar the state takes. (Did I mention he is an academic?)

What of the poor, who will be hit hardest by this tax and the cost of everything going up while wages are depressed? A Dr. Bill Heckle, representative of those informed and therefore outraged voters our policymakers dismiss as rabble, wrote in a letter published by the *Cincinnati Enquirer,*

> One thing we can conclude is that to facilitate any significant reduction of atmospheric CO_2, the economic impact would also be significant. Even more disturbing is that the poor and disadvantaged are not mentioned in the economic analyses. According to the latest census, 37.3 million Americans are living below the poverty level. What would the economic impact of reducing CO_2 levels be on them? The cap-and-trade part of the Waxman-Markey bill is essentially a tax on energy, and the poor will be disproportionally "taxed" because a higher proportion of their income goes for energy costs.[47]

Don't worry, we were told, the lowest rungs on the socio-economic ladder will get some of the cost refunded. Just like in Britain. Great. But also consider one of Obama's "green jobs" models, Germany. The *Washington Post* wrote of the impacts there of Obama-style power grabs: "A kilowatt of electricity costs three times as much [in Germany] as it does in the United States, supercharged with high taxes to discourage use and to help fund renewable energy development."[48] This, and eco-taxes driving gasoline to (at present exchange rates, after the Euro's plunge) a mere $7 per gallon, hurts German families, like the Pokropp family of three whom the *Post* cites as an example. To get by, the family "unplugs all their appliances but the refrigerator at night, avoids driving and limits steam baths—a favorite German custom. 'We have no choice,' said Andreas Pokropp, a former coal refinery worker. 'We have to be green, even if we can't afford it.'"[49]

Although a non-transparent tax, cap-and-trade manages the rare feat of also being a rationing scheme—that's the "cap"—under which the state decides how much of something the private sector can have. This cap on greenhouse gas emissions from burning coal, oil, and natural gas (which provide over 80 percent of U.S. and global energy) operates akin to World War II-style rationing of, say, gasoline or nylons, but instead, it rations the burning of gasoline and electricity produced by disfavored sources—in other words, the ones that work. The distinctions between this and the World War II scheme are that cap-and-trade allocates the allowances according to political considerations, and allows covered emitters to buy and sell ration coupons on the open market instead of a black market.

Hence the misnomer of cap-and-trade being a "market mechanism," just because buying and selling are involved. Where the allowances go, at first, are actually divvied up in the legislation, therefore, politically. The market doesn't kick in until after the ration coupons are handed out, seemingly according to which groups have the best lobbying operation.[50] It is a clever way of saying that the well-connected get to sell that which is given them by the state, while the state restricts other poor saps without Gucci-shod lobbyists. So this is no "market mechanism." It is corporate welfare, in fact, the biggest corporate welfare scheme in our nation's history.

The cap is lowered each year—by roughly 2 percent in the House and Senate bills. So if you think it's bad, just wait until the next year.

Here are some of the things said by Obama and his Democrat and green group allies in cheerleading their scheme:

President Barack Obama: "Under my plan of a cap and trade system, electricity rates would necessarily skyrocket.... So, if somebody wants to build a coal plant, they can—it's just that it will bankrupt them, because they are going to be charged a huge sum for all that greenhouse gas that's being emitted."[51]

Oh, and "That will also generate billions of dollars."[52]

Then the president was joined in this call by House Speaker Nancy Pelosi: "I believe we have to [pass cap-and-trade] because we see that as a source of revenue."[53]

Democratic Senator Benjamin Cardin, a man who knows his tax hikes, having served for years on the House Ways and Means (tax-writing) Committee before joining the Senate's tax-writing Finance Committee, said cap-and-trade is "the most significant revenue-generating proposal of our time."[54] In Washington, since 1993, we ceased having tax increases. We have "revenue enhancements" or other euphemisms, but whatever one you choose, it is the most significant of our time.

But don't worry, we're assured it doesn't cost anything.

Remember this: Obama was correct, energy price hikes are "necessary" under cap-and-trade. They are the entire purpose of the exercise of cap-and-trade. Price hikes are not—as some particularly eely political creatures have insisted, with the occasional aid of self-styled truth-squads—some side effect they've figured out how to avoid.[55] Of course, taking them at their words beggars the reality that if it didn't cost anything, it wouldn't convince anyone to change their behavior and reduce emissions. Obama told the truth when he promised "skyrocketing" energy costs and bankrupted industries.

Representative John Dingell, the longest-serving Member of the House and therefore a man who knows taxes, great, big, and otherwise, said, "Nobody in this country realizes that cap-and-trade is a tax, and it's a great big one."[56]

Indeed, economists have long called carbon cap-and-trade a tax. Consider the CBO, which has, at least as far back as 2001, called it a regulatory tax. "The economic impacts of cap-and-trade programs would be similar to those of a carbon tax: both would raise the cost of using carbon-based fossil fuels, lead to higher energy prices and impose costs on users and some suppliers of energy."[57] The results are the same: energy and consumer prices rise; output, employment, and real wages fall. Except unlike a transparent tax, cap-and-trade transfers wealth from individuals to well-placed constituencies. If you want to know who, look at the groups lobbying for the scheme, some of whose interests and efforts are detailed later.

This is no different than the brazen stunt the same crowd pulled in advocating a state seizure of the health care insurance and delivery systems. A bill sold on the implausible grounds that it would lower costs was revealed by expert analysis as certain to increase costs. So it was then promoted on the fallback grounds that it would provide subsidies for many of those hardest hit by a price hiking-measure adopted in the name of cutting costs, but in fact, ultimately driven by the desire to seize control.

The same ritual has played out with the similarly disingenuous cap-and-trade. The sales pitch was a lie, and they didn't stick with it for all that long, for the apparent reason that those spouting it knew it was untrue. The issue wasn't the issue. These people cannot tell you what they seek to do and expect you to go along with it.

Worse, as taxes go, cap-and-trade is also a very expensive tax, actually four to five times as costly as a transparent tax.[58] This makes it particularly hard on the middle class whose taxes Obama vowed he would not raise—of any kind—not to mention seniors and the poor. But of course, transparent taxes threaten those few jobs of which elected politicians are particularly solicitous: their own. So we get sneaky backdoor tricks instead.

WHO PAYS?

With the Democrats still unsure of how to deal with the cost figures reaching the public eyes and ears, they began saying that these costs of cap-and-trade were to be paid not by you and not by me, but by the guy behind the tree, as the old Washington ditty goes. But check out what Obama's Office of Management and Budget Director Peter Orszag said in 2008 congressional testimony while still running the Congressional Budget Office:

> Under a cap-and-trade program, firms would *not* ultimately bear most of the costs of the allowances but instead would pass them along to their customers in the form of higher prices. Such price increases would stem from the restriction on emissions and would occur regardless of whether the government sold emission allowances or gave them away. Indeed, the price increases would be essential to

the success of a cap-and-trade program because they would be the most important mechanism through which businesses and households would be encouraged to make investments and behavioral changes that reduced CO_2 emissions.[59] (emphasis in original)

Orszag's successor as CBO's Director also testified the next year that those price increases will "be passed through to the cost that consumers face on energy products but also all other products that are made using fossil fuels . . . I don't know if there any goods that use no energy in their production. It seems to me unlikely."[60]

In a fit of candor or lapse of language, Democratic Rep. Charles Rangel, chairman of the House Ways and Means Committee, said on May 14, 2009: "Whether you call it a tax, everyone agrees that it's going to increase the cost to the consumer."[61]

Before joining Obama's Climate Service, Orszag was also rather candid about the economic ravages of cap-and-trade rationing. For example, consider other remarks in his April 2008 testimony: "[F]irms would ... pass [the costs] along to their customers (and their customers' customers) in the form of higher prices. By attaching a cost to CO_2 emissions, a cap-and-trade program would ... lead to price increases for energy and energy-intensive goods and services, the production of which contributes the most to those emissions."[62]

Inadvertently admitting a little too much, the Senate bill's co-author, San Francisco's own Boxer, introduced the idea of "recycling" the taxes paid for energy-use ration coupons, vowing that "the vast majority of allowances will go to consumers to keep them whole."[63] That won't get them their jobs back, although it does acknowledge that the bill that don't cost nuthin' is somehow still painful. But upon scrutiny, what this will mean in practice is that most of these "allowances" will still be given away to big business special interests. This vow of trying to return some of the bill's energy cost increases, incidentally, puts the lie for all time to the claims that cap-and-trade revenues will be "recycled" to the middle class. Several billion dollars from the ones that are sold to Americans so they can use energy will then be sent overseas as aid to satisfy Obama's Copenhagen "political commitment."

Still, Orszag had already warned us, "Regardless of how the allowances were distributed, most of the cost of meeting a cap on CO_2 emissions would be borne by consumers, who would face persistently higher prices for products such as electricity and gasoline. Those price increases would be regressive in that poorer households would [have] a larger burden relative to their income than wealthier households would."[64]

All of these assessments are true, and Orszag's are the words of a technocrat before he became a political operative.

When it comes to the impact of this scheme on agriculture, the president of the American Farm Bureau, Bob Stallman, says the cap-and-trade bill alone will create an artificial energy shortage for his association's 6.2 million member families, by imposing myriad additional costs on them.[65] This puts them at a disadvantage against other nations producing for our market, as well as for their vast export market, since America still feeds much of the world. In fact, farming families in this country export about one out of every three acres of their agricultural production.

For now, that is. What this means for America's farm communities is that their markets dry up as we become less competitive in agriculture as in every other field, particularly those requiring massive energy or natural gas inputs, such as fertilizer. Terrific quantities of energy are necessary in the chemical process that is fertilizer manufacture; fertilizer is, of course, a major requirement for America's farmers. Cap and trade is designed to force fuel-switching in the near-term from coal to natural gas as the only proven reliable fuel source that would deliver sufficient quantities of reliable energy and lower emissions (other than nuclear, which remains in political limbo), until some alternative not foreseeable today springs from the fore-head of Zeus, which is as likely as any other prospect that will soak up taxpayer money through the boom in federal grants to develop pixie dust.

As such, the cost of natural gas—therefore fertilizer, and conse-quently, farming and food—go up. Agriculture has long been a target of the greens, who will never forgive us for managing to feed all of those people whom the enviros insisted would starve if they, horror of horrors, managed to be born.

When Obama's Department of Agriculture computer model assessments of cap-and-trade's impact revealed that it would encour-age farmers to plant trees for carbon credits instead of food—thereby driving the cost of food even higher still—the administration told the modelers to change the assumptions to get a different result.[66] Funny, when it comes to their computer models projecting warming even as we experience observed cooling, they tell us there must be something wrong with the observations—the "me or yer old lyin' eyes" argu-ment—because the models must be respected. But of course, everyone knows that models predicting the weather—and even the behavior of the vastly larger and more complex climate system, a cen-tury out no less—are very reliable. Trillion-dollar-policy reliable, apparently.

The well-established economic consulting firm CRA International (formerly Charles River Associates) found in a study prepared for the National Black Chamber that "businesses and consumers would face higher energy and transportation costs under [the bill] which would lead to increased costs of other goods and services throughout the economy. As the costs of goods and services rise, household disposable income and household consumption would fall. Wages and returns on investment would also fall, resulting in lower productivity growth and reduced employment opportunities."[67] That should help the economic recovery along.

In short, CRA International found that "even after accounting for green jobs, there is a substantial and long-term net reduction in total labor earnings and employment," which the authors argue is the logical outcome of energy rationing policies. "This is the unintended but predictable consequence of investing to create a 'green energy future.'"[68]

Consider also what some other sources, beyond the Obama squad, have said about this scheme. They indicate that not only is cap-and-trade a tax, paid by you, but a scam to reward well-heeled constituencies lobbying for it, which puts us all at risk of yet another financial scandal and meltdown.

The *Houston Chronicle* cited "Robert Shapiro of the left-leaning think tank NDN [as saying] the cap-and-trade system would create 'trillions of dollars in new, asset-based financial instruments.' Backers of the plan on Wall Street 'see emissions-permit trading as a lucrative new market that could earn them billions in new fees, commissions and, while it lasts, speculative gains.'"[69] Unsaid was that these, too, are ultimately borne by the consumer, ratepayer, and taxpayer: in other words, you.

You will pay for these risks in more ways than you might imagine. Old Red herself, *The Guardian*, dared publish the following heresy in February 2009. Under cap-and-trade, "[t]he market must be unashamedly rigged to force supply below demand," and it leaves the state "like medieval pardoners handing out unlimited indulgences. . . . Europe's whizz-bang carbon market is turning sub-prime."[70]

This parallels eerily with the 2008 financial collapse, whose rubble we were just crawling out from under when Wall Street advocates rushed to Washington to promote new governmental ministrations rewarding them with billions in skim, but no actual innovative, productive economic activity. Fully aware of this, the green pressure group Friends of the Earth began a searing "Subprime Carbon" campaign which managed to be the one green campaign ignored by the press. "Unfortunately, the federal cap and trade proposals put forth so far would create a system that poses almost identical challenges as those in the mortgage-lending industry," Friends of the Earth said in a March 2009 piece.[71]

Clearly, cap-and-trade is a scheme designed to raise energy prices which is, in turn, certain to put vastly greater numbers of people out of work than the number of jobs that could ever be generated to satisfy and administer to its inefficiencies. It is also specifically chosen and designed to enrich rent-seeking lobbying interests.

So, when the House bill was being considered in the Energy and Commerce Committee, Republican opponents sought to build in some statutory triggers to prevent what they suspected, but liberal proponents denied, would occur. They offered three amendments to suspend cap-and-trade if:

> Gasoline hit $5 a gallon;
> Electricity prices increased 100 percent; or
> Unemployment reached 15 percent.

All were defeated on near-party-line votes.[72]

OUT OF THEIR MINDS, PUTTING YOU OUT OF WORK

After the president's candor about "skyrocketing" energy costs and "bankrupting" those he doesn't care for—now, there's a just and proper use of the state—came back to haunt the debate over "climate" legislation, he decided to take a slightly different approach. Okay, a completely different approach, showing a certain flexibility with what he is willing to say: "Make no mistake, this is a jobs bill."[73] Huh.

We know that "green jobs," "security," and other comforting phrases are the new hooks to rebrand and distract from the reality of many aspects of Obama's drive to expand government, not merely cap-and-trade. The "green jobs" canard is dismantled in chapter 6, but consider how, for example, certain jobs are sure to be created. The same scheming, expensive, incompetent government would do quite well under the scheme, with the Congressional Budget Office projecting a boom in bureaucrats costing $7.5 billion over the next decade, starting at a whopping $540 million per year immediately.[74] Of course, you pay for that, too.

Anyhow, complying with this law, if enacted, should be easy under Obamanomics. As Senator John Kerry said, "Let me emphasize something very strongly as we begin this discussion. The United States has already this year alone achieved a 6 percent reduction in emissions simply because of the downturn in the economy, so we are effectively saying we need to go another 14 percent."[75] Recession being the sole established way to significantly reduce emissions over any period of time, he was saying that, heck, the collapse has brought us a third of the way there.

It is worth noting that, as the CBS Evening News reported, "As the US economy struggles, we're not just losing jobs, we're losing manufacturing jobs, the kind that pay well, have benefits and provide a comfortable middle-class lifestyle. Of the nearly 8.5 million jobs lost since the recession began, more than a quarter were in manufacturing and getting them back may require a big change in attitude about working with our hands."[76] More than 17 million Americans were employed in manufacturing in 2000. By 2009, the number was fewer than 12 million.[77] Now, it seems, they just need to make things worse.

As Nick Loris of the Heritage Foundation wrote facetiously, "If the trade off is a 6 percent reduction in emissions for a 3.5 percent reduction in unemployment in one year alone, we could get to a 20 percent reduction in carbon dioxide by October 2011 and push the unemployment rate to 18 percent."[78] Please, don't give them too many ideas, though this may add some texture to the Obama economic strategy of imposing all sorts of mandates and taxes to make recovery that much harder.

Cap-and-trade promoters do seem to be all too aware of the relationship between emission reductions and job loss, as each and every scheme has included wealth transfers to offset the cost of living increases, as well as up to three years of assistance for workers displaced by the law's restrictions on key economic activities.

The House-passed bill requires the Secretary of Health and Human Services to provide monthly cash payments in "adjustment assistance" to energy producing and transforming industries; industries dependent upon energy industries; energy-intensive manufacturing industries; consumer goods manufacturing; or "other industries whose employment the Secretary determines has been adversely affected by any requirement of title VII of the Clean Air Act."[79] We would call those "the American workforce," excluding lawyers, bureaucrats, and lawmakers.

Then there's the relief for the lowest-income households— at or below 150 percent of the poverty line, going to about one-fifth of U.S. residents—to help offset their estimated "loss in their purchasing power" resulting from Obama's national energy tax.[80] These new welfare payments, or "energy stamps" as some House Republicans began calling them, would go to an estimated 65 million individuals, making it a larger government aid program than welfare, food stamps, or even Medicaid, creating the largest welfare program in our nation's history for displaced workers.[81]

These are odd features running through these supposed "jobs bills." Displaced workers can apply for payments equal to 70 percent of the average weekly wage of that worker "for a period of not longer than 156 weeks," or 3 years.[82] A job-search allowance of up to $1,500, relocation assistance in the same amount, and other job retraining programs are also included, because the number of workers forced into a career change as, say, windmill repairmen, will be extensive.[83]

Too extensive, in fact, to be supported by the relief schemes accompanying the harms. Congressional Budget Office estimates that the program to help displaced workers will be funded up to $4.3 billion over ten years.[84] That is insufficient. Economic analysts CRA International also estimate a net loss of jobs from the bill of about 2.5 million each year.[85] Run the numbers and you see that each worker, if equally treated, should expect about $1,500 to offset 70 percent of his annual, lost wages. Meaning those who lose their jobs had better be those who were earning about two grand a year.[86]

Some of these bills, like the "Dingell-Boucher Discussion Draft" circulated at the end of the previous Congress in 2008, openly acknowledge that the money put aside for this assistance will not be sufficient, arranging for *pro rata* reductions in the welfare once the funds begin to dry up.[87] The accepted insufficiency in funds put aside to assist displaced American workers does not stop the same bills from transferring billions of the revenues generated from selling Americans energy use ration coupons to India, Mexico, and China for tree planting programs—just so you know these lawmakers aren't entirely without compassion.

So we would also be guaranteeing that the global warming legislation and program will need a federal bailout, too. Already, according to the *Washington Post*, forty of the fifty states will run out of unemployment funds over the next two years and will have to borrow $90 billion from the federal government to pay for benefits.[88] So what the heck, why not really go long on the stupid?

With lawmakers behind these schemes admitting they are job-killers, it seems the targeted audience believes them. A poll in *Manufacturing & Technology eJournal* revealed an estimated 20 percent of manufacturers would shut their doors here under the measure.[89] But what do people actually engaged in making things know?

However, the obvious impact of hitting manufacturing economies the hardest is also behind the plea made by numerous Democrat senators from America's heartland, that any bill must include provisions starting a trade war against countries not following suit.[90] Not only is that a prescription for economic disaster, if history is any guide, but it admits the economic harm in store for America if cap-and-trade is adopted. That they find it necessary to make this condition should tell you (and them) all we need to know about whether to engage in such climatically meaningless gestures.

All of this explains the *Wall Street Journal* writing of the debacle certain to result:

> [I]n addition to all the other economic harm, a cap-and-trade tax will make foreign companies more competitive while eroding market share for U.S. businesses. The most harm will accrue to the very U.S. manufacturing and heavy-industry jobs

that Democrats and unions claim to want to keep.... [it] would be the greatest outsourcing boon in history.[91]

HOUSE OF CARDS

Despite all these downsides well-known to anyone versed in the issue, the political threat to lawmakers from voting instead on a less costly but transparent "carbon" or energy tax was just too great. So in the House, the Democrat leadership bull-rushed the sneaky cap-and-trade bill, cramming it down while rushing to escape work for their 2009 Fourth of July "recess." Lead author Henry Waxman of Beverly Hills vented his outrage at Minority Leader John Boehner for insisting on reading—*aloud*, gasp!—provisions from the more than 300 pages added to the bill at 3:00 a.m. the very morning before the vote.[92] Waxman erupted that, if Boehner insisted on such transgressions, why, members would miss their flights!

Foreshadowing the sleazy vote-buying that occurred to pass the "health care" bill, those additional, early morning pages, fleecing the taxpayer to pay for expensive goodies in members' districts, apparently did the trick to secure enough votes. The 1,510 page bill passed the House on June 26, 2009, by 219 to 212.[93] Forty-four Democrats voted No. Eight Republicans voted Yes.[94] Members caught their planes. You caught the shaft.

Among the Republicans voting for the bill—who were apparently not reachable with economic arguments and somehow couldn't even figure out how to say, "I'm with Friends of the Earth on this, it is setting up an enormous financial scandal the likes of which we just experienced," or "I'm with Greenpeace on this, *it's climatically meaningless*"—was one Leonard Lance of New Jersey. This bright bulb, who said "aye" to "skyrocketing" electricity prices and pushing energy-intensive jobs abroad, shall be deeply missed when his voters figure him out. He employed a particularly despicable approach to calm his furious constituents, saying it is time for the rest of the states to have Washington place on them the same burden that New Jersey had already placed on itself, by "level[ing] the playing field."[95] Not by straightening out New Jersey's disastrous burdens, but exporting them. Only fair, you know.

Indiana Governor Mitch Daniels captured the sentiment of those victimized by this ploy of the coastal elites. "It's become clear that the Pelosi bill has little to do with a cooler planet and everything to do with raising money for the out-of-control federal spending now under way in Washington. Please excuse us Midwesterners for feeling a bit like the targets of an imperialistic policy, devised in places like California, New York, and Massachusetts for their benefit, at our expense."[96]

After such political blowback hit members of Congress, who up to that moment when voters began paying attention had had about the easiest six-figure, perk-heavy job in the world, the Senate sought to spin their own effort. Thus was born the initial 821-page Kerry-Boxer energy-rationing bill, which oddly didn't mention global warming or cap-and-trade.[97] In fact, co-author Senator John Kerry openly insisted that "I don't know what cap-and-trade means."[98] What he is likely saying is that he heard most of you have gotten wind of what it means, and aren't thrilled. So in his bill, S. 1733, cap-and-trade is now called "pollution reduction and investment."[99]

OBAMA'S "WINDOW INSURANCE"

Confronted with political opposition at home and the prospect of insufficient Euro-adulation at those December 2009 Copenhagen

"Kyoto II" talks, the Obama administration unveiled its backdoor plan to impose Kyoto-style energy suppression through the Environmental Protection Agency (EPA) without express congressional authorization.[100] In early December, EPA announced the finding that six greenhouse gases including carbon dioxide "threaten the public health and welfare of current and future generations" by contributing to "greenhouse gas pollution."[101] This was taking advantage of a judicial stretch of a law drafted in the 1970s and last amended in 1990 (the Clean Air Act) which quite plainly was never intended or structured for such a purpose. In the absence of any statutory framework detailing how they can address these gases, until checked by the courts, the Environmental Protection Agency can basically regulate these gases however they see fit—which would tend to benefit their friends and harm those not in line with their agenda.

Obama wants "climate"—suddenly renamed "energy"—legislation. And if he doesn't get it, well, EPA might just have to make some rulings that require them to take on unprecedented levels of oversight in the business community—until business, seeking relief, begs for legislation regulating unofficial cap-and-trade policies. Or, possibly, EPA can be aggressive in its threat of doing so, to the same end. This would provide the sort of political "cover" Congress has needed, so leading lawmakers have gone along with the routine. It is a reprehensible form of mobster-like "insurance," more like, *Better pay me to protect you from my lunatic friend here; sure would be a shame if something happened to you like, say, if EPA got loose on some sort of CO_2 regulatin' spree.*

Toward this end, the Environmental Protection Agency's 2011 budget request includes $43.5 million to regulate greenhouse gases. The rest of the Left, all the way up to the White House, has not been shy, making insinuations about how terrible the EPA doing this would be.[102] Democrats in the Administration, in Congress, and elsewhere have argued that EPA regulation would be extremely problematic. For example:

EPA regulation would be "one of the largest and most bureaucratic nightmares that the U.S. economy and Americans have ever seen,"[103] said Rep. Colin Peterson, Democratic chairman of the House Agriculture Committee.

EPA regulation would be a "glorious mess" and "it seems to me to be insane that we would be talking about leaving this kind of judgment... to a long and complex process of regulatory action,"[104] said Democratic Rep. John Dingell, an author of the Clean Air Act (CAA).

"Making the decision to regulate CO_2 under the CAA for the first time is likely to have serious economic consequences for regulated entities throughout the U.S. economy, including small businesses and small communities,"[105] warned an internal OMB document.

These concerns appear to be heartfelt, but generally they came as a warning that the threat of EPA regulation presented Congress with the imperative to legislate, to preempt the Environmental Protection Agency doing this[106]—when, of course, Congress could simply pass a line item prohibiting the regulation and giving itself time to deliberate, were this concern sincere. In less guarded moments, members of Congress openly stated that the Environmental Protection Agency would be far more harmful than if people just accepted Congress' more orchestrated assault.[107]

As at least one senator remarked before a private audience of policy-types I participated in that he could not recall any instance of bureaucrats announcing that what they were proposing was so terribly awful that Congress really needed to step in and stop them from doing it.[108]

So, Obama angrily demands that holdout businesses join schemers like GE to give him and the Democrats political cover on the biggest tax increase and regulatory intervention in American history. And he threatens that unless opposition to him and pressure on Congress to do the right thing by rejecting cap-and-trade legislation are stopped, he will use the Environmental Protection Agency to impose extraordinarily intrusive and expensive rules by which they will regulate the entire economy, down to livestock, construction, and retail stores.

You may be wondering why the Environmental Protection Agency would begin a regime of global warming regulations knowing that Congress never voted for or approved such a thing. It is because the Supreme Court, in *Massachusetts v. EPA* (April 2007), decided to instigate the agenda from the bench.[109]

In that case, green groups teamed up with activist state attorneys general to get around Congress's continuing resistance to openly adopting the Kyoto agenda. As my CEI colleague Marlo Lewis, PhD, writes, "They found five willing accomplices on the Court, who essentially ruled that Congress authorized EPA to regulate GHGs for climate change purposes when it enacted the [Clean Air Act] CAA in 1970—decades before global warming became a public concern. The Court's decision—an affront to common sense—all but ensured"[110] the parade of horrible policies spewing out of the Environmental Protection Agency at an increasing pace, each triggered as a matter of statutory necessity by the one before it.

Sadly, the Court paid no heed to the domino effect that would necessarily ensue should they rule as they did. Had they examined this, at least one of those five justices would surely have recognized that the 1970 Congress never intended the Clean Air Act to be used this way. (At that time, in fact, the public—or rather the sensationalist media and science establishment—were in a *cooling* panic.[111]) Admittedly, only some of the specific statutory consequences were addressed in any detail in one among the numerous briefs filed on the case—an inherent risk given how topics are parceled out among allied sides in such cases. But in this case, the terrific wave of consequences should the Court rule incorrectly was not a significant consideration, despite it being possibly the most economically consequential ruling of the court for decades—if not the past century. (Full disclosure: I represented the "skeptic" scientists in that case, but our brief was focused on the science, not Clean Air Act minutiae).

The ruling from *Massachusetts v. EPA* in 2007 found that the Environmental Protection Agency could classify CO_2 as a pollutant if it chose. One major consequence which was not even raised was that , if it did, this would make many small facilities subject to the Clean Air Act and onerous requirements for obtaining "prevention of significant deterioration" permits—that regulate supposedly dangerous emissions, but drain small businesses of costly man-hours. Lewis notes that these include "millions of office buildings, apartment complexes, big box stores, enclosed malls, heated agricultural facilities, small manufacturing firms, even commercial kitchens."[112] Environmental attorney Peter Glaser, who did address some of the likely consequences to the Court, declares this will cover "office buildings, apartment buildings, warehouse and storage buildings, educational buildings, health care buildings such as hospitals and assisted living facilities, hotels, restaurants, religious worship buildings, public assembly buildings, supermarkets, retail malls, agricultural facilities... and many others."[113]

The Environmental Protection Agency now agrees, estimating that the outcome of this kind of regulation means that applications for Clean Air Act "prevention of significant deterioration" permits to construct those facilities would "necessarily skyrocket," to borrow a phrase, from 280 to 41,000 each year, and the number of "Title V" permit applications for permits to operate them would spike from 14,700 to 6.1 million.[114] Incidentally, it does seem that these applications would largely have to be rejected yet, even were that not the case, this burden alone should freeze the regulatory beast's ability to process applicants, either way putting a freeze on new construction.

The EPA publicly argues that they were forced by the Court to regulate carbon dioxide, thereby imposing this economic albatross on us all. This is untrue. They were merely given the authority by the Court—it was the agency's choice, and the Obama administration's decision, to exercise it.

As if this rule's origin and certain impact are not sufficiently perverted, consider how intellectually corrupt the approach became. Supporters shrilly insisted that EPA regulation would extend only to those mean, *big polluters* such as power plants and refineries, disparaging claims to the contrary. For example, even Obama's EPA chief Lisa Jackson decried as "myth" the claim that the rule would be expansive, sneering at the idea that "EPA will regulate cows, Dunkin' Donuts, Pizza Hut, your lawnmower and baby bottles."[115] (So, they brag about coming after your light bulbs and small appliances. But small businesses? *What are you, some kind of conspiracy kook?*). But then, because of what the Clean Air Act actually says—that "pollution" from a source which passes a threshold of 250 tons should be regulated, which is an insanely small amount when it comes to carbon dioxide—they found themselves forced to (unlawfully) "tailor" what the Act actually said, proposing another rule to functionally read the amount at a much higher level of *25,000* tons in order to prevent the inclusion of the very small businesses they had angrily denied would be affected.[116] Clearly that is not only an admission they'd been less than honest, but also a tacit admission that the Act wasn't actually written for the purpose of regulating carbon dioxide, which is not a pollutant.

Then in May 2009, the Office of Management and Budget in the White House released a memo acknowledging that regulating carbon dioxide would have serious economic consequences. According to the head of the U.S. Chamber of Commerce's environment and regulatory affairs, William Kovacs, "the memo 'confirms almost everything we've been saying on the spillover effects of regulating greenhouse gases.'"[117]

"Well, well," the *Wall Street Journal* wrote. "In a speech in February, Obama EPA Administrator Lisa Jackson ridiculed those of us who warned about these consequences. . . . Her routine got a big laugh from the like-minded Georgetown audience, but the new draft rule is a flat-out admission that the critics are right."[118]

This raises yet one more problem with this effort by Obama to bully business into dropping its opposition, or Congress into passing a more orderly chaos on top of EPA's threatened nightmare. His administration clearly sought to avoid taking public responsibility for the same accomplishments it boasted to its ideological base about, to the point of transparently making up law as it went.

To recap, the Environmental Protection Agency plan was to propose an unlawful re-reading of the statute it wants to use as a "global warming" law, purporting to limit its regulatory reach to just those big, nasty polluters. The greens won't stand for it, of course—they want all emitters of CO_2 included, no matter how small. At least one green group made clear it plans to use the courts to "halt" greenhouse gas emissions.[119] Why would even that group hold off on their new-found ability to blackmail the federal government until a less ideologically attuned administration was inaugurated? Even collec tivists go rogue every now and again.

For example, as Senator James Inhofe of Oklahoma pointed out in a speech on the Senate floor, The Conservation Law Foundation, in their comments on EPA's Advanced Notice of Proposed Rule-making (ANPR) on greenhouse gas regulation under the Clean Air Act, did ask the Agency to regulate such sources. Moreover, some groups already made the case in their comments that the Environmental Protection Agency is required by law to apply that "prevention of significant deterioration" program to sources emitting above 100 or 250 tons of CO_2 per year. No exceptions. Scary indeed. The Center for Biological Diversity argued, "While it is uncontroversial that EPA should prioritize the largest pollution sources first, one of the reasons that the [Clean Air Act's] program will be such an effective tool for reducing GHG emissions is that it applies to a wide array of sources that will emit in excess of the applicable statutory thresholds of 250 or 100 tons per year."[120] Which means just about everything.

A court presented this challenge would agree, given that what Obama's EPA is doing is, on its face, a violation of the Clean Air Act's clear language. 100 to 250 tons doesn't mean 25,000, even if the lower numbers were ignored to avoid what the agency admits would prove "absurd" in practice. This would generate an unprecedented regulatory cascade covering nearly all businesses—yes, down to donut shops, apartment buildings, and small construction jobs.[121] The EPA's ploy is to present itself as having tried to be nice and make things up as they went along for a more politically palatable outcome. It was all the fault of the courts. Swear.

In other words, they either think you're stupid, or that the media won't do their job and accurately tell this story.

Incredibly, Obama's cram-down then got even worse. Jackson soon admitted the plan was actually to use the backdoor of existing Clean

Air Act provisions as a global warming law regardless of whether Congress passed cap-and-trade.[122] "Climate Czar" Carol Browner then told the pressure group National Resources Defense Council the same thing, saying "we want comprehensive energy legislation, because we need all the pieces of the puzzle."[123] The appeal for legislation so EPA wouldn't have to do this to America was really a little tap-dance to disguise that the legislation would still allow them to do most of it anyway. Jackson simply needed her congressional allies to oblige by making sure the bills didn't preempt all EPA authority. And lo and behold, neither of the bills did.

Finally, as noted already, EPA formally made this finding as Team Obama and others flew off to the Copenhagen "Kyoto II" confab, obviously to get some Euro-love while denying the timing was anything but coincidence, only to then send an all-staff email[124] to EPA employees admitting how, boy, they really put on a show by this orchestration.

All of this desperate incoherence is illustrative of how arrogant and relentless this crowd is in their determination to quickly impose their long-delayed agenda while laying the blame at someone else's feet (they're very big on blaming others, as you may have noticed).

OBAMA'S BACKDOOR KYOTO IN PRACTICE

So Obama's plan is to secure, one way or another, a legal obligation by the United States to regulate carbon dioxide emissions ever more tightly downward. One more problem arises, however—one of the "absurd" results the Environmental Protection Agency warns will occur after the greens have this "tailoring" rule thrown out. As outlined previously, the Clean Air Act (CAA) as written triggers a series of regulations elsewhere in the Act once the Environmental Protection

Agency declares carbon dioxide a "pollutant." Once there is no unlawful "tailoring" going on, one of these regulations sets out National Ambient Air Quality Standards, or NAAQS. NAAQS for carbon dioxide would mean that the United States unilaterally accepts legal responsibility, which green groups can enforce through the courts, for cutting our contribution to the global atmospheric concentration of carbon dioxide—even if it costs our economy.

This would be all pain, no gain, so far as the climate goes, but if the Kyoto experience and Europe's experience of exporting economic activity under a similar, even more forgiving scheme are any indication, it is also sure to lead to an increase in global emissions as economic activity leaves for other shores.[125]

NAAQS set a standard of parts per million (ppm) of CO_2 in the atmosphere, measured around the country, to determine if a state is in "attainment."[126] Every state will begin this process wildly out of attainment, because the computer models and advocacy campaign on which Obama's plan is based demand some atmospheric concentration well below the current level. Bear in mind that the U.S. cannot control this level, which represents a *global concentration* of CO_2.

In fact a rogue, litigious green group has already filed a petition (with the next step being federal court), asking the Environmental Protection Agency to impose carbon dioxide NAAQS—just in case you're wondering how likely it is that these scenarios could come true.[127]

On its face, this would mean the United States must close a coal-fired power plant for each one opened in China or India. But under Clean Air Act Sec. 179B, states do not have to actually attain NAAQS that transboundary pollution from a foreign country prevents them from attaining; they only have to reduce emissions as much as would be necessary to attain NAAQS if there were no transborder pollution.

In the case of CO_2, America would, as the Center for Biological Diversity (CBD) argues, "only" have to do its proportional share of the global reductions required to attain NAAQS.[128] Well, that's comforting. Particularly from greens whose threshold argument is that the U.S. disproportionately uses everything, particularly energy. "Our share" will not be a small thing to those doing the suing.

Contrary to the Pollyanna-like claims by CBD and its group 350.org, however, this Sec. 179B would not prevent NAAQS for CO_2 from being a nightmare. 350 parts per million (ppm), which is what they seek based on those farcical IPCC computer models, is 100 ppm lower than the stabilization target for 2050 proposed by the Waxman-Markey cap-and-trade bill, the EU, and IPCC (450 ppm). Nobody knows how to stabilize at that higher 450 level without extreme economic sacrifice. Moreover, under the Act, NAAQS must be attained in five, or at most ten, years. So here you see the grounds for Obama's window-insurance threat, reminiscent of old-time thugs hinting that maybe you should pay Congress with some political cover to legislate the agenda, to protect you from bad things that might happen.

The solution is not to roll over to this juvenile policymaking. Rather, we need to affirm with a simple, one-page piece of legislation—which exists and is known as the Blackburn bill,[129] co-sponsored by nearly every House Republican and (as of this writing) not one Democrat—stating that the Clean Air Act was not written to be used this way. Of course, once you remove the false urgency, the energy rationing "global warming" issue dies.

As my colleague Dr. Lewis writes of the petition by CBD and 350.org, "Not even a global economic depression sustained over many decades would be enough to stabilize atmospheric CO_2 levels at 350 ppm—the goal of the CBD-350.org petition. For example, even if the world's governments could somehow dial back global CO_2 emissions to 1957 levels, when the global economy was smaller than one-third its present size, and then hold CO_2 emissions constant for the next nine decades, global concentrations would still increase to 455 ppm by 2100."[130]

Remember, atmospheric concentrations are not the same as emissions: the atmosphere includes massive quantities of "natural" CO_2 from plants decaying, volcanic gases, and animal emissions, as well as the CO_2 emitted by all the nations of the world. Unlike most actual "pollutants," the atmospherically essential CO_2 is rather well mixed, so you would not find CO_2 "pollution" uniquely elevated near its man-made sources in urban areas as you would, say, sulfur dioxide.

Unlike real pollutants, called "criteria" pollutants in CAA lingo, carbon dioxide cannot be "scrubbed" out or similarly reduced, but is, instead the very objective of burning coal—it is a basic principle that the more efficiently you combust a hydrocarbon (oil, coal, or gas), the more CO_2 you produce. So the solution of using less is actually very simple, even if the objective of the U.S. bringing down a global concentration of something that the rest of the world will ensure rises for decades, and natural processes nonetheless dominate, is impossible.

So in Obama's vision, we are to be the world's patsy. Despite massive projected Chinese, Mexican, Indian, and other growth—as well as volcanic eruptions and other natural processes, given we're dealing with something mostly produced by sources other than humans—our economy alone will incur a legal obligation of futile gestures.

And of course NAAQS levels also stand a chance of being ratcheted downward by green groups using the courts and pronouncements from the political body that somehow has been granted a monopoly on climate "science," the UN's IPCC. Meanwhile, as we hobble ourselves by insanely regulating our most abundant energy source—coal—out of our domestic energy mix, China is rapidly building coal-powered plants, and has every intention of continuing to do so. As does India, whose "8 percent economic growth rate is powered by coal."[131]

The bottom line: your own government is working feverishly to doom you to massive self-sacrifice in the name of the vainest gesture imaginable.

CHAPTER 5

PICKING YOUR POCKETS FOR POLITICAL PAYOLA

A popular aphorism holds that the American Republic will endure until the day Congress discovers it can bribe the public with the public's own money.[1] To one extent this prophecy was slightly too pessimistic, as Congress quite obviously discovered this ability some time ago. Yet the Republic remains, if on increasingly unsteady terms. Our current lawmakers' revelation is not that they can bribe the public, but how much more cravenly they can do so.

Barack Obama's inauguration ushered in a new era of such tie-ups between Washington and well-heeled constituencies. Politicians now not only create and then bribe constituencies with confiscated wealth, but do so brazenly claiming that their actions are urgent, imperative, and just the beginning of much more to come. These bribes extend to individual corporations and ad hoc coalitions, which in turn lend their credibility, prestige, and finances to advancing a shared agenda.

The environmental issue generally, and particularly global warming, have exposed with disturbing clarity how big business and special interests scratch politicians' backs so that together they can pick your pockets. It is difficult to imagine a more glaringly obvious or expensive push for state control of our freedoms than this campaign to limit the availability of energy in the name of saving the world. Yet our free press has proved worse than negligent in performing their watchdog role here. Blinded by their sympathy for a shared ideology, the establishment media are fully and actively complicit in the burgeoning corruption of our system.

You would think that flagrant collaborations between big business and government made in shady backroom deals, at the expense of the little guy and with the added element of national security implications, would make the media want to investigate. But quite the opposite is true. The media not only cover for this ugly revival of corporatism and policy corruption, but cheerlead the deals, at best deigning to raise the obvious questions just to shoot them down with industry/politico/green-supplied talking points.[2] Even the most nauseating "green" political payola is news only in a perverse fashion, touted not as scandalous, but as a wonder of supposedly strange bedfellows agreeing to work together in ways unimaginable but for the dire emergency against which they valiantly and selflessly set aside their differences to defend.

Emboldened by the lack of media inquiry into the shady relationships, and the absence of headlines like, say, "Climate Fat Cats: Big Business Lobbies to Increase Your Taxes, Energy Costs, and Threaten

Your Jobs," the government's corporate pals increasingly boast of their efforts. So, too, do politicians, Obama foremost among them.

THE ORIGINS OF THE GLOBAL WARMING INDUSTRY

Big business was actually one of three founding principals of the anti-energy, anti-liberty agenda, which Barack Obama now pushes so aggressively as the vehicle for much of his desired "fundamental transformation" of America. Thanks to the keen eye of a few pioneers such as Enron's Ken Lay, industry saw the enormous financial potential in joining the anti-growth, anti-people ideologues for a ride.

As Lawrence Solomon of Canada's *Financial Post* wrote as part of a series exposing such behavior, Enron was the early ringleader of the global warming industry and originator of its current tactics:

> Enron Chairman Kenneth Lay...saw his opportunity when Bill Clinton and Al Gore were inaugurated as president and vice-president in 1993. To capitalize on Al Gore's interest in global warming, Enron immediately embarked on a massive lobbying effort to develop a trading system for carbon dioxide, working both the Clinton administration and Congress. Political contributions and Enron-funded analyses flowed freely, all geared to demonstrating a looming global catastrophe if carbon dioxide emissions weren't curbed. An Enron-funded study that dismissed the notion that calamity could come of global warming, meanwhile, was quietly buried.
>
> To magnify the leverage of their political lobbying, Enron also worked the environmental groups. Between 1994 and

1996, the Enron Foundation donated $1-million to the Nature Conservancy and its Climate Change Project, a leading force for global warming reform, while Lay and other individuals associated with Enron donated $1.5-million to environmental groups seeking international controls on carbon dioxide.[3]

An internal Enron memo written to Ken Lay on the heels of the 1997 Kyoto negotiation noted,

> [This treaty] is exactly what I have been lobbying for.... This agreement will be good for Enron stock!!...if implemented, this agreement will do more to promote Enron's business than will almost any other regulatory initiative outside of restructuring of the energy and natural gas industries in Europe and the United States.... Enron now has excellent credentials with many "green" interests including Greenpeace, [World Wildlife Fund], [Natural Resources Defense Council], German Watch, the U.S. Climate Action Network, the European Climate Action Network, Ozone Action, WRI, and Worldwatch,... This position should be increasingly cultivated and capitalized on (monitized) [sic].[4]

Guaranteed, and indeed windfall profits and the transfer of many hundreds of billions of dollars in consumer, ratepayer, and taxpayer wealth easily clouds the thinking of even the most ardent capitalist. *Help our natural enemy out now, throw them under the bus later* seems an apt description of the philosophy shared by Enron and the green groups with which Enron, BP, and others worked to impose the Kyoto agenda on America. These are trailblazers whose commitment was actually less capitalist than traditional Progressive.

Writing in *National Review Online,* my colleague Iain Murray notes,

> Playing the bootleggers in a bootleggers and Baptists alliance, these businessmen have realized that they can get the government to increase their profits by means of "cap and trade" and similar regulatory interventions, at the expense of other businesses and the paying public. Ordinarily, such shenanigans would have the corporate watchdog groups in arms, but by getting the "Baptists" of the green movement on their side, they have shielded themselves from public disgust.[5]

Now, the bootleggers who coalesced with their green Baptists have turned venally corporatist. Realizing Obama cannot impose the ideological agenda otherwise, they have leveraged their own power and locked in schemes funneling your money both directly to them and through the state as a condition of their support in the form of hundreds of millions of dollars in lobbying, advertising, and other political resources. So they provide financial and political cover for Obama's power grab, with tremendous payoffs waiting for them along the way, and vastly more if they succeed.

Consider other, more public admissions of major-player chief executives affirming the wealth transfer—from you to them—which they so selflessly call for. For example, the Chicago-based utility Exelon. Exelon, by chance White House counselor David Axelrod's first "AstroTurfing" client, to all appearances maintains their ties to Axelrod, given their leadership in an orchestrated campaign of companies leaving the U.S. Chamber in a huff of faux environmental principle over the Chamber's opposition to cap-and-trade. Further, as *Forbes* magazine detailed in an issue bearing the subtle tease on the cover, "Exelon's Carbon Advantage,"

> Obama's chief of staff, Rahm Emanuel, helped create Exelon. Emanuel was hired by [Exelon CEO John] Rowe to help broker the $8.2 billion deal between Unicom and Peco when Emanuel was at the investment bank Wasserstein Perella (now Dresdner Kleinwort). In his two-year career there Emanuel earned $16.2 million, according to congressional disclosures. His biggest deal was the Exelon merger.
>
> Emanuel emailed Rowe on the eve of the House vote on global warming legislation and asked that he reach out to some uncommitted Democrats. "We are proud to be the President's utility," says Elizabeth Moler, Exelon's chief lobbyist. "It's nice for John to be able to go to the White House and they know his name."[6]

Investment analysts Sanford C. Bernstein and Co. projected that Exelon would reap about a billion dollars per year in windfall profits under the scheme. Exelon's CEO Rowe found little about this assessment to disagree with. In fact he openly noted, "We don't flinch from the charge that, yes, some of our motivation and enthusiasm comes from the fact that we should make money on it if it happens."[7] Real, big money is surely a real, big part of that enthusiasm.

In fact, according to *Forbes*'s interview with Rowe, "Exelon needs that legislation to happen sooner rather than later. Without a carbon price of some sort, Exelon's fortunes aren't so bright...." Rowe acknowledges that "There's nothing that's going to drive Exelon's profit in the next couple of years wildly. It just isn't going to happen.' Except, of course, carbon legislation. And because of that, the company views spending on lobbying for legislation almost like a capital expense."[8] (Adding insult, it is not uncommon for the regulated utilities pushing this tax to be permitted to recover from ratepayers half of the "public affairs and regulatory policy" bill for increasing the ratepayer's burden.[9])

Around the same time as these Exelon revelations, Michael Morris, the CEO of America's largest coal burning utility, American Electric Power (AEP), told *Forbes* that the scheme—which, by chance he, too, is promoting—would add billions in additional costs to his company, certainly, but he chuckled at the beauty of it: they get to pass those billions on to the ratepayer, with a little something on top for themselves.[10] Under cost-recovery schemes giving a percentage for their troubles, the more it costs, the better.

These billions, which come from you—at least so long you don't or can't leave the energy companies, as Morris notes in his interview—would also in some cases be for no additional capital expenditure or other outlays or obligations on their part, outside of the army of lobbyists—er—"public affairs specialists," working feverishly to get this burden enacted into law. "Exelon would gain simply because a price on carbon would raise the cost of production for fossil-fuel-powered electricity. Most of that would be passed on to customers, raising the wholesale price of power. Exelon's revenues would rise, but its costs wouldn't."[11]

Exelon is the biggest provider of nuclear power in the United States. On behalf of the National Association of State Utility Consumer Advocates, Sonny Popowsky, Pennsylvania's state consumer advocate, addressed the fact that certain utilities like Exelon, lobbying for this scheme, are poised to receive windfalls. He explained that for a few reasons endemic to the utility industry, the nature of meeting "peak" demand, and nuclear's attributes, "Nuclear power plants will receive literally billions of dollars . . . even though they incur zero carbon compliance costs."[12]

So here you have admissions of billions in forced wealth transfers from you, with much of it going to well-placed lobbying interests, in the name of saving the planet—but with no feasible climatic impact under any scenario.[13] One might think that, aside from the loopiest greens, any American, whatever his or her ideology, would by now have had enough of this, and would demand that Team Obama drop the "end is nigh!" approach to policymaking and honestly answer basic questions, such as "what will it do?" "at what cost?" and "is that in our interest?"

p. 343

THE PROGRESSIVE HERITAGE OF
THE ENRON/OBAMA AXIS

This industry scheming proved critical, as the global warming movement—first percolated among population nags, socialists, academics, and other leftists—only took off once big money interests adopted it as their own vehicle to lock in profitability, disadvantage small business (and otherwise potential competition), and ensure an orderly future for themselves.

It is support from these interests that drives Congress to promote this scheme, which is also dear to the heart of Obama's far-Left ideology in its transfer of wealth and power to the state. This collaboration is not a new invention, but the latest twist on an old political philosophy (as well as a far older profession). Media personality Glenn Beck on his television and radio shows, writer Jonah Goldberg in his best-selling book *Liberal Fascism*, and others have drawn the parallels between modern American "liberals"—including particularly, as Beck has pointed out, Team Obama—and the early twentieth century Progressives. In an amusing unwillingness to simply stick to a name and persuade the public about one's own ideas and agenda, modern American liberalism has rushed to the refuge of the Progressive label, desperate to shirk a thoroughly tarnished and disfavored brand, after having previously discredited and subsequently dropped "Progressive," in favor of "Liberal." It's slash-and-burn political marketing, if with a limited repertoire.

Regardless of such re-branding exercises, there is certainly much in common between the operating mechanisms of the earlier Progressives and the Left's newest vehicle, "climate change." The Progressives were not crusading consumer advocates so much as partners in imposing regulatory regimes at the behest of entrenched industry desiring to organize the marketplace. We see in Obama's green agenda and sundry power grabs less a Left versus Right conflict than a combination of corporate and ideological interests, leading to a modern spin on the old corporatism that found such favor, say, among our European friends in the 1930s, as Goldberg reveals so well.

Historian Gabriel Kolko wrote about this in his book *The Triumph of Conservatism: A Reinterpretation of American History 1900–1916*, as did James Weinstein in *The Corporate Ideal in the Liberal State, 1900–1918*. Both leftists, these authors detailed how, under Progressivism, big business turned to the state for favors to manage their problems, which included competition, both real and anticipated.

Weinstein wrote of how such cutting-edge collaboration sought to orchestrate "the ideal of a liberal corporate social order."[14] Kolko explained, "It is business control over politics (and by 'business' I mean the major economic interests) rather than political regulation of the economy that is the significant phenomenon of the Progressive

Era."[15] He noted that when competition was reducing rates and profitability, "The railroad men turned to political solutions. . . . They advocated measures designed to bring under control those railroads within their own ranks that refused to conform to voluntary compacts."[16]

Kolko described this objective of the business-government collaboration as entailing "the elimination of internecine competition . . . I mean by the term, rather, the organization of the economy and the larger political and social spheres in a manner that will allow corporations to function in a predictable and secure environment permitting reasonable profits over the long run."[17]

In practice, this means locking things up for themselves. Notice the one party not "at the table" in this calculation: the customer, consumer, taxpayer—however you style it, it means you are the one left out.

This tactic extended to telephone, steel, oil, meatpacking, and other industries where large players desired effective immunity from competition and market forces, in return for a pact in which they ceded to the state some of their own ability to compete, made unnecessary anyway due to the barriers to entry for competitors and agreements between existing interests.

Similarly, by their advocacy of these schemes, "climate" rent-seekers like Duke Energy and Exelon give every indication that they have determined that the notion of a deregulated, competitive market for electricity is an alarming prospect. They've even mocked up the old model of voluntary association between unrelated industries with the U.S. Climate Action Partnership (USCAP)—today's equivalent of the old National Civics Federation, which pushed a big business-government alliance. USCAP seeks a pact with the governing class and ideologues to secure their own future and (for many of them and depending on the plan adopted) billions in windfall profits at the ratepayers' expense. The group was even credited with providing the "blueprint" for the Waxman-Markey House cap-and-trade bills.[18] At least these companies got something for their reported $100,00 entrance fees.[19]

Kolko demonstrated the parallels when he wrote, years before there was a global warming industry or business-government axis trying to cram this particular agenda down: "Progressivism was initially a movement for the political rationalization of business and industrial conditions, a movement that operated on the assumption that the general welfare of the community could be best served by satisfying the concrete needs of business."[20] Under Progressivism, "regulation itself was invariably controlled by leaders of the regulated industry, and directed toward ends they deemed acceptable or desirable," partly "because the regulatory movements were usually initiated by the dominant businesses to be regulated."[21] Similarly, Enron led a select few peers at the vanguard of inventing the global warming issue as a policy matter in the United States.

By pushing the global warming agenda, the rent-seekers are replicating what Roy Childs, in his 1971 essay titled "Big Business and the rise of American Statism," described as past practice by leading industrialists, "faced with seemingly insurmountable problems, who initiated the drive for federal government regulation of their industry."[22] Competition was forcing these businesses to charge less. They wanted to put a stop to it, and codify a lucrative living.

These climate capitalists push the global warming agenda in one of two ways: either as an offensive strategy to gain state-mandated "rents" (subsidies, mandates for their goods or services, and other booty), or to a lesser, but equally enabling and therefore dangerous degree, simply as linguine-spined capitulators thinking they're cutting a better deal than would be handed them. One might summarize the former as promoting a philosophy of "What's good for GM is good for America." The latter capitulators are like those (possibly apocryphal) "weepers" supposedly assigned to ride the French trains during the 1939–1940 "phony war," sobbing, dispiriting the population, and sapping its will to fight. The modern weepers parade through Washington, D.C., conference rooms uttering vacuities such as "It's inevitable," "Well, you can't just say 'no,'" and "You've got to be at the table or you're on the menu." Such useful idiots naively seek to employ government defensively against something much, much worse which they fear will otherwise surely come.

Finally, and without fail, when the inanity of their talking points is patiently revealed to them, today's climate rent-seekers ritually defend their attempts to impose the biggest regulatory intervention in our nation's history as justifiable in order to provide "certainty."[23] While the economy does react negatively to uncertainty, that is actually the result of this lobby's efforts to impose the agenda. This is nevertheless the newest tweak on political capitalism and early Progressivism, which claimed to employ the machine of government for purposes of "stability."

So, now as before, the relevant conflict is not so much corporate interests against the individual (as Marx would have it), but between the interests of the large capitalists and small businesses. Like the inevitable fall-out among thieves splitting the loot in an old cowboy Western, it is the wrangling among businesses—and very little else—that has kept the Statist agenda from being imposed for more than a decade. Even while squabbling among themselves, these global warming looters uniformly manifest the equivalent of what Childs described as the railroads "gleefully hand[ing] over control to the government in return for guaranteed rate increases and guaranteed profits."[24] Out of this came not just more centralized industry, but labyrinths such as the Federal Trade Commission, which was described at the time as being in every way to the benefit of the barons of the age.[25]

Today, the greens and their pals in banking and finance seek institutionalization of their carbon "offset" racket through FTC and Securities and Exchange Commission regulation. (Though Obama's SEC "guidance," requiring publicly traded companies to "disclose"—given the crumbling scientific case, this means "completely make up"—supposed "climate change" risks including from regulations, posed by their operations, was a big wet kiss to the trial lawyers and green pressure groups.)[26] Once the ration coupons have that sort of bureaucratic and Wall Street constituency in place, rewarded annually, the edifices will not go away any time soon.

Such regimes are vastly simpler to create than to dismantle, a fact of which our rent-seekers are surely aware, considering they and their allies frantically insisted, after anxious Senate Democrats balked at repeating the House cap-and-trade political disaster, on adopting *anything* just to get it in place. Tightening and entrenchment to follow. Never forget how, at the earliest dawn of the Progressives' era, we also saw the birth of the Interstate Commerce Commission, finally disbanded in 1995 after decades of obsolescence (and most of its functions merely transferred to another bureaucracy).

COSTLY, SINKING SHIP OF FOOLS

Just as with the Progressives, today we see big business rushing for "a seat at the table" with Obama in order to help write "global warming" or "clean energy"—but, in effect, energy rationing—rules, impeding new entrants or competition to their benefit, and at your expense. But business got suckered, and the greens and Obama must be laughing now at these rubes who pretended to be sage with their "not at the table, you're on the menu" talking points, oblivious to the warm gravy bath and the apple stuffed in their maw.

Did no one read the identical language buried in both the House and Senate "global warming" bills, which otherwise are so distinct as to be six hundred pages different in length, ensuring that *all laws* on the books shall now be construed as "global warming" regimes and *shall* be employed to that end? I know Section 707—which does indeed require the executive branch to use all existing laws to keep CO_2 concentrations below a level they will have surpassed by the time the law goes into effect—is awfully far down to read when you're hurrying to get a scheme in place before people catch on, but the very notion that each successive year's version of the legislation has included hundreds and hundreds more pages should have sounded alarms that there were some troubling things buried in there besides the goodies for favored industries. [27]

If these bills are enacted, there is no need to bother with ongoing court battles over whether the National Environmental Policy Act, an originally sleepy law which now not only governs but significantly restricts all major federal permitting decisions and activities (such as resource development and highway construction), is really a global warming law as pushed by litigious greens. Should this measure pass, as the Democrat leadership plans to do either stealthily in 2010, or more likely—if their majorities survive—in 2011, then every statute on the books in the United States Code now or in the future should be read as intended to reduce or avoid greenhouse gas production. Even in the event that a non-radical, less enamored of this sort of agenda finds his or her way to the Oval Office, the mandatory language of the law would prevent it being softened in the Executive Branch. That way, the greens will always have the courts. This dynamic is not new, only the breadth of the reach is, but now more than ever it represents Washington where simple people have the ability to sell our future to those who are more clever in return for the bag of magic beans called "certainty."

OBAMA'S GLOBAL WARMING TROUGH

The cap-and-trade legislation is by no means the sole initiative in Obama's power grab relevant to the business-government alliance. "Green jobs" also promises preferences, mandates, and handouts. They serve as just another road to the same place, in the event cap-and-trade and the Environmental Protection Agency's backdoor regulating are somehow shut off. Cap-and-trade is the most brazenly high-profile among them, however, and so serves as our example here.

Again quoting Lawrence Solomon, "The financial stakes are enormous in the global warming debate—many oil, coal and power companies are at risk should carbon dioxide and other greenhouse gases get regulated in a manner that harms their bottom line. The potential losses of an Exxon or a Shell are chump change, however, compared to the fortunes to be made from those very same regulations."[28]

Democrat Senator Barbara Boxer, shepherding the Senate climate bill as a co-sponsor and chair of the Environment Committee, laid things out rather plainly when explaining the purchase of votes and political cover to ram the thing through. "There's so much revenue that comes in from a cap-and-trade system that you can really go to a person in a congressional district and get enough votes there by saying, 'What do you need? What do you want?' You can really help them."[29]

"There's so much revenue" from the biggest tax increase in American history, most of which is given away to big business for the first decade—yet somehow, as the administration and its congressional, green group, and industry allies calmly tell us, it won't cost anything.

This is why Senator Bob Corker of Tennessee, speaking of the House-passed version, told *National Review*'s Rich Lowry, "If you had a government relations person working for you and you didn't make money off the deal, you didn't have a very good government relations person."[30]

Phil Kerpen of Americans for Prosperity (AFP) wrote,

> This disastrous bill, which will send energy prices skyrocketing while having no discernible impact on global average temperature will only get worse as even more special interests are bought off at the expense of taxpayers. It's a scam, an enormous tax-and-spend bill concealed in a cloak of green political correctness. The real purpose of the plan is to dramatically enhance the power of Washington politicians by giving them control over vast swaths of the U.S. economy.[31]

And as the *Washington Times* noted in an editorial on the heels of the House adoption of cap-and-trade, this scheme for which Boxer was buying cover with your hard-earned money smacks eerily of the gangster capitalism of Russia as that country transitioned from a newly liberated economy to one of corrupt cronyism. It would "centralize an inordinate amount of power in Washington and generate vast fortunes for people with friends in high places.... Because the credits will be distributed by the government, the key question is who will decide who gets them. As we have seen recently with the stimulus bill, Troubled Asset Relief Program (TARP) bailouts, the automotive fiasco and the federal budget generally, only those with friends in high places will have a place at the trough. Those with pull will profit; those without will be run out of business."[32]

The dispensation of climate loot surely does offer parallels with post-Communist privatization deals, under which formerly state-owned industries were conveniently centralized in the hands of a few well-connected types, made instant billionaires with more than a whiff of corrupt deal-making. As the *Times* wrote: "Under cap-and-trade, we will soon see the rise of the carbon oligarchs. These people will make vast fortunes on this legislation by trading influence and rule-making that benefits them at the expense of the rest of us. These energy brokers and carbon-offset middlemen will produce nothing and make no contributions to society but will become rich based on political preference and other insider influence."[33]

Cap-and-trade riches are to be the fruit of a panic manufactured by a very deliberate universe of ideologically motivated actors now controlling nearly all levers of power in American government. A (at best) social democrat president, possibly the most radical Congress ever, and increasingly activist courts are being aided by business, pressure groups, and other interests, who receive billions in sops picked right from the public's pockets.

This global warming industry became self-perpetuating and attracted more supporters as potential beneficiaries crowded the halls of Congress. The Center for Public Integrity claims that by the time cap-and-trade hit the House floor, according to official disclosure records, more than 880 businesses and interest groups had filed lobbying registration papers citing climate change as their issue of interest[34]—a deceptively low figure given that subsequent lobbying registrations at the end of the year revealed the real figure had been

1,747 entities.[35] By the time of that House vote, there were more than four "climate" lobbyists for every Member of Congress,[36] all of whom heard Senator Boxer's casting call for cheerleaders.

Although the media claim this money generally—and with respect to utilities and oil and gas companies, particularly—is spent on blocking the bills, that line of argument reveals either breathtaking ignorance or dishonesty. The largest utilities and related interests (Duke, Exelon, AEP, AES, NRG) are promoting the legislation, and most of the oil and gas companies weighing in are seeking adoption of the legislation, promoting particular provisions for their own parochial reasons. BP and Shell actively lobby for cap-and-trade, while ConocoPhillips and BP switched from the pro-cap-and-trade USCAP to promoting a different scheme, to cite four of the "majors."

So, in fact, the biggest boys in the energy industry, styled in the template coverage of this issue as cynically blocking legislative "progress," actually argue only that it must be the *right* legislation, as they each develop their own scheme for windfalls or at least work to ensure the cost falls most readily on the consumer and not on them. Shell and BP had long funded the home of "ClimateGate," the alarmist outfit the Climatic Research Unit at University of East Anglia.[37] "Big Oil" just fled USCAP when it became obvious that they had gotten fleeced: utilities got just about the same amount of allowances or ration coupons as their emission totals, while refiners got 2 percent of theirs. Time to devise a new scheme.

"The American Wind Energy Association paid $5 million for lobbying in 2009, compared with $1.7 million the previous year, the highest amount ever for the association and a sixth of the $30.1 million spent by all renewable companies combined,"[38] according to *Greenwire*. Add to this green pressure groups, unions (for reasons

described elsewhere in these pages), the finance and banking interests pushing the bill and, of course, backers of pixie dust companies
that, like "renewables," can never compete so long as the measuring
sticks for success are performance, supply, and reliability, and you
have one vast lobbying industry.

ALL THE PRESIDENT'S MEN

Tom Borelli is the president of the Free Enterprise Project at the
National Center for Public Policy Research. He has been a leading
voice calling out chief executives who rush down this path of a cor-
porate-business alliance, enriching themselves or merely ensconcing
their power at the expense of your money and freedoms. One of his
efforts was to detail Obama's insidious and unseemly move to bring
those with a clear and direct stake in one of his highest priorities into
his advisory sphere. These people in return provide the patina of capitalist support to Obama's power grab.

Borelli recognizes that "Fundamentally, Obama and Waxman are
fostering a form of Corporatism in which a collection of powerful
special interest groups join together to advance their world view. The
losers are everyday Americans who cherish their individual liberty,
consumer choice and standard of living—all of which will be reduced
thanks to the adverse consequences" of "green" schemes. Toward this
end, politicians on the Left "have found big business to be a crucial
ally in their quest for a national cap-and-trade law to limit carbon
emissions. Corporate backing greatly enhances the global warming
bill's prospects of passing, but it also reveals a key feature of Obama's
political strategy: a new era of special interest politics in which major
corporations work in concert with liberal politicians and advocacy
groups to advance the left-wing agenda."[39]

For example, Obama created a President's Economic Recovery Advisory Board (PERAB) to provide, in theory, "an independent voice on economic issues." In practice, however, the board gives a prestigious home to willing corporate partners to help advance the corporate-government alliance's agenda. After its very first meeting, the group cranked out a (very public) memorandum to the president endorsing a carbon cap.[40] Consider the disgracefulness of this move by an "economic recovery" body, given that the entire purpose of such a scheme is to raise the price of energy—to have it "necessarily sky-rocket," in Obama's formulation.[41]

Obama elevated CEOs Jeffrey Immelt of GE and Jim Owens of Caterpillar to the group, providing them both with prestige and access; they both also happened to be pushing Obama's initiatives. Both were members of the United States Climate Action Partnership (USCAP) with green pressure groups to scheme cap-and-trade into place. Borelli particularly pressured Owens for this stunt, as Caterpillar would, in fact, be greatly harmed under cap-and-trade, simply because its customers would be "bankrupted"[42] (if we are to believe Obama). Borelli writes how, ultimately, after expressing such confusion about his own stance and the rationale behind it, "At the 2009 Caterpillar shareholder meeting, Owens acknowledged he opposed the Waxman-Markey bill because it could harm his business."[43] He then pulled Caterpillar out of USCAP in early 2010.

The *Los Angeles Times* revealed that USCAP companies helped to push this enormous energy tax hike past the finish line in the House, singling out Duke Energy and Alcoa for "marshaling votes on Capitol Hill, working behind the scenes with committee negotiators and providing what House leaders call a blueprint for compromise."[44] In his victory lap, bill co-author Edward J. Markey of Massachusetts cited this cynical profiteering/toadying, calling their support "indispensable."[45]

The rent-seekers' next move, inescapably coordinated at some level with the White House, was to try to neuter the U.S. Chamber of Commerce. The Chamber, though it is occasionally a partner in schemes increasing the size and scope of government (like most every Washington lobby), showed sentience and resolution in its opposition to the global warming, anti-energy agenda.[46] That didn't sit well with some larger member companies hoping to cash in on "global warming" laws.

Larger companies pay larger association dues, and therefore have outsized influence no matter the safeguards put in place to minimize this. Among the USCAP companies pressuring the Chamber quietly (and some not so quietly) was Johnson & Johnson, which, like Caterpillar, supported this complex if enormous tax scheme for reasons at which one can only guess. (Maybe it has something to do with "early action credits," a legislated windfall for a company's having made certain decisions in the absence of a mandate, presumably on their economic merits.[47]) But the biggest peacock of them all was Exelon. If Axelrod's firm was not directly involved with Exelon yet again, the White House itself was closely working with Exelon and the rest to surely orchestrate the pressure campaign that caused the Chamber to soften, but not abandon, its opposition.[48]

By throwing their hats in the arena with the Statist, power-grabbing Left, these companies lend the prestige of their names and provide vast resources to the environmentalist movement. This includes, as Borelli wrote, "the almost unlimited resources of a corporation—lobbying, public relations and advertising to promote its political agenda. With GE, the liberal movement also acquires the

company's media units (NBC, MSNBC and CNBC), which aggressively push the green agenda in news coverage and network
programming."[49]

In a remarkable parallel to these millions spent by industry in support of Obama's "green" agenda, Roy Childs described the results of
the Progressives' business-government partnership: "Big business
acted not only through concrete political pressure, but by engaging
in large-scale, long-run ideological propaganda or 'education' aimed
at getting different sections of the American economy united behind
statism, in principle and practice."[50] His treatment deserves reading
in its entirety, it is so breathtakingly indicative of what we are wit-
nessing with today's global warming industry.

But consider the cynicism underlying Obama using his creation,
the President's Economic Recovery Advisory Board (PERAB), to promote wildly expensive, inefficient drags on the economy that
climatically are no more than gestures. It was at an event touting this
group that the president rolled out the "green jobs" line of argument
for his various social engineering/corporate welfare plans, including
the cap-and-trade ration-and-tax scheme.

GE's Immelt and John Doerr of the Silicon Valley venture Capital
firm Kleiner Perkins Caufield & Byers are two individuals highly
financially invested in this promotion of massive subsidies and mandates for otherwise uneconomical goods and services. Both are
interesting choices as poster children for corporate American promoters of Obamunism.

Under Immelt's leadership, a once mighty and profitable company
sank to its knees as he redirected its business strategy to almost purely
relying on policy-driven purchases by its customers, particularly the
"green" agenda which is almost entirely a shower of governmental
policy favors for those it doesn't take down. In fact, White House vis-

itor logs showed Immelt met with Obama's inner circle "roughly a half dozen" times in Obama's first year in office, according to the Associated Press[51] in a brief wire story about the administration releasing its records over the holidays and which, oddly, went to the trouble of downplaying the influence of "climate" lobbyists.

Is that what lies behind Immelt saying things like, "We're all Democrats now"?[52] Could it be that GE has expectations of hauling in as much as $192 billion in the next three years from Obama priorities? Possibly, as Borelli says, "GE secured hundreds of millions of dollars from President Obama's $787 billion 'American Reinvestment and Recovery Act' for its utility customers Duke Energy, Exelon and FPL Group—all USCAP members."[53] Let's assume Immelt was raised believing in markets, as opposed to the market socialism he and so many others like him are now parroting. If so, he has made a dramatic turn as, after some questionable decisions and surely a fright put in them by the recession, GE has decided to cast its lot with a model dependent upon stimulus and other taxpayer monies. These generally, and under Obama specifically, mean products and services dictated by politics or ideology, not performance. When this mentality pervades, it is not a good sign for a country.

Whatever it is, Immelt's got the Obama Kool-Aid moustache, also saying in late 2009, "The government has moved in next door, and it ain't leaving. You could fight it if you want, but society wants change. And government is not going away."[54] And don't forget to have a seat at the table—where you can't say no.

Doerr is a partner in what is now Al Gore's investment firm, whose other principals are surely a major source of the $300 million Gore boasts of having been given to re-brand global warming into a "climate crisis." Gore is not required to disclose specifically where he got this money, and he doesn't—despite smearing all opponents as selling their services to donors or being otherwise driven by money. Regardless, Doerr, Gore, and the rest of the partners stand to benefit handsomely if the warm-mongers succeed in parlaying this faux crisis into further mandates and wealth transfers.

For a moment, ponder the outcry if Halliburton and ExxonMobil sat on a similar Bush inner circle of advisors, let alone if they were traipsing into the White House. Might we hear from the Left that these two conflicts are outrageous and need to be a topic of endless scrutiny and public discussion? Have we heard that about GE and Doerr?

While palling around together on Obama's PERAB, Immelt and Doerr took to the pages of the *Washington Post* on the need for the United States to implement low carbon policies to fix America's "competitiveness crisis."[55] Did you know that America is losing its edge because its energy prices are too low, and it has too few wealth transfers and governmental intrusions into the economy? Well, you do now. The long and the short of this public relations coup for Obama's agenda was that these guys agreed the United States needs new policies so that Kleiner Perkins Caufield & Byers and GE can make more money. Ah, fresh ideas and "change."

Among the claims and admissions in the *Post* item was that "Kleiner Perkins has invested $680 million in 48 of the most compelling new clean-energy technologies, with $1.1 billion more to invest." So it's clear why they would argue for the global warming agenda. And indeed, these gambles haven't paid off for one simple reason: "our government's energy and climate policies are our principal obstacle to success."[56]

What they really mean is the *absence* of certain policies is what stands between them and their fortune. But here you see the clever use of language in Obama's service toward energy rationing and old-school Progressivism.

BEHIND THE GREEN DOERR

GE's interest in profiting under these energy scarcity, tax, and subsidy regimes is fairly well-aired—thanks to their windmills, gas turbines, "green" jet engines (given a preference by Obama legislation), "smart grid" technologies,[57] a Greenhouse Gas Services joint venture in carbon credits,[58] and the use of NBC to promote it all.[59] For the gory details, follow D.C. *Examiner* columnist Tim Carney's bird-dogging of all that GE has received for its most expensive lobbying operation in the country, particularly in his book *Obamanomics: How Barack Obama Bankrupts You and Enriches His Wall Street Friends, Corporate Lobbyists, and Union Bosses.*[60] There are many hundreds of millions of reasons that Immelt wrote that the Obama administration will be a profitable "financier" and "key partner."[61]

John Doerr, however, has largely escaped scrutiny. He came into high demand as a congressional hearing witness in Washington, D.C., after Obama's inauguration. When appearing, he is generally identified on the agenda and in media reports simply as a wealthy investor. His usefulness is tied to a shared agenda to be sure, but it is due mostly to his ability to play the swashbuckling capitalist.

Doerr appears to spend most of his professional time with his venture capital firm, whose portfolio includes companies researching developments in solar, biofuel, geothermal, and other energy sources. None of these, of course, make money in the absence of government schemes—meaning left to the forces of supply, demand, and traditional market considerations. Oh, and his wife is on the board of directors of the Park Avenue-founded green pressure group Environmental Defense Fund.

Portfolio magazine was about the only outlet showing any suspicion about this wealthy investor's promotion of the global warming agenda. It took a peek at the man in 2007, back before Doerr was an Obamaphile but after he had begun chumming with Gore, in a piece cleverly titled "Behind the Green Doerr." The subhead read, "If John Doerr has his way, greentech will be Silicon Valley's new new thing—and taxpayers will foot the bill."[62]

"Greentech" means those gadgets that the Obama and global warming agenda throw a fortune of your money at, pretty much without regard to their performance, and certainly without regard to economic considerations you might have if left to your own devices with that money.

Author Russ Mitchell contrasted Doerr's agenda with his past successes investing in actual breakthroughs such as Compaq, Intuit, Sun Microsystems, AOL, Amazon, Netscape, and Google—all of which were profitable because they satisfied demand by enabling consumers to become more efficient and productive. "Greentech, however, is a very different animal than Silicon Valley is used to," Mitchell writes. He continues:

> None of the alternative energy sources being developed today—solar, wind, geothermal, or biomass—is close to financial sustainability, which means that the supersize returns V.C. funds depend on will require massive government subsidies, regulations, and mandates. Of course, government interference runs against Silicon Valley's libertarian grain. But money is money, and since venture capital

funds typically have a 10-year life span, the clock is already ticking.[63]

Doerr does tend to change the subject and distract from the relevant merits of the arguments, tossing up chaff about American ingenuity, seemingly to disarm anyone who challenges his strange policy priorities as somehow doubting Yankee Exceptionalism. But ingenuity doesn't require mandates and subsidy schemes, particularly in rather hare-brained plots. Doerr asked a Senate committee, "What do Amazon, eBay, Google, Microsoft and Yahoo have in common?" Answering himself, he said, "They are all American."[64] Ergo, supposedly, we can somehow defeat the laws of physics and make windmills and solar panels serious substitutes for energy sources that work. Even if for now, as he moans, GE is the only American windmill manufacturer of much standing. As a Republican committee release asked afterward in response:

> eBay, Google, Microsoft, and Yahoo have something else in common: they came about not because of regulation, or anything like cap-and-trade—they arose from the creative minds of entrepreneurs trying to meet a market need. This is something Doerr should know. In 1974 he joined Intel, just as the company invented the legendary 8080 microprocessor, and he later became a leading Silicon Valley pioneer. He faced nothing like the behemoth of cap-and-trade, and his success was rewarded by the free market. If one hopes for a new Silicon Valley of clean energy technology—which we do—it won't happen under the most burdensome regulatory scheme since the New Deal. By removing barriers to

innovation and opening access to our domestic energy resources, America can compete and win the race.[65]

But as Mitchell quoted CATO's Jerry Taylor piquantly exposing Doerr's line of reasoning: "Did we need subsidies to bring DVDs or iPods to market? If subsidies worked, we'd have nuclear power too cheap to meter, and our cars would be filled with synthetic fuel."[66]

Mitchell also noted, "In essence, Doerr is helping to create the biggest new market the world has seen since the dawn of the oil industry—and asking for taxpayer dollars to do it."[67] Or as Doerr put it, "It's probably the largest economic opportunity of the 21st century,"[68] which coincides nicely with the admission by Senator Cardin that cap-and-trade is "the most significant revenue generating proposal of our time." From one perspective Doerr's claim is true, though Mitchell's illumination of what is meant by "opportunity" is equally so, making the admission rather indelicate.

As to whether this next government-dependent boondoggle will end (as all such efforts must when they have no real market) Mitchell writes that "Doerr admits, 'It's possible.' He pauses and rubs his forehead before repeating, 'It's possible.' Kleiner Perkins partner Ray Lane, a sage 60-year-old, goes further. 'A bubble? You can almost count on it,' he says. 'Bubbles are common. They end badly for those who come in late. For those who come in early, it's not that bad.'"[69] Which brings us back to where we began, with Enron's plan.

Doerr, Gore, and Kleiner Perkins have various irons in this fire. For example, they are promoting emissions-tracking software into which they have sunk capital, which will be for all intents and purposes squandered in the event there is no "climate crisis" and no policies premised therein (but will be lucrative if such a crisis is codified). The *New York Times* wrote an article in 2009 headlined "Expecting New

Tax, Firm Prepares to Track Carbon," which noted, "If Congress passes legislation that puts a price on carbon emissions, companies will need to track and report the waste from their operations."[70] By "expecting" such a legal regime, of course, the *Times* means "aggressively lobbying for, supporting a private advocacy campaign for, and insinuating itself into governmental policy advisory roles for the purpose of advancing."

When the Department of Energy (DOE) came through with $3.4 billion in "Smart Grid" grants, even journalists quickly discovered what DoE claimed it had no idea of, that Gore and Kleiner Perkins were the primary investors in Silver Spring Networks, a company making the products whose utility clients received $75 million of the haul.[71] Nice due diligence. Or else very, very lame lying. Such is the "greentech industry," built on sand, government connections, and your hard-earned money. Then there's that curious episode of the Department of Energy lending $529 million to a Kleiner Perkins-backed company developing an electric car—in Finland—so the super wealthy can survive anti-automobility restrictions in a carbon constrained world by driving a trinket that costs nearly six figures.[72] Crisis means opportunity, right, Al?

THE REST OF THE CARNIES

We've touched upon Duke Energy, which has coal, nukes, and gas, and is notorious for pushing this scheme, particularly through and thanks to its CEO Jim Rogers, who is, coincidentally, a former Enron executive. The *Washington Post* reported, "In the final two weeks of drafting the legislation, Duke Energy chief executive James E. Rogers consulted with [House bill chief authors] Congressmen Waxman, Markey and Boucher, talked with Obama's energy and climate czar

Carol M. Browner, and addressed a private meeting of the Blue Dog Coalition, a group of fiscally conservative House Democrats, to ease their concerns."[73]

Interesting points about Duke include their growing stable of windmills, which, of course, need government intervention to be profitable. And of course, there was that time when, during one of Rogers's lobbying trips to D.C. to push the Waxman-Markey bill in June 2009, Duke Energy was also busy asking the North Carolina state utility regulators to approve a 13.5 percent rate increase, expressly citing the apparent, imminent passage of cap-and-trade legislation. For which it, by chance, also was the leading corporate cheerleader and which nicely positioned Duke in its ration coupon scheme, awarded to electricity retailers—like Duke—ostensibly on the grounds that doing so would insulate ratepayers from increases.[74] Got that?

Consider also how the gas industry has long advocated this agenda to varying degrees since the issue's inception, and with Enron, even though the industry will ultimately be made extinct should the agenda ever be fully implemented. (You don't reduce hydrocarbon emissions 83 percent as promised and keep burning gas in any appreciable quantity, certainly outside of heating and cooling government buildings.) Now, major players in the gas industry are actively promoting the windmill and solar panel boondoggles, paying handsomely for advertisements openly admitting that more of those things mean more gas because, after all, people want their lights on when the sun doesn't shine and wind doesn't blow, and this requires gas plants to back 'em up. Also, when it appears that the lights are on the way to going out and the politicians panic, a new gas-fired plant is the only thing one can possibly get online in under two years, which the guys with gas certainly know.

Displeased with the insufficiency of the House bill's wealth transfer, twenty-seven independent gas companies decided to increase their initial, early year bet of $300,000 for lobbyists. Creating a somewhat appropriate acronym for themselves, ANGA (America's Natural Gas Alliance), they then dove in with both fists, and spent something over a million for the year.[75] *Congressional Quarterly* reported in September 2009 that ANGA's "campaign ... will target Democrats and promote new alliances with liberal and environmental groups.... Now natural gas producers are trying to build ties with Democrats and promote their fuel as a cleaner alternative to rival fossil fuels in a world threatened by climate change."[76]

THE OFFSET SCHEMERS

The examples of GE, Gore, and Doerr illustrate the interest of many large companies and individuals in promoting the global warming agenda and, by coincidence, wetting their beaks. The rest of the global warming industry have similar tales, if with varying details. Other names you know who have cast their lot with this agenda include George Soros—benefactor of the Center for American Progress—and his longtime colleagues Stanley Druckenmiller and Julian Robinson, as well as T. Boone Pickens and others who recognize this new artifice for profiting from policy favors, the world's second-oldest profession.

Those names, and others, include the Wall Street and finance players calling for a "new playground," which is how one European carbon trader famously described the EU Emissions Trading Scheme to a reporter[77]—the cap-and-trade program which Europe now admits did not cut emissions, but did raise the cost of everything while providing some windfalls for well-connected industries. Carbon traders, of course, are parasitic, feeding off this creature of the state, not creating new wealth, but siphoning it off by the imposition of an economic inefficiency.

The *Wall Street Journal* cited an estimate by the broker Raymond James & Associates and claimed that, "Assuming federal cap-and-trade legislation passes the Senate, exchanges could reap $200 million or more in annual revenue from the market."[78] That profit is merely siphoned-off productive economic activity, in the name of changing the climate (which it will not do), while advancing the belief that the government can create economic growth by adding inefficiencies.

The recent economic rubble was brought down on us by the Wall Street derivatives-types gaming different, while at the same time highly similar, federal programs designed to advance an ideology. As already noted, even the pressure group Friends of the Earth warned that the cap-and-trade payoff to Obama's pals was scripting a replay of the recent market meltdown, calling it "Subprime Carbon."[79]

As the traders climbed out from under the mess in March 2009, several grabbed reporters to tout cap-and-trade as their next big thing. Illuminating comments included that there are "bucks to be made," "I can see nirvana coming," and this will be the traders' new, "huge playground."[80]

It is surely a coincidence that the banks most heavily leveraged in the carbon scheming led the way down in late 2008. Iconoclastic UK journalist Brendan O'Neill called on us to also

> [R]emember that the green-industrial complex's business interests played a role in bringing about the recession. The company whose collapse precipitated the credit crunch, Lehman Brothers, enthusiastically embraced the idea of car-

bon trading, which is held up by all members of the green-industrial complex as the way forward. In its 2007 report, The Business of Climate Change: Challenges and Opportunities, Lehman expressed hope that it might become a "prime brokerage for (carbon) emissions permits," meaning it aspired to make money not only from speculating in mortgages but also from trading in thin air. Lehman was inspired by European carbon-trading schemes.[81]

Lehman was the bank for Al Gore's schemes, led by the green activist and Gore partner Theodore Roosevelt IV.

As Australia's indefatigable Joanne Nova detailed in "Climate Money," "carbon trading" worldwide reached $126 billion in 2008.[82] Banks are now calling for laws to coerce us into more carbon-trading, which experts predict will make "hot air" the largest single commodity traded, absorbing anywhere from $2 to $10 trillion.[83]

Rachel Morris wrote a detailed piece on this boomlet in the left-wing *Mother Jones* magazine, titled "Could Cap and Trade Cause Another Market Meltdown?" with the subhead: "The same Wall Street players that upended the economy are clamoring to open up a massive market to swap, chop, and bundle carbon derivatives."[84]

Morris wrote:

> Cap and trade would create what Commodity Futures Trading commissioner Bart Chilton anticipates as a $2 trillion market, "the biggest of any [commodities] derivatives product in the next five years." That derivatives market will be based on two main instruments. First, there are the carbon allowance permits that form the nuts and bolts of any cap-and-trade scheme....In addition to trading the

allowances and offsets themselves, participants in carbon markets can also deal in their derivatives—such as futures contracts to deliver a certain number of allowances at an agreed price and time.[85]

By biggest, do we also mean this fictional "market" is thus "too big to fail"? For fail, it certainly will. Like the Fannie/Freddie mess, this too will have been created by the state, and therefore surely would be bailed out by the taxpayer.

So it fell to a nominee to the Federal Energy Regulatory Commission to tell a Senate committee that it might take 1,400 new bureaucrats to oversee the carbon-trading market that the House's climate change bill seeks to establish.[86]

With banks like J.P. Morgan and Goldman Sachs running with this scheme cooked up in great part by Enron (with the able counsel of Goldman) in the 1990s, the *Financial Times* commented, "It is perhaps not surprising, therefore, that so many carbon traders used to work at Enron. Louis Redshaw, who is now the head of environmental markets at Barclays Capital, spent four years working for Enron in London and set up its renewable energies desk. Enron alumni have also ended up on trading desks at other investment banks."[87]

In a May 2009 "GS Sustain" (Goldman's "Sustainability" investment practice) research alert titled "Change is coming: A framework for climate change—a Defining Issue of the 21st Century," the investment house touted the industries to which it was directing money to capitalize upon the climate agenda, which it also was pushing. Though ostensibly an investment-advice document, the "sustainability"-types couldn't contain themselves; it reads like an alarmist eco-group tract, warning of the population explosion causing climate change, the looming "tipping point" (always just over the horizon), and other environmental horrors.[88]

Oddly for a company so closely identified with Democrats, Goldman came in for (alternative) media inquiries into its scheming. Almost as if he had read "Behind the Green Doerr," Matt Taibbi writes of Goldman's *modus operandi* in *Rolling Stone*: "The plan is (1) to get in on the ground floor of paradigm-shifting legislation, (2) make sure that they're the profit-making slice of that paradigm and (3) make sure the slice is—a big slice. Goldman started pushing hard for cap-and-trade long ago, but things really ramped up last year when the firm spent $3.5 million to lobby climate issues."[89] This neatly summarizes the firm's ground-level work with Enron to create the cap-and-trade scheme from which both would skim millions in perfectly legal profits.

As *New York* magazine noted about the firm it calls "Tenacious G,"

> [It] will take a lot more than [Goldman's recent, subprime mortgage unsavoriness] to truly dampen Goldman's influence in Washington. As financial writer Michael Lewis recently said, the Obama administration, led by Geithner and the White House's National Economic Council director, Larry Summers, continues to operate from an economic worldview shaped by people who "believe that the world can't function without Goldman Sachs." Goldman also has a key ally in Obama's chief of staff, Rahm Emanuel, a former investment banker and onetime adviser to Goldman Sachs who frequently solicited campaign funds from the firm while working with the Clintons. And... the administration quietly hired Robert Hormats, another Goldman executive, as an economic adviser to Secretary of State Hillary Clinton.[90]

The latter, of course, is responsible for negotiating the specifics of Kyoto II, which, by chance, is considered by negotiators as an economic instrument.

We should not be surprised that fraud in carbon trading is on the rise in Europe, where such trading has been required of the sort that Obama seeks to mandate here. A Copenhagen *Post* headline read, "Denmark rife with CO_2 Fraud,"[91] and Reuters offered "Forest-CO_2 scheme will draw organised crime: Interpol." The latter story noted how "Organised crime syndicates are eyeing the nascent forest carbon credit industry as a potentially lucrative new opportunity for fraud, an Interpol environmental crime official said on Friday."[92]

The *Telegraph* reported: "[T]he very nature of carbon credits makes them 'an incredibly lucrative target for criminals', Rafael Rondelez, who was involved with the Europol investigation, has warned."[93] In fact, Interpol reports that in some EU countries, as much as 90 percent of the carbon trading is tainted by fraud of some sort. "Now 10 percent fraud-free!" isn't a bad pitch among the relative universe of Enron legacies.

Carbon Control News—the existence of a publication with such a title being itself proof that this enterprise has gone too far—wrote how "European Union (EU) governments are taking drastic steps to thwart potential fraud in the EU's emissions trading scheme—steps that may themselves be illegal—after it was revealed carbon traders are exploiting Europe's complex tax policies to bilk purchasers of carbon permits of hundreds of billions of dollars." The paper kindly cited U.S. "concerns about the potential for market manipulation of the type that led to the recent collapse of the global financial system."[94]

Now why would that be? Possibly the same reason that in Europe the windmill syndicates have been taken over by the Sicilian Mafia.

All of these state interventions pretending to control the weather—but which really just impose further burdens on the economy if while simultaneously helping out some buddies—create steady streams of guaranteed payments. This revenue comes both from individuals forced to buy the phony-baloney cure-all tonics, regardless of their actual performance or economics, and from the state. The mob, of course, likes guaranteed revenue streams as much as the taxman. *and legal !*

Please remember that such outcomes are not likely to have discouraged the scammers who conjured the idea of carbon cap-and-trade. These are not side effects the promoters had no idea would actually come about. Enron, like certain others we see who have followed in their footsteps, had a yen for get-rich-quick schemes that didn't really require them to do anything. In fact, many of the major utilities pushing the scheme share a record of being prosecuted for illegal market manipulation arising out of the California crisis that Enron and others helped nudge along and capitalized upon with the help of clueless politicians.[95]

Finally, it would be remiss to ignore those various commodity exchanges set up to play bookies in these carbon offset rackets, which annually tout just how much money passes through them *without* formal energy rationing, as proof not only of their success but, somehow, that we need laws mandating that ever more people buy their wares.

One of these logically confused advocates is the Chicago Climate Exchange (CCX), set up by none other than one Richard Sandor, about whom a Bloomberg headline read, "Sandor Got Obama's Nod for Chicago-Style Climate Law." There, chronicling the organization's rise, we learned how "it doesn't hurt that the six-year-old market got $1.1 million of seed money from the city's Joyce Foundation, whose board included a little-known state senator named Barack Obama.

Now the 44th president is determined to enact America's first limits on greenhouse gases. . . . 'Obama was on the foundation that gave us the grant,' Sandor said. 'We know him well.'"[96]

Bloomberg helpfully noted that Obama's energy rationing law "would create a mandatory national program to cut greenhouse-gas emissions. . . . To release each ton, companies will need to own either a government-issued permit or a carbon credit of the kind traded over-the-counter or on the Chicago exchange."[97] Huh.

Things weren't always quite so . . . organized for these Friends of Barack and their clientele. There was some confusion at first, for instance, over whether to recognize "investments" made some time ago in unconventional schemes like purchasing "credits" from farmers who "plant[ed] seeds using special knives instead of conventional plows, to disturb as little soil as possible."[98] The confusion was clarified. These pass muster.

So, with the House bill having blessed these bets, you better have kept those lottery tickets showing you paid a farmer in Lower Absurdistan to stay mired in inefficient production techniques. Your gamble, which, one must admit, at the time looked pretty crazy, will indeed pay off. After all, the planet is on the line. Really.

CHAPTER 6

GREEN EGGS AND SCAM: THE WHOLESALE FRAUD OF "GREEN JOBS"

The new "Green Jobs!" battle cry is merely the rebranding of an old campaign. Having failed, pure statism was reborn in the late twentieth century as environmentalism, which in turn is now manifesting itself as a fight to steal your economic freedoms and take your wealth to subsidize the uneconomic investments of the Al Gores of the world, lock in more favors for unions, and other noble causes.

We need only dare to take the word of President Obama's erstwhile "green jobs czar," Anthony K. "Van" Jones, who crowed, "The slogan of 'green jobs' is the banner under which all of the pro-democracy forces can gather for the next big assault."[1] David Foster, the director of a rather opportunistic coalescence of unions and green pressure groups calling itself the "Blue-Green Alliance" (as in blue-collar jobs; more on the unions' scheme later), helpfully chimed in about the cap-and-trade "global warming" legislation sold as a "green jobs" measure. He said, "It is an economic restructuring bill for the global economy. We should not pretend that it isn't."[2]

Before the idea set in that Jones-style candor wasn't likely to help things—outside of the fever-swamps and community organizing rallies—that self-styled radical and Communist plainly laid out a larger agenda and strategy, captured on audio and now archived courtesy of our friends at HotAir.com:

> Right now we're saying we want to move from suicidal gray capitalism to some kind of eco-capitalism where at least we're not, you know, fast-tracking the destruction of the whole planet.
>
> Will that be enough? No it won't be enough. We want to go beyond systems of exploitation and oppression altogether, but that's a process.
>
> And I think what's great about the movement that's beginning to emerge is that the crisis is so severe in terms of joblessness, violence, and now ecological threats that people are willing to be both very pragmatic and very visionary.
>
> So the green economy will start off as a small subset, and we're going to push it, and push it, and push it, until it becomes the engine for transforming the whole society.[3]

There we go again with that whole need to transform American society. Jones's radicalism is (by his terms) really more of an incremental move to his other adopted "-ism," and "green jobs" is just a vehicle. Also, of course, "it" is never enough, whatever "it" is. As the old labor leader once noted, heeded by today's Left, what you want after getting what you demand is simple: more.[4]

In the words of a man rather Van Jones's opposite, Phil Kerpen of Americans for Prosperity, "Green jobs are not economic jobs but political jobs, designed to funnel vast sums of taxpayer money to left-wing labor unions, environmental groups, and social justice community organizers."[5]

At last, the long-sought kumbaya moment of harmony and agreement. We are one in our common understanding that the "green jobs" agenda offers a Potemkin village of supposed employment and economically stimulating programs, while actually serving as the vanguard in the campaign to impose the Left's larger agenda.

A way to economic prosperity, however, it most certainly is not.

A young reporter who shall remain nameless emailed me something he heard and was trying to figure out. He said that, at a late 2009 panel discussion, "a top labor official was discussing the push for green jobs, cap-and-trade legislation and the like. The panel discussion was specifically about 'Buy American' requirements in the economic stimulus law, but Robert Baugh, executive director for the Industrial Union Council of the AFL-CIO, said 'Buy American' is only one plank in a 'much larger discussion' about transitioning the U.S. economy to deal with climate change. 'It's called industrial policy. And for people who are offended by that term, I call it environmental economic development policy.'" I explained to the young man that people are offended by that term because it is a synonym for central planning, meaning socialism or worse, and it is dedicated to directing vast sums of wealth from those who earned it to those whose politics are correct.

People who decide such things have determined that the environmental movement is the artifice for pushing this larger agenda, the latest excuse for the series of policy demands waved about for decades in the name of every claimed threat. The environmental schemes are simple, sleight-of-hand proxies for the "wrenching transformation of society" Al Gore prescribes.[6] The transformation is from one premised in individual liberty to one in which the benevolent state wisely guides the minority to provide for the majority, fattened to its commanding size on a steady diet of government programs insidiously leaving them looking to become even more dependent.

Pushing this agenda requires deceiving voters who are neither blessed nor burdened with the greens' insight, who can't see the warming that's surely hiding behind the cooling, and so on. In short: who just need to be told what the problem is by those who know best.

IT'S A SCAM

"[J]ust remember these four words for what this legislation means: jobs, jobs, jobs and jobs. Let's vote for jobs," huffed House Speaker Nancy Pelosi on the floor of Congress in remarks urging passage of the Waxman-Markey cap-and-trade legislation.[7] She didn't mention that these jobs were in China, Mexico, India, and elsewhere—not here.

How many job-creation schemes include massive unemployment assistance for the people they put out of work? As already covered, this one does. The truth is that every single iteration of these supposed jobs bills pushed in the name of "global warming" has, buried deep inside, an admission of the truth, providing years' worth of aid to workers displaced by the bills' restrictions. This is not simply "just in case." Job loss is the direct, logical, and expected result of shackling the economy with an energy tax and rationing scheme. As such, calling the statists' global warming schemes "jobs" programs is more than just another scam; it is an outrage. There is no credible case to be made for the claim.

It's just that Democratic pollsters, most famously Bill Clinton's former pollster Stanley Greenberg, came out in 2009 and warned the team to re-brand the enterprise, and to drop the term "cap-and-trade"—which itself was conjured as a way to avoid saying "energy tax." The pollsters plainly advised: re-brand the same schemes instead as "green jobs."[8]

For reasons that are not entirely clear, this happy talk became too much for the *New York Times*, which complained in an editorial that "when [Obama's] aides talk about the issue, they talk about things that are easy to sell—'energy security' and 'green jobs'—rather than pushing for tough measures needed to cap emissions." This is a nice way for the *Times* to admit that its allies' implausible, soothing pitch for these painful measures fails the Left's threshold test for glum earnestness.

Europe has proven the painful outcome of these policies, and to some extent even learned it. Dr. Michael Economides, University of Houston economics professor and publisher of *Energy Tribune*, writes how, in the context of the "Kyoto" international process for imposing this agenda,

Germany's Angela Merkel has already insisted on major exemptions for German heavy industry . . . . Italy[9] also rocked the EU climate boat by insisting on exemptions for its own energy-intensive industries at the turn of the year. . . . In June, deputy head of Poland's Solidarity trade union, Jaroslaw Grzesik, estimated that the EU's climate policy would cost 800,000 European jobs. The think-tank Open Europe has already estimated that the same policies will cost the UK $9 billion a year,[10] leaving an extra 1 million people in fuel poverty by 2020.[11]   July 2009

At home, even the Democrats' usually reliable Brookings Institute predicted the House bill imposing a similar scheme would reduce America's Gross Domestic Product by 2.5 percent.[12] That's what counts as a "jobs bill" to an environmentalist.

THE INCOHERENCE OF GREENSPEAK

"Green jobs" cheerleaders carry on like slightly less credible carnival barkers or sport gambling touts pushing their "lock of the week." Listen to the activists' unified field theory and wonder why they don't also promise to cure teenage acne and end world hunger: "Properly designed legislation," declared the Natural Resource Defense Council's Frances Beinecke, "will encourage innovation, enhance America's energy security, foster economic growth, improve our balance of trade, and provide critically needed U.S. leadership on this vital global challenge."[13]

That's all? Of course not. It's also super fast-acting! Pass the miserable global warming bills in Congress, and "millions of clean energy jobs would be created, starting right away."[14]

The "stimulus" bill experience is very relevant, however. Unemployment shot up to over 10 percent after the Obama administration vowed the stimulus billions would cap the figure at 8 percent. Even the Associated Press eventually reported that the stimulus bill's similar effort at throwing money at transportation infrastructure projects didn't help reduce unemployment.[15] According to the Government Accountability Office (GAO), this is primarily because of the aforementioned National Environmental Policy Act (NEPA), and

Davis-Bacon Act (described below), as well as other federal requirements attaching to the expenditure of taxpayer funds.[16] There is no reason to expect these politically selected pork schemes to prove any different than "stimulus bill" make-work such as spending $1.1 million to fix a guardrail "near a manufactured lake in a desolate patch of the Oklahoma Panhandle."[17] These projects share the trait of being selected for political and not any economic considerations.

So, as is also now well-ridiculed, the Obama administration chose to change the subject through changing the emphasis, instead touting that it had "created 640,329 jobs" (not 640,330, mind you; somehow artifice is more convincing when it eschews rounded numbers).[18] Obviously, with unemployment skyrocketing at the same time, this was not a net-jobs figure, exposing how such claims are used deceptively.

Given the amount of money borrowed, that would translate to a $247,850 taxpayer subsidy per job, which is similar to what can be expected as the subsidy for a windmill job.[19] While many of those stimulus jobs proved to be phony, many others were simply jobs dishonestly classified as "saved or created"; similarly, the tag "green jobs" is even being assigned to, say, existing steel jobs on the argument that windmills require steel. It will generally mean foreign steel, but in any event, that doesn't mean those jobs were created or saved by a "green jobs" scheme.

California's oddball governing class, having already committed hari-kari on these issues, still had to include everything from public relations representatives to marketing managers, accountants, and brick-layers to claim that "green jobs" account for something like 1 percent of employment.[20] (Meanwhile, a draft report by a state advisory committee estimated that California's new greenhouse gas laws could cost the state economy more than $143 billion over the next decade on top of the rest of the pain.)[21]

It's all gimmickry. Then there was the familiar fact that many of those stimulus jobs were temporary, which is also inherently the case with "green jobs." In short, if you liked the "stimulus," you'll love "green jobs" schemes.

Typically, after all of that stimulus money earmarked for "green jobs" was spent, few "green jobs" resulted—funny how giant pots of money not conditioned on performance tend to disappear into black holes like that. The Obama administration announced in November 2009 that it was spending tens of millions more to conduct studies looking for them.[22] And they did not appear to be joking.

WHAT IS A GREEN JOB?

No official definitions of a "green job" exist, but the trade-news site *Greenwire* notes that "The White House has broadly defined 'green jobs' as positions that benefit the environment, pay 10 percent to 20 percent more than other jobs and are more likely to be unionized."[23] Except that this clearly includes, according to our president, tasks such as changing light bulbs and caulking, at least according to a speech he gave at a campaign rally in College Park, Maryland.[24] "Green jobs" are often menial, generally make-work positions hardly commanding great pay as promised. If you do pay above-average scale for that, you're just digging a deeper economic hole.

More enlightening is research led by Andrew Morriss of the University of Illinois College of Law, the Property and Environment Research Center, and George Mason University's Mercatus Center. His team found that "the green jobs literature often defines a job as 'green' based on the inefficient use of labor in a production process. In other words, they prefer increasing the number of jobs, even if it means using a less efficient means of production."[25] Similarly, and affirming other economic literature, the old-line, state-funded economic think tank Rheinisch-Westfälisches Institut Wirtschaftsforschung (RWI-Essen) wrote in October 2009 about the German experience swooned over by President Obama:

> Proponents of renewable energies often regard the requirement for more workers to produce a given amount of energy as a benefit, failing to recognize that this lowers the output potential of the economy and is hence counterproductive to net job creation. Significant research shows that initial employment benefits from renewable policies soon turn negative as additional costs are incurred. Trade and other assumptions in those studies claiming positive employment turn out to be unsupportable.[26]

All of which naturally pricks up the ears of organized labor, as discussed later.

The term is also broadly applied to, for example, jobs installing "smart meters" or any of the host of programs pushed by companies and statist nags riding the "global warming" agenda. But politics in the United States have dictated that "green jobs" do not include the greenhouse gas-free hydroelectric power, as dams are disfavored for being mean to fish and an affront to Gaia's design. CO_2-free nuclear power derived from uranium is also a no-no.

So "green jobs" in practice means requiring more man-hours to produce the same kilowatt hour (or other unit) of energy. That is, it is what directly results from mandating a form, and level of use, of less efficient and therefore inherently more expensive energy. These energy sources—windmills, solar panels, and other things we ditched more than a century ago as our main sources of energy once we found things that worked better—are also intermittent, meaning they don't work continuously. They are unreliable. As such, they are even more expensive still, as you have to build the same production capacity twice. This also means you still have to use, though intermittently and therefore inefficiently, the disfavored sorts of energy (meaning those that work). All of this increases the cost of anything requiring energy to produce—which is everything—which also puts people out of work.

This invokes the key fallacy underlying "green jobs." As noted by Economides,

> The basic assumption is that technology per se *generates* jobs. Mostly, it does not. Rather, technology *enables* jobs— real and sustainable jobs—based on how useful the technology is to the marketplace. To generate real *industrial* jobs, however, you need a basic commodity to trade, and in the energy business this has meant oil, gas or coal. Yet "green" politicians and eco-lobbyists expect to create a revolution in green jobs based on alternative energy sources. The trouble is that alternative energy sources remain ... inefficient, offering a very poor to mostly negative return on investment. Cut off the flow of massive public subsidies and the alternative energy industrial revolution would grind to a halt tomorrow—as the European experience already bears out.[27] (emphases in original)

More on Europe's disaster later, but as Morriss et al. summarized:

> A group of studies, rapidly gaining popularity, promise that a massive program of government mandates, subsidies,

and forced technological interventions will reward the nation with an economy brimming with "green jobs." Not only will these jobs allegedly improve the environment, but they will pay well, be very interesting, and foster unionization. These claims are built on seven myths about economics, forecasting, and technology. Our team of researchers from universities across the nation surveyed this green jobs literature, analyzed its assumptions, and found that the special interest groups promoting the idea of green jobs have embedded dubious assumptions and techniques within their analyses. We found that the prescribed undertaking would lead to restructuring and possibly impoverishing our society.[28]

Dubious assumptions to push a massive government program? Shocked, shocked.

Morriss et al. concluded that "These green jobs studies mistake any position receiving a paycheck for a position creating value. Simply hiring people to write and enforce regulations, fill-out forms, and process paperwork is not a recipe for creating wealth. Much of the promised boost in green employment turns out to be in non-productive—and expensive—positions that raise costs for consumers."[29] This supposed economic jolt is actually a drag.

Even some left-of-center think tanks are unable to defend what energy policy advocate Chris Tucker calls "Obama's green-jobs-qua-economic-ambrosia rhetoric" anymore, citing a study by Sam Sherraden at the lefty New America Foundation admitting that green jobs are a negligible factor in employment and will likely be so for the foreseeable future.[30] Sherraden warned that policymakers should avoid "over-promising about the jobs and investment we can expect from government spending to support the green economy."[31]

Still, the greens' desperation to spin, dissemble, and otherwise distract from how these schemes really operate must explain why the cheerleaders sputter so much nonsense when muttering the term, draping it with every meaningless catch-phrase in the Washington, D.C., handbook (but telling us nothing other than that they have no idea what they are talking about).

Consider the Center for American Progress's (CAP) Andrew Light, whom I will use as our green guinea pig for these purposes, having by chance viewed him repeating his movement's vacuous catch-phrases to FOX News late in Obama's first year in office while I was pulling material together for this book. There he stammered, either naively or disingenuously, "If you sort of are going to move the world towards a fundamentally new suite of mechanisms for creating energy, that's—we need people to do that and that's how you make and create jobs."[32]

Is it possible that the greens actually think that that is the sum total of these mandates' impacts?

Of course not. These people are ideologues, not complete idiots (even if they seem to think you are). If mandating things is beneficial to employment and the economy, why stop at adding these new great ideas? Let's mandate many, many more things in the name of global warming. If we wanted to "move" (feel free to say "force," or otherwise use the full weight of government to coerce) the world onto, say, a vegan diet and stop all of that destructive bovine flatulence, why, that would create jobs making tofu and selling it in vegan food stores, too. Same is true for rickshaws instead of automobiles, both of which are logical extensions of the "green jobs" case. We'd be the richest country in the world, if only we could get beyond old ways of thinking and our resistance to success. There are no downsides at all to this free lunch, and all it will produce is jobs, jobs, jobs.

Readers over the age of thirty may recall that this sort of ministration of the economy by our superiors has been tried in Eastern Europe, and worked so well they had to build a wall to keep all the millionaires in.

Further, this philosophy is absurd on its face, given that it tells us that Hurricane Katrina, the Chicago Fire—and other disasters global warming is supposed to bring more of—are actually good for the economy. After all, they require that workers rebuild and replace things, which employs people. Paging Frédéric Bastiat. Good heavens, people, when you are mocked rather well in advance by a nineteenth century French economist—you might want to reassess. He wrote of similar morality in the case of a glazier paying young boys to smash windows in order to create work—and ridiculed the mentality by also suggesting that cutting off one's right hand would create a wealthier world, since more difficulty means more work, which means more wealth.

One glaring problem here is that by making make-work *de facto* or *de jure* union work, you are adding inefficiency and cost. This is because the jobs must never end, as satisfying the constituencies you've nurtured and even created requires constant taxpayer infusions. This leads to a bubble, which must burst. Thus the silver lining of the economic clutter will simply be more boom-bust jobs like the ethanol boondoggle which left so many Midwestern communities on the verge of being ghost towns.

Then there's the free-lunch fallacy on which "green jobs" depends, and which our policy sages ignore. After, in effect, mandating the destruction of windows in order to replace them, everyone is left with a full window pane, if lighter in the wallet, liberated from the confiscated wealth they would otherwise put to productive uses. But, that wealth was transferred to the Burgomaster's glazier brother-in-law, in whose faltering alternative-window business the town's former vice president heavily invested before running around warning towns-people about the horrors of old windows causing hellfire to be rained down on the village. Which, under this theory of economics, would actually be beneficial.

"Green jobs" legislation would be the ultimate cash for clunkers program, except that cash for clunkers as applied to automobiles simply moved September's likely vehicle purchases up to August without actually creating new demand. Green jobs programs do create new demand, if via mandates, for that which otherwise is not demanded (hence the mandate). Therefore, this involves moving forward purchases not of what would be purchased later, but what was unlikely to ever be purchased. It would be like mandating car purchases—for the Amish.

HOW MANY UNIONIZED SLACKER FEDERAL BUREAUCRATS DOES IT TAKE TO CHANGE A LIGHT BULB?

Delving further into the President's intentions with this green jobs mantra, we turn to that campaign speech in College Park, Maryland, exhorting the youth vote with what might be one of the most inane sales pitches of all time. In this speech, Obama seized the mantle of "hope-monger"—in contrast to those other "mongers" among us (you know who you are!). He then proceeded, through three separate stanzas about global warming, to reveal he is also a warmmonger, breathlessly crafting a message of climatic catastrophe.[33]

As we soon learned was quite typical of our leader, he prescribed Inside-the-Beltway nostrums, which are also particularly tiresome from someone pitching himself as a sainted outsider determined to bring revelatory change to our national politics. One of his money lines on this day was: "We are going to spend billions of dollars on solar, wind, and biodiesel."[34] Yes. It's criminal that we haven't done that yet. Except for the approximately $50 billion in taxpayer money[35] already cast down those rat holes, that is. Still, one can't go a day in Washington, on a college campus, or even in front of the television, watching those utterly vacuous BP "man on the street" commercials, and not hear some form of the talking point that *It really is it time we start investing in these.*[36]

The details of how Obama hopes to spend those billions proved no more amusing than how the tens of billions already squandered have yielded only more promises of future promise: "We will hire young people who don't have a trade and give them a trade making homes more energy efficient, insulating homes, changing light bulbs, reducing our dependence on dirty power plants."[37]

Yes. He really said that. Jonah Goldberg noted the oddity of how the greens "get teary-eyed about their mythical 5 million 'green jobs,' most of which would involve temporary gigs weatherizing granny's attic, replacing light bulbs at the DMV, and hiring ACORN to shake down businesses that use too much air conditioning."[38] So it is that the idealistic, modern-day version of the "ask not what your country can do for you" consists of telling slackers that the government will provide windmill and light bulb-changing jobs after graduation.

That's not Camelot; it's a strange New Deal. Oddly enough, global warming alarmism never took hold during FDR's roaring 1930s—though it was warmer then than now. I suppose we should just be thankful President Roosevelt never stumbled upon the excuse. Then the state might really have gotten big.

"GREEN JOB" MEANS "TEMPORARY JOB"

The "stimulus" analogy bears numerous intrinsic similarities, like accumulating enormous debt and concomitantly allocating the borrowed money inefficiently to politically favored recipients and agendas. Incurring unprecedented new levels of stimulus debt, put to questionable use, surely chased investment away from our shores, just as it is likely to stunt future economic growth.[39] This is true even if we cannot be sure of how much never arrived, being sent instead to more reliable economies, and we are too embarrassed by the administration's precedent at fudging their own figures to pretend to make our own up. It is also likely that by suddenly mandating that all manner of projects be *de facto* or *de jure* union projects—another trait shared with "green jobs"—real jobs were lost or avoided.

But the most glaring similarity, and indeed feature of "green jobs" is that they are temporary. Before you find comfort in this, recall that the unions don't stand for such notions, and the enactment of green jobs schemes ensures further infusions of taxpayer money into the bubble to make the make-work permanent.

We saw how some jobs supposedly created under the "stimulus" actually reflected funding of a position that lasted, in some cases, only a week. The reason you hear of enormous numbers of projected jobs is because those pushing them do not "homogenize the data." Homogenizing, or harmonizing, the claimed green jobs figures annualizes them, translating the thousands of days-, weeks- or months-long gigs (i.e., "jobs created") into the equivalent of full-time jobs. So a sexy claim of half a million jobs, which are 60-day installation contracts, is homogenized at around 75,000 "jobs created."[40]

But make-work and mandating that federal buildings get new caulk is not creating positive economic activity, or growth, as few if any of those jobs will exist in a year without a doubling down on the subsidy just to keep the wards of the state going. Regardless of its intellectual integrity, this is a favorite game of the statist set hell-bent on pretending the state is the source of wealth creation and good times.

This is given deeper meaning when you consider, as detailed later, the real jobs both avoided and outright killed from this sort of make-work. Consider Obama's serial calls touting "green jobs" in 2008 and 2009, for Americans to "think of what's happening in countries like Spain [and] Germany,"[41] directing our gaze to these European models for the economic miracle he hopes to stick us with.

Researchers in those countries took a look, and found that "green jobs" are indeed overwhelmingly short-term hires requiring a continuous stream of subsidies to turn them into anything connoted by the term a "job created." Some German academics heeding Mr. Obama's call found that "It is most likely that whatever jobs are created by renewable energy promotion would vanish as soon as government support is terminated, leaving only Germany's export sector to benefit from the possible continuation of renewable support in other countries such as the US."[42] For pointing out this very reality, the lead author of a research team at King Juan Carlos University was assailed by the head of that country's renewable energy lobby, not for being substantively wrong but for being "unpatriotic." This gentleman's argument against exposing Spain's disastrous experience was that only if the United States fell for it, too, would the mandarinates created in Spain by these boondoggles have a chance to survive, by providing them a new market.

Dr. Gabriel Calzada's team there found among other things that, "Only one out of ten green job contracts were in maintenance and operation of already installed plants, and most of the rest of the working positions are only sustainable in an expansive environment related to high subsidies."[43]

The jobs' temporary nature inherently led to the creation of a bubble needing the constant infusion of taxpayer money just to keep it stable; growth only meant ever higher wealth transfers.

That bubble burst in Spain when the state had to admit that it had run out of other people's money. Calzada testified to Congress that these results were affirmed in a Royal Decree of April 30, 2009. The government declared that <u>the electricity "rate deficit," or debt created</u> <u>by shielding ratepayers from the full cost of "green energy,"</u> "is deeply harming the system and puts at risk not only the financial situation of the electric sector companies but also sustainability of the system itself. This dis-adjustment turns out to be unsustainable and has grave consequences since it deteriorates the security and financial capacity of the investments necessary for providing electricity at the levels of quality and security the Spanish society demands."[44] The politicians naturally then promised to actually increase the subsidies.

As noted elsewhere, it seems that a humiliated and rather unhappy Obama administration set Van Jones and its other apologists out to nonetheless say that this study was, e.g., "debunked by the *Wall Street Journal*,"[45] and that "The analysis by the authors from King Juan Carlos University represents a significant divergence from traditional methodologies."[46] Both claims are nonsense.

Upon scrutiny, the claim that the *Wall Street Journal* played a key role is reduced to the fact that a *Journal* blogger posted a green group activist *ad hominem* attack against the study's lead author Calzada and indicated rather ignorantly that opportunity costs (jobs avoided by wasting the money) aren't actual economic costs.[47] The claim that the study's methodology was "non-traditional" came in a white paper rebuttal by two young non-economist staffers with the taxpayer-funded National Renewable Energy Laboratory. That is the one already mentioned which was farmed out to the wind energy's lobby and Center for American Progress for assistance in coming up with this cronyish, political retort to an academic assessment.

What this principal argument turned out to mean was that the Spanish authors used methods generally employed by people committing their own resources, to the exclusion of the input-output (or Leontief) methodology designed for central planning in which all is assumed as knowable, controllable, and static. That is to say, the Calzada team's sin, according to the administration's non-economists tasked with rebutting the study, was to eschew an analytical method discredited outside of social democratic government agencies and select, associated interests.

GREEN'S UNSEEN: KILLING JOBS WITH FREE LUNCHES

"Renewable" energy as acceptably defined in the "green jobs" campaign means energy sources that we left over a century ago because we could. With plentiful hydrocarbons, or "fossil fuels," renewables are simply too expensive and, regardless, are inescapably intermittent and unreliable. That is why they require subsidy and mandate schemes in order to exist on any meaningful commercial scale. As a result, here, as elsewhere, the statists' campaign to pick winners and losers—ok, to pick losers—inherently prescribes turning losers into winners, but only by government fiat and at taxpayer expense.

Indeed, Europe's experience to which the president refers us also proves that the economic costs of "green jobs" schemes extend beyond the direct financial costs of the subsidies.

A mandate that we obtain a certain percentage of our electricity from running on giant hamster wheels, accompanied by a billion dollars in subsidies to giant hamster wheel manufacturers to bring down the consumer cost of hamster-wheel electricity, will indeed create jobs in the giant hamster wheel manufacturing and hamster wheel electricity industries. No one disputes that.

The jobs that are created would seem to be net jobs—in other words, the overall employment result is positive. However, the truth is rather uglier. Mandating inefficient, non-economic energy sources costs jobs. Taking wealth from producers inherently keeps them from using it productively, as they otherwise would, to create or support jobs that are self-sustaining—unlike those created by mandate, which cannot make it without continued infusions of cash and the reinforcement of artificial demand.

As the authors of the aforementioned German study explained:

> While employment projections in the renewable sector convey seemingly impressive prospects for gross job growth, they typically obscure the broader implications for economic welfare by omitting any accounting of off-setting impacts. These impacts include, but are not limited to, job losses from crowding out of cheaper forms of conventional energy generation, indirect impacts on upstream industries, additional job losses from the drain on economic activity precipitated by higher electricity prices, private consumers' overall loss of purchasing power due to higher electricity prices, and diverting funds from other, possibly more beneficial investment.[48]

This reply to Obama's implicit call that we should follow Germany's example is not an outlier, but is rife with citation of other papers throughout the economic literature whose findings it affirms.

The Spanish study articulated the same result through two separate methods: the policy machinations creating 50,000 jobs prevented the creation of more than twice as many, because the inefficient state spends more than two times the money to create one phony job that the private sector spends to create one real job. That's on top of the energy-intensive manufacturing jobs that left windmill-obsessed Spain for coal-rich America, among other places, after these schemes were adopted. According to the study's lead author Dr. Calzada, testifying before the U.S. House of Representatives' "Special Committee on Global Warming":

> Our study sought to answer the seminal question—what was the price of Spain's attempt to lead the world in a clean energy transformation? Our research shows that that price was very high. Here are some highlights from our study:
>
> - For every 1 green job financed by Spanish taxpayers, 2.2 jobs were lost as an opportunity cost. . . .
> - Those programs resulted in the destruction of nearly 110,500 jobs.
> - Each "green" megawatt installed on average destroyed 5.39 jobs elsewhere in the economy, and in the case of solar photovoltaics, the number reaches 8.99 jobs per megawatt hour installed.

Calzada then noted, to the rude and vocal displeasure of the Democrats assembled (Republicans, as is so often the case, left the room, and their invited witness was stranded to be disrespectfully treated with no support), "Spain has already attempted to lead the world in a clean energy transformation. But our research shows that Spain's policies were economically destructive."[49]

In fact, taking Obama's instruction and looking at what's happening in Spain and Germany affirms how "green jobs" schemes do create jobs, but only in countries smart enough to avoid the schemes.

For example, green jobs schemes in Spain created those steel jobs in Carroll County, Kentucky, exported within just a year of Europe's cap-and-trade scheme going into effect. The UK not only lost the steel jobs at Corus to India (also mentioned in chapter 1), but did so after paying producers a windfall fortune, via free cap-and-trade allowances to sell to others, during the "transition" period which turned out to be just a period to transition from the UK to friendlier environs. This is because green jobs mandates chase away real jobs in manufacturing sectors that require a significant and reliable electricity supply and, in a global economy in which most of the world rejects this foolishness, they can and will move.

Yes, "windmills require steel!" As do giant hamster wheels. Good luck, however, producing steel with electricity made by running on such wheels (or by using windmills). Your domestic steel industry will ultimately find it cannot operate in a system that so punishes energy-intensive activity. Businesses pass on costs to consumers until they can't, and then they leave. These are some "unseens" of these mandates. British journalist Dominic Lawson writes of how English steel mills are already proving "unable to compete globally, even at current domestic energy prices," thanks to this suite of policies. Indeed, the Teesside community lost 1,700 workers to India, exposing as painfully true Lawson's claim that this impact on employers is a poorly kept secret, and that "deliberately to make them uncompetitive is industrial vandalism—and even madness...a futile gesture...and immoral."[50]

What Lawson refers to is that other insidious corruption of the supposed vehicle for "green job" creation: cap-and-trade. As the *Wall Street Journal* noted, the largest UK steelmaker "Corus is essentially being paid to lay off British workers.... The Corus story also shows that cap and trade isn't really a free market. Markets develop to efficiently allocate resources and capital. Carbon cap and trade is a government-rigged market, in which carbon allowances are dispensed based on political influence. Such a system is ripe for manipulation, and Corus is merely the latest example."[51] In one of a series of similar crafty moves out of countries riding the massive scam that is Kyoto, Corus was purchased by Indian steel giant Tata Group. Tata also endows something called the Tata Energy Research Institute, or TERI. You may be interested to know that the UN International Panel on Climate Change's (IPCC) "chief climate scientist" Rajendra Pachauri—he's actually that Indian economist and railway engineer by training mentioned earlier, but he's a rather hysterical promoter of climate alarmism, so it's all good—happens also to receive money from TERI—climate profiteer—by serving as chairman of the IPCC—climate cheerleader. Odd, that.

Steelmakers are by no means alone. Facing reality, energy-intensive Spanish manufacturers representing nearly one-fifth of Spain's electricity consumption with more than one hundred facilities across industry lines—metallurgical, cement, chemicals, ceramics—formed an association to alleviate the inexorable higher march of that country's high energy prices caused by the same vaunted policies.[52] They made clear this was destroying their competitiveness with other countries where the cost of electricity is not so punitive. Some openly threatened that they had no choice but to leave the country if resolution to the madness were not forthcoming.

Adios, amigos. And with Mexico, China, and India, along with 150 other countries sitting the Kyoto-style nonsense out and thereby ready and eager to take our own unwanted, energy-intensive manufacturing and other jobs, we have no reason to expect any different result here.

Such truths run counter to claims made by, for example, CAP's Andrew Light. When asked by FOX in the aforementioned interview whether these supposed job-creating schemes will actually move jobs overseas, he demurred, saying that this won't occur if the United States takes the lead,[53] which is gibberish. Somehow when the Europeans took the lead, with an economy that incidentally is larger than ours, they failed to persuade the rest of the world to jump in. But they chased their own jobs out.

This talking point, of course, merely parrots the "first actor" myth, a staple of "green jobs" advocacy. The German experience Obama wants us to follow affirmed that "claims about technological innovation benefits of Germany's first-actor status are unsupportable. In fact, the regime appears to be counterproductive in that respect, stifling innovation by encouraging producers to lock into existing technologies."[54]

Ritual accusations, that even such unlikely suspects as European academics were just performing partisan hit jobs, were thrown at all studies which exposed Obama's rhetorical exhortation of European successes as farcical. But such accusations are nothing but partisan sniveling in their own right.

The "green jobs" cheerleaders promoted reports challenging the lessons from Europe, produced by parties with fairly predictable tendencies to tout benefits and dismiss costs of their desired agenda. These included the Worldwatch Institute and the Political Economy Research Institute at the University of Massachusetts-Amherst (PERI)—the latter also quietly enlisted by Obama's Department of Energy to help dismiss the Spanish study, according to emails unearthed by Freedom of Information Act requests. PERI produced a paper for Team Soros (the Center for American Progress, also brought into the process by Obama's Department of Energy; the coincidences abound when dealing with this lobbyist-free administration). Also joining the fun of free-ice-cream economics was the contract firm Global Insight. In a paper for the U.S. Conference of Mayors, Global Insight became an aggressive advocate for the global warming agenda.

The Beacon Hill Institute at Suffolk University in Boston examined these papers and found that these authors routinely make wildly, insupportably optimistic assumptions, mistakenly argue that a cost is actually a benefit, and fail to account for jobs destroyed or not created.[55]

The truth about "green jobs" schemes is their unadvertised impacts, proven in the very countries we are to model. Europe's experience tells us that green jobs schemes are not only distorting, but also highly destructive. Green jobs mean pink slips. This means we need to hope Team Obama fails in its vow to create five million green jobs[56]—"millions and millions and millions" of green jobs (in former President Bill Clinton's irrationally exuberant cheerleading, after saying in the same speech that we need to slow our economy down to stop global warming)[57]—for the simple reason that we should expect just the jobs avoided ("opportunity costs") alone to actually be more than twice those created.[58]

CAN MAKE-WORK "GROW THE ECONOMY"?

Sadly, however, such impacts, whether "opportunity" costs or otherwise, are not pressing considerations in Washington. No, we are now told that by mandating that the American economy be driven by all manner of energy sources that cannot stand on their own, we will "grow the economy." That is the new, favorite phrase of my young Democratic congressman, Tom Perriello. Mr. Perriello, like a host of lawmakers desperate to find cover for their 2009 vote in support of the disastrous Waxman-Markey "cap-and-trade" bill, has since dedicated countless hours on the House floor and elsewhere to spread this tawdry exposition of economic illiteracy to those masses he and his colleagues hope are desperate or inattentive enough to fall for it.

Mere days after his "aye" vote, Mr. Perriello regaled a Charlottesville, Virginia, radio audience with some strange talk about how people who say the cap-and-trade and "green jobs" schemes will chase away jobs "aren't living in the real world." In the real world, the enthusiastic sage held forth, America is "hemorrhaging jobs" to China and India precisely because they've already passed Waxman-Markey style legislation.[59]

As with so many of the "global warming" talking points, this one is pure fiction and also certainly news to India and China, who have otherwise been quite busy telling Europeans and Obama administration-types to go stuff their bossy demands that Indians and Chinese do themselves such harm. Perriello's other talking point to advance these welfare programs in the name of economic growth was that many more green jobs are in the offing than exist in, say, the coal industry. This is simply more uninformed, wishful, or disingenuous free-ice-cream thinking. Mandating labor-intensive energy sources, by its very nature, requires more labor to produce less energy. It also displaces workers employed in the industries producing the sources under regulatory assault—mostly coal. Both of these outcomes harm the economy, not grow it.

Leading greens even go so far as to claim that the pittance generated by "green" energy today already requires more workers than does the key contributor, coal. But, as is generally the case with these claims, this one is balderdash, and as the University of Colorado's Roger Pielke Jr. notes, it is lucky for them that it is.[60] Pielke and the *Christian Science Monitor* both observed, if in their own way, that more renewable-energy workers than coal-energy workers would bring into stark relief the spectacular expense and inefficiency of renewables. Imagine the audacity of crowing how you require more employees to produce about one percent of our electricity than are needed to produce about fifty percent with coal.

An amusing, related claim was that made by five Democrat senators boasting of their pet projects' inefficiency, naturally in the context of calling for more taxpayer subsidies. Signed by Senators Bob Menendez of New Jersey, Debbie Stabenow of Michigan, Michael Bennet of Colorado, Ron Wyden of Oregon, and Kirsten Gillibrand of New York, trade-outlet *Greenwire* writes how the letter "highlights that solar technology 'creates more jobs per megawatt of energy produced than any other form of energy.'"[61] Good heavens, and you want me to pay for that? How about instead we sprint in the other direction as its supporters cannot help but tell you that it is the most labor-intensive, inefficient source around?

And, predictably, Al Gore leapt into the fray with bogus job-comparison figures, specifically as the basis for an op-ed in the *Financial Times* co-authored by United Nations Secretary General Ban Ki moon calling for the world to get on board with that stuff Gore's invested in. Their argument (that vastly greater numbers of jobs already exist in the wind-energy industry than in the coal industry) was soon enough debunked by the *Christian Science Monitor* (CSM)[62]—if accidentally so, as *CSM* was specifically dismissing a very similar claim made on *Fortune* magazine's blog[63] (which was soon corrected, a desperately needed but uncommon practice for Mr. Gore).

In their call for more taxpayer-funded green pork, Gore and Ban falsely stated that "globally, with 2.3m people employed in the renewable energy sector, there are already more jobs there than directly in the oil and gas industries. In the US, there are now more jobs in the wind industry than in the entire coal industry."[64] But as *CSM* pointed out, the key to the "bogus comparison" is that the very same wind energy report from which such claims are derived makes clear that "those 85,000 jobs in wind power are as 'varied as turbine component manufacturing, construction and installation of wind turbines, wind turbine operations and maintenance, legal and marketing services, and more.' The 81,000 coal jobs counted by the Department of Energy are only miners. Their figure excludes those who haul the coal around the country, as well as those who work in coal power plants."[65] In fact, there are 133,000 workers directly employed in the U.S. coal industry. So Gore's comparison was not of apples to apples, but an entire basket of lemons to one orange.

Taking this more global viewpoint, consider research published by the National Mining Association, claiming[66] that every two of those mining positions creates seven more jobs on railways, barges, and elsewhere in the economy. Comparing something closer to apples with apples, you must then make the relevant number of coal-related jobs more likely around 450,000 workers employed as a result of bringing coal-fired electricity to market. In fact, Penn State University research shows that each coal job supports up to eleven other jobs in the worker's community. Now recall that this source accounts for half of our electricity, and windmills something between under one-half of one percent and a percent-and-a-quarter.[67]

You see why they have to make things up. The truth is highly damaging. Still, it's pretty bad when even the falsehoods one concocts to advance a case actually defeat it.

Incidentally, Mike Carey of the Ohio Coal Association has testified in Congress that his state's coal workers make on average more than $64,000, nearly $25,000 more than Ohio's average yearly income.[68] In West Virginia, the gap is even wider, and yet coal remains our most economical energy source (even after a three-decade war against its use).[69]

Speaking of funny business, consider the two studies that gained the most traction in support of this "grow the economy" line, suggesting net job increases from the leading "green jobs" vehicle of cap-and-trade. These were both led by David Roland-Holst, an adjunct professor at, of all places, Cal-Berkeley's Center for Energy, Resources and Economic Sustainability. His team's November 2009 paper "Clean Energy and Climate Policy for U.S. Growth and Job Creation" claimed that the cap-and-trade bill would grow the economy by $11 billion, creating an additional 918,000 to 1.9 million jobs. They even went so far as to answer the logical question of *why stop here?*, concluding, "Indeed, a central finding of this research is that *the stronger the federal climate policy, the greater the economic reward*"[70] (emphases in original). Again, might as well tell a whopper.

Here's how you get there, according to Heritage Foundation economist David Kreutzer, who analyzed the effort. By raising the price of energy, people then use less. This is axiomatic, despite energy's rather inelastic demand (that is, people need it and will pay for it, absorbing more economic pain than they would for other cost increases by foregoing other purchases or activities in order to maintain a certain level of energy use, for wealth creation or comfort).

Imagine you sell frozen goods. The state increases your energy costs enough to coerce you into using less energy, then also requires the purchase of an expensive new, highly efficient, smaller freezer. So you pay much more to be able to move less product. The greens (and appliance manufacturers, who, to no surprise, are also pushing the agenda) love these latter mandates, insisting that if the state makes people purchase expensive new equipment, they will actually save a few dollars in the long run from lower electricity bills. As with hybrid cars, such claims are routinely exposed as generally, even wildly unsupportable unless, of course, the cost of energy is raised drastically. Which the greens also demand. Possibly as a way to make their other demands appear less cruel.

So, the Berkeley authors then tally the additional costs coercing you into using less energy as "savings" to the economy. They multiply it by the new, higher price of electricity and declare that that's how much people have saved to spend on other things (even though this lower amount of energy may still be costing people more, leaving them with less). Then this phantom free money is run through their macroeconomic model multipliers and, *Voila!*, it produces higher income and more jobs.

This generally also assumes that people do not wish to save money unless the government makes them—an assumption that perfectly embodies this agenda.

But all of this is absurd. Kreutzer notes that if it were medicine, it would bring down a torrent of malpractice lawsuits. And in its absurdity, it reveals the complete and total absence of arguments available to support the position that these schemes "grow the economy."

The truth is that even inherently biased administration studies of the "green job" scheme cap-and-trade, by EPA, the Energy Information Administration (EIA), and the Congressional Budget Office, as well as the independent Brookings Institute, the Heritage Foundation, the American Council for Capital Formation, and CRA International, agree that these cap-and-trade bills must reduce overall employment and lead to lower incomes than can be had without them. EIA, for example, said that the Waxman-Markey cap-and-trade bill destroys 2.3 million jobs *on net* when fully implemented (in 2030), 800,000 of them manufacturing jobs.[71] Not one cap-and-trade scenario modeled by any of these entities produced net job or income growth from cap-and-trade.

Reckless and disingenuous though the claim is, agenda-driven whizzes in Washington insist that throwing away a billion dollars, confiscated from today's and future generations, grows the economy—simply because they see a giant hamster wheel research facility go up in their district. But the claim that this will "grow the economy" is made up. These actions will do the opposite.

The government can give us nothing that it has not taken from us. The politics of envy, which underlies much of the "green jobs" hooey, have never been as strong in the United States as in Europe—and that fact gave us a chance for longer than the Europeans to stand firm against all of the promises of free ice cream. Now we are told to look to Europe, but ignore the actual lessons. Instead, accept a fairy tale.

Our German experts summarized for us:

> German renewable energy policy, and in particular the adopted feed-in tariff scheme, has failed to harness the market incentives needed to ensure a viable and cost-effective introduction of renewable energies into the country's energy

portfolio. To the contrary, the government's support mechanisms have in many respects subverted these incentives, resulting in massive expenditures that show little long-term promise for stimulating the economy, protecting the environment, or increasing energy security.[72]

GREEN JOBS IN RED CHINA

What might be the most embarrassing aspect of this con is that the same policies supposedly ensuring that particular, politically desired goods will be produced here, because their use is mandated here, actually ensure they'll be made somewhere else.

President Obama likes to use rhetoric about "green jobs that can't be shipped overseas" (what about down to Mexico?). This can only mean one of two things. The first, imposing protectionist walls to keep other countries' goods out of America, seems unlikely, as Obama appears sincere in his opposition to shrugging off our existing, binding commitments in the realm of international trade law and instead sparking a trade war as so many in his base call for. Already the Department of Energy has had to waive those Buy American portions of the stimulus bill with respect to energy efficient lighting, saying, "The determination of inapplicability under the Recovery Act section 1605 [the Buy America portion of the stimulus bill] for [LEDs, fluorescent electronic lighting ballasts, and CFLs] is based on extensive market research and a thorough investigation of the domestic manufacturing landscape. This research revealed that these three products are manufactured almost exclusively in China and Mexico."[73] This decision was issued by Al Gore's recently former CEO Cathy Zoi. Possibly she could mention this next time they talk.

What this leaves us with, then, is that those jobs that cannot be shipped overseas are the temporary installation jobs. This does make sense.

What it does not do is make a case for imposing the mandates. The smaller number of jobs manufacturing the wind and solar contraptions, if we mandate the machines, will still mostly be found elsewhere. This is one of the lessons from the Danes' experience of massive windmill deployment, which has not only been a tremendous waste of money, but one with fleeting employment benefits.[74] It turns out that even this, Obama's third model for us to follow—quickly becoming the substitute for Spain when the truth about that latter country came out—showed that the manufacturing jobs, the kind that Obama implies are the ones he is speaking about (judging by the locations he has chosen to give these speeches), will not stay much longer.

Big Danish windmill manufacturer Vestas also proved elsewhere in Europe that windmill manufacturing jobs will most certainly be exported once the schemes mandating their product raise electricity prices as intended. Vestas shipped manufacturing jobs from, for example, the Isle of Wight, to among other places the United States, when that appeared to be a savvy marketing gesture, and also possibly to take advantage of stimulus programs and promises of more such programs to come.[75] But these operations can easily leave town, and they generally do.

This is a rather intellectually amusing conundrum. The job loss occurs even when industry's power bill is subsidized to protect them from the costs they are involved in increasing (for others), try to keep their jobs from fleeing. This was the case in several European locations which bled jobs to the more accommodating business climate of China, whose energy prices are unburdened by cap-and-trade and other idiotic mandates.

The lede in a November 5, 2009, *Boston Globe* story captured the situation well: "Little more than a year after cutting the ribbon at a new factory in Devens built with more than $58 million in state aid, Evergreen Solar said yesterday that it will shift its assembly of solar panels from there to China."[76] Ouch. It seems that "In exchange for receiving $58.6 million in grants, loans, land, tax incentives, and other aid to build in Massachusetts, Evergreen pledged that it would add 350 new jobs," which it did. Briefly, only to then "write off $40 million worth of equipment at Devens because of the production shift to China." The company cited the cost of production here not faced if they build their machines elsewhere. No one told them it wasn't polite to prove the president wrong, and send green jobs overseas, to make things for use back home in response to mandates making it more expensive to produce here, prompting others to move overseas. Boy, Obamanomics can be exhausting.

Wash, rinse, repeat, but notice more and more hair circling the drain each time.

The same held true for many other companies. For example, President Obama said at a January 2010 visit to Ohio that the wind and solar industries were "about to collapse" until taxpayer-funded wealth transfer was made available to them through the stimulus bill.[77] Still, amid the massive disgorging of that borrowed or confiscated taxpayer wealth for these schemes, in late 2009 the Gamesa wind turbine plant in western Pennsylvania announced it was laying off nearly half its 280 workers,[78] General Electric said it would close a solar panel factory in Delaware,[79] and we learned that the largest solar plant in the United States, the DeSoto Solar Center in Arcadia, Florida, which once employed 400 workers, actually by then only boasted two full-time "green jobs."[80] The company's parts were almost exclusively manufactured abroad—including the critical solar panels (Philippines) because, let's face it, it's too expensive to make things here anymore—even the agenda's required trinkets—thanks in part to our escalating green agenda.

Green protests notwithstanding, producers go where it is most economical to operate, and in a modern and global economy they can satisfy, from overseas, the product demands of any poseur's policy peacocking. This raises another demerit to Obama's schemes: parts made where it's cheapest, say in Asia, are installed in America, but to the bottom line benefit of a Spanish company. As the *Wall Street Journal* reported, "While the wind farms and solar installations are in the U.S., the profits from these projects are flowing mainly to European companies and developers owned by private-equity investors."[81]

When it became among the first to catch on, the *Washington Times* editorialized,

> Of the $1 billion in clean-energy stimulus money spent since the beginning of September, $850 million has gone to foreign wind companies. It doesn't take a bunch of experts at a hastily planned "jobs summit" to discover this isn't the way to bolster employment in America. Indeed, the 11 U.S. wind farms that received stimulus money from the Treasury have imported 695 of the 982 wind turbines to be installed, creating 4,500 jobs overseas. That's far more overseas work than the stimulus money has created in the United States.[82]

As the *Dallas Morning News* wrote about the planned U.S. Renewable Energy Group $1.5 billion wind farm in West Texas for which the stimulus bill paid about a third, "There would be perhaps 330 jobs created in Texas. Most would be temporary construction jobs. Meanwhile, thousands of Chinese workers in the northeastern industrial city Shenyang would build the labor-intensive turbines."[83]

It is for reasons such as this that former Senate Majority Leader and current Center for American Progress appendage Tom Daschle says, "It's just wrong when 70 percent of components for clean energy in this country come from abroad."[84] It's also pretty wrong when U.S. taxpayers' hard-earned money is confiscated then politically squandered, as detailed in a Bloomberg story aptly titled "China's labor edge overpowers Obama's 'green' jobs initiatives," revealing that "President Barack Obama is spending $2.1 million to help Suntech Power Holdings Co. build a solar-panel plant in Arizona. It will hire 70 Americans to assemble components made by Suntech's 11,000 Chinese workers."[85]

Whether it was using an Australian company to build a wind farm in Texas using turbine parts from Japan, or other companies using Chinese parts,

> Money from the 2009 stimulus bill to help support the renewable energy industry continues to flow overseas...[with] more than 80 percent of the first $1 billion in grants to wind energy companies [going] to foreign firms. Since then, the administration has stopped making announcements of new grants to wind, solar and geothermal companies, but has handed out another $1 billion, bringing the total given out to $2.1 billion and the total that went to companies based overseas to more than 79 percent.[86]

> In fact, despite receiving this windfall of "stimulus" cash, the U.S. wind manufacturing sector actually lost jobs in 2009, according to a year-end report by its professional association.

Also, most of the jobs "created or saved" in America have been temporary construction positions, or "management" hires. The real job creation (or job salvation, to use Obama's disingenuous math) has taken place beyond our borders.... In case the trend isn't clear, America's massive investment in "Green Jobs" has been a colossal, costly failure—unless you're looking for work overseas. For all the promises of the Obama administration, here at home these taxpayers' billions have amounted to little more than a few thousand temporary construction positions and a few hundred management jobs. In fact, there's a good chance that the government employees hired to promote "Green Jobs" outnumber the actual permanent "Green Jobs" created.[87]

So, how do we not ship jobs overseas when mandating those parts? Should we mandate that they be made here? We cannot do that and, as noted, President Obama has rejected resorting to protectionism (on this issue) as a way to guarantee that green jobs cannot be sent overseas. The inherent conflict and inanity (or disingenuousness) in this is typical of the issue. This is just talk as they find their precious policies causing more real-world problems, and solving none.

RWI-Essen concluded its study by agreeing with Mr. Obama, at least in part, imploring us to, *Ja, bitter,* do take a close look at how this supposed European model has worked out:

> Policymakers should thus scrutinize Germany's experience, including in the US, where there are currently nearly 400 federal and state programs in place that provide financial incentives for renewable energy.

Although Germany's promotion of renewable energies is commonly portrayed in the media as setting a "shining example in providing a harvest for the world" (*The Guardian* 2007), we would instead regard the country's experience as a cautionary tale of massively expensive environmental and energy policy that is devoid of economic and environmental benefits.[88]

That's rough stuff for European academics trying not to be mean to a guy who campaigned so hard there. But again, the issue is not the issue, and the proclaimed goal really isn't the goal. Green jobs schemes are about limiting access to energy, handing out expensive favors to preferred constituencies, and enhancing dependence upon the state for economic activity.

WE CAN QUIT ANY TIME WE WANT

Confronted by all of the above ugliness, we are told that the overwhelming majority of those who have looked into the matter are wrong because *upon adoption of these schemes, green energy will soon become competitive* with actual, functioning sources of power. This, of course, is the same thing the green-jobs lobby has been peddling in order to keep the subsidies flowing, with far too much success, for decades.

It was only recently that they turned to the desperate play of going for it all, claiming that green jobs schemes are actually the way out of the economic mess. Falling for this again, now, is a dangerous folly when you realize the "bubble" these schemes create in return for debt, requiring continued infusions, meaning more debt, simply to keep the game going. Also remember that for all intents and purposes, wind is as advanced as it ever will be. The exorbitantly more expensive solar energy is even more unlikely to carry a significant energy load in our lifetimes, if ever. Centuries of research have produced just about everything that will be produced, with improvements coming at the margins. Marginal improvements won't ever allow these inherently intermittent sources to replace the energy we receive from coal and gas, let alone oil for transportation.

But also consider what this really means. As the *Wall Street Journal* reported in late 2009 about a study by the bank HSBC, "Traditional, onshore wind power breaks even with gas at $8.33 or oil at $92. Offshore wind still needs a push: It requires gas at $17.14 or oil at $189. In contrast, solar thermal needs to see natural gas at $35.66 or oil at $393. And good old photovoltaic solar, like the kind on rooftops? Natural gas needs to be at $59.61 or oil at $657 a barrel. Quick reality check: Gas today is at $3.93 and oil is at $66."[89] (At the dawn of 2010 these were around $6 and $78, respectively, or about 10 percent of the way towards what they would need to be.)

That is the objective of various "green jobs" schemes: make everything else so expensive as to give life to what is uneconomical. But that is incredibly economically harmful.

Also, note what President Obama said in his September 2009 UN "global warming" speech:

> Most importantly, the House of Representatives passed an energy and climate bill in June that would finally make clean energy the profitable kind of energy for American businesses and dramatically reduce greenhouse gas emissions.[90]

He repeated this in his 2010 State of the Union speech, and had actually rolled out the very deliberate formulation in his first address to

Congress (not technically styled as a State of the Union for a newly installed president).[91] The key word there is that lawmakers passed a scheme to make inefficient projects "profitable," not "cost-effective" or economical. That's corporate welfare. These mandates and subsidies would, however, add value to the investment portfolios of many leading lights among the Left, but distilled, it ultimately means raising the cost of all traditional sources of energy. Which as we have seen, and even heard in his own words, is his intention.

Recall the sage from Team Soros, Mr. Light, who assures us that these mandates are "gonna spur new innovation, which is gonna reward smart investment, and which is gonna make alternative energy sources competitive"[92] with things that actually work. No. The laws of physics remain undefeated. All these government programs will do is impose the agenda admitted to by Van Jones and his Blue-Green allies, and seize your wealth to reward the purely speculative among Obama's Wall Street supporters underwriting the green campaign.

CHAPTER 7

OBAMA'S "BAPTISTS AND BOOTLEGGERS": UNIONS AND GREENS SELLING OUT AMERICA

How can you suppress Wealth crea-creation and still have any wealth to redistribute, pray tell??

We know that job loss is the direct, logical, and expected result of Obama's plans to ration energy, seize control of our means of energy production, and otherwise shackle the economy with his green boondoggles. Even studies by the "green jobs" industry and its component parts, the labor unions and environmental groups, confirmed that those programs kill existing jobs to pay for the new, heavily subsidized, and temporary ones. These admissions were memorialized in a report by Senator Christopher "Kit" Bond of Missouri, the senior Republican on the Senate's—wait for it—Subcommittee on Green Jobs and the New Economy[1] (seriously).

Bond looked into the "grow the economy!" cheerleading and revealed how "a coalition of environmental and labor organizations including the Sierra Club, Teamsters, and SEIU found...that state and local taxpayer subsidies of tens of millions of dollars often times produced only a few hundred jobs. At this rate, taxpayer green jobs subsidies cost tens of thousands, and sometimes hundreds of thousands of dollars, per green job."[2]

That harms employment and the economy, present and future. So why, precisely, would unions team up with green pressure groups to lobby for such an agenda? Why have they pooled resources to become among the biggest pots of money promoting "global warming"?

David Foster, spokesman for the "Blue-Green Alliance," a labor-greenie group, admitted how it is a union priority to use "the environment" as a way to organize society and divvy the spoils. "It is an economic restructuring bill for the global economy. We should not pretend that it isn't."[3] No objections here. Possibly they hope to replicate the most recent success of intrusive government mandates making organized labor a partner of America's automobile manufacturing industry, culminating in the federal takeover. Regardless, we see both labor and the greens echo the claim by Americans for Prosperity's Phil Kerpen that the agenda creates "political jobs, designed to funnel vast sums of taxpayer money to left-wing labor unions, environmental groups, and social justice community organizers."[4] If nothing else, we know that an inarguable result of Obama's general agenda as well as specific environmental "salvation" is a massive increase in the size of the state. And the Blue-Green Alliance spent more than a million dollars last year lobbying for the agenda.[5] It even teamed up with Gore's campaign for a national bus tour pushing their agenda.[6]

Of course, government workers are unionized, and government-mandated programs effectively demand union labor. This is intrinsically a boon to their ranks (and their coffers). Unions, like the windmill lobby, have figured out that they only have one likely path to grow their respective bottom lines, and that path is through federal mandates. "Card check," "green jobs"—it all works.

BLUE AND GREEN: LIKE PEAS AND CARROTS

There is a certain, elusive similarity between the greens and unions. It goes beyond the obvious point, as my colleague Iain Murray noted in his book *The Really Inconvenient Truths*, that "Earth Day is held every year on April 22, a date deliberately chosen because it was Lenin's birthday."[7] It also extends beyond their both being special interest groups within the left-wing coalition whose extensive lobbying presence ensures that they receive policy sops harmful to the overall economy (meaning at the expense of the rest of the public). In fact, it seems that the principal difference between the greens and unions is that the greens' agenda less involves direct sops to them, at our expense—though they receive a windfall from the taxpayer under schemes like cap-and-trade[8]—than it seeks to impose their demands of how *others* ought to live, mandates on all of us satisfying the greens' anxieties, paranoia, and ideology.

Slight differences in their advocacy notwithstanding, these two groups are teaming up for adoption of a larger, harmful agenda ensuring direct benefits to one of them which will also funnel taxpayer money and mandates into the other's pockets.

LABOR'S BILL COMES DUE

According to the legislative newspaper *The Hill,* in May 2009 Vice President Joe Biden bluntly told one labor union, "We owe you."[9] Throughout Obama's first year in office, union leaders paraded through the White House to meet with the president and other members of his staff. The Service Employees International Union (SEIU) president Andy Stern boasted: "We spent a fortune to elect Barack Obama—$60.7 million to be exact."[10] His was far and away the most frequent name appearing in the White House visitor logs, until media attention cooled his heels a bit.

After the slight attention to Stern's White House visibility died down, Obama appointed him to, of all things, a panel to make recommendations on debt reduction.[11] Of Obama's four picks to the panel, joining SEIU's Stern was the CEO of a USCAP company pushing cap-and-trade.[12] Just as with the President's Economic Recovery Advisory Board, Obama ensured supposedly independent voices would be fully vested advocates for his agenda.

Al Gore insists that, specifically in the context of "global warming" advocacy, where one gets one's money dictates one's positions, motivations, and arguments. So it is worth noting that, as of mid-2009, the Center for Responsive Politics reported that over the course of his startlingly brief political career, Barack Obama had received at least $818,968 from organized labor. For perspective, over his significantly longer time in office Vice President Biden had received at least $345,249.[13] What does this tell Al Gore?

The unions are not letting the possibilities of this new entitlement go. They are employing their longstanding practice of ensuring that programs mandated or otherwise created by the federal government are, either as a matter of law or simply coercively in practice, union jobs. Indeed, the White House's broad definition of "green jobs" includes that they are "more likely to be unionized." *Politico* looked into the matter and reported that the unions' green kick was motivated at least in part by the desire to rebuild declining membership.[14]

THE UNION RACKET THAT IS "GREEN JOBS"

When Professor Gabriel Calzada in Madrid led the research team exposing Spain's windmill boondoggle, guess who teamed up to assail him, and not for the substance of what he said but very specifically because he dared say it? The windmill lobby and the trade union linked to the Communist Party.[15]

As was found by the aforementioned research team led by Andrew Morriss, "by focusing green job expenditures on economic activity with low labor productivity, resources can be forced to be shifted from capital to favored workers in line with these groups' political and economic priorities."[16] To achieve these goals, Morriss concludes, requires an inappropriate emphasis on promoting inefficient use of labor—and the political dynamic ensures that this is union labor—subsidized by taxpayers to the point of resembling a Ponzi scheme.[17]

All of this is to say that, one way or another, "green jobs" mean government jobs. This is because they don't exist without a government mandate, and will not remain in existence without government support schemes, despite the cry made for decades that "green" projects can become economical in, well, just another decade. Cue the unions.

Max Schulz reported on this matter in the *American Spectator*, noting that "organized labor is latching on to the green jobs movement with gusto. In August, a coalition of labor unions joined with environmental organizations to launch a 50-stop tour visiting 22 states to pressure Congress to pass cap-and-trade legislation." Schulz writes that, at the coalition's Good Jobs, Green Jobs conference, staged just after Obama's inauguration—why can't the rest of us get union guys to move that fast?—"The fledgling Obama administration sent Environmental Protection Administration chief Lisa Jackson to pump up the troops, while United Nations Undersecretary General Achim

Steiner and others talked up the notion of an emerging 'Global Green New Deal.'"[18] These are very big red flags.

This also took place as the stimulus bill was being written, so "organizers cut off the program at noon so that attendees could flood Capitol Hill."[19] That bill, by chance, ended up with over $40 billion of your money earmarked for "green" schemes, as well as "a treasure trove of items from Big Labor's wish list. One was a provision that applies Davis-Bacon wage mandates to all construction projects funded by the law, including the $25 billion appropriated to green the nation's schools and federal office buildings. It also applied Davis-Bacon to the Department of Energy's weatherization efforts, for which [the stimulus bill] coughs up $5 billion."[20]

Davis-Bacon, of course, is the Depression-era wage subsidization law explicitly put in place in part to keep blacks from taking jobs[21] the unions felt were theirs, if by a simple requirement that "prevailing wage rates...be paid on federally funded or assisted construction projects."[22] Translated into practice, that means it is used to ensure that federally underwritten jobs involving labor use labor that is unionized. As already noted, it is also a principal reason cited by the Government Accountability Office for why stimulus infrastructure projects had no impact on unemployment.

This unionization of "green jobs" continued with the global warming bills. In response, the U.S. Chamber of Commerce protested, in objection to "applying the Davis-Bacon Act, a law that in no way furthers the United States' ability to reduce climate emissions, and would result in diminished competition, shutting out many qualified minority, small, and non-union businesses from the entire market. Applying the Davis-Bacon Act to programs in [legislation] would increase costs to taxpayers, who would pay more to get less. The Davis-Bacon Act has been shown to increase public construction costs by anywhere from five to 38 percent above projected costs for the same project in the private sector."[23]

Notice, too, how Obama's first budget rushed to steer $8 million in the Bureau of Labor Statistics just toward measuring employment and wages for businesses whose main activities the White House defines as "green." Obama's request to Congress stated: "New information about green-collar jobs is needed to address key policy questions, such as 'how many green-collar jobs are there now and how many are being created?' and to provide data to answer questions related to job-training planning, such as 'what education and training do green-collar jobs require?' and 'what is the likely demand for workers in the green-collar occupations of the future?'" So, "To help inform the debate on both these fronts—and to meet the demands for information from State policymakers, businesses, and job seekers—the BLS proposes to work with other [Department of Labor] agencies and key organizations to define the green economy and then produce data on green-collar jobs."[24]

Uh-oh, I sense more phony administration claims of jobs created on the way. Forgetting for the moment the administration's miserable track record on that front, the above statement reveals a political motivation to simply take from you and then throw at unions even more money, but as pleasantly titled sops. The administration merely admits the obvious here, showing no apparent idea of what they meant by the call for lots of new "green" loot. When massive piles of federal taxpayer money are mandated to go to "green" projects, it will help get the money to the right places faster if one has an idea of what those beneficiary sectors will be. It makes even more sense to know this before you borrow or take the money from the taxpayer in the first place.

And as Schulz writes, Davis-Bacon and the already described sops are by no means "all labor wants in the new green economy. The federal government will spend billions of dollars to subsidize alternative energy production from wind, solar, biomass, and other industries. . . . Labor bosses want to ensure that these jobs pay union scale."[25]

We are talking about institutionalizing a pipeline of taxpayer money to union workers and, by extension, to unions and political campaigns of lawmakers who do the unions' bidding. All are premised on institutionalizing the inefficient use of labor. This should do nearly as much to increase organized labor's power as the more coercive "card check" proposal, which advocates abandoning workers' secret ballots in votes on whether to organize a facility's workforce.[26] With card check stalled, "green jobs" is certain to be the largest guarantee to the movement in our history. Obama also telegraphed it would be a signature message of the 2010 political campaign to reverse the Left's political fortunes.

And it gets worse. In the EU, the situation has so rapidly been perverted that British unions seem to believe they have a right to green jobs. In 2009, workers at that Vestas windmill turbine factory on the Isle of Wight barricaded themselves in as part of their pressure campaign to stop the jobs from being exported. You see, Mr. President, just like any other manufacturing job, "green jobs" *can* be sent overseas, and often are if left at least somewhat to market forces.[27] We have already seen the United Steel Workers president Leo Gerard single out[28] über-windmill welfare queen GE for buying parts for its wind turbines from countries having the lowest costs, like China or India. Hmm, possibly the state can be of some assistance? In step the unions and their buddies in government to demand permanence for this uncompetitive enterprise-slash-drain on the economy.

The shared idea here is to construct an enduring revenue stream through subsidies that reward a friendly constituency, or in this case two core constituencies. In turn, the beneficiary lobbies reward the helpful politicians with continued power in office. The cycle ensures that the next generation of politicians have no choice but to continue the mandarinate—because it's what their (noisiest) constituents want. This is a dangerous mix, combining unionization and demands of permanence with jobs that are, by their nature, almost universally temporary, requiring enormous per-job subsidies and constant infusions of money simply to maintain what was artificially created in the first place.

Creating those "millions and millions and millions"[29] of green jobs would take decades and, if it didn't, could literally bankrupt us. As one more sober, if still invested, voice in the green jobs industry cautioned, the growth potential of the new energy industries is not as it is being sold, and the taxpayer should be prepared for a very long march—one initiated on the promise of the programs providing immediate economic stimulus, mind you. Roger Bezdek, president of the Department of Energy contractor Management Information Services Inc., told *E&E News*: "You have to build a lot of windmills to replace what's happening in Detroit.... Green jobs aren't going to turn the economy around this year or next year. That hype is way overblown.... It will take incentives, policies, R&D over two decades to move the economy in these new directions."[30]

COSTLY BOONDOGGLE

The per-job cost for "green jobs," meaning the subsidy to create each one, is on a par for inefficiency and wastefulness with a "stimulus" job.

Although tremendous amounts can be spent creating each job, that does not mean the money goes to lavishly compensated windmill installers, form-fillers, and caulk-gunslingers. That money, which is often in the hundreds of thousands of dollars per job, goes to what we might call "overhead," meaning that it only makes sense that the unionized federal labor force will also proliferate under these mandates. As luck would have it, the government employee union, AFSCME, endorsed the radical green group the Apollo Alliance and its call for massive federal spending on "green jobs" and related boondoggles.[31]

We know that Obama told us to look at what's happening in countries like Spain and Germany. Oh, and Denmark, a tiny country with a population half the size of Manhattan, whose energy needs and system are somehow apparently a fair proxy for our own. In Spain, the taxpayer spent €571,138 ($753,778) for each "green job."[32] That the sum vastly exceeds a standard worker's wages was no exception. In Germany, solar panel-related "green jobs" carried per-worker subsidies as high as €175,000 ($240,000).[33] Again, that doesn't mean the worker was paid that. That's what it cost our always-efficient bureaucracies, meaning the taxpayer-underwritten servants, to create each job. In Denmark, each subsidized green job was a comparative steal, at the subsidy per job created of 600,000 to 900,000 Danish Kroner per year ($90,000 to $140,000).[34] This subsidy constitutes around 175 to 250 percent of the average worker's pay in the Danish manufacturing industry.

Senator Bond's report found similar costs in American programs, from as low as $30,000 in taxpayer subsidy per job created at a solar company, all the way up to $276,857 and $325,758 per job created at two others.[35] The White House claimed that stimulus "green" jobs, assuming all were real, cost $135,294 each.[36]

This is an awfully large transfer of wealth from individuals to the institutional framework supporting these programs. Yes, the ranks of windmill installers, et al., swell along with the unions' monthly haul. But much of it goes to expanding the bureaucracy of unionized federal employees. Even the *New York Times* reported that an audit of Florida's Sunshine Energy program found that more than three-fourths of the money went to administration and marketing.[37]

Of course, even if the subsidy per job did go to the broad array of what are called "green workers," that, too, would merely prove too much about enormously expensive job creation programs, particularly given what the private sector requires to create jobs producing reliable energy sources. Regardless, this also raises the matter of strange boasts like that of those Democrat senators begging for more subsidies, that solar power "creates more jobs per megawatt of energy produced than any other form of energy." Hundreds of thousands of dollars per job and more jobs needed per unit of energy: that's some *seriously* expensive energy. No wonder it takes the government to make it happen.

Further, Senator Bond's report detailed how, despite the often breathtaking subsidy, these "green jobs" can actually mean lower pay to the worker than for jobs producing energy from sources that work, and therefore are not relative burdens on the economy. But in the final analysis, more lower-paid union jobs still mean more union dues and more union political power. So, despite the often eye-popping per-job subsidies and promises that green jobs will be plentiful, interesting, enjoyable, and remunerative, the notion that "green jobs" are well-paying jobs is false.

As Morriss et al. concluded, "By promoting more jobs instead of more productivity, the green jobs described in the literature actually encourage low-paying jobs in less desirable conditions. Economic growth cannot be ordered by Congress or by the United Nations (UN). Government interference in the economy—such as restricting successful technologies in favor of speculative technologies favored by special interests—will generate stagnation."[38] They continue, "In a competitive market, factors of production, including labor, earn a return based on productivity. By focusing on low labor productivity jobs, the green jobs literature dooms employees to low wages in a shrinking economy."[39] Their research found that a very small number of high-paying jobs emerging from the scheme skew the average, allowing for the White House's gauzy assertion that green jobs—implicitly *in toto* and not *ad hoc*—are jobs paying 10 to 20 percent more than "other jobs."

But why aren't unions demanding with equal fervor policies allowing, if not mandating, creation of those far-better-paying oil, gas, and nuclear jobs domestically? As Jonah Goldberg notes, "Meanwhile, the oil industry is among the highest-paid professions in the United States (typical workers make double the national average). It employs 1.8 million people and indirectly supports another 4 million."[40] He cites an industry study projecting that opening those areas that are continuously blocked off from exploration and production would generate another 160,000 jobs in the next two decades and pour $1.7 trillion into the federal tax kitty.[41] (Industry has an interest in putting the best gloss on numbers supporting what it believes are productive activities. Just as the Obama administration enjoys touting their schemes demanded by their union and green-group base. The principal difference is that the latter have been exposed as making an awful lot of their employment claims up.)

The short answer is that the unions are in a political partnership with Obama and the greens. There are trade-offs involved. This was agreed as the more politically salable way to go, with the same net-net for the unions in the end.

SCORPIONS AND FROGS

That most of the enormous per-job subsidy goes to what we might call overhead (or supporting the state that supports these jobs) is to be expected when the job is designed to expand the state. Affirmation that the jobs are incredibly wasteful is found precisely in the fact that they exist under direct mandates or coercive policies. Mandating and coercing waste is what the government does.

And the unions continue to do what unions do. For example, when a project isn't mandated by the feds, sometimes it takes a little old-school organizing to make sure project developers know *who's watchin' dis block*. Organized labor quickly learned to use environmental challenges to threaten solar power facilities to, ah, do the right thing. In the Golden State, long riding at the vanguard of state intervention to force the economy into "going green," energy contractors claim[42] that they are being blackmailed—they call it "greenmail"—by union organizers stalling green energy projects unless they go union. Even the *New York Times* has reported on the phenomenon.

> As California moves to license dozens of huge solar power plants to meet the state's renewable energy goals, some developers contend they are being pressured to sign agreements pledging to use union labor. If they refuse, they say, they can count on the union group to demand costly environmental studies and deliver hostile testimony at public hearings. If

they commit at the outset to use union labor, they say, the environmental objections never materialize.[43]

The vehicle for this demand is called a Project Labor Agreement (PLA), which builders seeking to develop their own "green jobs" niche fear "will saddle the nascent industry with high costs and undermine its competitiveness."[44] Of course that's a strange concern given that these projects are inherently uncompetitive, but this is the *New York Times*, so we'll allow some leeway. " 'These environmental challenges are the unions' major tactic to maintain their share of industrial construction—we call it greenmail,' said Kevin Dayton, state government affairs director for the Associated Builders and Contractors of California." In that state, Dayton estimated these PLAs can raise costs on a project by about 20 percent.[45] Add 20 percent to uncompetitive, and you've got a real problem if the project *does* manage to go forward.

According to the website "The Truth about PLAs," one project subjected to the tactic was "what would have been the $850 million Victorville 2 Solar Hybrid Power Plant."[46] A group calling itself CURE (California Unions for Renewable Energy) legally intervened as a party in the power plant licensing process. Various data requests and other lengthy procedural hurdles ensued, including all manner of procedural objections and even a lawsuit, with the effect of throwing more sand into the gears of government permitting—as if there was not already enough.

The contractors' association, having become aware that the City of Victorville was considering use of a PLA as a way to escape this barrage of obstacles, pushed back, sending a mass mailing to residents detailing what was going on and the threat it posed. After this, the obstacles appeared to slowly clear as the union group was dealt several setbacks in the process, including having their suit tossed and the

California Energy Commission approving the application to build the plant.[47] But the damage seems to have been done, as the project stalled in the face of California's regulatory state, which increasingly seems designed to block energy production.

Unions and greens teaming up to push something that, in turn, the unions block until they are brought in is somewhat reminiscent of how green groups demand wind farms, solar collectors, and the rest only to then fight them just as vehemently as they do resource extraction, coal plants, transmission lines, and everything that works. What a confused bunch.

Nonetheless, unions are teaming with green pressure groups to push for massive federal "green jobs" schemes, which are bad for workers and employment, but good for unions. Both the unions and the "green energy" lobbies have realized this is likely their only formula for growth. When you cannot compete and succeed on your own merits, the world is viewed as a zero sum game, and whatever you get, you've got to take from someone else.

WHAT'S IN IT FOR THE GREENS?

These schemes promise a big wet kiss of ever more billions to the unions. But, what is in this for the green groups?

Imposition of their agenda remains the end goal. If the greens achieve their desired mandates, they will in effect finally codify lower levels of economic activity, individual wealth creation, and of course consumption. Supposedly viable substitute technologies demanded by the greens are incapable of reaching the scale or otherwise providing the energy necessary to meet today's demands, let alone those of tomorrow. We know from the Congressional Budget Office's serial forays into cap-and-trade, for example, that the scheme is expected to cause productivity, output, and wages to fall as energy prices rise.[48] Presumably this also discourages larger families, which is the Holy Grail for modern environmentalists.

You no doubt recall the outgoing leader of Greenpeace, Gerd Leipold, repeating the "western lifestyles must be stopped" objective spouted by the IPCC's Pachauri, when interviewed by the BBC in 2009. Surely you wondered about the urgent need he asserted for the suppression of economic growth in the United States and around the world. "We will definitely have to move to a different concept of growth.... The lifestyle of the rich in the world is not a sustainable model," Leipold said. "If you take the lifestyle, its cost on the environment, and you multiply it with the billions of people and an increasing world population, you come up with numbers which are truly scary."[49] You don't recall this? It was in an interview in which Leipold admits his group lies to frighten people into accepting its agenda. Wouldn't the media, so dependent on him and his kind for their lurid "climate porn," have spread the word far and wide? Of course, the media downplay the desire to stop our way of life. Though it might add quite a lot to the story and context, it really wouldn't help the cause, now would it?

In a piece in the *American Thinker*, the Heartland Institute's Joseph Bast brought our attention to some refreshing candor from Mike Hulme, an environmental activist at the UK's Tyndall Centre. In his 2009 book *Why We Disagree About Climate Change*, Hulme—who also participates in the UN's Intergovernmental Panel on Climate Change and does seem to be one of the more intellectually honest of his peers—explains on behalf of the larger global warming industry being recklessly abetted by the Obama administration that "we need to ask not what we can do for climate change, but to ask what climate change can do for us."[50]

And what climate change can do for activists is quite a lot: "Because the idea of climate change is so plastic, it can be deployed across many of our human projects and can serve many of our psychological, ethical, and spiritual needs." Also, "We will continue to create and tell new stories about climate change and mobilise them in support of our projects," Hulme adds, helpfully describing these myths as "transcend[ing] the scientific categories of 'true' and 'false'."[51] The myths he suggests they promote are Lamenting Eden, Presaging Apocalypse, Constructing Babel, and Celebrating Jubilee.

To be sure, "global warming" and its prescribed agenda of wealth suppression and redistribution through energy rationing has supplanted all other issues of the well-heeled green pressure industry, working so closely with the Obama administration to impose the anti-energy agenda on Americans. It is the best excuse for an agenda the Left have long insisted is *just the right thing to do*. Tim Wirth, a former Democrat Senator from Colorado who worked with Gore to launch the issue to prominence, and who now heads Ted Turner's UN Foundation, showed the hand of his ilk by saying in 1990, "We've got to ride the global warming issue. Even if the theory of global warming is wrong, we will be doing the right thing, in terms of economic and environmental policy."[52] Nearly twenty years later, former UK Prime Minister Tony Blair hectored[53] all of us during the Copenhagen talks on a Kyoto successor treaty that we simply must agree to the agenda even if the science is wrong, which is the same thing that Canada's then environment minister Christine Stewart said[54] at the time of the original Kyoto. And President Obama in his 2010 State of the Union speech—after touting "the overwhelming scientific evidence on climate change," to great laughter from about half the chamber—then lapsed into this old fallback of the agenda being "the right thing to do" anyway "even if you doubt the evidence," tacitly admitting the evidence is no such thing.[55] Again, the issue has never been the issue to these people.

In *The Politically Incorrect Guide™ to Global Warming and Environmentalism*, I detailed numerous such admissions among green activists, money-men, and high government officials throughout the rich and poor worlds, illustrating just how entrenched it is that this is the leading extant excuse—the vehicle—to achieve their "change." Just as it is for the labor unions.

But do not confuse the greens' disdain for commerce and capitalism with revulsion towards money, which actually happens to stick to them quite well. And there's plenty of it to be had through this collaboration. Much of the booty to the greens comes from the state in the form of grants, programs, and even "jobs created" by the various schemes. For example, the cap-and-trade bill that passed the House ultimately requires American businesses to buy 100 percent of the energy use "allowances," or ration coupons, which are created, required and, at first, politically allocated. That is not to say that 100 percent end up being auctioned by the state. Instead, the legislation actually set aside billions of dollars' worth of these certificates needed to use "fossil fuels," providing them for free to green "non-governmental organizations" (NGOs).[56] That is, community organizers and other pressure groups.

These favored parties, which of course are not covered by the law's requirement for such allowances and therefore have no apparent use for them, then raise revenue by selling this windfall to those horrid capitalists who need ration coupons in order to use that nasty energy they love so much. This is scandalous confiscation of hard-earned taxpayer money for use and redistribution in a way that no lawmaker would openly champion.

SEND IN THE COMMUNITY ORGANIZERS

Other schemes also emerged guaranteeing a heightened role for green NGOs in the effort to organize society, one notable program being an offshoot of the "Van" Jones push[57] to prepare "the environment" as the next vehicle for minority group activism, wealth transfer, and even litigation demanding environmental, social, or some other form of "justice." You are free to read the latter point as a legal "settlement" practice in which suits are threatened or brought with the idea of some sort of tribute being paid to end the unpleasantness. Even activist attorneys general do it now in the name of "global warming."

First, consider the revelations of Jacob Gershman in the *New York Post*, exposing the scandalously wasteful "green jobs" program called the Weatherization Assistance Program. It is worth excerpting at length:

> A child of the 1970s fuel crisis, WAP was designed to help poor Americans reduce their home energy consumption. As part of the stimulus bill, Obama and Congress are pouring $5 billion into the program—a nearly 10-fold increase in funding.
>
> It was sold as a vehicle for job creation, an investment in the environment and a means for low-income Americans to lower their heating costs. But it's a failure on every count.
>
> Here's how it works: If you're eligible, the government will pay to weatherstrip your doors, insulate your walls and ceilings, fix your windows and, in some cases, buy you a new refrigerator and heating system—all for free. You just have to sign up with a local community-action group, which will send over workers to do the repairs.

> It's proving a rip-off—the government is spending a for-
> tune for each household that benefits. A quarter of the money
> is squandered on a vast bureaucracy of regulatory field staff,
> administrators and training. Also inflating the costs are pre-
> vailing-wage mandates and provisions that encourage states
> to spend the most money on the fewest homes.[58]

What sort of rip-off? "With $400 million, New York state intends to repair 45,000 units, or *nearly $9,000* a home." A similar bog has been uncovered in (surprise!) Illinois. And columnist Deroy Murdock noted in a 2009 retrospective how, "So far, Texas has spent $1.8 million in federal funds and has treated seven homes, averaging $257,000 each."[59]

The contagion spread with the election of Mr. Green Jobs himself. As the *Los Angeles Times*'s Andrew Malcolm titled his blog post about some disturbing news out of the Government Accountability Office (GAO), "Obama's federal government can weatherize your home for only $57,362 *each*."[60] ABC News reported, "A $5 billion federal weatherization program intended to save energy and create jobs has done little of either, according to a new report obtained by ABC News on the one-year anniversary of President Obama's American Reinvestment and Recovery Act. Only 9,100 homes had been weatherized nationwide as of Dec. 31, according to the new report by [GAO]," which would be "a far cry from the 593,000 that the government plans to complete during the course of the Recovery Act, which runs through March 2012."[61] Among the culprits GAO cited was, to no surprise, the unions' pet demand of applying Davis-Bacon to projects using taxpayer money.

Now recall how the Obama administration also hurriedly sought to expand its "environmental justice" programs. These are premised on, as Van Jones famously described,[62] the idea that white people are forcing pollution into minority communities with nefarious intent. The Obama EPA raced to finalize a database to track pollution "scores" for minority and low-income neighborhoods which, you may be shocked to learn, reflect Mr. Jones's worldview. Of course, this calls for increased roles for ACORN-type groups and assorted other goons, and is another excuse for funneling taxpayer money to politically friendly and useful constituencies.

The Agency's Environmental Justice Strategic Enforcement Assessment Tool (EJSEAT) assigns "environmental justice" scores by Census tract,[63] a quiet but steadily growing practice-area of environmental advocacy percolating as the movement strives mightily at the same time to change its face from one of wealthy, western, white elites. Only upon instruction in—wait for it—Obama's stimulus bill did the project make strides toward completion.

At about the same time that this was announced, EPA administrator Lisa Jackson urged black journalists to, in essence, step up coverage of Jones's theory. She enlisted them to help the movement "tell the stories that need to be told" about the importance of environmental issues in poor African American neighborhoods. She told the audience at the National Association of Black Journalists' annual meeting: "You have a central role to play, because you are the keepers of the conversation," while also making plain her goal of changing the image of the environmentalism movement.[64]

On its face, this should have been an easy sell, at a meeting—of people describing themselves as journalists—somehow nonetheless titled "This Land is Our Land Too: Justice, Jobs, and Environmental Protection." What Jackson failed to explain clearly was why poorer communities should adopt the folly of the expensive gestures being imposed that make life harder on the poor and those seeking employment. It is, apparently, self-evident that all the downtrodden, say, those suffering from governmental malpractice in Detroit, should now gaze about and, deciding they don't have real, demonstrable, and remediable concerns, instead wring their hands in sympathetic obsession with the rich elites and convince themselves they should try to control the weather.

Jackson emphasized something called the Green the Block initiative, which was created, according to its website, "to educate and mobilize communities of color to ensure a voice and stake in the clean-energy economy."[65] It was launched at the White House by groups called Green For All and the Hip Hop Caucus (surprisingly, not really a congressional caucus), urging the scribblers to carry a message that "environmentalism goes hand-in-hand with traditional civil rights and social justice issues in our community."[66] Green for All, it turns out, was incorporated at the end of 2007 in California by our friend Van Jones as a 501(c)(3) nonprofit.

Green the Block and these constituent parts are dedicated to productive activities like joining ACORN to, in their eyes, take back September 11 from political foes who have somehow misappropriated it for unsavory patriotic purposes.[67] They instead envision a National Day of Service, because it was really carbon dioxide emissions which killed nearly three thousand on that day. Dismiss that now but, as I detailed in *The Politically Incorrect Guide™ to Global Warming and Environmentalism*, according to numerous sympathetic green pressure groups, for all intents and purposes, it was.

Seemingly in reference to Green the Block and the Hip Hop Caucus, Jackson insisted, "There are powerful voices in the black community calling for change in our economy, change in our health care, change in our schools."[68] Seeking to enlist the journalists as administration and movement cheerleaders, she vowed of these groups that "their committed advocacy can help ensure that our children's health is protected, and that the green and clean energy jobs being created are coming to our communities."[69] When it comes to pushing the message of environmental oppression and green mythology, she said, "That's where you come in. You fight to tell the stories."[70] Jackson seemed aware that there's nothing a journalist likes better than to see him or herself as a fighter, indispensible to the story.

Besides, as House Democrat Whip James Clyburn asserts,[71] the green movement is really all about remedying social inequities.

SHOWTIME AT THE APOLLO ALLIANCE

So upon even the slightest scrutiny, it becomes clear that the larger movement and strategy of green and other activist groups is to team up with politically powerful and seemingly incongruent Big Labor to push an agenda. As Jones said, "The slogan of 'green jobs' is the banner under which all of the pro-democracy forces can gather for the next big assaults."[72]

Jones was, of course, also on the board of the hard-left environmentalist group Apollo Alliance, which took credit[73] (with fairly strong justification) for dictating to Congress the relevant parts of the stimulus pork provisions on which the movement now feeds.

Apollo's website includes a lengthy analysis of the legislation with itemized reasons for its claim to influence, including recommendations for more money for those sketchy programs to fund community groups promoting energy efficiency, the aforementioned Weatherization Assistance Program—granting more than five times the amount Apollo sought—plus Conservation Block Grants. Maybe this was all coincidence and Apollo was preaching to the choir: it sought $50 billion on green jobs programs only to see the stimulus bill cough up $110 billion.[74]

As AFP's Kerpen wrote in a detailed exposé for Capital Research, a group which performed invaluable digging into the entire sordid operation and its influence,

> The Apollo Alliance unifies the three most powerful ele-
> ments of the political left: environmental groups, labor
> unions, and street organizers like ACORN, and points them
> toward a common goal that enriches all of them under the
> banner of "green jobs." Apollo and the Blue-Green Alliance
> (a similar group with overlapping membership) are out-
> growths of the Blue-Green Working Group, an informal
> coalition that for years has attempted to align the interests of
> environmentalists and union bosses.
> ...Apollo Alliance seized on the financial crisis as an
> opportunity to repackage the ideas it had long been promot-
> ing as a stimulus bill. Many of those ideas would be
> incorporated.... Senate Majority Leader Harry Reid specifi-
> cally credited Apollo....[S]ocial justice community
> organizers also stand to be funded by the stimulus bill.
> ACORN, the largest and most active social justice member of
> Apollo, and similar organizations are eligible to apply for as
> much as $4.19 billion of stimulus funding under the so-
> called "Neighborhood Stabilization Program" and are likely
> eligible for other stimulus programs as well.[75]

By chance, I was informed off-the-record by someone who would know that a major aluminum producer was threatened with a "social justice" campaign if it didn't protest the U.S. Chamber's opposition to the cap-and-trade bill that would, again by chance, fund many among the "social justice" network of groups. That push to drive businesses out of the Chamber was abetted by unseemly encouragement heaped upon it by none other than Obama's Energy Secretary Steven Chu, who described the companies walking out and pressuring for more to follow suit as "wonderful."[76]

The same person speaking to me on background also described similar claims against a company if it did drop out of a Baptist-Bootlegger group the U.S. Climate Action Partnership. The message was that, once you consummate the courtship, you are married to this mob.

Kerpen reminds us that Big Labor, including the AFL-CIO, AFSCME, the Service Employees International Union (SEIU), the United Steelworkers, and other unions representing transit workers, sheet metal workers, machinists, auto workers, and mine workers all endorsed Apollo, which is simultaneously promoted by Greenpeace and the Sierra Club, the League of Conservation Voters, ACORN, and other left-wing groups, as well as major left-wing foundations, law firms, venture capitalists (depending on the agenda to reward risk-taking), and, of course, wind and solar power industries.

By this point, you'll be surprised to learn that Apollo's key New York branch is run by none other than Jeff Jones, co-founder (with Bill Ayers) of the violent and radical 1960s to 1970s group the Weather Underground.[77]

Now, about the even more notorious ACORN. Before deciding in early 2010 to rebrand itself with new names in the wake of a series of scandals, ACORN decided to wet its beak in the highly lucrative global warming industry what with its former lawyer, Obama, running the show. He must surely be cognizant of the fact that, while he may not know a thing about climate change or even energy—calling windmills a "new" technology is a very bad start—he does know that this has been decided upon as a principal vehicle for imposing a radical agenda on America. The tireless work of Capital Research's Matthew Vadum brought unwanted attention to the alarmist Worldwatch Institute outing ACORN diversification into Big Green.[78]

Worldwatch cites Brian Kettenring, ACORN deputy director of national operations, spouting emotion-laden platitudes such as that the group "was inspired to join the Climate Equity Alliance and work with groups such as the Sierra Club after seeing the vulnerability of cities such as New Orleans to rising sea levels and more intense climatic events. The group, which lobbies for affordable housing and improved education in urban areas, is also encouraged by the hope of 'green jobs,' environmentally sustainable employment opportunities. . . . ACORN's contribution will include direct lobbying of Congress. In the long term, Kettenring expects more ACORN chapters to become involved in green jobs initiatives, such as efforts to collect federal funding for weatherizing urban buildings."[79] Who could have predicted that?

Consistent with such costly and wasteful uses of taxpayer money (suggesting also fraud and abuse), the House cap-and-trade energy tax bill doubled down, allocating taxpayer funds to groups just like ACORN to advise and train eligible "community development organizations" in how to reduce the carbon footprint of residents in "affordable housing." In plenty of time, Vadum directed lawmakers and staff to chapter and verse in the legislation, but nothing was done to prohibit the troubled group from wrapping its tentacles around this new pipeline that, if adopted, over the years will prove a nearly bottomless drain on taxpayer funds, possibly in the trillions.

CHAPTER 8

DOMESTIC DISTURBANCE: LOCKING UP OUR RESOURCES AND SHUTTING DOWN THE ECONOMY

Immediately upon taking office, President Obama rushed to seal off our domestic energy supplies from public access. In a frenzied offensive, he intensified the long-running, multi-front campaign by his allies seeking to block production and use of the abundant coal lying beneath the ground. Obama vowed new policies to "bankrupt" coal and cause energy prices to "necessarily skyrocket."[1] America's ability to supply oil and gas was already dangerously threatened by inane measures severely limiting domestic production. A few of these—executive and legislative moratoria on much offshore exploration and production, and the same regarding our enormous "oil shale" deposits on land—had only recently been lifted after long-overdue public outcry. Soon those were placed in limbo again by

Obama delaying a plan to manage the resources. Such political recklessness, not physical shortage, has already ensured potentially
dangerous gasoline and electricity scarcity.

Obama's political pandering to radicals pursuing a retrograde
obsession with privation causes productivity, real wages, and employment to drop, which ultimately drags the economy down with them.
Incredibly, all of that is also intentional, as are the real human consequences that flow from energy poverty, including deaths from cold
(and heat), harm to dietary intake, or any other result of diminished
economic circumstances. Harry Reid came under great fire in February 2010 for saying that when men are out of work, they become
more physically abusive, but at root he was actually on to something
long pointed out by those who sought greater consideration of the
economic impacts of regulation: the impacts of job loss and other
economic harm extend far beyond placing the employable on relief.

But in the statists' fevered minds, there is a war on, and such harms
are a natural part of it. As University of Oklahoma geologist David
Deming writes, "Without the inexpensive and reliable energy provided by coal, oil, and gas, our civilization would quickly collapse. The
prophets of global warming now want us to do precisely that." He
equates Washington's fetish with seizing control of individual energy
production and consumption decisions as akin to mass, organized
suicides in history led by other self-styled seers claiming to commune
with nature.[2]

With the anti-growth, anti-energy radicals now installed in the two
political branches of government, on top of increasingly activist
courts, Washington is aggressively doubling down on a long-sim-
mering war against our prosperity, freedoms, and safety. Left to their
own devices, so the philosophy goes at its core, free individuals would
only wreak unacceptable harms. Alternately, we have already visited

them upon ourselves; therefore, the current crisis demands radical action by the state and suspension of certain liberties. Either way, we must be brought into check. Apparently, if only given one more chance, their experiment in ideology would get its fair shake, this time without some tyrant stomping in to muddle their neatly organized society as did that unfortunate series of despots spoiling the fun in central and eastern Europe.

As individual Americans suffer now, and with our national security already imperiled by these policies (as detailed in chapter 9), much more of the same is being cynically pushed in the name of *enhancing* our security and returning us to prosperity. The only thing enhanced here at home is state control of power, in all senses of the term. We are scripting disaster for ourselves as the Left largely buries its schemes amid a massive push of other radical objectives. The "health care" fight over the state grabbing control of one-sixth of the economy might have been the only way to distract from seizing another equal part through gaining control over energy, short of all-out military conflict or similar emergencies necessitating more leeway to the feds. Still, the breadth, depth, and swiftness of Obama's rush to seize and restrict domestic energy supplies is alarming.

THE RUSH TO SHUT THINGS DOWN

Most breathtaking about Obama's power grab was how quickly upon taking office, and despite taking longer than any president before him to fill key slots to run the business of government, he and his allies in Congress began turning off the spigot of domestic resources by sealing off our reserves. In no time they were working with green activists, using existing laws and drafting new ones to bring us to heel in the name of their ideology.

The *Weekly Standard*'s Fred Barnes noted how, within Obama's first few months in office, he had "proposed removing all tax incentives to produce oil and gas, slapping a 13 percent excise tax on all energy derived from the Gulf of Mexico, and increasing the corporate tax rate by 3 percent on all companies that produce or process oil and gas."[3] Obama sought new taxes on drilling in his 2010 budget that could put small "mom and pop" producers out of business, according to the group representing "stripper wells"—those yielding only about fifteen barrels daily of harder-to-extract oil, but which cumulatively add up to over a million barrels per day. This one "energy independence" move alone would reduce domestic oil output by 15.4 percent and gas output by about 9 percent almost overnight, by attacking our small producers who lift about as much oil as we import from our friends the Saudis.[4] Brilliant.

Obama cannot bring himself to candidly address those tax incentives Barnes writes about, or the way he is further perverting our economy with them. Subsidies are distorting and not needed for any source of energy that, to truncate the analysis, "works." So Obama lifting indirect subsidies (tax incentives) on oil and gas production is not inherently a problem. Unlike windmills and solar panels, oil and gas would still contribute without subsidies, with the possible exception of those "stripper" wells (which, also unlike windmills and solar panels, at least work to lessen our dependence on foreign energy). But Obama then escalates subsidies for sources of energy that do not work. Obama's pouring hundreds of millions of more taxpayer dollars, most of them borrowed, into rat-hole technologies makes his call for an end to "fuel subsidies"[5] even more incongruous. With this disingenuous styling, he does not mean wealth transfers like those he quickly rushed through to windmill, solar panel, and pixie dust companies in which Al Gore and their shared allies are invested. Obama calls those "investments," which is code for something that cannot attract enough people to actually voluntarily "invest" their own money to support it. Usually for very good reason.

And while Obama has lately taken to showing a little rhetorical ankle when it comes to increasing supplies of oil and gas in North America, his policies do just the opposite. His clueless Secretary of the Interior, Ken Salazar, postponed a new offshore leasing program. As the *Washington Times* noted, "The secretary announced that a new offshore energy plan—written in the months after Congress allowed its offshore ban to expire—would have to wait an additional six months before his department would even consider looking at it again...."[6] He shortened the duration of drilling leases, retracted onshore oil and natural gas leases, and stopped programs supporting "unconventional" (but still hydrocarbon and abundant) resources like shale, oil sands, and heavy oil. Salazar also suspended governmental research and development of those unconventional sources even though they are produced in Canada, Mexico, and here at home. He and his allies are also coming after them by promoting a Low Carbon Fuel Standard (LCFS).

The LCFS is premised in the notion that the amount of carbon in fuel can be altered. Unfortunately, it can't. Crude oil contains the same amount of carbon regardless of its origin. Heavier sources require more energy to extract the fuel. So the idea behind an LCFS is to include in a fuel's carbon designation the CO_2 emitted in the process of extracting it from its source, thereby tarring (so to speak) certain sources of oil as supposedly dirtier than others. What this means is that Saudi oil would be declared the "cleanest," and we would import more oil from the Middle East to replace what a LCFS effectively bans—hence the acronym becoming rakishly known by others as the Less Competition For Saudis measure.

No one seemed concerned that in 2005, Congress had enacted a section of the Energy Policy Act declaring these sands (and oil shale, which the entire Obama administration is working to shut down after the executive moratorium was repealed and Congress failed to renew its own) as "strategically important," and that they "should be developed to reduce the growing dependence of the United States on politically and economically unstable sources of foreign oil imports."[7]

Canada may not be unstable but its largest energy source is apparently just too politically incorrect. Of course, the Chinese are no fools, and they rushed in with a $2 billion investment to get their meat hooks on about three billion barrels of our neighbors' massive resource just too icky and promising for the American Left, a dynamic played out with Gulf of Mexico oil and gas, too. Nearby and plentiful, but now being pursued by other countries instead of us.[8] And you thought that letting the Chinese buy Unocal might allow undue influence over our energy security by gaining access to assets of strategic importance. Of course, an LCFS is in the name of "global warming," so it's all good.

About our own shale deposits, the *Washington Times* bemoaned how in Salazar's first month he "shut down an oil shale leasing program that had begun to make serious strides toward more cleanly and efficiently producing American oil from shale—a potential recoverable resource three times the size of Saudi Arabia's oil supplies."[9] How smart is this from the man who tells us he is driven by ensuring American "energy independence"?

Well, "More than half the world's oil shale reserves lay in the Green River Formation, which covers portions of western Colorado, northeast Utah and southwest Wyoming. Some government and industry officials believe the formation contains as much as 1.5 trillion barrels of recoverable oil—more than three times the total that will ever be produced in the oil fields of Saudi Arabia.... The 'mother lode' of these domestic reserves sits ... mostly on federal lands overseen by the Bureau of Land Management, said Jim Bartis, a senior policy researcher at the Rand Corporation and lead author of an influential 2005 paper on policy issues associated with oil shale development."[10] From the Department of Understatement, we are told that "BLM has been cautious about promoting oil shale as a viable resource, and ... the Obama administration has placed greater restrictions on oil and shale R&D leases on public land."[11]

Obama also canceled the high-level nuclear waste repository that had been decades in the making.[12] After all, as senior administration officials blustered, thanks to stardust and moonbeams we actually have no need for any more nuclear power, and we also don't need to build any more coal-fired power plants because that production can be replaced by putting some windmills off the East Coast.

Obama even proposed regulations to hammer the ethanol and biodiesel industries that are pure creatures of the sort of mandate and subsidy schemes he prattles on about. He declared open war on Americans' access to all sources of abundant, reliable, and particularly the affordable energy, as well as the freedoms and prosperity that they bring. Remember, "We can't drive our SUVs and eat as much as we want and keep our homes on 72 degrees at all times. ... That's not going to happen."[13] Disregard that at least two of these things he does in excess.

Hardly two weeks after being installed, Obama's Secretary of the Interior Ken Salazar rescinded 77 already-awarded leases on 130,000 energy-rich acres in Utah, even though those deals, made in December 2008 and including some activity already underway, were the result of three resource management plans and seven years of work.[14] Although ostensibly rescinded just for review, none of these were reinstated when the review was completed. Instead, all that flowed were vague promises of possibly opening less than a quarter of them in the future, and an ominous vow that all future oil and gas leasing programs must require even more reviews.

Most revealing, Salazar indicated that these Utah revocations were just the beginning,[15] telegraphing his subsequent move to redirect his department charged with taxpayer-owned resources to focus instead on Regional Climate Change Response Centers,[16] to make up reasons and provide bureaucratic cover for keeping our resources in the ground. The *New York Times* gleefully editorialized about the Utah revocations as "one more sign that the Obama administration will take a more sensible approach to energy exploration on public lands"[17] than his predecessor. Toward these ends, ninety liberal members of Congress—from other than Utah—then pushed legislation to lock up more than nine million acres of Utah as wilderness, negating a 2003 agreement under which the feds agreed to stop designating lands as wilderness to shut them off from resource production.[18]

How's that working out? In just Obama's first year in office, two million more acres were slapped with the designation and an internal document leaked in early 2010 indicating a whole lot more land-grabbing was on the way, in eleven different states and mostly covering areas with energy potential.[19]

Incidentally, Utah only has ten million acres of private land. Electorally unfriendly places must be made into museums, it seems.

More subversive, if equally alarming: under Obama our policymakers cheered on efforts to use existing laws, like the National Environmental Policy Act (NEPA), to block domestic energy production and indeed all resource production.[20] He even had his White House Council on Environmental Quality issue a Guidance on revising (read: expanding) this stealthiest of all weapons as yet another "backdoor tool to regulate greenhouse gases [that] will stifle job creation and create greater uncertainty for the economy... [I]t will enable federal agencies to block or delay production of America's domestic energy resources."[21]

As noted elsewhere in these pages, the gargantuan "cap-and-trade" bills Obama sought to ram through Congress both contain an identical Trojan Horse of a provision mandating that all federal laws be used as carbon dioxide suppression measures, removing any resistance that the crowd bastardizing NEPA, the Endangered Species Act, and other laws were encountering in the courts. The same holds true for the tax code, anything requiring a federal permit, and so on. Everything.

Imagine the boon this is for green groups dedicated to stopping domestic energy production. Already in recent years, as Institute for Energy Research president Thomas Pyle has written, "According to the Department of the Interior, the number of suits filed in federal court to delay, defer or outright deny the development of domestic energy resources has grown more than 700 percent in the past decade; from 167 protests per year between 1997 and 2000, to 1,180 a year from then until now. And because petitioners don't actually have to win the case to delay energy development ad infinitum, why would anyone stop?"[22] They won't. In fact, 1,200 lawsuits a year—that's five blocking actions filed each and every day the courts are open—isn't enough. We're only 65 percent dependent on foreign oil, not nearly dependent enough on foreign gas, and still producing and using coal. Obama is giving them more tools to do more harm.

The point of these actions was to accelerate the process of starving us off what works, and what the Left despises for that very same reason. And delay with Obama means denial, which his administration lacks the courage to admit. To the contrary, he continues to allege a desire to see domestic energy production, and to insist that one job lost is too many.

As the chairman of the House Western Caucus Rob Bishop said, "The evidence is clear that this administration seems intent on restricting the development of American energy resources."[23] Rep. Doc Hastings of Washington wrote, "Although the President regularly expresses verbal support for a comprehensive energy plan, his Administration has demonstrated that no matter how many Americans are out of work, it will continue to take steps to proactively discourage certain types of economic development—including the creation of natural gas jobs, oil drilling jobs and nuclear jobs." Summing it up, Hastings concluded, "If this is his Administration's idea of support for comprehensive energy development, I would hate to see their idea of opposition."[24] We're seeing it. We're just being lied to about it.

IT GETS WORSE

As all of these land lock-ups indicate, Obama was in a hurry to sever more than merely energy resource production, hitting a diverse array of largely but not exclusively Western communities, nearly all of whom depend upon responsible resource production for their existence.

Surely you didn't expect Team Obama to resist waving the "spotted owl" flag immediately upon taking office, so you were not surprised when Obama cancelled a Bush-era logging rule on the grounds that allowing the continued timber harvesting violates the Endangered Species Act (ESA), immediately striking small Oregon communities.[25] His Interior Department front man on the issue, Tom Strickland, the assistant secretary for fish and wildlife and parks, said public forest management decisions are an opportunity to sequester more carbon.[26] In fact, the administration has gone as far as speaking in terms of people daring to log in "our carbon sinks."[27] No. They are forests, just as they were before the "climate" excuse for the Left's agenda was coined, although I suppose that's one way to view decisions harming families and destroying communities. But, of course, those are just people, not trees.

This was no isolated move. Under Obama—whose government must decide whether and how aggressively to defend against greenie litigation, and whether and how to appeal if they lose—we saw a refusal to ease enforcement of the heartless, at-whatever-the-cost ESA provisions in order to aid California farmers being denied water in the name of a fish.[28] We saw suspension of bureaucratic support for a large copper mine in Arizona,[29] a gravel mine expansion halted in the Puget Sound area,[30] and a cascade of many more decisions revealing a radical view of people, nature, and public resource management.

Team Obama made the menacing decision to work cooperatively with green groups using a variety of laws to shut down all manner of activity by tying it to claims of global warming, which means energy use, particularly that aforementioned NEPA decision to require all federal projects be evaluated on their supposed contribution to man-made global warming. Their willing accomplice, in fact the group egging them on with constant threats of litigation, is the Center for Biological Diversity (CBD), the group that managed to convince the Fish & Wildlife Service, with the assistance of the courts, to list the polar bear, which has proliferated during the supposed ravages of warming, as a threatened species under the rigid Endangered Species Act.[31]

CBD is famous for vowing to "halt"—note the word choice—greenhouse gas production,[32] which not only means use of energy sources that keep us free and safe, but activities such as logging that release CO_2 because, of course, once felled, trees do not hold all of the carbon nutrient. (This has long been called the "carbon cycle" for a reason; remember: trees absorb CO_2 from the atmosphere and produce oxygen; upon dying, decaying biological matter releases remaining, stored CO_2.) CBD opened a new Climate Law Institute to "use existing laws and work to establish new state and federal laws that will eliminate energy generation by the burning of fossil fuels—particularly coal and oil shale."[33] With Obama's friendly administration, the project's "initial" $17 million will go that much further.

POLITICS AND IGNORANCE

The administration and its allies raced to cram down these outrages all while sputtering about "energy independence," a fuzzy term that apparently means limiting not just foreign sources of energy, but domestic energy, too. The *Wall Street Journal* derided Obama's rhetorical window dressing which he laid out in a speech in Prague not long after his inauguration.

> Mr. Obama repeated his pledge to "confront climate change by ending the world's dependence on fossil fuels, by tapping the power of new sources of energy like the wind and sun." Never mind that neither the wind nor the sun are new sources of energy. It so happens that the U.S. gets about 2.3% of its energy resources from "renewable" resources of the kind the president advocates while fossil fuels account for about 70%.... Mr. Obama's energy policy goes something like this: Phase One: Inaugurate the era of "green" energy. Phase Two: Overturn the first and second laws of thermodynamics. Phase Three: Carbon neutrality![34]

Reading Obama's own statements, Australia's *Brookes News* economics editor Gerard Jackson wrote, "Obviously raising energy prices to lower living standards is part of his agenda."[35]

These steps were a parallel campaign with the effort by the Sierra Club, a group with an annual haul of about a hundred million dollars, to block all new coal plants and even force the retirement of existing plants, as detailed in Chapter 10. Coincidentally, a breakdown of Sierra's political giving in previous election cycles reveals a strong tilt in favor of Democrats: 96 percent to 3 percent (2006), 99 percent to 1 percent (2008), and as of this writing, 100 percent to 0 percent track in favor of Democrats for 2010.[36] Who says there's no such thing as a "friend" in Washington?

The Obama Left's war on energy is not new, but merely an acceleration of a hyper-partisan agenda representing an ideological hatred of individual and economic liberties and private control of that which ensures our freedoms—energy. Rep. Todd Akin of Missouri advances the following breakdown of relevant votes in the U.S. House of Representatives on expanding American-made energy, by issue (percentages given are by vote on each issue):

ANWR Exploration: Republicans: 91 percent Supported—Democrats: 86 percent Opposed

Coal-to-Liquid: Republicans: 97 percent Supported—Democrats: 78 percent Opposed

Oil Shale Exploration: Republicans: 90 percent Supported—Democrats: 86 percent Opposed

Outer Continental Shelf Exploration: Republicans: 81 percent Supported—Democrats: 83 percent Opposed

Increased Refinery Capacity: Republicans: 97 percent Supported—Democrats: 96 percent Opposed

In sum, just over 90 percent of House Republicans in recent years have supported increasing the production of American-made oil and gas, while 86 percent of House Democrats voted against doing so.[37]

So, the dogmatic passion is there, if not so much the substantive literacy. President Obama is joined in his windmills-are-a-"new"-technology insight by sages like House Speaker Nancy Pelosi, who appeared on *Meet the Press* to assuage fears about her fitness for the task of directing a radical overhaul of our energy infrastructure and policies. While some may argue about the nomenclature of calling the carbon-based matter buried underground "fossil fuels," there isn't any debate that, if that's what we call them, they include natural gas. Or, at least, there wasn't.

This woman who stands next in succession for the presidency after, ah, Vice President Joe "No New Coal" Biden,[38] revealed that natural gas is not actually a fossil fuel, after all. Instead, "I believe in natural gas as a clean, cheap alternative to fossil fuels. . . ."[39] Huh. Possibly Ms. Pelosi and her husband didn't do much homework when investing all of that money with T. Boone Pickens's outfit pushing a preference for the stuff in our energy policy?[40]

Dunno. But she insisted that is the case, reinforcing the claim with the qualifier, "Clean compared to fossil fuels."[41] As in, "San Francisco liberals are uninformed. Uninformed compared to the ignorant."

Interviewer Tom Brokaw didn't catch the misstep, either, and but for a pair of *Wall Street Journal* mentions, this minor oversight by a rather high policymaking official didn't make many waves.[42]

Less than a month prior, Pelosi's counterpart in the Senate, Majority Leader Harry Reid of Nevada, feverishly pouted, "Coal makes us sick, oil makes us sick. It's global warming. It's ruining our country, it's ruining our world."[43] Hmm. I wonder if he has considered living without either of them. I suggest Reid go to those countries not yet burdened with central coal-fired power. Or automobility. I call those countries "Haiti." Ask the Haitians for their thoughts on their air quality. Or the soil, water, levels of infant respiratory disease, and the number of young girls sentenced to spending their days deforesting and wading in dung to form patties for fuel. They will look at you in stunned amazement and then ask for help finding food, medicine and, yes, fuel. Fuel which, if abundantly available, would allow them to radically improve—dare I say "fundamentally transform"?—their lives, create wealth, and place an economic value on and prioritize environmental improvements. Reid might more sensibly suggest that central coal-fired electricity would save millions of these lives. Or at least that it stops men from beating their wives.[44]

Meanwhile, our governing crowd insists that the one thing we can't afford when it comes to their pet paranoia of global warming is debate. Their cocktail of ignorance and zeal threatens a cost far worse than their so-called climate models can credibly pretend is our fate if we refuse to succumb.

When asked, also on *Meet the Press*—what is it with their confessions of ignorance and this show?—whether the administration would "consider repealing any of the longer-term spending given the deficit problem," Obama's chief economic advisor Lawrence Summers revealed a tenuous grasp on our energy needs and the very basics of something which he is responsible for radically overhauling. "That's a hugely important investment in the future. No, the president's not going to think about repealing substantial increases in solar energy and wind energy which are crucial to reducing our dependence on foreign oil. . "[45]

You know, because of all those wind- and solar-powered cars clogging our roads. And all of that electricity we get from burning oil (an almost imperceptible 1.1 percent of supply in 2008,[46] which is almost precisely as immaterial as wind and solar combined).

Were the stakes, and these individuals' roles in the policymaking process, both not so high, this criticism might be slightly unfair. If they were, say, just spouting off at the table, haranguing a relative over Thanksgiving and a few too many, it would matter much less. But this is serious.

Incidentally, this is the same Larry Summers who got in trouble at Harvard for noticing that men and women are different, in case you were wondering whether politics dictates what constitutes "knowledge" to our educated elites. At least a little backpedalling was in order after Obama's Energy Secretary Steven Chu sputtered, when asked for his thoughts on the tangential little issue of an upcoming OPEC meeting, that whatever the oil cartel does is "not in my domain."[47] Ah. Then the Energy Department—founded by Jimmy Carter largely to reduce America's dependence on foreign oil after a cartel-driven oil embargo . . . did they cover that at orientation, Mr. Secretary?—does *what*, exactly? (Answer: hand out your money.) And does such confusion about DOE's mission explain its spectacular success at that task, through the curious means of imposing and enabling policies that steadily increased our dependence from a little more than one-third of U.S. consumption in 1974 to about two-thirds today?

Welcome to Washington. Even before the invention of "global warming," an entire suite of boneheaded and even cruel leftist policies led to domestic oil production declining steadily beginning in 1985—the Department of Energy works quickly when it wants to!—while a growing nation's demand also grew. Our imports of all energy, on net, have increased to between 25 to 30 percent of our use,[48] despite having the world's largest known and suspected domestic reserves. Close enough to success for government work, as the saying goes.

Is it possible that Team Obama really is this clueless? Of course it is. A more important question is whether or how much it matters. Chu, Summers, and their ilk of pointy-headed academics are only nominally in charge. The activists are really the ones running the show. "Energy and Climate Czar" Carol Browner has been given the policy reins. This leaves DOE to host events and hand out billions of taxpayer dollars in research grants to prop up technologies so woeful that investors can't be convinced to fund them, as well as grants to people inquiring into all sorts of global warming lunacy.

Among Washington's purveyors of proper policy, catch-phrases promiscuously fly, such as "Under my energy plan" or "He doesn't even have an energy policy!" The former has proven to generally mean an *anti*-energy plan, while the latter is typically thrown at any politician who wants to go with what works. That's deemed as having no energy plan at all.

FILL 'ER UP WITH SOLAR!

Leaving for the moment the disgraceful politics that have strangled offshore oil and gas exploration and production, what about those canceled and delayed leases onshore? In his first year, Obama worked on a new law with House Democrat legislators to, in the words of Dan Naatz of the Independent Petroleum Association of America, "make it more difficult to operate on federal lands at a time when they should be looking to make it easier and simpler," taking "a step in the wrong direction as we're trying to find more American natural gas and more American oil."[49] "After a year in the office, it's very clear there is a direction that has been decided, and it's anti-oil and gas," said Jack Gerard, president of the American Petroleum Institute.[50]

Naatz describes Obama's "greater bureaucratic delays and slowing down [of] the process."[51] A November report by the Independent Petroleum Association of Mountain States (IPAMS) cited new "irregularities" in the federal oil and gas leasing program reducing the acreage available for lease, including about $100 million in unissued and suspended leases in just three Western states. The Associated Press, of all outlets, took a look and found that the Bureau of Land Management are presently maintaining a hold on about $100 million in Rocky Mountain drilling leases already auctioned or sold since 2002, as a result of environmentalist protests and lawsuits.[52]

IPAMS spokeswoman Kathleen Sgamma told trade writers that "there are lots of situations where [the Interior Department] is seriously slowing down the natural gas and oil program."[53] And that is their objective, which they on occasion openly admit, as you will see.

After a court issued an injunction to put things in Utah on hold until complaints about allowing resource development were reviewed, Salazar saved the court and greens any more trouble by simply revoking the leases—in case anyone wondered what a sweetheart settlement looked like.

Environmental writer Bonner Cohen gently described the tactics as being "seen by some as a sign of the Obama administration's fundamental hostility to fossil fuels."[54] How are these dogmatic stunts playing for communities in the resource-rich Mountain West? Salazar's Utah cancellations prompted three counties to join producers to sue him to let go of what had already been auctioned off and duly paid for.[55] One producer noted that his company paid the feds hundreds of thousands of dollars for leases to drill for oil and gas, yet has still to install one rig thanks to this bureaucratic treachery. This not being the sort of change he could believe in, he dared confront Salazar at a "listening tour" stop with the outrageous assertion: "We think the government should issue the leases we purchased or give the money back."[56] Money back? Ack. A despairing Salazar, sobered by such cruel logic, then offered this *deal was already done, gotta respect property rights* plea to the greens who vocalized their displeasure over his daring to allow a few Colorado sales to go through.[57]

Even where Interior agrees to auction off smaller blocs of land, green groups pitched in to block them in court on the grounds of preserving "wildlife heritage." This occurred in Wyoming and the Roan Plateau in Colorado, not long after Obama's inauguration. In late 2009, the Obama Bureau of Land Management pulled all 148 parcels covering 71,000 acres of the Talladega and Conecuh national forests from auction, citing threatened legal action by a local environmental group.[58] This came on the heels of ordering the removal of nearly 1 million acres of land in southern Nevada from new mining claims for the next two decades, ostensibly in the name of a desert tortoise.[59] This staggered an industry trying to rebound from the economic downturn, taking off-limits a section of land they had seen as ripe for development. At about the same time, the Bureau of Land Management pulled more than 7,700 acres from planned oil and gas leases, although their allowing fewer than 10 percent of the planned parcels to go to auction still left green groups fuming. At least they could find comfort in the contemporaneous victory in Wyoming, managing to get that state's bureau of land management to remove fifteen oil and natural gas lease parcels and thousands more acres from auction.[60]

Despite "energy independence" and "reduce our foreign dependence" mantras, Obama's U.S. Fish & Wildlife Service rejected an offer in Alaska to swap land with the Athabascan Indians as part of a deal that would have legalized oil and gas drilling on an oil-rich part of the

Yukon Flats National Wildlife Refuge.[61] Oddly, the rejected trade would have sent oil- and mineral-rich lands to those who would like to produce on them, and 150,000 acres of bird-rich wetlands to the Fish & Wildlife Service, plus the future rights to 56,500 more acres.[62] Sort of sounds like it made sense. And it also simply could not be tolerated.

In May of Obama's first year in office, his allies in the Democrat caucus in Congress proposed increasing federal revenues from whatever quantity of oil and gas that domestic producers manage to squeeze out of public lands. Not by increasing production, mind you—in his first year Obama issued the fewest leases in history, in a recession no less—but just by increasing the royalties paid by producers for the privilege. This came from Rep. Nick J. Rahall II, West Virginia Democrat and chairman of the House Committee on Natural Resources, who welcomed Obama's inauguration by proposing royalty rate increases of 50 percent.[63] Helping along the campaign to simply cut off domestic production altogether, he would also cut the lease periods in half, to five years. As geology, laws, and labor make domestic production already higher-cost than in other parts of the world, this makes it more likely we will give way to lower cost producers in, say, the Middle East. Again, brilliant.

The administration jumped in and, on its own, raised the cost of operating on public lands substantially. Obama justifies this job-, investment-, and energy-killing approach of huge new taxes on energy production here upon the ludicrous contention that failure to do so could lead to "overproduction of oil and gas," which rather subjective and certainly odd characterization of the current state of affairs is "inconsistent with the Obama Administration's goals" about global warming and that sort of thing.[64] Good heavens.

The American Petroleum Institute's Jack Gerard said in a statement responding to such moves that "With America still recovering from recession and one in ten Americans out of work, now is not the time to impose new taxes on the nation's oil and natural gas industry. New taxes would mean fewer American jobs and less revenue at a time when we desperately need both. A robust U.S. oil and gas industry is essential to the recovery of the nation's economy."[65]

But Team Obama remains convinced that this will only force us to finally confront our greed and change our ways, or else overcome those laws of physics to invent the perpetual motion machine or at least pixie dust. As reported by the *Washington Times*, the environmental pressure group Natural Resources Defense Council crowed, "Mr. Rahall's plan fits neatly into the broader efforts of the Obama administration and congressional Democrats to make a 'dramatic shift' in energy production toward green sources."[66]

All of this, from slow-walking to revocation, is part an obvious strategy to buy time, halting as much energy from reaching the market as possible—during a budget crisis and economic slowdown no less—as the administration seeks to institutionalize new laws reducing domestic resource production. Assessing simply the resources that were until recently under formal moratoria—and which Obama has placed under political moratoria—the consulting and modeling company Science Applications International Corp. (SAIC) found that "U.S. gross domestic product would lose $2.36 trillion and American consumers would pay an additional $2.35 trillion for energy if oil and gas on federal lands remain" locked up.[67]

Daniel Simmons of the Institute for Energy Research cites the mounting examples and, noting the public mobilization behind the idea of "drill here, drill now" which so frightened elected policymakers as energy prices spiked in 2008, says, "The American people are demanding access to our vast energy resources, but so far the Obama administration has thwarted efforts to increase our domestic energy production."[68]

We obviously need more domestic energy, and Obama's rhetoric is designed to lead the average voter to believe he wants that, too, even if it is hard to navigate all the caveats with which he festoons the claim. But the truth is, while crying "climate change!," "environmental heritage," and even somehow pleading a "jobs" agenda as excuses to call things off, Obama simply doesn't want us to produce more energy. After all, we might use it.

CHAPTER 9

INSECURITY COMPLEX

The security implications of cap-and-trade, a low carbon fuel standard, green jobs boondoggles, and sealing off domestic resources are many. Foreign dependence, lack of resiliency, and economic uncertainty all make us more vulnerable. As Member of the European Parliament Nigel Farage wrote in outrage after learning of the scandalous closure of Corus's Teesside facility in the UK, mentioned previously as being in essence exported to India thanks to "global warming" laws, "It is Britain's last great steelworks and an essential national resource. Without it, we are at the world's mercy."[1] I am not one to support Euro-style "national champion" or other protectionism—which Farage's umbrage does not represent—but let's face facts: maintaining domestic steel production rates slightly higher in a nation's interests than ensuring the Chinese don't build more windmills than you do.

Few also dispute that higher energy costs harm the economy, and therefore harm people. Higher energy costs also make recession more likely—energy price spikes have preceded every such downturn in modern times—and harder to escape. They mean higher utility bills, higher prices at the pump, and higher costs for food. This reduces consumers' real wages and purchasing power, and signals higher inflation. It also offsets meager, targeted tax cuts pushed by administrations whose policies drive up these prices with the other hand, which essentially creates a tax hike. Energy tax hikes are among the most regressive, meaning they most hurt seniors and the poor.

In what should be no surprise, we see the highest real gasoline prices in the biggest basket cases among our states, which also happen to be long-suffering under environmentally possessed or otherwise liberal governance, such as Michigan, California, and New York. Europe has a policy of keeping gasoline more than double and even triple what Americans pay, and this doubtless contributes to their historically slower economic growth and higher unemployment rates.

Further, Obama's own (largely debunked) environmentalist dogma should tell him it is foolish for us to artificially concentrate a quarter of our entire domestic oil output, and more than ten percent of domestic natural-gas production, in Hurricane Alley, as we do currently. By imposing policies that make it difficult to change this, he ensures it will continue, just as we finally recognize the peril. This compounds the security-of-supply issues he mentions in his rhetoric decrying reliance on other countries for our energy. We have massive resources both on-shore and in less storm-prone areas, so this need not be the case, but for politics.

But Obama has said that our current policies (which he is making vastly worse) actually encourage "over-investment" in oil and gas production. This reflects a belief that energy security somehow comes from making energy more expensive. So you should not be surprised that Obama's energy secretary runs around the country saying things like we have to figure out how to triple the cost of a gallon of gasoline. He specifically cited Europe's prices as the goal—"Somehow we have to figure out how to boost the price of gasoline to the levels in Europe"[2]—whose prices at the time he said that averaged about eight dollars, and were over eleven dollars per gallon in some places when ours rose to four dollars. Since we all pay the same for a barrel of oil, Europe's punitive taxation is to blame for its extraordinarily higher prices.

Despite higher prices and cost of living, apologists for Euro-style governance claim that Europe actually proves the compatibility of Obama-style policies with better economic performance than our system premised on a much freer market.[3] However, America, with policies historically more geared toward energy abundance, has maintained a remarkably steady share of world economic activity for decades, despite very large and long-suffering "developing" nations making major leaps in recent years. Meanwhile, Europe's share has eroded.

As *Investor's Business Daily* noted in an editorial slamming the Copenhagen "Kyoto II" treaty talks, in a pompous 2000 internal treaty "the EU asserted it would 'leapfrog' the U.S. in productivity and output by 2010. By the time of its midterm review in 2005, however, the chest-thumping was over. It was clear the EU wasn't 'leapfrogging' the U.S.—or even staying up with it. Instead, its share of world output was falling at an even faster rate. From about 36% of world GDP in 1969, the EU today accounts for roughly 27% of the world's $47.9

trillion in output. That's just a tad higher than the U.S., though the EU has 80 million more people."[4]

Confronting this, and aware that Europe does not have the will or, possibly, the means to best us in a competition of free economies, Europe's plan—like Obama's—has increasingly become one of bringing us down to their level with shackles on our liberties and competitiveness. *Investor's Business Daily* noted, "They can't beat the U.S. So they want us to join them in their self-inflicted decline by hamstringing our economy with expensive regulations to slash carbon output and regulate businesses to death. In this effort, Europe has engaged the developing world as its ally. Egged on by EU elites, the so-called Group of 77 of developing countries are urging the same thing as the EU—massive taxes and wealth transfers from the developed nations (mainly the U.S.) to the Third World to alleviate the alleged impacts of global warming.... Their only hope—global warming welfare."[5]

Our public continues to have greater aspirations, but the Kyoto and related agendas are leading to great self-inflicted harms, consistent with what many of our trade competitors would prefer. A key symptom of this was our politicians' craven effort at pretending to try to resolve energy price shocks. In 2009, oil prices doubled, jeopardizing economic recovery. In response, according to *Politico*, Oregon Democratic Rep. Peter DeFazio proposed an increase in taxes to ease the volatility.[6] According to DeFazio's reasoning, if the price is high all the time, you'll feel price swings less. The fact that higher baseline energy prices harm the economy all the time, not just during price spikes, seems to have escaped both him and his green pressure group allies.

Of course, the only way to fit these square pegs of ideological illogic into a round and rational world is to convince one's self that we are running out of energy resources, thereby justifying a campaign to jealously hoard and ration them. While popular in certain salons, this is absurd and, when associated with the levers of power, dangerous.

Thanks to such inanity, the United States ranks *dead last* in energy security among major consuming nations, according to a recent Energy Security Index compiled by Energy Security News and the *Washington Times*.[7] Our oil sands-loving, drill-happy neighbors to the north, whose socialized health care we apparently can't get enough of (and neither can Canadians, come to think of it), at least have pro-energy policies, making Canada the most energy-secure nation.

The energy security report found that, as of early 2009, "the U.S. imported the most oil from Canada, 2.5 million barrels a day, followed by 1.3 million barrels a day from Mexico and around 1 million barrels a day from both Venezuela and Saudi Arabia."[8] Given their willingness to produce, all of these suppliers rank as more energy secure than the United States, with the sole exception of Mexico— which is pro-drilling but anti-liberal (in the classical sense), keeping foreign expertise and investment from helping Mexico help itself (a similar problem now confronting Venezuela after Chavez politicized the workforce).[9] Existing U.S. policies already—before the Obama administration worsened them—keep us less energy-secure even than numerous European countries (such as Poland), dirt-poor South Africa (where they were recently forced into rolling brownouts, a state of shortage versus complete loss of power, due to insufficient electricity capacity), India, and even the island state of Taiwan.

Meanwhile, Russia and China playing in our backyard reveal how they are taking the worldwide lead in acquiring massive new energy assets. China is in the midst of a spree of buying petroleum assets around the world, including refinery, oil, and gas properties in Asia, Russia, South America, and Africa. Obama went to China and signed

off on promoting shale gas investment *in China* through the US-
China Oil & Gas Industry Forum,[10] even as his administration is
seeking to block development of recent, enormous new shale gas
reserves at home, which, if exploited, are considered potential game
changers by some experts.[11] This is inexplicable.

Emerging, enormous market India announced in late 2009 that it,
too, was looking to join the fun. The *Financial Times* wrote that such
state-controlled exploration and development companies "have
exploited western groups' relative weakness to secure control of
resources. Emerging economy buyers, led by Chinese and Russian
companies, paid for $24.2bn of the total $48bn value of the 50 largest
oil and gas deals agreed in the second quarter, according to PWC, the
professional services firm."[12] That's up from about 20 percent the year
before.[13]

According to the Congressional Research Service (CRS), we pos-
sess the world's largest estimated combined recoverable natural gas,
oil, and coal endowments, completely disproving the vacuous talking
point that "America only has about 2 to 3 percent of the world's
proven oil reserves." The greens' stupid mantra is disingenuously
premised on our *proven* reserves of just 21 billion barrels, a rhetorical sleight of hand as this figure merely illustrates the results of
moratoria making it unlawful to go looking for resources where they
are most likely to be.[14] If they really had a problem with our proven
reserves, they would first swear off the moratoria forever. That they
support moratoria instead reveals a little more about their true objectives and concerns.

CRS simply compiled U.S. government estimates revealing an
expected supply of 167 billion barrels of recoverable oil, for example,
which is the equivalent of replacing America's current imports from
OPEC for more than seventy-five years.[15] As regards gas, a 2009

assessment from the Potential Gas Committee indicates at current consumption levels, roughly 90 percent of which we still manage to satisfy with domestic production, we likely have enough natural gas to meet American demand for nearly ninety years.[16] And of course, there's Old King Coal, of which the United States likely has a quarter of the world's supply, according to CRS.[17]

With this alternate perspective to the inane and deceptive talking point of "it's only six months' supply"[18] tossed at any suspected major U.S. resource deposit, bear in mind that thanks to Obama's allied politicians, judges, green groups, and lawyers, we confront an unstable prospect for future energy supplies despite these riches.

We are not going to actually run out of any of these energy sources for several lifetimes and, if history is any guide, innovative people and markets will ensure we continue discovering more efficient ways to find, lift, and use each of these sources. All of this adds context to Obama's press to find ways to take our own domestic energy security away from us, using any available rhetorical artifice culminating in a legal power grab.

So while we in the West are going nowhere fast when it comes to producing our own resources, despite sitting atop massive known and likely reserves, it should also come as no surprise that OPEC reports the cartel's market share is set for a healthy expansion. The energy sources are out there and educated guesses indicate they are spectacularly large.[19] According to BP's annual Statistical Review of World Energy, global energy reserves would supply the world for forty-two years at current production levels, though the number rises when adding Canadian oil sand deposits, which increase world reserves by more than 10 percent.[20]

The report also said that, in 2008, proven global oil reserves fell, if slightly, for the first time in a decade. Key factors behind that slight

dip in proven reserves included not only our own self-defeating policies, but a prohibition on investment and exploration by foreign firms
in Russia and Middle Eastern countries. Mexico's experience has
shown how closing one's fields to private, if foreign, investment and
expertise leads to declining production despite plentiful supply. As BP
Group Chief Executive Tony Hayward said in the Review's introduc-
tion, "The challenges the world faces in growing supplies to meet
future demand are not below ground, they are above ground. They
are human, not geological."[21] It's the politics, stupid!

But governmental interventions making it difficult to find the
energy doesn't mean it isn't there, as the Obamaphiles' rhetoric would
have you believe.

And there is every reason to believe that these projections are all
wrong, given that government (and many private) estimates of
energy reserves have historically fallen short of reality. *Reason* magazine's Michael Lynch describes past resource estimates as having
serially proven "wildly pessimistic."[22] Science writer Ron Bailey
looked at these estimates and, specifically referencing USGS figures,
concludes that since the beginning of time we've used about one-
sixth of the oil and gas we have found or now think we can locate
and lift.[23] That indicates that physical shortfalls are not even a near-
term concern, so long as we remain free to explore and produce,
though with the caveat that "The bad news is that much of the
world's oil reserves are in the custody of unstable and sometimes
hostile regimes" (again, informing a decision to get serious about
domestic production). And the betting man would bet that the estimated supplies will continue to increase with further developments
in technology.

National Review's Jonah Goldberg examined the issue and noted:

In 1995 the [U.S. Geological Survey] said that the Bakken formation, in North Dakota and Montana, had a modest amount of oil. It now believes there are 3 to 4 billion barrels there—25 times the 1995 estimate. The Minerals Management Service (MMS) insisted in 1987 that there were a "mere" 9 billion barrels of oil in the Gulf of Mexico. Twenty 20 years later that estimate is up to 45 billion. Prudhoe Bay in Alaska has already generated 15 billion barrels of oil and natural-gas liquids even though the government insisted the needle would hit empty at 9 billion. Right now, the MMS guesses that the Atlantic and Pacific Outer Continental Shelf (OCS) has 14.3 billion barrels of oil and 55 trillion cubic feet of natural gas. But that number is almost surely very low, because the government has kept oil companies from taking a serious look at what's down there, and they will spend tens or hundreds of millions of dollars looking for oil only if there's a good chance the government will let them drill for it.[24]

By touting his rigorous anti-exploration position, Obama also ignores progress, as those of his mindset tend to do. *Reason*'s Lynch fairly conservatively described the Potential Gas Committee's 2009 report, projecting a "70-year domestic cushion" of gas and demonstrating "how new technology (aka human ingenuity, what the late Julian Simon called the *ultimate resource*) *creates* resources, refuting the static fixity/depletion view of the mineral-resource world"[25] (emphases in original).

The scarcity and "limits to growth" crowd, led most prominently by "peak-oilers"—those who remain convinced, despite the evidence, that we simply must be running out of the stuff—may be proven partially right. If so, it will only be because politics yet again got in the way of plentiful physical supply. And this makes you less rich, less safe, and less free.

AN UNREFINED AGENDA

Remember the one item of leverage that President Obama felt he had over the Iranians: namely, their lack of capacity to refine crude oil to gasoline, which left them vulnerable to cutoff?[26] Not satisfied with his efforts to block domestic resource exploration and extraction, Obama immediately moved to increase our own reliance on foreign refined petroleum ever further by also pushing "cap-and-trade," which appeared to especially target refiners.[27] Refining is a cyclical and even something of a boom-and-bust business, with the economic slowdown temporarily shuttering capacity which will be needed when the economy recovers and grows. Ditto in the event that global flare-ups disrupt foreign countries and therefore our imports. So just as with crude oil, Obama is doubling down on our policies discouraging domestic refining capacity.

We haven't built a new refinery in the United States in decades, and the only one now on the books would be brought to a halt by that "low carbon fuel standard" Team Obama is crafting. This is because that new refinery was intended to process the Canadian supply, which the greens are working hard to keep from American use, apparently just because there is so much of it. (The greens imply it is somehow tainted for being "high sulfur,"[28] ignoring that we have laws managing sulfur emissions.) It may be too late anyway, as the Canadians have learned Mandarin for "Thanks, we'll take it."

In a move reminiscent of banana republics but increasingly familiar to U.S. resource and energy producers, in October 2009 Obama's

EPA shut down a project in Indiana to process heavy crude like that found in Canada's oil sands. Claiming it had new information, the Environmental Protection Agency objected to the state of Indiana granting an air operating permit to expand BP's Whiting Refinery in that state, a permit EPA had approved only months before.[29] It is merely a sign of things to come. Under Obama's "cap-and-trade" scheme, the refinery industry estimates that instead of expanding, one out of every six existing refineries will close within a decade as a result of the legislation's mandates. Gary Heminger, executive vice president of Marathon Oil Corp's refining subsidiary, told Reuters that this would cost us 1.5 million barrels per day in refining capacity, most directly affecting the U.S. Northeast, Midwest, and Gulf Coast regions due to refinery locations and the crude that they manage.[30]

That would increase our reliance on foreign refined gasoline—from countries smart enough to avoid subjecting themselves to these schemes, which is the vast majority of the world. The *Wall Street Journal* reported on an industry assessment of the impact, concluding, "By 2030, U.S. refining production could drop 17% from today's levels. . . . The drop would have to be made up by foreign imports, the study says, meaning the U.S. could end up relying on other countries for 19.4% of its refined fuel—nearly twice the amount it imports today."[31]

It takes a hyper-intelligent mind to see the wisdom in this, and we are fortunate to have several such intellects in charge at the moment.

Thanks to the Left, and frankly the public being very tolerant of such posturing, the United States has for years been too cool to bother tapping enormous resources lying beneath our own lands, preferring lazy sloganeering about working to "reduce our dependence on foreign oil!" while its policymakers flatly refuse to increase domestic production. But our new leadership is now compounding, not fixing, the problem.

OBAMA'S FRACTURED THINKING
ABOUT PLENTIFUL SHALE GAS

Technological advances in locating and extracting natural gas from newly discovered shale gas fields has led to an abundance of natural gas as an energy source. However, the process of extraction, known as "hydraulic fracturing," has been blocked by Obama and his buddies in Congress for no good reason. Their weapon was to try to place the practice under the jurisdiction of the Environmental Protection Agency. EPA's excuse for wresting control over the process, once it appeared capable of yielding previously unimaginable energy, is water contamination, despite lacking any historical evidence.

And the administration, when pressed, admitted as much. During a December 2009 hearing of the Senate Committee on Environment and Public Works, Senator James Inhofe asked three officials from the Environmental Protection Agency and the United States Geological Survey if they were aware of any documented cases of contamination from hydraulic fracturing. None of the three witnesses could provide a single example.[32]

That their demand to move authority from the states coincides with the boom in available reserves does leave one suspicious that this is not about anything other than snuffing out a practice that would pose the greens' biggest nightmare, of dramatic increases in affordable and reliable non-coal energy. The only reasonable reading of these actions is that the Left sought to give the Environmental Protection Agency control over this spectacular boon to our economic, energy, and national security in order to kill it.

Why would the Left kill an energy source? Especially now? The answer is, for the same reason they've committed themselves to killing coal and anything else that works: we've got a lot of it and can make it work reliably. Traced back further, it is explained by the same reasons behind their trying to stop every aspect of energy production, from exploration to transmission to combustion. Energy allows you to be independent.

To see the Left come so unglued about this is educational. Fracturing is a process that involves pumping water, sand, and viscous material commonly found in household soaps and detergents roughly two miles down a well or a hole in a rock, to create tiny fissures in the rock bed. This allows previously trapped natural gas to flow to the surface. The process, colloquially known as "fracking," has been regulated by states and conducted safely for sixty years in more than a million wells, and, as I write this, is aiding production from over 35,000 wells per year.[33] The process has already provided Americans 7 billion barrels of oil and 600 trillion cubic feet (Tcf) of natural gas.[34]

The National Petroleum Council reports that the overwhelming majority of all wells require fracturing in order to remain profitably in operation over the next decade, making it a necessary part of domestic energy production. The discoveries of new fields in combination with a few technological advances were game-changers, moving the U.S. natural-gas market from scarcity to abundance. The mere prospect of tapping this gas has kept prices down, helping the economy already.

The formula is very simple. Increased domestic energy production leads to increased domestic employment. An affordable domestic energy source provides jobs—not temporary make-work installing inefficient "green" sources—domestically, as opposed to providing more jobs for (and more power to) Russia, Iran, Libya, and others who continue to be enriched by our backward energy policies. Increased domestic supply decreases pressure on the price of gas.

Allowing the Environmental Protection Agency to try to stifle domestic energy production by preventing the harmless process it requires will continue to doom us to talking about increasing our energy independence and reducing our dependence on foreign sources, while uselessly sitting atop massive reserves.

Team Obama were apparently alarmed by more than a billion dollars being invested to begin production from gas fields in eastern Texas and northern Louisiana. Particularly unnerving was the Marcellus Shale formation running from West Virginia up into New York, possibly the largest in the world, and enough to provide for all the United States' gas needs for nearly two decades.[35] Penn State University geosciences professor Terry Engelder, in a published estimate, projects that the Marcellus Shale area would employ 100,000 more people just in Pennsylvania at salaries $20,000 above the average annual salary. Add to this the continuing discoveries of quality sources of natural gas in North Dakota and elsewhere in the country, and you'll see the price spikes that threatened the economy only a very few short years ago don't have to return.

These new gold mines, so to speak, have been made viable solely due to advances in "fracking," as fracturing is known. So that is what Team Obama is trying to snuff out with the help of its allies in Congress, led by Colorado liberal Diana Degette and, in the Senate, Bob Casey of Pennsylvania.[36] Environmentalists likely concluded they had no choice but to pay lip service to this alternative to coal, but their record reveals a belief that anything that we have this much of must be attacked and stopped in its relative cradle, and they soon acted on their instincts.

The American Petroleum Institute estimates that if the Obama administration is successful in killing this process, we would lose between 676,000 and 3 million jobs in five years, depending on which greenie twist on the idea the Environmental Protection Agency applied.[37] Imports would surge by 14, 30, or 60 percent in less than a decade, again depending on which approach is chosen. Through duplicative federal regulations, the number of new oil and natural gas wells drilled would drop by 20 percent in the next five years. Were fracturing eliminated, new oil and gas wells would drop by 79 percent. That would mean 45 percent less domestic natural gas production and 17 percent less domestic oil production.[38]

The hit to gross domestic product could be more than $370 billion in less than five years if the plan to kill fracturing is implemented, $170 billion if the Environmental Protection Agency simply restricted what fluids can be used to force the energy to the surface, or a mere $80 billion if the Agency kindly decided simply to regulate the practice, instead.[39] Now add that to the SAIC findings about the impact of keeping the resources formerly under moratoria locked up, as Obama clearly desires. Hard as it is on its face for many to understand, these actually are objectives of the "energy independence!" crowd.

Outright legislation imposing a ban on fracking "would be a disaster for us," in the words of North Dakota Democrat Senator Byron Dorgan, and "is potentially very threatening to the oil exploration and recovery activity underway" there according to the state's only congressman, Democrat Earl Pomeroy, who adds, "It's one of these pieces of legislation that is a solution in search of a problem."[40] Nice sentiments, but their constituents will see on whose side these gentlemen's political party really is, soon enough.

An editorial in the *Oklahoman* expressed similar sentiments, grasping at a familiar thread:

> Uncle Sam has grabbed control of much of the auto industry to financial sector. Why not oil and gas regulation as well? Dramatic increases in federal control of the private

sector and in regulation are becoming hallmarks of the Obama era. The latest power grab is an attempt to switch regulation of hydraulic fracturing from the states to the Environmental Protection Agency. This is what we in the opinion trade call a "DBI" issue—dull but important. Fracturing isn't a topic at the top of the minds of most folks, but it resides there for energy professionals, regulators and trade groups.... U.S. Rep. Dan Boren, D-Muskogee... says the regulatory shift would be "disastrous for the industry." This is a solution in search of a problem.[41]

It is also typical of this administration which, as is now abundantly clear, poses the biggest problem to resolving our energy needs.

INSECURITY BLANKET: BEING THE WORLD LEADER IN BEING THE WORLD LEADER

The other "energy security" argument Obama makes is that the United States is preparing to get its clock cleaned, and be less safe for it, if we don't match and raise every billion thrown at windmills by China. This is yet one more way Obama makes us less secure in the name of enhancing security. As the argument goes, it would be intolerable if we fail to achieve the status of being the "world leader" of things that don't work in the way that a modern society requires its energy sources to work. That of course makes no sense.

First, recall that China and others are throwing billions at making windmills and solar panels for the simple reason that rich countries have said they'll spend many billions more buying the things regardless of their relative performance or economics. They already cleaned up under Obama's stimulus and can hardly wait for more. In fact, on top of all of President Bush's reckless spending in a vain attempt to buy peace with environmentalists, President Obama vowed to spend another $150 billion over ten years pushing these dogs.[42] So you see how easy it is to look simple to others around the world in our desperation to appear sophisticated.

Mindless "world leader"-type talking points have come to the fore in an achingly stupid progression. Rich countries find themselves having created a bit of a monster by claiming that the weather is now our historical responsibility. We vow to "do something," only to find that actually reducing carbon dioxide emissions—which are a reasonable proxy for economic activity—is really quite difficult. The "planned recession strategy,"[43] as one internal briefing paper in the United Kingdom put it, isn't popular with the voters. So in the face of such political challenges, we commit to spend hundreds of billions of dollars on symbolic gestures—what is called "green technology." This translates into mandates to generate a certain percentage of one's electricity in a certain way.

So, rich countries promise to spend mind-boggling billions of dollars on windmills, not conditioned on their actual ability to deliver, be cost effective, or otherwise pass tests that the private sector generally applies to decisions requiring large sums of its own money. China, India, and other nations may be relatively backward in some respects, but they most assuredly are not stupid. They, in turn, promise to do their part and build the things to sell us.

The media leap to their feet, swooning over how *even China and India are going big into windmills, so you know it's a good idea!* In turn, American politicians, feeling the heat, promise to reclaim their status as "the world leader" in windmill technology because, suddenly, being the "world leader" in something—anything—is, in its own right, very desirable. The newspapers soon report, with slightly less fanfare, that the mafia have moved in to windmill syndicates, just like in Europe.[44] Mobsters and clever countries love large sums of guaranteed revenue.

Also, notice this strange desire among our thinking class to be the "world leader" in something just for the sake of being the world leader. Now, I wasn't under the impression that we had identity crises like certain small European nations who once, an awfully long time ago, were really quite the global players. I suppose this is no more absurd than demanding we move terrorists captured on foreign battlefields or elsewhere on foreign soil to New York for a criminal trial so we can show the world what a shining example we are.[45] Both reflect a sad desire to pose and gain the approval of those in other nations who, generally, will never approve.

A related and increasingly grating talking point is that *unless we mandate (something uneconomical) here, why, our domestic producers will be left behind!* This assumes that one need harmfully mandate the frivolous in order for one's companies to be "world leaders" in frivolity. Yet, for example, and apparently as part of his sales pitch that we need to follow their lead, Germany's ambassador to the United States touted at a 2009 Washington dinner how the leading supplier of solar panels for his own country's fetish happens to be an American company.[46] Not that this means the jobs producing their expensive and most of the time useless gadgets will therefore necessarily be in America (or Germany).[47]

This anecdote unwittingly debunked the domestic lament (employed to mandate more expensive energy here) that, unless we hobble ourselves with a national windmill mandate, why, we might get shut out of being a world-leading windmill manufacturer. And for some reason, policymakers aren't throwing lobbyists making this argument out of their office. Apparently, windmills are a strategic and critical industry.

But—and pardon me for asking—if we're not a world-leading windmill power, so what? And, if we were, how does that make it worth doing? Further, is this not the ultimate proof that there is not a substantive argument anywhere to be found for such boondoggles?

History actually is checkered with policymakers running off vainly with billions of taxpayer dollars in the earnest pursuit of "world leadership" in something that they've decided simply must be led, and by them. For example, a European policy-wonk colleague of mine noted in an email, responding to my pointing out the German ambassador's tale and soliciting his experience with the argument, (insert sarcasm font)

> Yes, the United States has paid the price for failing to develop technologies that other governments subsidized, like the Concorde (UK and France), and the UK's Advanced Passenger Train, civil Hovercraft, Magnox nuclear reactors, in fact just about anything invested in by its National Research and Development Corporation in the '60s and '70s. Such "good ideas" fail with the same frequency as the "bad" ones. Putting a networked computer terminal in every home is a good idea. Building Minitel,[48] however, probably hurt France's chances of becoming an Internet hub.

Closer to home, as Gregg Easterbrook pointed out in the pages of none other than the *New York Times*,

> Government is good at basic research, poor at commercial-scale applied energy technology. The Synthetic Fuels Corporation, a heavily subsidized attempt begun by the Carter administration to manufacture gasoline substitutes,

flopped without ever producing a marketable gallon. The Energy Department has also financed such overpriced, unrealistic projects as the MOD-5B, a wind turbine that weighed 470 tons and stood 20 stories tall: it looked like a gigantic propeller intended to push the earth to a new star system. It ended up being sold for scrap.[49]

Get used to it.

Remember, with exceptions regarding marginal efficiencies, windmills, solar panels, and other centuries-old "new" technologies have come pretty much as far as they're going to go, and in the absence of breakthrough battery storage technology, their role is clearly limited. There are no windmill breakthroughs imaginable. Private equity markets are actually pretty good at finding winners. Government isn't. In fact, government inherently is drawn to losers, always politically choosing its targets for support and always when there is insufficient interest among people who are investing their own money.

What's really going on here is this: U.S. rent-seekers, demanding that we adopt Euro-style inefficiencies, simply adopted the classic Euro-style argument (put forth by a political gathering desperate to find an identity) of needing to claim world leadership in something—*anything*—whatever it might be. This is the same way the Europeans arrived on the climate kick: many pols I have spoken to and read admit they simply selected an issue on which to claim "leadership" and to distinguish themselves from the United States.

In serious times like these, or frankly otherwise, we have no need for policy based on such vacuous advocacy. So maybe we won't be among the world leaders in an industry that has proven it cannot compete without government mandates and subsidies. We should instead—at least in happier times—be content to watch *others* pour money down this rat hole and, where we find comparative advantage, contribute whatever we can make profitably. But we need not imitate the behavior. Older countries should be better at older technologies, and wind's age was many moons ago. We might as well aspire to remain competitive with French guillotine craftsmen as waste billions on keeping our windmills, ahem, "modern."

As Steve Hayward of American Enterprise Institute wrote on the blog of AEI's magazine, *The American*:

> The 1960s "war on poverty" finds its analogue today in what might be called the "war on carbon," and the endless clichés that government spending for, and heavy regulation of, the energy sector will deliver millions of "green jobs" probably ought to be called "the Great Energy Society...." And sure enough, the old "send a man to the moon" cliché has made a comeback. Al Gore has invoked it, saying we can "re-power" America with non-carbon energy in 10 years, just like the Apollo project put a man on the moon inside a decade.
>
> No one ever seems to ask a simple question about moon landing analogies: Why did we quit going to the moon? Because, to use the environmentalists' favorite term, it was unsustainable. Proving that something is technically achievable, whether moon rockets or hydrogen cars, doesn't mean that it is affordable or economical. We quit going to the moon because it wasn't cheap, and probably not the best use of scientific and engineering talent, either.[50]

Sure, we can spend a fortune on things the idea of which make elites feel really good. But none of this changes that phony markets created by government fiat rather than demand only continue the transfer of wealth from the private sector. These industries are essentially wards of the state and, it turns out, cost jobs both in opportunity costs—the private sector creates twice as many jobs for every "green job" the state[51] creates using confiscated wealth—but also directly, when industry flees because energy is now unreliable, too expensive, or both.

Such reckless squandering of resources leaves us more vulnerable, not less.

CHAPTER 10

HTS OUT:
DIM BULBS
EE BLACKOUTS

ously warned: "We can't drive our SUVs

we want and keep our homes on 72

..and then just expect that other coun-

hat's not leadership. That's not going to

who has control of your thermostat, what

is that he is going to coerce or force you

own ideological and political purposes.

zar" Carol Browner's slip to *US News* of the goal to "get to a system where an electric company will be able to hold back some of the power so that maybe your air conditioner won't operate at its peak.'" "You'll still be able to cool your house," she continued, if only as much as Browner, Obama, and company believe is necessary and appropriate. Utilities would exercise the newfound right to hold back some of the power if they were made to by law, or by physical scarcity.

Both Browner and Obama are here speaking about *de facto* or *de jure* energy shortages. The *de jure* part can be overturned after political resistance. The *de facto* shortages, however, are not so easily undone and therefore are a critical part of their agenda.

In that same formulation, Obama also set forth the dangerous belief that leadership is demonstrated by asking other countries what's okay. And what they have told him is that it is only okay if we adopt energy-scarcity policies now served up alternately in the name of jobs, national security, global warming, and the old fall-back: it's just the right thing to do.

Having his taxpayer-funded White House thermostat on "orchid" (according to his own staff) is, well, somehow acceptably different.[3] I get that part. But despite his crowd's insistence that we drive, say, little electric cars—even as Obama openly scoffs at the notion that a man with his unique needs arrange for even hybrid transportation— they have no idea what that means other than that you would plug it in. To the wall. Where electricity comes from, apparently.

The truth is, moving the transportation sector onto the electricity system is the last thing we can manage, because we can't produce the juice we are projected to need in coming years.[4] This will yield bitter fruit when the economy recovers to a significant degree. As Senator James Inhofe implored his colleagues on the Senate floor,

> The need to grow our domestic energy supply is clear. The Energy Information Administration projects that our demand for electricity will increase by 26 percent by the year 2030, requiring nearly 260 gigawatts of new electricity gen-

eration. Every source will need to grow and produce more energy to meet that demand. Curtis Frasier, executive vice president of Americas Shell Gas & Power, recently warned that the recession could be masking a global energy shortage: "When the economy returns, we're going to be back to the energy crisis," he said. "Nothing has been done to solve that crisis. We've got a huge mountain to climb."[5]

The Left's disregard for consequences seems worse now than ever. Who can in good faith deny that Team Obama appears oddly, or else consciously, blind to the continued and expanding threat from the fiscal house of cards which they are building ever higher with each successive "stimulus" and "jobs" bill? Cap-and-trade and other "green" tomfoolery will only worsen our economic situation. Yet they persist in their assault on the engine that drives our economy: the delivery of energy. The power to create is bound up in our very way of life. But the mere word "energy" drives too many Americans to sleep—unless it's buried in solipsistic calls to "energy independence" or "reduce our dependence on foreign sources of energy!" So to get your attention, let me just call energy what it is: freedom.

Americans treasure their freedom, and so hair-shirt environmentalism flopped with Jimmy Carter, prompting the new rallying cry, "save the planet." Under Obama, in the face of cooling global temperatures, this morphed into a campaign touting national security concerns. This shift in strategy requires a very limited short-term public memory, as the "global cooling" panic of the 1970s or the greens' rather tenuous history of concern for national security would reveal this newfound concern as disingenuous. The consequences of engineering energy poverty, of the lights going out, are of the economic, national security, and of course human varieties.

It is time for the Left to begin considering the ancient philosoph-
ical conundrum of what happens when the dog catches the car he's
chasing. The anti-energy movement channeled by Obama has a long
history of making demands and instituting hare-brained policies
reflecting no apparent thought about practical implications. America gets half (49 percent) of its electricity from coal and sits on top of
about 250 years of supply at present levels of use.[6] But we are increasingly unable to burn it and are now racing toward a regime where
that's all but illegal. The rest of our electricity comes from disfavored
nuclear (19.4 percent), natural gas (21.5 percent), and supposedly
anachronistic dams (6 percent).[7]

Windmills and solar power together account for something like
0.5 percent of our electricity production. "Renewables" *in toto*
amount to maybe 2.3 percent, including twelve categories of sources,
not just wind and solar but wood, biomass (excrement and stuff that
grows), and so on.[8] Consequently, Obama's earnest vow to double
their use in his first term is climatically meaningless, although the
stuff of exorbitant expense.[9] Even that is a pipe dream due to the
reality that Obama's allies have ensured that nothing could be built
for years because of endless litigation and delays in issuing permits.
Our overall reliance on coal and gas, even after thirty years of
bureaucratic and legal war against them, tells you how futile the pursuit of "renewables" is. Obama's larger promise of mandating that 25
percent of our electricity come from these niche or boutique con-
tributors (to take economic roost on his successor's watch), is just
plain madness.

Very much like us, Europe gets about 50 percent of its electricity
from coal, and even more from nuclear (as much as 30 percent overall).[10] But its push for renewables—what I'll call "clean energy," as
that is Obama's 2010 catch-phrase to mask the agenda—leaves Euro-

pean residential customers paying about twice what we do.[11] Researcher Richard Soultanian of NUS Consulting Group, USA, writes that the eight most expensive electricity markets are European.[12]

Recall also that Europe's brand of social democracy has left it with its share of the super-wealthy, and an enormous indigent class that they rhetorically pretend social democracy has cured, separated by a middle class generally poorer than ours. As such, on the whole, Europe's electricity prices are even more punitive than they appear in direct comparison, as the top two classes pay for the indigents. Also recall that some governments like Spain set the price far below the cost of production, thereby hiding actual cost factors and kicking a ballooning "rate deficit" down the road to future ratepayers and taxpayers to pay off.[13]

Europe is hardly finished eroding its citizens' freedoms through restricting access to energy, either, but is desperately trying to tighten the screws ever more. Of course, the European public might finally choke on internal government admissions, such as the UK's "planned recession" global warming strategy[14] asserting that the next phase of "green energy" mandates may cost seventeen times any benefits it might produce.[15]

Not all EU countries are being quite so persistently reckless as Spain and the UK. One can only imagine the horror on the *New York Times* editor's face when reading his staffer's story on our environmental superiors succumbing to the crushing reality of green posturing, in an April 2008 article:

> Over the next five years, Italy will increase its reliance on coal to 33 percent from 14 percent. Power generated by [Italian utility] Enel from coal will rise to 50 percent.

And Italy is not alone in its return to coal. Driven by rising demand, record high oil and natural gas prices, concerns over energy security and an aversion to nuclear energy, European countries are expected to put into operation about 50 coal-fired plants over the next five years, plants that will be in use for the next five decades.

In the United States, fewer new coal plants are likely to begin operations, in part because it is becoming harder to get regulatory permits and in part because nuclear power remains an alternative. Of 151 proposals in early 2007, more than 60 had been dropped by the year's end, many blocked by state governments. Dozens of others are stuck in court challenges.[16]

Ignore the silly claims about the availability of nuclear power being a reason we're issuing permits for fewer coal plants here. We have not permitted a new nuke here in thirty years. The only real energy option we currently have is running what we've got a little harder, a strategy with limitations obvious to most, if not *New York Times* reporters. The hard truth is that Obama's EPA is already using the finding that global warming "endangers" the planet to impose onerous demands on energy producers. At this writing, the Environmental Protection Agency has refused to give permits to coal-fired plants in the Navajo Nation, in Kentucky, and in Arkansas, claiming the very idea of building a coal plant showed that the parties hadn't considered Best Available Control Technology (BACT).[17]

Best Available Control Technology (BACT) is a pollution control standard mandated by the Clean Air Act. It is the standard that the Environmental Protection Agency uses to determine how much of a particular "pollutant" will be allowed from a site and how it will be controlled. One way it is enforced is through "fuel switching capability"—the ability of a manufacturing establishment to use alternative sources of energy if they become available.

Here's the rub: the Environmental Protection Agency said this about state of the art coal production, with the latest in pollution controls; there was no technology more advanced. Obama's EPA simply declared that, despite Congress never having made this enormous leap (and the Environmental Protection Agency still hasn't formalized any such regulations), carbon dioxide must be controlled. As natural gas emits less carbon dioxide than coal when burned, per EPA, then using natural gas to generate electricity would be the Best Available Control Technology for coal-fired power.

Just imagine when they get their agenda in place. Stock up on candles.

So, new coal power actually is less likely in the United States because of an ideological jihad against its use that even Europe, in practice, has not bested. Of course, natural gas wasn't even used for electricity generation until the war on coal gained traction. Moving us off coal onto something that so many industries use as "feedstocks"—raw material in their manufacturing processes—was foolhardy. That strategy directly raised the cost of electricity as well as the price of manufactured products as massively increased demand for natural gas resulted in often serious price spikes.

As *E&E Daily* wrote,

> Congress has long been undecided about where natural gas should fit into the energy-supply pie. Coal has dominated as a fuel source for electricity generators. More than 100 nuclear plants supply about 20 percent of U.S. power, and natural gas supplies about 20 percent.

Industry estimates and policymakers' assumptions about gas supply and its role in cleaning the air shift decade to decade. At the end of the 1970s and into the 1980s, gas was considered a precious commodity with a short, 10-year domestic supply. But starting in the late 1990s and through much of the past decade, utilities built gas-burning power plants to the exclusion of coal-fired plants to help them comply with clean-air mandates.[18]

Yet now that they've moved us onto gas, green groups aren't shy about insisting that it, too, fails their test and can only be a "bridge" to as yet undiscovered breakthrough energy sources that will carry the load. Apparently, since you have to punch holes in the ground to get natural gas, no amount of economic harm can justify its use to the enviros.

STUPID IS AS STUPID DOES

Through a combination of taxes, regulation, and state-enabled litigation, the anti-energy establishment has curtailed our freedom by blocking new energy production, including nuclear and even potentially spectacular sources of natural gas. Dams are simply out of the question. When existing dams are broken down due to age and/or pressure from greens, the (rarely) proposed replacements are blocked by environmentalists and allies in state bureaucracies—even with all of the bells and whistles the greens have come up with, such as "fish migration and passage technical assistance." This just happened in Ohio, a state as unlikely as any other to be self-sustaining with wind power, uniquely unsuited for solar power, but rich in coal—which they're supposed to leave in the ground.[19]

Incidentally, you'll notice the greens' somewhat challenged argument: coal states need to get off coal; but they won't be able to produce the other stuff, either. This is standard absurdity, but when it comes time to renew permits or build replacement capacity, the joke's no longer funny. The lights will go out and people suffer.

Instead of coal, nuclear, gas, dams, or even windmills, it seems we are to just rely on electricity instead.

Good luck with that. Anyone here speak Italian? Because before wising up, Italy confronted precisely this dilemma, which made itself known when a tree fell on a power line from Switzerland one winter day, blacking Italy out. Its effect was felt in hospitals, roads, and commerce, which was nearly brought to a standstill.[20] All because the Italians were too pure to smash atoms or build coal-fired power plants. Someone else could do that.

Except that they might not. Those others Italy depends on to export nuclear power, like France and Switzerland, have their own political issues to confront, which they may do in ways that don't conform with Italy's interests. For example, the French economy will ultimately need the power that they have been sending Italy. This is predictable.

As is the case if a tree falls, a year is dry and the dams produce little, and so on. California and a few other states have embraced this idea of just relying on others to produce electricity for them. But if everyone passes the buck to their neighbors, then no one produces energy.

Electricity and total energy use are closely tied to economic growth. When our economy grows, so does the demand for energy. A lack of one ensures a lack of the other. Our policymakers not only are not listening, but the ones in power have a plan to take advantage of this crisis —which will only make it worse.

THE REGICIDE OF OLD KING COAL

The United States is called the Saudi Arabia of coal, referencing the estimated centuries' worth of domestic supply. Coal can be turned into a gas or liquid to burn, too, expanding the realm of its applications. Nothing so abundant can be allowed by the greens, however, so the energy source representing our energy security is under furious assault.

On Christmas Eve 2009, green sympathizers received a gift via the media. As *Climate Wire* stated, "The end of 2009 marks another year in which utilities abandoned new coal-fired power plants at a breathtaking pace. Environmentalists say it signals a trend, and they smell victory in their ongoing war on coal. . . . The coal slowdown came as the Sierra Club, along with many other green groups, battled new plants vociferously at protests and in courtrooms."[21] David Victor, a professor of international relations and Pacific studies at the University of California, San Diego, said that "essentially no new plants are gaining approval." With coal by far the single largest payload for freight rail, even planned rail expansions have been shelved as a result of this campaign.[22]

This disgraceful campaign to bury coal forever has the Obama administration's aggressive participation. Candidate Obama famously boasted to the *San Francisco Chronicle* editorial board that he would "bankrupt" coal. Killing our domestic coal industry is surely a principal reason Obama brought in radicals like Carol Browner and Van Jones through the back door of phony "Czar" positions with direct access to the president. The inescapable fact is that their shared climate agenda seeks to impose energy poverty on our country. The first step is to finally kill Old King Coal.

It doesn't matter that we burn coal more cleanly than we could ever have imagined possible. The environmentalists find the mere act of taking it from the ground as offensive as they find the freedoms it enables.

The Obama administration's close ally, the Sierra Club, now boasts of having killed 100 planned coal-fired power plants since 2001.[23] This is out of what Sierra says was 150 total plants slated for development. Sierra Club attorney Bruce Nilles came out and told *National Journal* that Sierra's litigation strategy is not merely to stop new coal-based generation, but now also to retire "the existing coal fleet." With some help. "We are gearing up to show very strong support for the administration," he said, citing the Environmental Protection Agency's efforts to stop certain mining practices and make it more difficult for power plants to obtain permits to operate.[24] The greens are clear that they expect Obama's "cap-and-trade" rationing scheme will do precisely that trick for them.[25]

One Sierra Club attorney and frequent spokesman acknowledged in a closed conference call his belief that lawmakers would never let the lights go out through anything directly attributable to their own actions (which, of course, doesn't take inaction into account). Therefore, Sierra's counsel concludes that turning the lights off is understood to be the job of the pressure groups.

In keeping with this, Sierra soon announced a campaign to shut down power plants which provide heat, air conditioning, computing power, and other services on sixty college campuses. College campuses, of course, are generally hotbeds of mindless Sierra Club-style environmentalism, so it's fitting in its own way and might be one area in which we could wish them success. Nothing might help turn around such a detached constituency as faculty lounges than having them try to get by on windmills.

It seems relevant to note that these green groups are indispensible to and beneficiaries of people heavily invested in either making traditional energy sources more expensive or regulating them out of the picture altogether. For example, in late 2009 we learned that a David Gelbaum regretted that he could no longer fork over millions to the Sierra Club's campaigns, facing tough times of his own due to being so heavily invested in struggling alternative energy projects. In the letter communicating his despair, Gelbaum claimed to have anonymously given Sierra Club $47.7 million from 2005 through 2009. According to the *Wall Street Journal*, "Mr. Gelbaum, a major donor to the Democratic Party, didn't identify the clean-energy investments, but Quercus Trust, the fund that Mr. Gelbaum runs, was down almost 57% over the 18 months to late November, according to PlacementTracker."[26]

So Sierra has received millions each year from this gentleman and, we should assume, others like him who are banking on the success of alternative energy. Their hope is certainly going to be that Sierra's anti-fossil fuel campaign will so greatly increase the cost of energy to regular Americans that their investments in alternative energy become economic. This parallels the aforementioned Enron strategy.

Any enemy of the United States would dream of shutting down our electricity generation and transmission system. In fact, the Chinese already plan for that contingency, a key component of what's called asymmetrical warfare.[27] Yet, for all intents and purposes, this is also what the greens seek, although you would never know this from the treatment their proposals receive in the media.

Sierra's line is that no new coal plants will be built, and anyone who invested in building them would be a fool. Meaning, don't bother. Don't dare. *Be a shame if we came after you, too*, isn't stated, most likely because it doesn't need to be.

And their tactics are clearly working. The one hundredth plant blocked, per Sierra Club, was the Desert Rock Energy Company facility in the Four Corners (New Mexico) area, on Navajo land. Following an increasingly familiar script, the Environmental Protection Agency issued the air quality permit to the 1,500-megawatt plant, only to have the greens lead a lawsuit to block it. As has also become a familiar scenario, once the Obama administration was ensconced, the Agency decided to rescind the permit. That's how we spell s-w-e-e-t-h-e-a-r-t, as in "deal." It should also be the end of the project, since the green groups have raised the projected costs to bring the plant on line to $4 billion.[28]

The Desert Rock example was just one of three large power plants planned by Sithe Global Power, whose investors Sierra and a double-digit gaggle of greenie groups went after.[29] The other two planned facilities blocked were the 750-megawatt Toquop plant near Mesquite, Nevada, and the 300-megawatt River Hill waste-coal plant in Clearfield County, Pennsylvania.[30] The latter cleans up waste piles by putting the stuff to use. Bad, very bad.

According to the *Arizona Republic*, Sierra casualty #100, Desert Rock, would have been "fueled by coal from a new mine, bringing more jobs and revenue to the Navajos." And now it won't. The greens are also pushing the Environmental Protection Agency to impose new costs on the Navajo Generating Station near Page, Arizona, which the Navajos say will lead to its closure. Sierra's spokesman reassured the paper of the righteousness of the cause. "If we want to take care of global warming, coal power plants are the low-hanging fruit. We can't just continue with business as usual if we want to protect the planet."[31] But stopping this and every other coal-fired plant in America would have no detectable impact on climate, according to any alarmist computer model. So here the greens again showed their compassion for minorities, as they did in 2005 when a nearby coal mine closed to sell emission credits generated by its being shut down.

The then-Navajo Nation president Joe Shirley Jr., who is also an anti-nuke activist, reminded the reporter that his people suffer from more than 50 percent unemployment—85 percent in some areas—and have average annual incomes under $15,000. He complained that they have been victimized by greens forcing closure of a tribal sawmill and helping to shut down the Mohave Generating Station near Laughlin, Nevada, that received coal from Navajo land. He told the *Republic*, "They just shut us down, put more people into impoverishment. You want me to accept that?"[32] No. But our president does. Well, actually he's going to put you all to work soon in temporary jobs building windmills. If you join a union.

In fact, the spin on this is that a wind farm is indeed projected on Navajo land, with short-term installation contracts possibly going to Navajos (or possibly not), and maybe even some of the far smaller number of jobs in maintenance and administration that research shows are the only ones not inherently temporary.[33] Nice trade. Get used to it.

The earnest and glum greens' sales pitch is along the lines of "got wind?," in what seems a bit of a parody of a PETA ad haranguing you to subsist on tofu and the like (if decidedly without the frolicking, scantily-clad models). Pleading to swap out coal for "renewables" contraptions offers a spectacularly false choice, as solar panels can no more replace coal-fired power than a tender, juicy filet can match a plate of sprouts, no matter how "organic" the hippie at the counter insists they may be.

It's a fool's errand, which the greens seemingly recognize by also working to substitute their noted investment acumen (paging David Gelbaum) and industry expertise for that of the people whose own capital is actually at stake. They regularly if incredibly claim that they're just doing a favor for the energy companies' shareholders, as the greens have run the numbers and it turns out that all electricity production from more efficient sources really would lose money. They swear.

These aren't harmless teen pranks, especially with the mounting evidence that the greens are working in tandem with Team Obama. As the Sierra Club's 100-plants boast indicates, generation has been blocked all over the country, threatening our security and way of life, with the full and often active participation of the greens' man in the White House. One of the groups involved writes on its web site: "The EPA, under the Obama Administration, is quite clearly shifting gears," citing a litany of Obama efforts to impede energy supply. "These regulatory interpretations and legislative actions are going to make it more difficult for projects like Desert Rock to be permitted, financed and constructed."[34] You all must be so proud.

This is but one approach to make it harder for coal operators to tap the capital markets, which itself is just one of the greens' tactics in stifling our energy infrastructure, the obvious result of which collapse would be the state rushing in to, ahem, save us. It is the Left's "Cloward-Piven" strategy from the 1960s—creating a crisis by overwhelming an existing system through their demands and schemes, then calling for crisis-type state intervention and usurpation in the face of system failure—which Obama clearly studied as part of his "community organizing" background.[35] Rather than not letting a crisis go to waste, as Rahm Emanuel has urged,[36] why not just create the crisis in the first place?

A campaign by Rainforest Action Network and other international pressure groups reveals a related tactic. They are tag-teaming with Obama to stop banks from lending to businesses engaged in what is called mountaintop coal removal. This has caused such pathetic operators as Bank of America to run shrieking from the practice (losing my banking and investment business to the more freedom-friendly BB&T in the process).[37] Add to this the pressure campaigns against utilities to not buy that coal. Ultimately the cost of capital for energy projects rises and then, the greens hope, is cut off altogether. Soon it will be obvious the state needs to be in the electricity business.

As the *Washington Times* reported, just in time for Christmas, Pittsburgh-based coal company CONSOL Energy announced it would lay off nearly 500 of its West Virginia workers after a judge suspended its permits, though noting that this outcome did not result "from any wrong-doing on the part of the mining companies." CONSOL's CEO Nicholas J. DeIuliis said he was forced to do this because, on top of the economy's problems, green activists were driving costs up and using bureaucracies and the courts to block projects. He stated: "It is challenging enough to operate our coal and gas assets in the current economic downturn without having to contend with a constant stream of activism in rehashing and reinterpreting permit applications that have already been approved or in the inequitable oversight of our operations." The constant assaults also made them an unreliable vendor, and DeIuliis said this was causing potential customers to shy away from doing business with them.[38]

Surely you will be surprised to learn that the Sierra Club was among the groups behind the legal challenge CONSOL credited for its decision to let these workers go. Stung by the attention drawn to their success at such a time of economic uncertainty and, of course, time of year, the greens actually waved off credit for doing precisely what is their objective—killing these and other coal jobs. No, the greens said,[39] it wasn't them, but a big bad coal company that cynically blamed them wrongly for layoffs the company wanted to undertake. Layoffs the greens actively seek and celebrate, and that

Obama has promised are his objective, too (unless he envisions lay-off-free bankruptcies?).

So, greens, were all of the other jobs you've killed mere accidents?

Obama hurried to jettison a Bush administration rule covering the mountaintop extraction practice as being "legally defective," asking a court to let the administration revise things more to its liking. The court tossed this stunt as impermissible freelancing.[40] Nonetheless, Team Obama not only moved quickly to rescind the 2-year-old permit for the ongoing Spruce Fork mountaintop operation, the largest projected project in West Virginia, but vowed to rewrite the rules anyway. (The Environmental Protection Agency's suspicious behavior bordered on the ostentatious as it claimed "new information" as its rationale for doing so.[41]) As the *Times* noted, "CONSOL Energy's political problems are not unique to the mining industry, which has suffered under the Obama Administration."[42]

The Senate Republicans on the Environment and Public Works Committee (EPW) wrote in a report released January 14, 2010, that the Environmental Protection Agency's "approach is both odd and troubling, considering that the Spruce permit was issued in 2007 after a 10-year process, which culminated in a detailed environmental impact statement."[43] The report of the Environmental Protection Agency's actions noted that the Spruce Fork mine was projected to provide 253 mining jobs and 298 indirect jobs; coal from the mine would generate electricity for 74,500 homes for each year the mine was in operation.

Republican EPW counsel Matt Hite said the EPA has held up 190 mining permits for ongoing review, leaving companies that have made substantial investments in coal development unable to move ahead with their projects.[44] In fact, as *E&E News* reported, "The regulatory push has had an impact on West Virginia coal production, which fell more than 11 percent in the past year, the federal Energy Information Agency said."[45]

My colleague William Yeatman writes that it turns out that Obama's EPA

> is intervening on behalf of a bug. Recent EPA research suggests that discharge from "fills"—piles of dirt and rock moved in the process of mining coal—hurts populations of mayflies, an insect that typically lives for less than a day. Other research suggests that populations of hardier insect species grow in the wake of the mayfly's decline, but this doesn't deter the EPA. During testimony before the Senate last summer, John Pomponio, an EPA official with jurisdiction over surface-coal-mining permitting in Appalachia, said that it is "critical that EPA re-invigorate its oversight role" in light of the mayfly study. In practice, a "re-invigorated oversight role" means that President Obama's EPA has outlawed surface mining practices that had been acceptable for decades. In this business environment—beholden to capricious and arbitrary EPA rules—coal-mining companies can't raise capital. After all, you can't mine without a permit.[46]

For this and many other reasons, Massey Energy CEO Don Blankenship has said the Obama team is actively trying to drive coal under, and to say otherwise is "either naïveté on the politicians' part or just looking after themselves."[47] In fact, even liberals who understand the potential damage are speaking against Obama's radicalism. Democrat Senator Jay Rockefeller of West Virginia slammed the Environmental Protection Agency for the threat to retroactively yank the Spruce Fork permit—the first such retroactive move since the Clean Water Act was passed in 1972. Rockefeller cited this, according to greenie outlet *E&E News*, "as proof that the Obama administration is being less than honest about its support for coal. Rockefeller said EPA Administrator Lisa Jackson was insincere at a recent House hearing in which she said the administration was not anti-coal. 'I think she proved it by undoing a permit that they'd already approved,'" or, rather, which had been approved in 2007 before this gang got to town.[48]

Later, at a hearing on Obama's budget, Rockefeller again slammed Obama for paying only lip service to supporting coal, while acting against mining to the harm of Rockefeller's constituents.[49] *E&E News* continued to report, "Rockefeller said his concerns snowballed when he considered recent U.S. EPA decisions on mountaintop-removal coal mining and work on regulations to control greenhouse gas emissions across the economy."[50] One of those factors included the EPA announcing it would begin second-guessing state permit authorizations for the first time, apparently circumventing a court order in doing so, clearly dedicating themselves to back out of "mountaintop's" more than 10 percent of U.S. coal production.[51]

Toward that end, during a Friday afternoon burial-ground for news announcements—in fact on Friday, September 11, leaving every chance it would be crowded out of the news—the Administration announced it was sneaking back in to look at and possibly rescind eighty such permits in West Virginia, Kentucky, Ohio, and Tennessee. The Environmental Protection Agency sniffs that maybe these permits violate the Clean Water Act and require "enhanced" review—or what the Agency euphemizes as an "enhanced coordination procedures."[52] And the greens defer credit to the mayfly.

Surface-mined coal offends the greens and obviously the Obama administration, providing a visible reminder of the activity, until the mined land is reclaimed and restored. According to Penn State's Dr. Frank Clemente, "The increasing availability of surface coal has been the prime mover in allowing electricity consumption in the United States to grow from 1,535 billion kWh in 1970 to over 4,100 billion kWh in 2008."[53]

All of which is to say that greens believe surface mining in particular must be brought down. As one industry player noted to me, the greens have already perfected the use of "section 404" (of the Clean Water Act [CWA], the "wetlands" provision) to engage the U.S. Army Corps of Engineers to block surface mining. If the industry tries to mine underground, they are blocked through the Mine Safety and Health Administration (MSHA). That "wetlands" provision is actually a key tool used to regulate surface mining, extended to the point of absurdity over the decades by activist bureaucrats, greens, and courts. Now, with Obama administration cover, the Left seeks to enable full-blown abuse by formally striking the statutory limit to the federal statute and its regulatory powers of covering only "navigable waterways," which has decreasingly afforded judicial restraint since the provision's 1972 adoption. Then came Supreme Court decisions in 2001 and 2006 ruling that "only navigable, permanent water bodies merited federal protection,"[54] indicating that sanity might soon be returned to this grandest of all regulatory overreaches.

Apparently terrified by the prospect that the law might be implemented merely as written, congressional liberals have seized their moment of complete control and are pushing legislation simply writing the word "navigable" out of the Clean Water Act. This would grant authority to the federal government over effectively all water in the United States, and strike a further blow to an already beleaguered mining industry by inserting the Environmental Protection Agency into more of its operations. Don't leave your hose on, now, if you don't want your driveway subjected to the Agency's "enhanced review." But to then also allow EPA authority over all waterways, designed so broadly, would invite the Agency in to regulate activities with purely local (intrastate) consequences. With surface coal mining among the environmentalists' number one targets, they surely intend to use this overreach to slow and ultimately stop surface coal production.

Fighting back against Obama's war on coal, Senator Inhofe decried the administration efforts to, in effect, "restrict local economic development in the Appalachian region." He charged in a statement this "is putting 77,000 good-paying jobs at risk, particularly those in the Appalachian coal region, where communities rely on mountaintop mining to fund their schools and other services."[55]

The greens getting saddled with blame for what they are clearly trying to accomplish would devastate them throughout a region where they actively recruit locals to work against their own interests. The Appalachian coal region includes Ohio, West Virginia, Virginia, and Pennsylvania and so is politically crucial for Obama's reelection chances. Media outlets report tension within the green movement over some of them having an itchy trigger finger for using the Endangered Species Act to require more reviews before issuing mine permits. Other green groups want to avoid turning the locals against them for having killed more jobs, referencing a local bumper sticker that said, "Save a Coal Miner, Kill a Tree Hugger."[56]

Further, the impediments to building new plants have left some U.S companies' fleets of coal-burning utilities, which provide about 50 percent of our electricity, averaging forty years or more in age. As investments, this brings them right up to the end of their expected lives. The plants have already undergone significant upgrades, but litigation and regulation have ensured that even simple maintenance

operations can trigger expensive "new source review" provisions—
cited by one of the green groups quoted above as yet another tool to
impose the global warming agenda—making their continued operation uneconomical.[57] And the Obamaphiles have not yet run out of
tricks.

After a stalemate of many years, in late 2009, Gang Green suc-
ceeded in convincing several federal appeals courts to let them sue to
block power plants (or seek damages) on the grounds of nuisance—
the nuisance being that they change the climate. Forget the collapsing
science for the moment; it was also of insufficient concern to our
robed wonders that even if they accepted the alarmists' claims, no
remedy the court could ever conceive of would, according to anyone,
abate the alleged nuisance. No power plant can be tied to causing
climate change even under the alarmists' own fantastic computer-
modeled scenarios. It was a desperate legal claim, and it worked. So
far. This approach, increasingly pursued by activist state attorneys
general, is mostly a ploy to extract windmill and other political con-
cessions out of power generators as they slow-walk to the gallows,
bringing our economy and energy security with them.

One brazen example came to the attention of the *Wall Street Journal*, which described how:

> Connecticut Attorney General Richard Blumenthal and
> seven state AG allies plus New York City are suing American
> Electric Power and other utilities for a host of supposed eco-
> maladies. A native village in Alaska is suing Exxon and 23 oil
> and energy companies for coastal erosion. What unites these
> cases is the creativity of their legal chain of causation and
> their naked attempts at political intimidation. "My hope is
> that the court case will provide a powerful incentive for pol-

luters to be reasonable and come to the table and seek affordable and reasonable reductions," Mr. Blumenthal told the
trade publication Carbon Control News. "We're trying to
compel measures that will stem global warming regardless of
what happens in the legislature."[58]

The good news is that these cases raise the issue of whether there
really is a federal common law of "global warming." They are candi-
dates for review by the Supreme Court as early as 2010. That is always
a dicey proposition, especially after the Court's 5 to 4 decision in *Massachusetts* v. *EPA* to allow carbon dioxide be declared a pollutant, a
decision from which, as Justice Scalia noted in his dissent, "It follows
that everything airborne, from Frisbees to flatulence, qualifies as an
'air pollutant.'"[59] Still, this may be the principal case putting the corrupted and falsified "global warming" claims underlying most of this
campaign under scrutiny. (*Massachusetts* v. *EPA* turned on a reading
of the Clean Air Act, and did not actually rule on the science, about
which there was scandalously little discussion in oral argument.)[60]

These new cases will also give the justices a chance to un-ring the
bell to some degree, as a practical if not legal matter, on the Environmental Protection Agency's overreaching regulating spree unleashed
by *Massachusetts* v. *EPA*. Given that judges read the papers, too, as the
old saying goes, this must have come to their attention by now. Even
noted liberal constitutional law professor Laurence Tribe of Harvard
has weighed in with a paper signaling the disaster that the courts are
teeing up by making determinations that belong to the executive and
legislative functions of our government.[61]

Still, we must confront that the next green group litigation will be
abetted by an Obama Justice Department sure to largely sit these key
cases out when their duty is to properly limit the state's reach within

the laws. When they don't, they are certain to argue against, e.g., the Supreme Court hearing the matter. The bottom line remains, however, that if we are unable to replace the capacity the greens are chasing off the board with litigation, the consequence is clear. Spout all of the happy talk you like about windmills somehow replacing coal and pixie dust being just around the corner; the lights are still going to go out.

GO NUCLEAR

Like coal, nuclear power is a major contributor to America's electricity supply, with 104 domestic reactors providing one-fifth of our electricity. Nuclear power is also a greenie target even though one 1,000-megawatt nuclear plant built in lieu of burning coal supplants 110 rail cars of that fuel per day.[62] This fails to move the greens because, although they shriek that coal is the greatest threat facing mankind, it turns out that they really mean *except for all the others*. As we see, nuclear power, dams, tree farms, and windmills anyplace the elites must look at them every day are all greater threats than "the greatest" threat. What the Left really hate is access to energy. Obama apparently shares this worldview, if only because promoting it inherently promotes his statist objectives.

On the basis of such inanity, politicians have abrogated their responsibility to get tough on the biases in our system against increasing domestic energy production. No new reactors have been ordered since 1978.[63] Construction was halted on those that were in the works in the late 1980s, including some that were underway, because of an injury-free accident seized upon by the Left,[64] a timely Hollywood movie,[65] and a compliant press. Despite rumblings for years about a nuclear renaissance prompted by the anti-energy crowd's focus on carbon dioxide as the main excuse to block reliable coal, construction has yet to begin on any among the more than twenty new reactors presently sought in the United States.[66] Even those projects still in development are a small fraction of what Obama's economic analyses implausibly build into their assumptions to support a claim that "cap-and-trade" wouldn't devastate our economy.[67]

This aversion makes the United States a Luddite outlier. Quite the opposite of Obama's model Denmark, France pays the lowest-pre-tax price for electricity in Europe,[68] producing more than three-fourths of their electricity from (heavily subsidized) nuclear power.[69] France illustrates one way of using more practical politics to decide on a national energy mix, chosen in their case by people who live in a rough neighborhood. France decided to put frivolity aside, at least when it comes to the matter of whether to depend on an otherwise reliable energy source (coal) which sits under their soil in large quantities, but on the side of the track closest to certain neighbors with a dodgy past record of behavior. Thus was born responsible French energy policy.

Numerous coal-rich countries are also big on nukes. And of course island nations and those otherwise not blessed with abundant resources like Japan, Taiwan, and South Korea, have, like France, put adults in charge of energy decisions, for the most part, and decided that reliable nuclear power beats no power and other unpleasant alternatives.[70] As the *Washington Post* reported in late 2009, "The number of plants being built is double the total of just five years ago.... As opposition recedes, even nations that had long vowed never to build another nuclear plant—such as Sweden, Belgium and Italy— have recently done an about-face."[71] Meanwhile, our policymakers insincerely wring their hands about catch-phrase agendas like "global warming" and "energy independence" while ignoring what would be the easy solution in front of them, if they believed their own rhetoric.

In a 2010 letter to Obama's chief science advisor John Holdren (whose official title is Director, Office of Science & Technology Policy, Executive Office of the President, as discussed in chapter 3), about 225 signatories from among science, military, and other policy fields pleaded with him to advise the president to move nuclear power in the United States forward, stating that "the world is leaving us behind. At present, 58 new nuclear plants (including two fast reactors, one in Russia and one in India) are under construction in 14 countries. Of these, 20 are in China, 9 in Russia, 6 each in India and South Korea. Only one is in North America, and that is resumed work on a plant that was mothballed in 1988 when it was 80% finished."[72]

The continuing anti-nuclear hysteria underlying this madness here at home is best illustrated by Al Gore's testimony before Congress that "I've *been* to Chernobyl. I've *been* to Three Mile Island," failing to distinguish between the ravages of a typically Soviet catastrophe and, well, no harm.[73]

Nukes provide three-fourths of our CO_2-free electricity, with dams supplying most of the rest.[74] Even though a massive, if politically infeasible, crash construction course of nuclear power would put us in a state of Kyoto Protocol grace by reducing our emissions as the treaty seeks, the administration's view of the energy source, as summed up by the *Weekly Standard*'s Barnes, is "the policy is, in effect: Forget it."[75]

It is true that, while speaking in Prague, President Obama intoned, "We must harness the power of nuclear energy on behalf of our efforts to combat climate change, and to advance peace and opportunity for all people."[76] Yet, Obama's rhetoric runs starkly in contrast to his actions. His budget zeroed-out the Yucca Mountain program for storing spent nuclear material before the Nuclear Regulatory Commission could publish its long-awaited review for suitability, after the taxpayer and ratepayer combined to pour over $13 billion down the drain over more than two decades.[77]

Sure, the President's 2010 State of the Union address called for more nuclear power, seemingly to recruit support for his stalled climate change bill that would force us off hydrocarbons faster than replacement technology could be brought to market.[78] He then followed this up with a promise of loan guarantees for up to two reactors at one site in Georgia.

Here's a little reality check on this announcement that, by this, Obama is somehow, in the words of the White House, "making good on a commitment to meet Republians [sic] half way" on an energy bill (that being the current euphemism for the cap-and-trade, cap-and-dividend, whatever your label for hydrocarbon energy rationing).[79] Obama's spokesman followed this with "republicans who advocate for nuclear power have to recognize that we will not achieve a big boost in nuclear capacity unless we also create a system of incentives to make clean energy profitable," which, if you recall the discussion of his word choice there, is pretty sleazy. No, the White House is not calling nukes "clean energy." It is instead playing a little economic blackmail saying *you'll only get more if you go along with my green porkulus schemes.* The same schemes we have seen in these pages as tremendously economically harmful, not to mention their posing as cynical attempts to impose an ideological agenda through the back door.

But, again, Obama's own economic assumptions for cap-and-trade assume 100 new nukes in the next two decades. So despite these (and many more) loan guarantees being called for by the 2005 Energy Policy Act, he is really just engaging in spin, recasting a minor overture as fulfilling his own non-carbon energy promises. Barack vs. Barack, one calling for 100 nukes, the other countering after a year with loan guarantees for two. Who will win?

The truth is that Obama said to Iowa voters in October 2008 that he was "not a proponent" of nukes, and it is unlikely that anything changed his core position.[80] But for the obstacles Obama and his team ensure remain in place, spending the money to try to advance new nuclear power would finally seem to be an attractive bet. Demand is projected to rise just as political intervention is foreclosing other sources that could meet this demand. Meanwhile, this uncertainty is cited by the anti-energy set as all the more reason to take such decisions out of the private sector's hands and rest them with the all-knowing state.

Further affirmation of Obama's dangerous worldview is found in his handpicked FERC chairman Jon Wellinghoff, who as described earlier publicly blabbers ideological pap about our just not needing any more nuclear plants, despite the administration's vow to cease man-made carbon dioxide emissions almost entirely. Secretary of Energy Steven Chu, despite a history of fever-swampism, did promise senators that "Nuclear power... is going to be an important part of our energy mix," given that the 20 percent it provides represents the critical "baseload. So I think it is very important that we push ahead."[81]

Of course, this sort of temporary sanity came courtesy of the Senate confirmation process, which also unveiled the previously unknown strict constitutional constructionist, Sonya Sotomayor. So it may be that the administration's internal conflict is not as great as Chu's profession would indicate.

Obama's newfound, hedging support for nuclear power is contingent upon finding an "acceptable" place for and manner of storing spent fuel, or finally recycling it. Such slippery subjectivity ("sure, so long as it's 'safe' and 'acceptable'") is the way these folks have masked what is, in truth, an unyielding opposition to most energy projects and sources.

Waste must be stored. All existing plants store the waste on-site, and new ones will be able to do so, too. Geologic disposal—burying it—might reasonably be viewed as a reaction to over-hyped concerns, and fears have also been stoked about the waste traveling around the country on its way to disposal (encouraged by those who fret about terrorists stealing it). But Obama's mantra has also been a staple of the anti-energy greens for decades, tirelessly proving unable to find anything safe or any place or manner acceptable. With green activists having ensured for decades that reclamation of spent fuel from our civilian reactors was unlawful in the United States—despite their general obeisance to the mantra of "reduce, reuse, recycle" and the success of other nations in doing so—this is a cynical way to oppose something while claiming to support it.

William Tucker, who wrote *Terrestrial Energy*, points out that France requires simply the basement of one building to store the waste from its reactors, despite producing so much nuclear power that "[i]t provides 80 percent of the country's electricity at the lowest rates in Europe. It gives France the second-lowest level of carbon emissions in Europe, behind only Sweden, a smaller country that is half hydro, half nuclear. It provides France's third largest import [sic: he means export], behind only wine and agricultural products."[82] Which illustrates why the greens need to block reprocessing and ensure a waste problem. (Whether our long-overdue reprocessing facility finally going forward in South Carolina survives this administration awaits to be seen.)

Because every viable energy source must be headed off at every pass, the hits to nuclear keep on coming. Who can be surprised that the investors required for long-term, multi-billion dollar investments to build each plant are leery about any such commitments? First, the permitting process requires what you might call patience. The ten years it takes from the license application process until the plant becomes operational is, as Senator Inhofe pointed out in a speech on the Senate floor, "two and a half presidential administrations and five Congresses. Few companies will make these sizeable investments if they fear their projects will be left twisting in fickle political winds."[83] And that is the point of imposing these costly delays.

The bureaucracy's interminable delays in issuing permits to the backlog of applications to build new plants in the United States have prompted Republican Senators Inhofe and David Vitter to press for Government Accountability Office oversight of the regulators. In a letter to the GAO, the two wrote that, "At this time, the [Nuclear Regulatory] Commission (NRC) itself does not appear to have developed the detailed schedules of how the agency, especially the hearing boards and the Commission, will consider and issue decisions on combined Construction and Operating Licenses (COLs)."[84] In short, it appears that they're sitting on these applications.

Again, according to Inhofe, "there appear to be no actual dates when any of the new plant licenses will be issued.... How can a utility prepare for construction without a firm date on which they can expect to receive their license? How can an investor judge the risk of a project without being able to evaluate progress in the regulatory process?" If we got moving, "[g]iven construction estimates of four to five years, the first two reactors could be operational in 2016, with 14 more potentially operational by 2018. Sixteen new reactors will be a good start toward rejuvenating an industry that has been stagnant for over 30 years."[85]

Until just after his State of the Union rhetorical conversion, the Obama administration had also slow-walked nuclear by denying loan guarantees—even specifically excluding nukes from receiving energy project loan guarantees in the so-called stimulus bill—despite the fact that industry has come to rely on the guarantees as a result of the legal morass our greens and policymakers have jointly created.[86] Former member of the Nuclear Regulatory Commission Peter Bradford told the *Christian Science Monitor* that "funding nuclear power on anything like the scale of 100 plants over the next 20 years" (as Obama's economic analyses assume), purely for convenience's sake, "would involve an intolerable level of risk for taxpayers," because of the enormity of federal loan guarantees required.[87] An accurate prediction or not, dependence on the state is precisely the plan for all energy sources and, despite the largesse provided in many forms for "renewable" sources, on this issue more than any other we see that while the Left hand giveth, the Far Left hand taketh away.

USEC (formerly US Enrichment Corp.) operates the only uranium enrichment facility in the United States.[88] Six months into office, Obama's Department of Energy (DOE) told USEC to withdraw its loan-guarantee application for construction of an Ohio plant to produce uranium fuel for nuclear reactors. Obama's DOE simply decided that the request was "not technically or financially ready to complete," a decision USEC said forced it to "demobilize" the project.[89]

USEC's application for the American Centrifuge Plant in Piketon, Ohio, had been pending for a year, after extensive testing. This would have been the only fuel-fabrication plant to use U.S. gas centrifuge technology. USEC's CEO revealingly noted, "It is unclear how DOE expects to find innovative technologies that assume zero risk."[90] Whether that is likely is found in the fact that, as a presidential candidate, Barack Obama said during a campaign stop in Ohio that he *supported* the loan guarantee for USEC.[91] This must have been what he meant when promising "change," as that's not the same sort of thing he said in Iowa. *P 296*

That certainly meant change for those already employed or expecting to find work in the more than 8,000 new jobs projected to be created by the project.[92] But no worries, the Obama administration said it would create 800 to 1,000 temporary, new cleanup jobs in the area with stimulus money.

Pressure groups masquerading as objective voices, and even as mere disinterested information clearing houses such as the "Nuclear Information and Resources Service," "Institute for Energy and Environmental Research," and a "Nuclear Energy Information Service" crow about, and, on occasion, claim to have been instrumental in, blocking states including Minnesota, Illinois, Kentucky, West Virginia, Wisconsin, and Hawaii from opening themselves up to nuclear power, and from making it easier to bring new capacity on line in Indiana, Arizona, and Missouri. They bemoan that permit applications at the state level slipped through, in Georgia and Florida[93]—leaving the decision now with Obama—but the greens vow not to give up fighting a nuclear renaissance.[94]

Obama's first few months in office also oversaw the Tennessee Valley Authority's scaling back its plans from up to four units at a nuclear plant in northeast Alabama to just one reactor.[95] Greens are suing to block expansion of TVA's Watts Bar Nuclear Power Plant in Tennessee.[96] And the Southern Alliance for Clean Energy cited concerns over low-level contamination (tainted wood, paper, plastics, etc.) to successfully stall Unistar's Calvert Cliffs, Maryland application and Dominion Power's North Anna application in Virginia.[97] Amusingly, these same economic sages dedicated to raising the price of electricity, while also insisting that windmills and solar panels are cost-effective, argue that commercial reactors be rejected because they cost too much to build.[98]

In Maryland, the mere fact of an anti-nuclear White House appeared to stir the regulators to life, seeking to re-examine a permit already approved for the proposed Calvert Cliffs 3 reactor, which had been considered a leader in the nuclear power industry's hopes.[99] Sadly, these examples reveal the process and outcome that we should expect, barring significant change of a different kind in Washington.

Given the emphasis on all of the jobs that would be created if we clobber the economy with a massive renewables mandate, consider the jobs that would be created if we broke the stranglehold on our *de facto* nuclear freeze. These jobs, of course, would not come at the expense of, say, domestic manufacturing jobs, but would instead help save them. Senator Inhofe, in another floor speech, cited a union official's support for nukes, which the senator attributed to the jobs that "just one new nuclear plant would provide, including 1,400 to 1,800 jobs during construction; 400 to 700 permanent jobs when the plant begins operating, with salaries 36 percent higher than the local average; and 400 to 700 additional jobs providing goods and services."[100]

TRANSMISSION DIFFICULTIES

Say we manage to somehow overcome all of this Obama anti-energy orchestration and generate the electricity we need to avoid blackouts. How do we get it anywhere? We have already seen that the greens are working with the administration and the courts to kill transmission lines. But those efforts are only part of Team Obama's plans.

Our electrical grid is actually a system of 200,000 miles of power lines divided among 500 owners, and it is simply not up to the task of meeting predicted energy needs (even in the absence of mandating electric cars).[101] Already our (insufficient) electricity generation is growing four times as fast as the rate of building out new lines of transmission.[102] You don't need one-to-one, but we need to keep up faster than that.

But don't bank on it happening. By the September 2009 deadline for applications, nearly two dozen "climate" and other "public interest" lobbies had asked the Department of Energy for money which, as luck would have it, was set aside in that Van Jones-assisted stimulus. They have successfully made you pay to staff-up activist groups to stick their snouts into controlling something you need and they hate.[103] Apparently, it's now government policy that including anti-energy activists is critical in any new energy planning decisions—decisions which, you might sense by now, aren't something bureaucrats should be running in the first place. This should turn out well.

CONCLUSION

Columnist George Will accurately notes that America's abundance of energy resources "horrifies people who relish scarcity" precisely because scarcity is a foundation for "government to ration what is scarce and to generally boss people to mend their behavior. . . . Today, there is a name for the political doctrine that rejoices in scarcity of everything except government. The name is environmentalism."[1] Environmentalism seeks to use the state to create scarcity as a means to exert their will, while expanding the state's authority over your life. Obama wants to use environmentalism for the same reason.

Will aptly captures the mindset of the Obama administration and its ideological and financial backers seeking to "fundamentally transform America." If Obama's environmentalist dogma were sound—if Man-made global warming were real and as bad as he insists there is overwhelming scientific evidence to support—Obama's schemes in the name of addressing it would surely be a strange way to respond. They would not, according to anyone, do anything. Even after decades of these planned trillions of dollars in tax hikes, after jobs lost and families so deeply harmed, the temperature will be whatever it was going to be. All that would change is that the Left would have its long-frustrated demands put in place, despite being rejected by the American people when sold more closely on their own merits than with the cynical "do what I want or people die!" line.

So now, in the face of that "global warming" rationale cratering, the Obama administration tells us that all these prescriptions are really about jobs. Yet there is nothing in the record and very little even in theory to suggest this is a reasonable expectation. When the practical realities of energy production, consumption, and those undefeated laws of physics come into play, there is simply no reason to believe that economic growth can result. This is only one of many reasons why we should not cause all the harm that Obama demands in his call for the state to cause "necessarily skyrocketing" energy prices and "bankrupt" industries, and this agenda to strip you of your freedoms.

As a third line of attack, Team Obama desperately demands we adopt their policies in the name of national security, insulting our intelligence in the process. In a vacuum, sending less money to the Saudis is a good idea. However, what Obama touts as an energy plan not only causes energy prices to increase by design (definitely not a security measure), but it directly and indirectly attacks domestic producers. It would move higher-cost energy producers out of the market to the inevitable benefit of the lower-cost producers such as the Arab states. Making us more vulnerable by sealing off our resources, which are the greatest in the world, helps nothing, and clearly harms us in many ways.

The economy-weakening, resiliency-sapping increased dependence on foreigners for all manner of energy resources intrinsically weakens our security. If dependence on foreigners is a bad thing, why increase it? We will still find a way to obtain and use energy, though at greater expense, and at risk of worsening the trade deficit, among other consequences. Fight back and demand that they not do this.

Obama and his allies have made up claim after argument after excuse for why we must do what they say, and cede freedoms to the state. None of these withstand scrutiny. So, taking a page out of the playbook the Left has used for decades, they come back to hammering that their agenda is just "the right thing to do." In no way is this true.

With public inspection and opposition causing them such problems, there is only one thing too expensive for Obama and his allies to consider: removing the artificial urgency of threatened regulations (or environmental catastrophe, always just over the horizon), to proceed deliberately, with open and honest debate.

Analysis does not treat his claims or arguments kindly, so his response is, "We must act now!" Yet again we see politicians, joined in the coalition described in these pages, crashing into the news shrieking that you must accept the following because, if you don't, why, there may be no tomorrow. That's when you know to demand a time-out on "action." After the disastrous 2008 bailouts gave way to more of the same in 2009, and then to promises for yet more emergency measures this year, there can be no doubt that this claim is the biggest red flag of all, yelling eco-crisis in a crowded recession. Fortunately, only the Left is panicking as the voters calmly head for the exits.

All that this craven approach means is that the Left cannot make their case for, and cannot afford to let you deliberately consider, what they demand. Statists, seeking to seize control of our access to abundant, affordable, and reliable energy that drives our society, our wealth, and our health, have shrieked for more than a decade that we *must...act...now.* Meanwhile, the beaches and the skies, if not all of our freedoms, remain just where we left them. Predictably, the doomsday cult rushes out, only to return waving their papers declaring they have recalculated their figures, and catastrophe is right on (readjusted) schedule, just around the next corner.

In sum, it is clear that, as is so often the case with this crowd, the issue really isn't the issue. This is not about the climate, it is not about jobs, and it is not about national security. At least not as they argue. And these messengers' sudden concern about America's economy and national security is not credible. Possibly they might prove their sincerity if they also agreed to and promoted with equal vigor upgrades to our refineries, transmission lines, nuclear power fleet, and ability to tap and consume domestic resources—but they don't.

The reasonable conclusion is that this agenda is about what it *would* do. Implementing this long-sought list of policy demands, offered by the larger umbrella of Left-wing activists for decades, in the name of every threat, "greatest" and otherwise, will simply transfer decisions from individual producers and consumers to the state. It would give them power. It would give them your wealth. And "they" are the Left's broad coalition of organized labor, organized green, organized Big Government.

These people do not like your lifestyle, or your ability to continue it without paying the costs they demand, which are to slowly coerce you out of it if they cannot impose the "wrenching transformation of society" that Al Gore and his movement have long insisted upon. They have never believed that you can be trusted with freedom. And there is nothing that they see as unreasonable in the pursuit of this goal.

So those are the things that this agenda is determined to do. The goal of Obama's power grab is to grab your power: your wealth, economic liberties, and personal freedoms.

You aren't falling for it any longer. And this is causing Obama and his allies to become more desperate, and to push harder, to steal your freedoms faster.

Events and the American character have conspired to bring about a moment of decision, one that will be discussed in future political discourse analyzing the current age.

The time to choose has arrived. Whose freedoms are they? If they're yours, you are going to have to fight to keep them. Because as things stand now, Barack Obama has ushered in and is rapidly moving forward with expansion of a vast partnership between the state, left-wing activists, wealthy ideological activists, and corporatists, all seeking to impose an agenda making you less rich, less free, and less safe.

But these freedoms are not theirs to take from you. Fight back. And tell your kids and grandkids what you did in this war.

NOTES

Chapter 1

1. Kenneth Walsh, "Carol Browner on Climate Change: 'The Science Has Just Become Incredibly Clear,'" *US News & World Report*, March 9, 2009; available at: http://www.usnews.com/articles/news/energy/2009/03/09/on-climate-change-the-science-has-just-become-incredibly-clear.html.

2. "Europe's Dirty Secret: Why the EU Emissions Trading Scheme isn't working," OpenEurope, August 2007; available at: http://www.openeurope.org.uk/research/etsp2.pdf.

3. "Study of the effects on employment of public aid to renewable energy sources," Universidad Rey Juan Carlos, Madrid, March 2009; available at: http://www.juandemariana.org/pdf/090327-employment-public-aid-renewable.pdf. This quote is from the House testimony of the research team's leader, "Testimony of Gabriel Calzada álvarez, PhD before the House Select Committee on Energy Independence and Global Warming," September 24, 2009; available at: http://globalwarming.house.gov/files/HRG/092409Solar/calzada.pdf.

4. See, e.g.: "North American Stainless to expand operations in Carroll County: NAS represents the largest Spanish investment in the United States," press release, Commonwealth of Kentucky, Cabinet for Economic Development, November 16, 2004; available at: http://www.thinkkentucky.com/ newsarchive/ ArchivePage.aspx?x=11162004_NorthAmericanStainless.html (accessed February 3, 2010).

5. Barack Obama, in a January 8, 2008, meeting with the editorial board of the *San Francisco Chronicle*. See video at: "Obama on cap and trade: 'electricity rates would necessarily skyrocket,'" Examiner.com; available at: http:// www.examiner.com/examiner/x-268-Right-Side-Politics-Examiner~ y2009m6d26-Obama-on-cap-and-trade-electricity-rates-would-necessarily- skyrocket.

6. "We are five days away from fundamentally transforming the United States of America," Barack Obama, campaign speech in Columbia, Missouri on October 30, 2009; video available at: http://www.youtube.com/watch?v=_ cqN4NIEtOY (accessed February 3, 2010).

7. Christopher C. Horner, *Red Hot Lies: How Global Warming Alarmists Use Threats, Fraud and Deception to Keep You Misinformed* (Washington, D.C.: Regnery Publishing, Inc., 2009).

8. See, e.g.: Christopher Booker, "What links the Copenhagen conference with the steelworks closing in Redcar?" *Telegraph* (UK), December 12, 2009; available at: http://www.telegraph.co.uk/comment/columnists/christopher- booker/6798052/What-links-the-Copenhagen-conference-with-the- steelworks-closing-in-Redcar.html.

9. Ibid.

10. "We are five days away from fundamentally transforming the United States of America," op cit.

11. Barack Obama, in a January 8, 2008, meeting with the editorial board of the *San Francisco Chronicle*. See video at: "Obama on cap and trade: 'electricity rates would necessarily skyrocket,'" op cit.

12. Brendan O'Neill, "After Copenhagen: Hands off the human footprint!" *Spiked! Online*, December 21, 2009; available at: http://www.spiked-online. com/index.php/site/lowgraphicsarticle/7860/.

13. Scott Wilson and Juliet Eilperin, "In Adviser's Resignation, Vetting Bites Obama Again," *Washington Post*, September 7, 2009.

14. See, e.g.: "Obama announces emissions rules," *Boston Globe*, May 19, 2009; and "Obama Announces Terms Of Latest Auto Industry Bailout," Getty Images; available at: http://www.gettyimages.co.nz/detail/85703661/Getty-Images-News (accessed February 3, 2010).

15. "Obama Pledges Climate Push After Health Care; Senate Timing in Flux," *New York Times*, October 16, 2009 (accessed February 3, 2010).

16. CNN, "Transcript of Second McCain, Obama Debate," October 7, 2008; available at: http://www.cnn.com/2008/POLITICS/10/07/presidential.debate.transcript (accessed February 3, 2010).

17. See, e.g.: Don Lee and Elizabeth Douglass, "Chinese Drop Takeover Bid for Unocal," *Los Angeles Times*, August 3, 2005.

18. See, e.g.: Marguerite Reardon, "Telecom tax imposed in 1898 finally ends," CNet News, August 1, 2006; available at: http://news.cnet.com/2100-1037_3-6101004.html.

19. Fiona Harvey, "Elevenses with the FT: Emission statement," *Financial Times*, November 3, 2006.

20. Mark Steyn, "The emperor's new carbon credits," *MacLean's* (CA), December 17, 2009.

21. Ibid.

22. "Speech by Mr. Jacques Chirac, French President, to the VIth Conference of the Parties to the United Nations Framework Convention on Climate Change," The Hague, November 20, 2000; available at: http://sovereignty.net/center/chirac.html.

23. Al Gore, remarks to the Smith School World Forum on Enterprise and the Environment, Oxford, video embedded in "Al Gore invokes spirit of Churchill in battle against climate change," *The Times* (UK), July 8, 2009; available at: http://www.timesonline.co.uk/tol/news/environment/article6658672.ece (accessed February 3, 2010).

24. "Intervention of H. E. Mr. Herman Van Rompuy, New President of EU Council," European Union Mission to the United Nations, November 19, 2009; available at: http://www.europa-eu-un.org/articles/en/article_9245_en.htm.

25. Melanie Phillips, "By the waters of denial they sit and weep...," *The Spectator* (UK), February 2, 2010; available at: http://www.spectator.co.uk/melaniephillips/5745566/by-the-waters-of-denial-they-sit-and-weep.thtml.

26. Christopher C. Horner, *Red Hot Lies*, 209–56.

27. Rupert Read, "Rupert's Read: Thoughts for the Day," October 15, 2009; available at: http://rupertsread.blogspot.com/2009/10/thoughts-for-day.html.

28. See, e.g.: Lenore Taylor, "Penny Wong cheered, Hugo Chavez cheered," *The Australian*, December 17, 2009; available at: http://www.theaustralian.com.au/politics/penny-wong-jeered-hugo-chavez-cheered/story-e6frgczf-1225811179614.

29. James Randerson, "Western lifestyle unsustainable, says climate expert Rajendra Pachauri," *The Observer* (UK), November 29, 2009; available at: http://www.guardian.co.uk/environment/2009/nov/29/rajendra-pachauri-climate-warning-copenhagen.

30. Roger Helmer, "European Parliament Welcomes IPCC Chairman," December 2, 2009; available at: http://rogerhelmermep.wordpress.com/2009/12/02/european-parliament-welcomes-ipcc-chairman/.

31. George F. Will, "Ray LaHood, Transformed," *Newsweek*, May 16, 2009; available at: http://www.newsweek.com/id/197925.

32. Jeff Goodell, "Geoengineering the Planet: The Possibilities and the Pitfalls," *Yale Environment 360*, October 21, 2009; available at: http://e360.yale.edu/content/feature.msp?id=2201.

33. "EPA Administrator optimistic about new laws," National Public Radio, April 28, 2009; available at: http://www.npr.org/templates/transcript/transcript.php?storyId=103582546.

34. Ibid.

35. "We are five days away from fundamentally transforming the United States of America," op cit.

36. "How Should Planners Promote Livable Communities?" *National Journal Online*, October 5, 2009; available at: http://transportation.nationaljournal.com/2009/10/how-should-planners-promote-li.php.

37. Ken Orski, "The Administration's 'Livability' Initiative Stirs Up Debate About How Americans Should Live and Travel," *Innovation Newsbriefs*, No. 9, October 16, 2009, quoted by Peter Gordon in Peter Gordon's blog, "Sin in the suburbs," October 16, 2009; available at: http://www-rcf.usc.edu/~pgordon/blog/archive/2009_10_01_petergordon_archive.html.

38. Terrence Jeffrey, "Obama's Transportation Secretary Says He Wants to 'Coerce People Out of Their Cars,'" CNSNews, May 26, 2009; available at: http://www.cnsnews.com/PUBLIC/content/article.aspx?RsrcID=48578.

39. See, e.g.: Damon Root, "Putting a Stop to Congressional Overreach," *Reason*, November 13, 2009; available at: http://reason.com/archives/2009/11/13/putting-a-stop-to-congressiona.

40. George F. Will, "Ray LaHood, Transformed," op cit.

41. Nick Schulz, "Government Planning is Back," June 30, 2009, The American Blog, American Enterprise Institute, June 25, 2009; available at: http://blog.american.com/?p=2505.

42. See, e.g.: Matt Cover, "Democrats' Cap-and-Trade Bill Creates 'Retrofit' Policy for Homes and Businesses," CNSNews, July 1, 2009; available at: http://www.cnsnews.com/PUBLIC/content/article.aspx?RsrcID=50365.

43. Jessica Leber, "U.S. EPA learns 'Energy Star' products are sometimes beaten by Brand X," *Climate Wire*, December 2, 2009.

44. James Randerson, "Western lifestyle unsustainable, says climate expert Rajendra Pachauri," op cit.

Chapter 2

1. Thomas L. Friedman, "The Copenhagen that matters," *New York Times*, December 23, 2009; available at: http://www.nytimes.com/2009/12/23/opinion/23friedman.html.

2. See, e.g.: Chris Horner, "Something Rotten in the *NYT*," *National Review Online*, March 27, 2008; available at: http://planetgore.nationalreview.com/post/?q=MmMwNzE2NWZkMWE2ZGU0OGIxZDJiOGNj MzVlOGI3NGY.

3. Robert Bryce, "Denmark is 'Energy Smart'? Think Again," *US News & World Report*, December 17, 2009.

4. Ibid.

5. "Electricity prices for second semester 2008," Eurostat, Report 25/2009, published July 14, 2009; available at: http://epp.eurostat.ec.europa.eu/cache/ITY_OFFPUB/KS-QA-09-025/EN/KS-QA-09-025-EN.PDF.

6. Hugh Sharman and Henrik Meyer, "Wind Energy—the Case of Denmark," Center for Politiske Studier (CEPOS), Copenhagen, Denmark, September 2009, at p. 19; available at: http://www.cepos.dk/fileadmin/user_upload/Arkiv/PDF/Wind_energy_-_the_case_of_Denmark.pdf.

7. William Tucker, "Going Nuclear," *National Review Online*, October 15, 2000; available at: http://article.nationalreview.com/375078/going nuclear/william-tucker.

8. See, e.g.: Noelle Straub and Peter Behr, "Energy Regulatory Chief Says New Coal, Nuclear Plants May Be Unnecessary," Greenwire, *New York Times*, April 22, 2009; available at: http://www.nytimes.com/gwire/2009/04/22/22greenwire-no-need-to-build-new-us-coal-or-nuclear-plants-10630.html.

9. See, e.g.: National Legal and Policy Center's efforts to bring accountability to the LSC; available at: http://www.nlpc.org/legal-services-monitor.

10. Data available at: http://www.ferc.gov/about/com-mem/wellinghoff/wellinghoff-bio.asp (accessed February 6, 2010).

11. See, e.g.: Wayne Parry, "Offshore Wind Power Could Replace Most Coal Plants In US, Says Salazar," *Huffington Post*, April 6, 2009; available at: http://www.huffingtonpost.com/2009/04/06/offshore-wind-power-could_n_183593.html.

12. Dr. Robert Peltier, "Gone with the Wind," *Power* Magazine, June 1, 2009; available at: http://www.powermag.com/renewables/wind/Gone-with-the-Wind_1928.html.

13. Ibid.

14. See, e.g.: Kate Sheppard, "Blowing in the Wind," *Mother Jones*, December 4, 2009; available at: http://motherjones.com/politics/2009/12/john-kerry-cape-wind.

15. Ibid.

16. Ibid.

17. Email from Dan Kish, Institute for Energy Research.

18. Quoted at Penny Rodriguez, "Wind Farm May Violate Endangered Species Act," *Environment & Climate News*, September 2009, Heartland Institute Chicago IL; available at: http://www.heartland.org/full/25804/Wind_Farm_May_Violate_Endangered_Species_Act.html.

19. Hugh Sharman and Henrik Meyer, "Wind Energy—the Case of Denmark," op cit., p. 23.

20. Gillian Caldwell, "My chat with President Obama: Don't be stubborn about it—or we will be!" 1Sky, February 5, 2010; available at: http://www.1sky.org/blog/2010/02/my-chat-with-president-obama-dont-be-stubborn-or-we-will-be.

21. Peter Behr, "NUCLEAR: Vt.'s veto of reactor renewal may throw a cloud over nuclear 'resistance,'" *E & E News*, February 25, 2010.

22. "Eastern Wind Integration and Transmission Study," National Renewable Energy Laboratory, January 2010; available at: http://www.nrel.gov/wind/systemsintegration/pdfs/2010/ewits_executive_summary.pdf.

23. Michael Morgan, "Industrial wind – the perfect energy solution for 1810," Allegheny Treasures, January 25, 2010, quoting at length an analysis by wind expert Jon Boone; available at: http://alleghenytreasures.wordpress.com/2010/01/25/industrial-wind-the-perfect-energy-solution-for-1810/.

24. Dr. Robert Peltier, "Gone with the Wind," op cit.

25. William Tucker, *Terrestrial Energy: How Nuclear Power Will Lead the Green Revolution and End America's Long Energy Odyssey* (Savage, MD: Bartleby Press, September 18, 2008).

26. R. A. Dyer, "Power grid narrowly averted rolling blackouts," Ft. Worth *Star-Telegram*, February 28, 2008; available at: http://www.wind-watch.org/news/2008/02/28/power-grid-narrowly-averted-rolling-blackouts/.

27. Christopher Martin and Mario Parker, "Wind Promises Blackouts as Obama Strains Grid with Renewables," Bloomberg News, August 7, 2009; available at: http://www.bloomberg.com/apps/news?pid=20601072&sid=arb-Hcz0ryM_E.

28. Hugh Sharman and Henrik Meyer, "Wind Energy—the Case of Denmark," op cit.

29. Ibid.

30. Arthur Robinson, PhD, "Mr. Obama, tear down this wall!" *Environment and Climate News*, September 2009, Heartland Institute (Chicago, IL); available at: http://www.heartland.org/publications/environment%20climate/article/25799/Mr_Obama_Tear_Down_This_Wall.html.

31. Ibid.

32. Ibid.

33. Ibid.

34. Ibid.

35. Ibid.

36. Ibid.

37. Ibid.

38. Ibid.

39. See, e.g.: "Nuclear Power: An obstacle to rapid development," Greenpeace International, 2009; available at: http://www.greenpeace.org/raw/content/international/press/reports/nuclear-power-an-obstacle-to.pdf.

40. Jim Tankersley, "Wind energy job growth isn't blowing anyone away," *Los Angeles Times*, February 2, 2010; available at: http://www.latimes.com/news/science/environment/la-fi-green-jobs2-2010feb02,0,3585090.story.

41. Ed Crooks, "Resources: The power bill arrives," *Financial Times*, February 3, 2010; available at: http://www.ft.com/cms/s/0/dd4572b8-1034-11df-841f-00144feab49a.html.

42. Fred Barnes, "No Energy from this Executive," *The Weekly Standard*, June 15, 2009; available at: http://www.weeklystandard.com/Content/Public/Articles/000/000/016/588tpmuu.asp.

43. See, e.g.: Elizabeth Souder, "Texas Panhandle's Palo Duro Canyon at center of debate over wind-power transmission lines," *Dallas Morning News*, December 20, 2009; available at: http://www.dallasnews.com/ sharedcontent/dws/bus/industries/energy/stories/DN-paloduro_20bus.ART0.State.Edition1.3cfbc42.html.

44. Scott Streater, "Bird and bat collisions continue to perplex researchers," Land Letter, *E&E News*, August 13, 2009; article available at: http://www.eenews.net/ll/2009/08/13/.

45. Guy Darst, "You're blocking my view," *Wall Street Journal*, May 25, 2007; available at: http://online.wsj.com/article/SB118005789405914255-search.html.

46. News Release, "US Fish and Wildlife Service Says Core Sage Grouse Habitat Areas Must Remain Protected—Even From Wind Development," Wyoming Game & Fish Department, July 8, 2009; available at: http://gf.state.wy.us/downloads/pdf/wind%20in%20core%20areas_1.pdf.

47. Scott Streater, "Idaho wind proposal would sever wildlife habitat, critics say," Land Letter, *E&E News*, October 29, 2009.

48. Jim Efstathiou Jr., "Prairie Chicken Mating Dance Threatens Texas Projects," Bloomberg, August 26, 2009; available at: http://www.bloomberg.com/apps/news?pid=20602099&sid=aldysneqgVeA.

49. Associated Press, "Feinstein: Don't spoil our desert with solar panels," March 21, 2009; available at: http://www.foxnews.com/politics/2009/03/21/feinstein-dont-spoil-desert-solar-panels/.

50. Stephanie Tavares, "Dirty Detail: solar panels need water," *Las Vegas Sun*, September 19, 2009; available at: http://www.lasvegassun.com/news/2009/sep/18/dirty-detail-solar-panels-need-water/.

51. Louis Sahagun, "Solar energy firm drops plan for project in Mojave Desert," *Los Angeles Times*, September 18, 2009; available at: http://articles.latimes.com/2009/sep/18/business/fi-solar18. The Department of Energy, however, provided BrightSource a $1.37 billion loan guarantee for the project in late February, 2010. Joel Kirkland, "Mojave Desert solar project gets $1.37 billion nod from DOE," *Climate Wire*, February 23, 2010.

52. See, e.g.: Floor speech, Congressman Dan Burton, U.S. House of Representatives, transcript/video, C-Span, June 1998; available at: http://www.c-spanarchives.org/congress/?q=node/77531&id=8788088. This caused a stir among Democrats (see, e.g.: http://www.c-spanvideo.org/congress/?q=node/77531&id=8785782), one of whom, Representative Henry Waxman, went to the floor to decry that there was "no evidence that there is any connection between the designation of this land as a monument and Riady group or any other contributions." Just fortuitous delight. Not a quid pro quo.

53. Colin Sullivan, "RFK Jr., enviros clash over Mojave solar proposal," *E&E News*, September 8, 2009; available at: http://www.eenews.net/public/Greenwire/2009/09/08/2.

54. Ibid.

55. Louis Sahagun, "Solar energy firm drops plan for project in Mojave Desert," op cit.

56. Louis Sahagun, "Environmental concerns delay solar projects in California desert," *Los Angeles Times*, October 19, 2009; available at: http://articles.latimes.com/2009/oct/19/local/me-solar19.

57. Paul Taylor, "Green group bad faith," *Los Angeles Examiner*, November 9, 2009; available at: http://www.examiner.com/x-3089-LA-Ecopolitics-Examiner~y2009m11d9-Green-group-bad-faith?cid=exrss-LA-Ecopolitics-Examiner.

58. Phil Willon and David Zahniser, "L.A. utility shelves plans for solar farm near Salton Sea," *Los Angeles Times*, December 16, 2009; available at: http://articles.latimes.com/2009/dec/16/local/la-me-la-solar16-2009dec16.

59. Noelle Straub, "Groups Sue U.S. Over Energy-Transmission Corridors on Public Lands," Greenwire, *New York Times*, July 8, 2009; available at: http://www.nytimes.com/gwire/2009/07/08/08greenwire-groups-sue-us-over-energy-transmission-corrido-17235.html.

60. Cheryl K. Chumley, "Environmentalists oppose Oregon wind farms," *Energy & Climate News*, Heartland Institute, Chicago IL, September 2009; available at: http://www.heartland.org/full/25801/Environmentalists_Oppose_Oregon_Wind_Farms.html.

61. This is actually a long-running issue. See, e.g., "Wind power is dividing enviros and spurring some odd alliances," *Grist*, January 10, 2010; available at:

http://www.grist.org/article/asmus-windfarm/. That's not to say there isn't already an awful lot of bird carcass there from other wind projects. See Robert Bryce, "Windmills are killing our birds," *Wall Street Journal*, September 8, 2009; available at http://www.robertbryce.com/node/301.

62. Patrick Reis, "Lawmakers push bill to address bird population decline," Environment and Energy News, July 11, 2008.

63. Robert Bryce, "Windmills are killing our birds," op cit.

64. "Summary of Wind Turbine Accident Data to 31 December 2009"; available at: http://www.caithnesswindfarms.co.uk/accidents.pdf.

65. For a listing and discussion of numerous projects being held up in this region see Virginia Wind, http://www.vawind.org/ (accessed February 6, 2010).

66. For discussion see, e.g.: "Windmills vs. Endangered Species," *West Virginia Highlands Voice*, January 7, 2010; available at: http://wvhighlands.org/wv_voice/?p=2268.

67. Ibid.

68. According to an analysis sent by email, Frank Maisano of Bracewell & Giuliani in Washington, D.C., December 2009.

69. "First Wind Cascade Wind Farm," Project, No Project, U.S. Chamber of Commerce; available at: http://pnp.uschamber.com/2009/03/first-wind-cascade-wind-farm.html.

70. "Biomass Gas & Electric Tallahassee Renewable Energy Center," Project, No Project, U.S. Chamber of Commerce; available at: http://pnp.uschamber.com/2009/03/biomass-gas-electric-tallahassee-renewable-energy-center.html.

71. William L. Kovacs "Activists' Failure to Agree on Energy Sources Jeopardizes Economy," *Environment & Climate News*, August 2009, Heartland Institute Chicago, IL; available at: http://www.heartland.org/ policybot/results/25678/Activists_Failure_to_Agree_on_Energy_Sources_Jeopardizes_Economy.html.

72. Memo, U.S. Chamber of Commerce, sent to me January 25, 2010.

73. Ibid. See also data available at: http://pnp.uschamber.com/ (accessed February 6, 2010).

74. Memo, U.S. Chamber of Commerce, sent to author January 25, 2010.

75. See, e.g.: "Fort Irwin earmarks $6.9 million for tortoise relocation," Victorville (CA) *Daily Press*, June 5, 2007; available at: http://www.encyclopedia.com/doc/1G1-164534817.html.

76. April Reese, "Army proposes moving more Mojave Desert tortoises from Calif. Base," Land Letter, *E&E News*, August 13, 2009.

77. Ed Crooks, "Resources: The power bill arrives," op cit.

78. Robin Pagnamenta, "Energy giants turn up the heat for dirty power," *The Times* (UK), February 16, 2010; available at: http://business.timeson-line.co.uk/tol/business/industry_sectors/utilities/article7028321.ece.

79. Ed Crooks, "The power bill arrives," op cit.

80. See, e.g.: http://change.gov/newsroom/entry/president-elect_obama_speaks_on_an_american_recovery_and_reinvestment_plan_/.

81. Jenny Mandel, "Germany slashes solar tariff, spurs debate about industry impact," *E&E News*, January 22, 2010.

Chapter 3

1. "Delay In Appointing Medicare Chief Baffles Lawmakers," *Medical News Today*, August 19, 2009; available online at: http://www.medicalnewstoday.com/articles/161125.php.

2. Jerome R. Corsi, "Holdren says Constitution backs compulsory abortion," *World Net Daily*, September 22, 2009; available at: http://www.wnd.com/index.php?fa=PAGE.view&pageId=110720, citing the 1977 book *Ecoscience: Population, Resources, Environment*, co-written by Holdren and Paul and Anne Ehrlich.

3. Michelle Malkin, "Van Jones, Valerie Jarrett, Barack Obama & do-it-yourself vetting," September 3, 2009; available at: http://michellemalkin.com/2009/09/03/van-jones-valerie-jarrett-barack-obama-do-it-yourself-vetting/ (accessed February 4, 2010).

4. See, e.g.: the photo in the lower left of http://therealbarackobama.files.wordpress.com/2009/04/jones-van.jpg (accessed February 21, 2010.)

5. "The New Republic: America's Future Recap," GlennBeck.com, September 2, 2009; available at: http://www.glennbeck.com/content/articles/article/198/29831/.

6. Daniel Kessler, "Gore's Green Group Loses CEO Cathy Zoi to the Obama Administration," TreeHugger.com, March 28, 2009; available at: http://www.treehugger.com/files/2009/03/zoi-goes-to-dc.php.

7. See, e.g.: Glenn Beck, "Speak Without Fear," Fox News, August 26, 2009, available at: http://www.foxnews.com/story/0,2933,543341,00.html.

8. Van Jones, "The Stimulus: A Down Payment on a Green Future," *Huffington Post*, February 17, 2009; available at: http://www.huffingtonpost.com/van-jones/the-stimulus-a-down-payme_b_167681.html; see also, Glenn Beck, FOX News Channel, August 26, 2009, video at 5:25–5:30, at "American Council on Renewable Energy," August 27, 2009; available online at: http://www.dipity.com/timeline/Van-Jones-Quotes/list (accessed February 4, 2010).

9. Gabriel Calzada álvarez, "Study of the effects on employment of public aid to renewable energy sources," op cit.

10. "Think of what's happening in countries like Spain, Germany and Japan, where they're making real investments in renewable energy," quoted in "Green Stimulus Money Costs More Jobs Than It Creates, Study Shows," CNSNews, April 13, 2009; available at: http://www.cnsnews.com/Public/Content/ Article.aspx?rsrcid=46453. Regarding the administration and related responses, see Chris Horner, "Friends of Spain and the Freedom of Information," *National Review Online*, December 4, 2009; available at: http://planetgore.nationalreview.com/post/?q=NTc3MTA5NjI5OGMyMmYw NTMwYTAzZDdhOTI4NjBmOTE=.

11. Christopher C. Horner, "Grande Gobierno: Obama Uses Feds to Protect His 'Green Jobs' Fantasy," BigGovernment.com, September 28, 2009; available at: http://biggovernment.com/chorner/2009/09/28/grande-gobierno-obama-uses-feds-to-protect-his-green-jobs-story/.

12. Internal Email from Avi Gopstein, copying *inter alia* EERE COO Steven Chalk, David E. Rodgers EERE Director of Strategic Planning and Analysis, and Deputy Assistant Secretary EERE Jacques Beaudry-Losique, April 17, 2009.

13. This conclusion is drawn from telephone conversations with the NREL FOIA officer between November 2009 and January 2010 about the request's progression through the administration and DoE EERE's response in particular, and is current as of February 22, 2010.

14. Robin Bravender, "Bold Initiatives Spur Calls for New EPA Watchdog," Greenwire, *New York Times*, October 15, 2009; available at: http://www.nytimes.com/gwire/2009/10/15/15greenwire-bold-initiatives-spur-calls-for-new-epa-watchd-86411.html.

15. "The White House Fires a Watchdog," *Wall Street Journal*, June 17, 2009; available at: http://online.wsj.com/article/SB124511811033017539.html.

16. Tim Dickinson, "The Eco-Warrior: President Obama has appointed the most progressive EPA chief in history—and she's moving swiftly to clean up the mess left by Bush," *Rolling Stone*, January 20, 2010; available at: http://www.rollingstone.com/politics/story/31820267/the_ecowarrior.

17. See Luke Popovich, director of the National Mining Association, accused the administration of circumventing the court order," cited in Patrick Reis, "Interior expands oversight of mountaintop removal," *E&E News* PM, November 18, 2009.

18. William Schambra, "Obama and the Policy Approach," *National Affairs*, no. 1 (Fall 2009).

19. See Robin Bravender, "GOP concerns about climate regs ensnare air nominee," Greenwire, *New York Times*, May 8, 2009; available at: http://www.nytimes.com/gwire/2009/05/08/08greenwire-gop-concerns-about-climate-regs-ensnare-air-no-10572.html, noting how Ms. McCarthy emphasized these relationships in questioning during her confirmation hearing, Senate Committee on Environment and Public Works, May 5, 2009. See also Ian Talley, "EPA Nominee Suggests New CO_2 Rules May Expose Small Emitters," *Wall Street Journal*, May 6, 2009; available at: http://online.wsj.com/article/SB124164614659693239.html#printMode.

20. "Prevention of Significant Deterioration and Title V Greenhouse Gas Tailoring Rule, 40 CFR Parts 51, 52, 70, and 71, EPA-HQ-OAR-2009-0517; RIN 2060-AP86," U.S. Environmental Protection Agency, September 30, 2009; available at: http://www.epa.gov/NSR/documents/GHGTailoringProposal.pdf, page 1.

21. "EPW Policy Beat: Absurd Results," Senate Committee on Environment and Public Work blog, October 5, 2009; available at: http://epw.senate.gov/public/index.cfm?FuseAction=Minority.Blogs&Content Record_id=255e2baf-802a-23ad-4737-f80f3065607d; see also "The 'Absurd Results' Doctrine," *Wall Street Journal*, October 4, 2009; available at: http://online.wsj.com/article/SB10001424052748704471504574447090218534138.html.

22. John D. Podesta, "The Great Transformation: Climate Change as Cultural Change," Essen, Germany, June 9, 2009; available at: http://www.greattransformation.eu/images/stories/downloads/podesta_text.pdf.

23. Data available at: http://www.socialistinternational.org/viewArticle.cfm?ArticleID=1843&&ModuleID=34 (accessed January 5, 2009), has been altered since to remove Browner.

24. Edward John Craig, "An Early Thaw," *National Review Online*, January 5, 2009; available at: http://planetgore.nationalreview.com/post/?q= YmFmYmZjNzRjYTQ0OWNkMTVmZjM2MDA0Y2I3ZTQ3MWY.

25. Andrew Napolitano, "What Can Obama's Czars Legally Do?" FOX News, September 8, 2009; available at: http://www.foxnews.com/opinion/2009/ 09/08/judge-napolitano-czars-obama/.

26. Rich Galen, "Hillary Needs a New Deal," Mullings, July 19, 2009; available at: http://www.mullings.com/2009_07_01_archive.html.

27. Igor Kossov, "Byrd Calls Obama's Czar's Dangerous," *Political Hotsheet*, CBS News, February 25, 2009; available at: http://www.cbsnews.com/blogs/ 2009/02/25/politics/politicalhotsheet/entry4828759.shtml.

28. "Al Gore's New Campaign," *60 Minutes*, CBS News, March 30, 2008; available at: http://www.cbsnews.com/stories/2008/03/27/60minutes/ main3974389.shtml; see also Albert Gore Jr., *An Inconvenient Truth: The Planetary Emergency of Global Warming and What We Can Do About It* (Rodale Books, 2006), 263.

29. For a history of Browner's involvement see, Myron Ebell, "Socialist International Meets, but Carol Browner Can't Make It," OpenMarket.com, Competitive Enterprise Institute, October 16, 2009; available at: http://www. openmarket.org/2009/10/16/socialist-international-meets-but-carol-browner-can%E2%80%99t-make-it/; see also, "From a High Carbon Economy to a Low Carbon Society," *Socialist International*; available at: http://www.socialistin-ternational.org/viewArticle.cfm?ArticleID=2032.

30. Kathy Shaidle, "The Rule of the Green Czar," *Front Page Magazine*, January 16, 2009; available at: http://97.74.65.51/readArticle.aspx?ARTID=33743; she also quotes Stephen Dianan, "Obama climate czar has socialist ties" (see note 32).

31. Jean-Marie Macabrey, "Top E.U. legislator fears Europe's emissions trading system could fail, unless modified," *Climate Wire*, March 9, 2009.

32. Stephen Dinan, "Obama climate czar has socialist ties," *Washington Times*, January 12, 2009; available at: http://www.washingtontimes.com/news/ 2009/jan/12/obama-climate-czar-has-socialist-ties/print/.

33. "Madeleine Albright: USA No Longer Intends To Be World's No.1 State," *Pravda*, September 18, 2009; available at: http://english.pravda.ru/busi-ness/finance/109362-1/.

34. Data available at: http://www.sourcewatch.org/index.php?title= Albright_Group.

35. Data available at: http://change.gov/learn/policy_working_groups (accessed February 4, 2010).

36. John Bresnahan, "Byrd: Obama in power grab," *Politico*, February 25, 2009; available at: http://www.politico.com/news/stories/0209/19303.html.

37. Lois Romano, "Energy Czarina has list of Bush policies to undo," *Washington Post*, January 15, 2009.

38. "Opening Statement of Senator James M. Inhofe, Environment and Public Works Committee," "Hearing on the Nomination of Gary Guzy to be Deputy Director of the Office of Environmental Quality," August 4, 2009; article previously available at: http://epw.senate.gov/public/index.cfm? FuseAction=PressRoom.PressReleases&ContentRecord_id=E5B5DBC0-802A-23AD-4145-4BE2272506B6.

39. Max Schulz, "Browner and Greener," *National Review Online*, December 11, 2008; available at: http://article.nationalreview.com/380716/browner-and-greener/max-schulz.

40. Jack White, "How the EPA Was Made to Clean Up Its Own Stain— Racism," *Time*, February 23, 2001; available at: http://www.time.com/time/nation/article/0,8599,100423,00.html. The judge subsequently reduced the fine to a paltry $300,000.

41. Ibid.

42. See "Notification and Federal Employee Antidiscrimination and Retaliation Act of 2001, Hearing before the Committee on the Judiciary, House of Representatives, One Hundred Seventh Congress, First Session, On H.R. 169," May 9, 2001; available at: http://commdocs.house.gov/committees/judiciary/hju72302.000/hju72302_0f.htm.

43. Mike Spitzer, "AP: EPA Head Browner Asked for Computer Files to Be Deleted," Associated Press, June 30, 2001; available at: http://www.mail-archive.com/ctrl@listserv.aol.com/msg70823.html.

44. "On March 7, 2001, the [U.S. Attorney's Office] stated to Landmark [Legal Foundation] that Browner's office had been searched, but reported on March 27 that it had not been searched." Memorandum Opinion, Judge Royce Lamberth, U.S. District Court for the District of Columbia, July 24, 2003,

Landmark Legal Foundation v. Environmental Protection Agency, Civil Action No. 00-2338; available at: http://www.landmarklegal.org/uploads/jl1.htm.

45. Associated Press, "EPA held in contempt over documents," *Deseret News*, July 25, 2003; available at: http://www.deseretnews.com/article/998899/.

46. Memorandum Opinion, Judge Royce Lamberth, U.S. District Court for the District of Columbia, July 24, 2003, *Landmark Legal Foundation v. Environmental Protection Agency*.

47. Michelle Malkin, "Down on Browner," *National Review Online*, December 12, 2008; available at: http://article.nationalreview.com/380776/down-on-browner/michelle-malkin.

48. Mark Tapscott, "'Put nothing in writing' Browner told auto execs on secret White House CAFE talks; Sensenbrenner wants investigation," *Washington Examiner*, July 8, 2009; available at: http://www.washingtonexaminer.com/opinion/blogs/beltway-confidential/Put-nothing-in-writing-Browner-told-auto-execs-on-secret-White-House-CAFE-talks-50260677.html#ixzz0ebP1tT8N.

49. Ibid.

50. Andy Cohglan, "Obama to restore science to its rightful place," *New Scientist*, January 20, 2009; available at: http://www.newscientist.com/article/dn16452-obama-to-restore-science-to-its-rightful-place.html.

51. U.S. Senate Committee on Environment and Public Works, Press Update, "Democrats History of 'Politicized Science' Under the Clinton Administration"; available at: http://epw.senate.gov/public/index.cfm? FuseAction=Files.View&FileStore_id=e19271e4-4796-4a2c-a2b9-c0ba6d89a1cb, citing, *Morning Edition*, National Public Radio, June 27, 2000.

52. Pranay Gupte and Bonner R. Cohen, "Carol Browner, Master Of Mission Creep," *Forbes*, October 20, 1997; available at: http://www.forbes.com/forbes/1997/1020/6009170a_2.html.

53. Editorial, "EPA—Clean It Up," *Cincinnati Enquirer*, December 26, 2000.

54. Press release, "EPA Censorship of Video Raises New Questions about Suppression of Science," House Select Committee on Energy Independence and Global warming, November 13, 2009; available at: http://republicans.globalwarming.house.gov/Press/PRArticle.aspx?NewsID=2734.

55. Kimberley Strassel, "The EPA's Paranoid Style," *Wall Street Journal*, November 12, 2009; available at: http://online.wsj.com/article/SB100014 2405274870368380457453202275745200.html.

56. Pranay Gupte and Bonner R. Cohen, "Carol Browner, Master Of Mission Creep," *Forbes*, October 20, 1997; available at: http://www.forbes.com/forbes/1997/1020/6009170a_2.html.

57. Jonathan Adler, "Environmental Protection Payoffs," *The Washington Times*, May 24, 1996.

58. Kathy Shaidle, "The Rule of the Green Czar," op cit.

59. Editorial, "EPA—Clean It Up," *Cincinnati Enquirer*, December 26, 2000.

60. "Commentary: Political Science At The EPA," *The Electricity Daily*, June 19, 2000.

61. Passed as part of the Treasury and General Government Appropriations Act for Fiscal Year 2001, Public Law 106-554 (H.R. 5654), Section 515.

62. Michael Fumento, "More Hot Air from the EPA," *The Weekly Standard*, October 2, 2006; available at: http://www.fumento.com/epa/lawn.html.

63. Christopher C. Horner, "The Lawnmower Police are Coming," *Human Events*, September 9, 2008; available at: http://www.humanevents.com/article.php?id=28441.

64. Kenneth Walsh, "Carol Browner on Climate Change: 'The Science Has Just Become Incredibly Clear,'" op cit.

65. William Yeatman, Competitive Enterprise Institute Web Memo, "Dr. John P. Holdren: 'De-development' Advocate is the Wrong Choice for White House Science Adviser," January 13, 2009; available at: http://cei.org/cei_files/fm/active/0/William%20Yeatman%20-%20Holdren%20WebMemo.pdf.

66. Christopher C. Horner, *Red Hot Lies: How Global Warming Alarmists Use Threats, Fraud and Deception to Keep You Misinformed* (Washington, D.C.: Regnery Publishing, 2009).

67. Ibid., 116–24.

68. Ibid., 90–94.

69. Ibid., 93.

70. Cited in Ed Morrissey, "Obama science czar: Redistributionism as the cure for American exceptionalism," HotAir.com, September 9, 2009; available at: http://hotair.com/archives/2009/09/09/obama-science-czar-redistributionism-as-the-cure-for-american-exceptionalism/.

71. Mark Hemingway, "Mark Hemingway on why eyebrows should be raised by Obama science czar's support for eugenics," *Washington Examiner*, July 15, 2009; available at: http://www.washingtonexaminer.com/opinion/columns/OpEd-Contributor/Science-czar_s-support-for-eugenics-should-raise-eyebrows-7971354-50765207.html, referencing Paul Ehrlich, Anne Ehrlich, John Holdren, *Ecoscience: Population, Resources, and Environment* (San Francisco: W.H. Freeman and Company, 1977).

72. David Freddoso, "Obama's science czar suggested compulsory abortion, sterilization," *Washington Examiner*, July 14, 2009; available at: http://www. washingtonexaminer.com/opinion/blogs/beltway-confidential/Obamas-science-czar-suggested-compulsory-abortion-sterilization-50783612.html# ixzz0ec9hjNhP.

73. Ibid.

74. Chris Mooney, "Hold Off On Holdren (Again)," *Science Progress*, July 15, 2009; available at: http://www.scienceprogress.org/2009/07/hold-of-holdren-again/.

75. Amanda Carpenter, "Population Czar," Hot Button Column, *Washington Times*, July 15, 2009; available at: http://www.washingtontimes.com/news/ 2009/jul/15/hot-button-40981162/print/.

76. David Harsanyi, "Science Fiction Czar," *Denver Post*, July 15, 2009; available at: http://www.denverpost.com/harsanyi/ci_12837799.

77. John Tierney, "U.S. Climate Report Assailed," *New York Times*, June 18, 2009; available at: http://tierneylab.blogs.nytimes.com/2009/06/18/us-climate-report-assailed/.

78. John Tierney, "Holdren's Ice Age Tidal Wave," *New York Times*, September 29, 2009; available at: http://tierneylab.blogs.nytimes.com/2009/09/29/ dr-holdrens-ice-age-tidal-wave/.

79. Paul R. Ehrlich, Anne H. Ehrlich, and John P. Holdren, *Ecoscience: Population, Resources, and Environment*, 686.

80. "I only came to this operation 25 years ago—a relative youth [age 29]— in 1973 at the conference in Aulanko hosted by Jorma Miettinen, who is here tonight. That was my beginning in Pugwash—a wonderful meeting—and many other of the people in the room were there. . . . In any case, it has been a wonderful run. It changed my life, going to that Pugwash conference and meeting this extraordinary array of personalities, committed to improving the human condition, to reducing the nuclear danger." John Holdren, "Speech on behalf of International Pugwash, at a dinner at the Royal Society of London held to celebrate the 90th birthday of Sir Joseph Rotblat, 7 November 1998, London England"; available at: http://www.pugwash.org/reports/nw/nw3a. htm (accessed February 4, 2010).

81. "EUGENICS: THE DISTILLED ESSENCE OF THE ANTI-LIFE MENTALITY," American Life League; data available at: http://www.ewtn.com/library/PROLENC/ENCYC105.HTM.

82. Michelle Malkin, "Study in contrasts: Christian scientist vs. eco-mad scientist," MichelleMalkin.com, July 15, 2009; available at: http://michelle-malkin.com/2009/07/15/study-in-contrasts-christian-scientist-vs-eco-mad-scientist/.

83. Paul R. Ehrlich and John P. Holdren eds., *The Cassandra Conference: Resources and the Human Predicament* (College Station, TX: Texas A&M University Press, TX, 1988).

84. Transcript, "Senate confirmation hearings: NOAA and Science Advisor," February 12, 2009; available at: http://scienceblogs.com/authority/2009/02/senate_confirmation_hearings_-.php.

85. "As University of California physicist John Holdren has said, it is possible that carbon-dioxide climate-induced famines could kill as many as a billion people before the year 2020." Paul Ehrlich, *The Machinery of Nature* (New York: Simon & Schuster, 1986), 27.

86. John Holdren, "Global Thermal Pollution," in Holdren and Paul Ehrlich, eds., *Global Ecology* (New York: Harcourt Brace Jovanovich, 1971), 85.

87. John Holdren and Paul Ehrlich, "What We Must Do, and the Cost of Failure," in Holdren and Ehrlich, eds., *Global Ecology*, 279.

88. William Yeatman, Competitive Enterprise Institute Web Memo, "Dr. John P. Holdren: 'De-development' Advocate is the Wrong Choice for White House Science Adviser," January 13, 2009.

89. Quoting Holdren, "'One change in (legal) notions that would have a most salubrious effect on the quality of the environment has been proposed by law professor Christopher D. Stone in his celebrated monograph, "Should Trees Have Standing?"' Holdren said in a 1977 book that he co-wrote with Paul R. Ehrlich and Anne H. Ehrlich. 'In that tightly reasoned essay, Stone points out the obvious advantages of giving natural objects standing, just as such inanimate objects as corporations, trusts, and ships are now held to have legal rights and duties,' Holdren added." Christopher Neefus, "In the 70s, Obama's Science Adviser Endorsed Giving Trees Legal Standing to Sue in Court," CNSNews, July 30, 2009; available at: http://www.cnsnews.com/public/content/article.aspx?RsrcID=51756.

90. Ibid.

91. William Yeatman, Competitive Enterprise Institute Web Memo, "Dr. John P. Holdren: 'De-development' Advocate is the Wrong Choice for White House Science Adviser," January 13, 2009.

Chapter 4

1. "Everyone in Britain could be given a personal 'carbon allowance,'" *Telegraph* (UK), November 9, 2009; available at: //www.telegraph.co.uk/earth/environment/carbon/6527970/Everyone-in-Britain-could-be-given-a-personal-carbon-allowance.html.

2. "Europe's Dirty Secret: Why the emissions Trading Scheme isn't working," op cit.

3. Rebecca Lefort, "Large rises in cost of gas and electricity as winter bills loom," *Telegraph* (UK), December 6, 2009; available at: http://www.telegraph.co.uk/finance/newsbysector/retailandconsumer/6738608/Large-rises-in-cost-of-gas-and-electricity-as-winter-bills-loom.html; see also, "Big jump recorded in excess deaths last winter," BBC, November 24, 2009; available at: http://news.bbc.co.uk/2/hi/health/8375884.stm.

4. "Gordon Brown calls for new group to police global environment issues," *The Times*, December 21, 2009; available at: http://www.timesonline.co.uk/tol/news/uk/article6963482.ece.

5. For examples see, "Former Tory Peer Is New Leader Of Ukip," *Sky News*, November 27, 2009; available at: http://news.sky.com/skynews/Home/Politics/Former-Conservative-Peer-Lord-Pearson-Elected-As-New-Leader-Of-UK-Independence-Party-Ukip/Article/200911415475385?f=rss; see also "Former Hague aide defects to UKIP," BBC, December 8, 2006; available at: http://news.sky.com/skynews/Home/Politics/Former-Conservative-Peer-Lord-Pearson-Elected-As-New-Leader-Of-UK-Independence-Party-Ukip/Article/200911415475385?f=rss.

6. Data available online at: http://eastangliaemails.com/.

7. Mark Steyn, "The Dog Ate My Tree Rings," *National Review Online*, November 29, 2009; available at: http://corner.nationalreview.com/post/?q=NjZkM2I0MWNlMTYwNzUwNzAxOTQ0ZDAxN2ZlNzAzMjA.

8. Paul Taylor, "Happy Earth Day?" *Los Angeles Examiner*, April 15, 2009; available at: http://www.examiner.com/x-3089-LA-Ecopolitics-Examiner~y2009m4d15-Happy-Earth-Day.

9. "Transcript: Obama's First State of the Union Speech," January 28, 2010; available at: http://www.cnn.com/2010/POLITICS/01/27/sotu.transcript/index.html.

10. For example, see: Lisa Friedman, "U.S. bound by Obama's Copenhagen emissions pledge—U.N. official," Greenwire, *New York Times*, January 20, 2010; available at: http://www.eenews.net/public/Greenwire/2010/01/20/3.

11. Heather Zichal, "A year laying the foundation for the Clean Energy economy," The White House Blog, January 11, 2010; available at: http://www.whitehouse.gov/blog/2010/01/11/a-year-laying-foundation-clean-energy-economy.

12. Ibid.

13. Ibid.

14. "Endangerment and Cause or Contribute Findings for Greenhouse Gases," U.S. Environmental Protection Agency, December 7, 2009; available at: http://epa.gov/climatechange/endangerment.html.

15. Heather Zichal, "A year laying the foundation for the Clean Energy economy," The White House Blog, January 11, 2010; available at: http://www.whitehouse.gov/blog/2010/01/11/a-year-laying-foundation-clean-energy-economy.

16. Ibid., see discussion of standards in "Taxing and Grabbing Your Power."

17. "Barack Obama endorses low carbon fuel standard," Reuters, January 12, 2007; available at: http://www.reuters.com/article/idUSN1229186820070613.

18. Heather Zichal, "A year laying the foundation for the Clean Energy economy," The White House Blog, January 11, 2010; available at: http://www.whitehouse.gov/blog/2010/01/11/a-year-laying-foundation-clean-energy-economy.

19. Ibid.

20. Rasmussen Reports, "68% Favor Offshore Oil Drilling," December 16, 2009; available at: http://www.rasmussenreports.com/public_content/politics/current_events/offshore_drilling/68_favor_offshore_oil_drilling.

21. "Shhh: Public Favors Drilling," *Wall Street Journal*, February 4, 2010; available at: http://blogs.wsj.com/washwire/2010/02/04/shhh-public-comments-favor-drilling/.

22. Chris Horner, "Kyotophiles Read the Papers, Too," *National Review Online*, January 23, 2010; available at: http://planetgore.nationalreview.com/post/?q=YWY0MmRiMWNhNTc3NjllNTllYjdhZjE0MTM0NzY2ZDk=.

23. See, e.g.: Darren Samuelsohn, "Sen.-Elect Brown's Win Adds More Question Marks to Senate Climate Debate," Greenwire, *New York Times,* January 20, 2010; available at: http://www.nytimes.com/cwire/2010/01/20/ 20climatewire-sen-elect-browns-win-adds-more-question-mark-48190.html?pagewanted=2.

24. See, e.g.: "Senate bill would cut emissions 20% by 2020," PBS, September 30, 2009; available at: http://www.pbs.org/newshour/updates/ environment/july-dec09/climate_09-30.html.

25. Press Release, "Boxer Says Goal is to 'Soften the Blow' from Cap-and-Trade," U.S. Senate Committee on Environment and Public Works Minority, July 16, 2009; available at: http://epw.senate.gov/public/index.cfm?FuseAction=Minority.PressReleases&ContentRecord_id=850753f9-802a-23ad-48ea-b618f97ee450.

26. Press Release, "Kerry, Boxer Introduce Clean Energy Jobs and American Power Act," U.S. Senate Committee on Environment and Public Works Majority, September 30, 2009; available at: http://epw.senate.gov/public/index. cfm?FuseAction=Majority.PressReleases&ContentRecord_id=0c00344c-802a-23ad-4f4d-edb0c9408d2e.

27. See, e.g.: J. R. Pegg, "Navy Sonar v. Whales Argued in U.S. Supreme Court," NBC News, January 7, 2010; available at: http://www.nbcnewyork. com/news/green/Navy_Sonar_v__Whales_Argued_in_U_S__Supreme_ Court.html; see also Gordon Jackson, "Conservation groups sue to block Navy training range," *Florida Times-Union,* January 30, 2010; available at: http:// jacksonville.com/news/georgia/2010-01-29/story/conservation_groups_sue_ to_block_navy_training_range.

28. See, e.g.: Kathleen Margareta Ryder, *COMMENT: Vieques' Struggle for Freedom: Environmental Litigation, Civil Disobedience, and Political Marketing Proves Successful,* Summer 2004, 12 Penn St. Envtl. L. Rev. 419; available at: https://litigation-essentials.lexisnexis.com/webcd/app?action=Document Display&crawlid=1&doctype=cite&docid=12+Penn+St.+Envtl.+L.+Rev.+ 419&srctype=smi&srcid=3B15&key=d032270a207394848dd904d0d5f5e123.

29. "Groups sue Navy over underwater explosion," Grist, July 30, 2008; available at: http://www.grist.org/article/navy2/.

30. These were highly misleading, however, leading to much of the cost being ignored. See "Incomplete CBO Estimate Does Not Include All Costs of

Cap-and-Trade," Senate Republican Policy Committee, July 8, 2009; available at: http://rpc.senate.gov/public/_files/EnergyFactsCBOScore.pdf.

31. Douglas Elmendorf, "Cost Estimate for S. 1733 Clean Energy Jobs and American Power Act," Congressional Budget Office Director's Blog, December 17, 2009; data available at: http://cboblog.cbo.gov/?cat=7; cost Estimate at http://cboblog.cbo.gov/?cat=7.

32. Ibid.

33. Ibid.

34. Ibid.

35. See, e.g.: H.R. 1862: Cap and Dividend Act of 2009, 11th Congress (Van Hollen), and the "Carbon Limits and Energy for America's Renewal (CLEAR) act" (Cantwell, Collins) which numerous news reports describe as having been introduced as legislation but which remains, as of this writing, in draft form only, available at http://cantwell.senate.gov/issues/CLEAR%20Act%20-%20Leg%20Text.pdf.

36. See, e.g.: "Cigarette tax for SCHIP nips at Obama tax promise," *St. Petersburg Times*, April 2, 2009; available at: http://www.politifact.com/truth-o-meter/promises/promise/515/no-family-making-less-250000-will-see-any-form-tax/.

37. See, e.g.: David Kreutzer, "Discounting and Climate Change Economics: Estimating the Cost of Cap and Trade," Heritage Foundation, Washington, D.C., November 19, 2009; available at: http://www.heritage.org/Research/Energyandenvironment/wm2705.cfm.

38. See, e.g.: Declan McCullagh, "Treasury Docs: Enviro Taxes Could Reach $400 Billion a Year," CBS News, September 18, 2009; available at: http://www.cbsnews.com/blogs/2009/09/18/taking_liberties/entry5322108.shtml.

39. For the debate over largest tax increase in U.S. history, see "Is it really the 'largest tax increase in American history'?" *Politico*, March 10, 2008; available at: http://www.politico.com/blogs/thecrypt/0308/Is_it_really_the_largest_tax_increase_in_American_history.html, citing "Revenue Effects of Major Tax Bills," U.S. Department of the Treasury OTA Working Paper 81, revised September, 2006; available at: http://www.ustreas.gov/offices/tax-policy/library/ota81.pdf. Longtime Capitol Hill energy aide Dan Kish of the Institute for Energy Research notes in an email to me that this is far bigger than the tax increase to fight the Axis powers, according to that Treasury

assessment. Using those figures, Kish states that the $73.4 billion taxed annually to pay for WWII, which in Treasury-adjusted 1992 dollars, updated to 2007 dollars, equates to $107 billion. As such, in its cost in constant dollars Obama's expected cap-and-trade revenues would amount to the biggest tax increase in U.S. history, even near if not precisely at the lowest range of expected revenues.

The 2 percent of GDP figure is arrived at by dividing $300 billion into a U.S. economy of approximately $14.441 trillion as estimated by International Monetary Fund staff for the year 2008 (International Monetary Fund, World Economic Outlook Database, October 2009: Nominal GDP list of countries.) Data for the year 2008 available at: http://imf.org/external/pubs/ft/weo/2009/02/weodata/weorept.aspx?sy=2008&ey=2008&scsm=1&ssd=1&sort=country&ds=.&br=1&c=512,941,914,446,612,666,614,668,311,672,213,946,911,137,193,962,122,674,912,676,313,548,419,556,513,678,316,181,913,682,124,684,339,273,638,921,514,948,218,943,963,686,616,688,223,518,516,728,918,558,748,138,618,196,522,278,622,692,156,694,624,142,626,449,628,564,228,283,924,853,233,288,632,293,636,566,634,964,238,182,662,453,960,968,423,922,935,714,128,862,611,716,321,456,243,722,248,942,469,718,253,724,642,576,643,936,939,961,644,813,819,199,172,184,132,524,646,361,648,362,915,364,134,732,652,366,174,734,328,144,258,146,656,463,654,528,336,923,263,738,268,578,532,537,944,742,176,866,534,369,536,744,429,186,433,925,178,746,436,926,136,466,343,112,158,111,439,298,916,927,664,846,826,299,542,582,443,474,917,754,544,698&s=NGDPD&grp=0&a=&pr.x=35&pr.y=9 ("The World Bank: World Development Indicators database, 1 July 2009. Gross domestic product (2008)." World Bank, 1-7-2009; available at: http://siteresources.worldbank.org/DATASTATISTICS/Resources/GDP.pdf (accessed February 5, 2010). This is a higher figure than World Bank or CIA World Factbook (Field listing - GDP [official exchange rate]), CIA World Factbook; available at: https://www.cia.gov/library/publications/the-world-factbook/fields/2195.html (accessed February 5, 2010).

40. David Kreutzer, "Discounting and Climate Change Economics: Estimating the Cost of Cap and Trade," op cit.

41. Declan McCullagh, "Obama Admin: Cap And Trade Could Cost Families $1,761 A Year," CBS News, September 15, 2009; available at: http://www.cbsnews.com/blogs/2009/09/15/taking_liberties/entry5314040.shtml; see also

Declan McCullagh, "Treasury Docs: Enviro Taxes Could Reach $400 Billion a Year," op cit.

42. Analysis of The Waxman-Markey Bill, "The American Clean Energy and Security Act of 2009 (H.R. 2454) Using The National Energy Modeling System (NEMS/ACCF-NAM 2). A Report by the American Council for Capital Formation and the National Association of Manufacturers Analysis conducted by Science Applications International Corporation (SAIC)." National Association of Manufacturers and American Council on Capital Formation, Washington, D.C., June 26, 2009; available at: http://www.accf.org/media/dynamic/3/media_378.pdf.

43. Ibid.

44. Ibid.

45. Ibid.

46. The professor is John Reilly, whose advocacy downplaying the legislation's costs touched off a fierce partisan battle and was used by many media outlets to support its passage with little regard to his actual analysis and its assumptions. He nearly quadrupled the initial cost assessment defended with such vitriol after he acknowledged "a boneheaded mistake," but still left his analysis burdened by problems, including that described here. See John McMormack, "Fuzzy Math," *The Weekly Standard*, April 22, 2009; available at: http://weeklystandard.com/Content/Public/Articles/000/000/016/412cwueq.asp. McCormack writes, in pertinent part, "In other words, Reilly estimates that 'the amount of tax collected' through companies would equal $3,128 per household—and 'Those costs do get passed to consumers and income earners in one way or another'—but those costs have 'nothing to do with the real cost' to the economy. Reilly assumes that the $3,128 will be 'returned' to each household. Without that assumption, Reilly wrote, 'the cost would then be the Republican estimate [$3,128] plus the cost I estimate [$800].' In Reilly's view, the $3,128 taken through taxes will be 'returned' to each household whether or not the government cuts a $3,128 rebate check to each household."

47. Dr. William Heckle, Letter to the Editor, *Cincinnati Enquirer*, November 13, 2009. No longer available online.

48. Anthony Faiola, "In Germany, the high price of going green," *Washington Post*, November 22, 2009; available at: http://www.washingtonpost.com/wp-dyn/content/article/2009/11/20/AR2009112002893.html.

49. Ibid.

50. See, e.g.: "Winners and Losers in the Waxman-Markey Stealth Tax," Institute for Energy Research, May 22, 2009; available at: http://www.instituteforenergyresearch.org/2009/05/22/winners-and-losers-in-the-waxman-markey-stealth-tax/.

51. Barack Obama, in a January 8, 2008, meeting with the editorial board of the *San Francisco Chronicle*. See video at: "Obama on cap and trade: 'electricity rates would necessarily skyrocket,'" op cit.

52. Ibid.

53. Zachary Coile, "Pelosi sketches strategy on key issues," *San Francisco Chronicle*, January 22, 2009; available at: http://www.sfgate.com/cgi-bin/article.cgi?f=/c/a/2009/01/22/MN5Q15EJQ2.DTL.

54. Lori Montgomery, "Congress Approves Budget," *Washington Post*, April 3, 2009; available at: http://www. washingtonpost.com/wp-dyn/content/article/2009/04/02/AR2009040203473.html?hpid=topnews.

55. See, e.g.: "Democratic cap and trade plans have credits to offset electricity rate increases," *St. Petersburg Times*, November 17, 2009; available at: http://www.politifact.com/truth-o-meter/statements/2009/nov/17/sarah-palin/cap-and-trade-electricity-rates-fixes/.

56. Glenn Thrush, "Dingell: Cap-and trade a 'great big' tax," *Politico*, April 27, 2009; available at: http://www.politico.com/news/stories/0409/21730.html.

57. Congressional Budget Office, "An Evaluation of Cap and Trade Programs for Reducing US GHG Emissions," June 2001; available at: http://www. cbo.gov/doc.cfm?index=2876&type=0&sequence=2.

58. According to center-left economist William Pizer in a paper for Resources for the Future, "Prices vs. Quantities Revisited: The Case of Climate Change," Resources for the Future, Washington, D.C., Discussion Paper 98-02, October 1997; available at: http://www.rff.org/documents/RFF-DP-98-02.pdf.

59. "Statement of Peter R. Orszag, Director, Implications of a Cap-and-Trade Program for Carbon Dioxide Emissions before the Committee on Finance United States Senate," April 24, 2008; available at: http://www.cbo.gov/ftpdocs/91xx/doc9134/04-24-Cap_Trade_Testimony.1.1.shtml.

60. Press Release, "Camp-CBO Exchange on Cap-and-Tax Proposal," House Ways & Means Committee Republicans, Thursday, March 26, 2009; available at: http://republicans.waysandmeans.house.gov/News/DocumentSingle.aspx?DocumentID=116686.

61. Senator James Inhofe, "Inhofe: Climate Bill Is a Costly Non-Solution," *Roll Call*, October 19, 2009, quoting Rangel in May 2009 (see: http://www.gop.gov/wtas/09/05/14/chairman-of-house-tax-committee); available at: http://www.rollcall.com/features/Policy-Briefing_Energy-2009/energy_environment/39557-1.html.

62. "Statement of Peter R. Orszag, Director, Implications of a Cap-and-Trade Program for Carbon Dioxide Emissions before the Committee on Finance United States Senate," April 24, 2008; available at: http://www.cbo.gov/ftpdocs/91xx/doc9134/04-24-Cap_Trade_Testimony.pdf.

63. In an Orwellian headline diminishing cost increases in fact resulting from the very bill that supposedly has some balm to mitigate just how high it might raise them, see Juliet Eilperin, "Climate Bill Would Ease Energy Costs, Senator Says," *Washington Post*, October 2, 2009; available at: http://www.washingtonpost.com/wp-dyn/content/article/2009/10/01/AR2009100103908.html.

64. Congressional Budget Office Economic and Budget Issue Brief, "Trade-offs for Allocating Allowances in CO_2 Emissions," April 25, 2007; available at: http://www.cbo.gov/ftpdocs/80xx/doc8027/04-25-Cap_Trade.pdf.

65. See, e.g.: "Statement of the American Farm Bureau, Senate Committee on Environment and Public Works Regarding: Climate Change, Presented By Bob Stallman, President," July 14, 2009; available at: http://epw.senate.gov/public/index.cfm?FuseAction=Files.View&FileStore_id=20fd972a-1850-4ded-85e1-8de02eb056ee.

66. See, e.g.: "Farms-to-forest plan worries Vilsack," *Washington Times*, December 29, 2009; available at: http://www.washingtontimes.com/news/2009/dec/29/forests-vs-food-study-worries-agriculture-chief/.

67. "Impact on the Economy of the American Clean Energy and Security Act of 2009 (H.R.2454)," CRA International Prepared for the National Black Chamber, Washington, D.C., April 2009; available at: http://www.naw.org/files/Study.pdf.

68. Ibid.

69. Tom Fowler, "Draft of climate change bill leaves lots to be resolved," *Houston Chronicle*, April 1, 2009; available at: http://www.chron.com/disp/story.mpl/business/6354686.html.

70. Julian Glover, "A collapsing carbon market makes mega-pollution cheap," *The Guardian* (UK), February 23, 2009; available at: http://www.guardian.co.uk/commentisfree/2009/feb/23/glover-carbon-market-pollution.

71. "Subprime Carbon," Friends of the Earth, Washington, D.C.; available at: http://www.foe.org/subprime-carbon.

72. See, e.g.: "The Cap-and-Tax Fiction: Democrats off-loading economics to pass climate change bill," *Wall Street Journal*, June 25, 2009; available at: http://online.wsj.com/article/SB124588837560750781.html.

73. Jake Tapper and Sunlen Miller, "President Obama On Energy Bill: 'Make No Mistake, This Is A Jobs Bill,'" ABC News, June 25, 2009; available at: http://blogs.abcnews.com/politicalpunch/2009/06/president-obama-on-energy-bill-make-no-mistake-this-is-a-jobs-bill.html.

74. See, e.g.: "Cap-and-trade: Almost $8 billion in administrative costs?" *Wall Street Journal*, August 11, 2009; available at: http://blogs.wsj.com/environmentalcapital/2009/08/11/cap-and-trade-almost-8-billion-in-administrative-costs/tab/article/.

75. Darren Goode, "Senate Democrats Have Uncertain Path For Climate Measure," *Congress Daily*, October 1, 2009; available at: http://www.nationaljournal.com/congressdaily/cda_20091001_8002.php.

76. Cited by Melvin Shapiro, "The end of jobs?" Townhall.com, February 17, 2010; available at: http://melvinshapiro.blogtownhall.com/2010/02/17/the_end_of_jobs.thtml.

77. Ibid.

78. Nick Loris, "John Kerry: If You Enjoyed This Year's Recession, Just Wait for Cap and Trade," *Hawaii Reporter*, October 6, 2009; available at: http://www.hawaiireporter.com/story.aspx?5f42e1d8-8d45-430b-8d0b-01fc00f08dc9.

79. H.R. 2454: American Clean Energy and Security Act of 2009, Sec. 425, passed by the U.S. House of Representatives on June 26, 2009; available at: http://www.govtrack.us/congress/bill.xpd?bill=h111-2454.

80. Ibid., Sec. 2201.

81. See Legislative Digest, "H.R. 2454, American Clean Energy and Security Act of 2009," House Republican Conference, June 26, 2009; available at: http://www.gop.gov/bill/111/1/hr2454.

82. Ibid., Sec. 426.

83. Ibid.

84. Congressional Budget Office, "H.R. 2454 American Clean Energy and Security Act of 2009," June 5, 2009; available at: http://www.cbo.gov/ftpdocs/102xx/doc10262/hr2454.pdf.

85. "Impact on the Economy of the American Clean Energy and Security Act of 2009 (H.R.2454)," CRA International Prepared for the National Black Chamber, Washington, D.C., April 2009, p. 7.

86. See e.g.: "Kerry-Boxer's Bait and Switch: Manufacturing," Senate Republican Policy committee, October 6, 2009, http://rpc.senate.gov/public/_files/BaitandSwitchManufacturing.pdf. Here's how we know the authorized amount of relief falls woefully short of what it purports to provide. If you assume an average job loss from the scheme, per year, of 1.125 in the scheme's first twenty years of operation (a fair estimate using, e.g., the IHS/Global Insight U.S. Macroeconomic Model; see analysis by Heritage Foundation, "What Boxer-Kerry Will Cost the Economy," David Kreutzer, Ph.D., Karen Campbell, Ph.D., William W. Beach, Ben Lieberman, and Nicolas Loris, Backgrounder #2365, January 26, 2010; available at: http://www.heritage.org/research/economy/bg2365.cfm), you get 22.5 million individual work years killed. Grant relief for each of those workers who lose their jobs for three years and there are 67.5 work years to be compensated for from $4.3 billion. That's $1,480 available as relief per lost work year. So it is a pipe dream to come up with 70 percent of their wages from this pot, or else it's first-come, first-serve for the first few million then bupkas. We get the same approximate figure approaching matters another way. This means 3 years of relief x 1.125 million lost years each year = 3.375 million new work years to be compensated for each year, from $430 million per year, or $1,450 per worker. So long as he or she didn't make more than about 2,075 *per year*, this comes out just right as just enough money to pay 70 percent of lost wages for three years.

87. See, e.g.: Chris Horner, "The New Climate Entitlement," *National Review Online*, October 7, 2008; available at: http://planetgore.nationalreview.com/post/?q=ZDFhMjQ1YjdlMTkwOTJiZTAwMzE4NjAzZGMwN2NkMzk=. The draft provided "compensation, through the issuance of a monthly rebate, for the loss in purchasing power resulting from this Act and the amendments made by this Act." It also included a provision to reduce the transfers pro rata in the event the economic pain is so great that even the limited-in-scope Low-Income Consumer Climate Change Rebate Fund cannot handle it, the document itself has since been removed from the House web sites.

88. Peter Whorisky, "States' jobless funds are being drained in recession," *Washington Post*, December 22, 2009; available at: http://www.washingtonpost.com/wp-dyn/content/article/2009/12/21/AR2009122103269.html.

89. "Breaking News: Manufacturing & Technology eJournal Poll Shows Clean Energy Act Could Force Nearly 20 Percent of Manufacturers to Close," *Manufacturing & Technology eJournal*, July 2, 2009; available at: http://www.mfrtech.com/articles/2293.html.

90. Stephen Power, "Senate Democrats Want Climate Bill to Protect Manufacturing," *Wall Street Journal*, August 6, 2009; available at: http://online.wsj.com/article/SB124959044772212205.html.

91. "Cap and Trade War," *Wall Street Journal*, March 30, 2009; available at: http://online.wsj.com/article/SB123837276242467853.html.

92. See, e.g.: Mary Katherine Ham, "John Boehner Takes Over the Floor to Read Cap-and-Trade Amendments," *Weekly Standard*, June 26, 2009; available at: http://www.weeklystandard.com/weblogs/TWSFP/2009/06/john_boehner_takes_over_the_fl.asp.

93. H.R. 2454: American Clean Energy and Security Act of 2009, Sec. 425, passed by the U.S. House of Representatives on June 26, 2009; available at: http://www.govtrack.us/congress/bill.xpd?bill=h111-2454.

94. Data available at: http://www.govtrack.us/congress/vote.xpd?vote=h2009-477.

95. "Energy Bill Vote was in New Jersey's Best Interest," July 26, 2009; available at: http://lance.house.gov/index.cfm?sectionid=29&sectiontree=7,29&itemid=178.

96. Governor Mitch Daniels, "Government that Works, Republicans' Weekly Radio Address," Real Clear Politics, May 30, 2009; available at: http://www.realclearpolitics.com/articles/2009/05/30/republicans_weekly_address_government_that _works_96755.html.

97. Press Release, "Kerry, Boxer Introduce Clean Energy Jobs and American Power Act," U.S. Senate Committee on Environment and Public Works Majority, September 30, 2009.

98. Darren Samuelsohn, "Boxer, Kerry Set to Introduce Climate Bill in Senate," ClimateWire, *New York Times*, September 28, 2009; available at: http://

www.nytimes.com/cwire/2009/09/28/28climatewire-boxer-kerry-set-to-intro-duce-climate-bill-in-43844.html.

99. "Clean Energy Jobs and American Power Act: Pollution Reduction and Investment"; available at: http://kerry.senate.gov/cleanenergyjobsandameri-canpower/pdf/PRI.pdf.

100. "Endangerment and Cause or Contribute Findings for Greenhouse Gases," U.S. Environmental Protection Agency, December 7, 2009; available at: http://www.epa.gov/climatechange/endangerment.html.

101. Ibid.

102. See, e.g.: "Administration Warns of 'Command-and-Control' Regula-tion Over Emissions," FOX News, December 9, 2009; available at: http://www.foxnews.com/politics/2009/12/09/administration-warns-command-control-regulation-emissions/.

103. Rep. Colin Peterson, "Amendments to Climate Change Bill Were Nec-essary," Op-ed, July 16, 2009, available at: http://collinpeterson.house.gov/press/111th/Peterson%20Op-Ed—%20Amendments%20to%20Climate%20Change%20Bill%20Were%20Necessary.html.

104. "'A Glorious Mess,'" *Wall Street Journal*, April 12, 2008.

105. Ian Talley, "OMB Memo: Serious Economic Impact Likely From EPA CO2 Rules," Dow Jones Newswires, May 12, 2009; available at: http://epw.sen-ate.gov/public/index.cfm?FuseAction=Minority.Blogs&ContentRecord_id=3530046c-802a-23ad-401a-82f7edb11f26.

106. See, e.g.: comments by Congressman Ed Markey and Senator Barbara Boxer in "EPA greenhouse gas ruling makes US regulation likely," *Recharge News*, April 17, 2009; available at: http://www.rechargenews.com/regions/north_america/article176160.ece.

107. I was on a discussion panel on "Earth Day" April 22, 2009, sponsored by FD Communications in Washington, D.C., kicked off by U.S. Senate Envi-ronment Committee chair Sen. Boxer who made such a warning in her (unpublished) remarks.

108. Senator to Author in an off-the-record meeting.

109. *Massachusetts v. EPA*, 127 S. Ct. 1438 (2007); available at: http://www.supremecourtus.gov/opinions/06pdf/05-1120.pdf.

110. Marlo Lewis, "EPA's Tailoring Rule: Temporary, Dubious, Incomplete Antidote To 's Legacy of Absurd Results (Part 1)," Master Resource, January 7, 2010; available at: http://www.masterresource.org/2010/01/epas-tailoring-rule-temporary-dubious-incomplete-antidote-to-massachusetts-v-epas-legacy-of-absurd-results/.

111. Ibid.

112. Marlo Lewis PhD, "EPA's Tailoring Rule: Temporary, Dubious, Incomplete Antidote To 's Legacy of Absurd Results (Part 1)," op cit.

113. "Inhofe Calls EPA's Endangerment Finding a 'Ticking Time Bomb,'" Senate Environment and Public Works Committee Minority, May 1, 2009; available at: http://epw.senate.gov/public/index.cfm?FuseAction=Minority.PressReleases&ContentRecord_id=fd7a0056-802a-23ad-4798-d91c266c0bbd&Region_id=&Issue_id=.

114. (EPA's) Prevention of Significant Deterioration and Title V Greenhouse Gas Tailoring Rule; Proposed Rule, Federal Register, Vol. 74 No. 206, 55292-55365, October 27, 2009; available at: http://www.epa.gov/nsr/documents/GHGTailoringProposal.pdf, see pp. 19-20.

115. See, e.g.: "Terms of 'Endangerment,'" *Wall Street Journal*, September 3, 2009; available at: http://online.wsj.com/article/SB10001424052970204731804574388642894879438.html.

116. Proposed Tailoring Rule at 55295; see esp. 71, 104-106 at http://www.epa.gov/nsr/documents/GHGTailoringProposal.pdf.

117. Ian Talley, "OMB Memo: Serious Economic Impact Likely From EPA CO2 Rules," op cit.

118. "Terms of 'Endangerment,'" *Wall Street Journal*, September 3, 2009; available at: http://online.wsj.com/article/SB10001424052970204731804574388642894879438.html.

119. See Marlo Lewis PhD, "Kempthorne: Whistling Past the Graveyard," *National Review Online*, May 17, 2008; available at: http://planetgore.nationalreview.com/post/?q=MThhNjc2NjUxZDZiNTQxNDhmZWQ1Y2Y3NmVkZjU5MGU=.

120. "Inhofe Calls EPA's Endangerment Finding a 'Ticking Time Bomb,'" Senate Environment and Public Works Committee Minority, May 1, 2009.

121. Memo, "First (1st) Round of Office of Management and Budget (OMB) Comments to USEPA on the Proposed Findings," Office of Management and Budget, April 24, 2009; available at: http://www.regulations.gov/search/Regs/home.html#documentDetail?R=0900006480965abd.

122. Ian Talley, "UPDATE: EPA: May Want CO_2 Clean Air Act Power With Climate Bill," Dow Jones Newswires, October 27, 2009, detailing Jackson testimony that day before the Senate Environment and Public Works Committee.

123. James Gerstenzang, "Q&A: Carol Browner, Director of the White House Office of Energy and Climate Change Policy," On Earth, Natural Resources Defense Council, February 8, 2010; available at: http://www.onearth.org/carol-browner-qa.

124. Chris Horner, "So…Which Time Were You Lying?" *National Review Online*, December 12, 2009; available at: http://planetgore.nationalreview.com/post/?q=MWU5N2Y3NzY0MTJkNGE0NzBlOTY3MjNlND NmYmE5MDc=.

125. If there was any impact on the increase of CO_2 emissions since efforts to reduce them in rich countries, it was that the emission increase accelerated slightly after agreement to the Kyoto Protocol, and they are projected to continue rising steadily. See, "Energy-related carbon dioxide emissions," International Energy Outlook 2009, U.S. Energy Information Administration, May 27, 2009; available at: http://www.eia.doe.gov/oiaf/ieo/emissions.html.

126. For a description of what this means and entails see, Federal CAA Toolbox, "National Ambient Air Quality Standards (NAAQS)," Air Force Center for Engineering and the Environment; available at: http://www.afcee.brooks.af.mil/products/air/federal/compdet/naaqs.html.

127. See Marlo Lewis PhD, "NAAQS Petition Confirms Mass v. EPA Is Bottomless Well of Absurd Results," GlobalWarming.Org, December 3, 2009; available at: http://www.openmarket.org/2009/12/03/naaqs-petition-confirms-mass-v-epa-is-bottomless-well-of-absurd-results/.

128. "Petition to Establish National Pollution Limits for Greenhouse Gases Pursuant to the Clean Air Act"; available at: Center for Biological Diversity/350.org, http://www.openmarket.org/wp-content/uploads/2009/12/cbd-350org-petition.pdf.

129. H.R. 391 (110th Congress), specifically, "To amend the Clean Air Act to provide that greenhouse gases are not subject to the Act, and for other purposes." See: http://www.govtrack.us/congress/bill.xpd?bill=h111-391

130. Ibid.

131. Gayathri Vaidyanathan, "A roaring economy is hitched to a galloping addiction to coal," *Climate Wire*, February 4, 2010.

Chapter 5

1. This is alternately attributed, either as until Congress or "politicians" learn their power, to Alexis de Tocqueville and Alexander Fraser Tytler.

2. This is evident in the regular stream of coverage touting progress, or casting aspersions upon the challenge to "global warming" legislation winding through Congress, though an example of a credulous and even incurious media is found in the *Los Angeles Times*'s coverage, Jim Tankersley, "Industry leaders join Obama on emissions limits," May 18, 2009; available at: http://articles.latimes.com/2009/may/18/nation/na-climate18.

3. Lawrence Solomon, "Enron's Other Secret," *Financial Post* (Canada), May 30, 2009; available at: http://network.nationalpost.com/np/blogs/fpcomment/archive/2009/05/30/lawrence-solomon-enron-s-other-secret.aspx.

4. Memo from John Palmisano, "Implications of the Climate Change Agreement in Kyoto & What Transpired" (1997). It can be found on the "Master Resource" website run by former Enron policy advisor Rob Bradley; available at: http://www.politicalcapitalism.org/enron/121297.pdf.

5. Iain Murray, "Wanted: For Carbon Crimes," *National Review Online*, September 15, 2009. The phrase "Bootleggers and Baptists" was first coined by economist Bruce Yandle in a 1983 article in the May/June edition of the Cato Institute's *Regulation* magazine, "Bootleggers and Baptists: The Education of a Regulatory Economist"; available at: http://www.cato.org/pubs/regulation/regv7n3/v7n3-3.pdf; see also "Bruce Yandle, Revisited," *Regulation* 22, no. 3: 5–7. (1999); available at: http://www.cato.org/pubs/regulation/regv22n3/bootleggers.pdf.

6. Jonathan Fahey, "Exelon's Carbon Advantage", *Forbes*, January 18, 2010, http://www.forbes.com/part_forbes/2010/0118/americas-best-company-10-exelon-utility-tax-carbon-windfall.html.

7. Rebecca Smith, "For Exelon, Carbon Reductions Solve a Problem, Make Money," *Wall Street Journal*, October 19, 2009; available at: http://online.wsj.com/article/SB10001424052748703790404574471672160799790.html.

8. Jonathan Fahey, "Exelon's Carbon Advantage", *Forbes*, January 18, 2010.

9. See, e.g., Bruce Henderson, "Lobbying Pays Off for Duke," *Charlotte Observer*, October 9, 2009; available at: http://www.charlotteobserver.com/top-stories/story/992164.html. This arrangement is typical, generally found either in a state's utility law or tariffs, which are the individual companies' filings with the regulators in which the agreed rates, terms, and conditions of service are found. Meanwhile, what are clearly "lobbying" expenses are not permissibly recovered in rates. What activity is which is decided by state regulators on an *ad hoc* basis.

10. Jonathan Fahey, "Q&A: Utilities Could Cash In On Climate Bill," *Forbes*, June 16, 2009; available at: http://www.forbes.com/2009/06/16/aep-global-warming-business-energy-utilities.html.

11. Ibid.

12. Peter Behr, "Power Industry Infighting Heats Up Over Climate Legislation," *E&E News*, July 16, 2009; available at: http://www.eenews.net/public/climatewire/2009/07/16/1.

13. Making the case that no one alleges a detectable climate change from Kyoto, cap-and-trade, or the like is like proving a negative, but it has been established, establishment wisdom since just following the Kyoto negotiations. As Senator James Inhofe said on the Senate floor in an October 2007 speech, referencing advice famously given to then-Vice President Al Gore when Gore returned home having ignored unanimous Senate Article II "advice" and agreed to Kyoto, "First, going on a carbon diet would do nothing to avert climate change. After the U.S. signed the Kyoto Protocol in 1997, Al Gore's own scientist, Tom Wigley of the National Center for Atmospheric Research, calculated that Kyoto would reduce emissions by only 0.07 degrees Celsius by the year 2050. That's all. 0.07 degrees. And that's if the United States had ratified Kyoto and the other signatories met their targets." This analysis then appeared in Wigley, T.M.L. 1998. The Kyoto Protocol: CO_2, CH_4 and climate implications. *Geophysical Research Letters*, Vol. 25, No. 13: 2285–88.

14. James Weinstein, *The Corporate Ideal in the Liberal State, 1900–1918* (Boston, MA: Beacon Press, 1968), 1.

15. Gabriel Kolko, *Railroads and Regulation* (Princeton, NJ: Princeton University Press, 1965).

16. Ibid., 3–5.

17. Gabriel Kolko, *The Triumph of Conservatism: A Reinterpretation of American History 1900–1916* (Washington, D.C.: Free Press, 1977), 4.

18. Jim Tankersley, "Industry leaders join Obama on emissions limits," op cit.

19. Darren Samuelsohn, "Soul-searching follows U.S. CAP defections," Greenwire, February 22, 2010.

20. Gabriel Kolko, *The Triumph of Conservatism*.

21. Ibid.

22. Roy Childs Jr., "Big Business and the Rise of American Statism" in *The Libertarian Alternative*, ed. Tibor Machan (Chicago: Nelson Hall, 1974), 208–34. Originally delivered as a speech at the University of Pennsylvania, November 1969.

23. It should come as no surprise that this ritual refrain, offered to me even at the CEO level of major companies, is a talking point pushed by the alarmist industry. See, e.g.: "As companies look out 50 years and make the long-term investment decisions critical to their business operations, they need regulatory certainty. That's why corporate leaders are calling for passage of climate legislation in the US and agreement on a global climate deal here in Copenhagen." From the World Wildlife Fund press release, "'This Is the Time to Show Leadership and Make History': Corporate Leaders Call for Agreement in Copenhagen," December 13, 2009; available at: http://www.worldwildlife.org/who/media/press/2009/WWFPresitem146 60.html (accessed January 26, 2010).

24. Roy Childs Jr., "Big Business and the Rise of American Statism" in *The Libertarian Alternative*, ed. Tibor Machan (Chicago: Nelson Hall, 1974), 224.

25. Roy Childs Jr., "Big Business and the Rise of American Statism" in *The Libertarian Alternative*, ed. Tibor Machan (Chicago: Nelson Hall, 1974), 230–31, quoting J. W. Jenks (citation omitted).

26. SEC's "Interpretive Guidance on Disclosure Related to Business or Legal Developments Regarding Climate Change," announced January 27, 2010.

27. Sec. 707 "Presidential Response and recommendations" of both S. 1733, "Kerry-Boxer" and H.R. 2454, "Waxman-Markey."

28. Lawrence Solomon, "Enron's Other Secret," op cit.

29. Alexis Simendinger, "Will Key Chairmen Power Up For Energy Bill?" *National Journal*, June 6, 2009.

30. Rich Lowry, "Corker on Obama: 'He Personalizes Everything,'" *National Review Online*, July 31, 2009; available at: http://corner.nationalreview.com/post/?q=ZTUzMGY1YWYzM2VmNzM3OGQ3NWUyZDM5NTY4OTM0ZDE=.

31. Phil Kerpen, "Democrats' Big Green Scam," FOX News, June 23, 2009; available at: http://www.foxnews.com/opinion/2009/06/23/democrats-buying-energy-tax-opponents/.

32. Editorial, "The Rise of the Carbon Oligarchs," *The Washington Times*, July 13, 2009.

33. Ibid.

34. Marianne Lavelle, "The Climate Lobby's Nonstop Growth," Center for Public Integrity, May 19, 2009; available at: http://www.publicintegrity.org/investigations/climate_change/articles/entry/1376/.

35. Christa Marshall, "Climate and Energy Issues Send Hordes to K Street," Greenwire, *New York Times*, February 10, 2010; available at: http://www.nytimes.com/cwire/2010/02/10/10climatewire-climate-and-energy-issues-send-hordes-to-k-s-21839.html.

36. Marianne Lavelle, "The Climate Change Lobby Explosion," op cit.

37. "History of the Climatic Research Unit," www.cru.uea.ac.uk/cru/about/history/.

38. Anne C. Mulkern, "Influence spending by wind, all renewables soared in 2009," Greenwire, February 22, 2010.

39. Tom Borelli, "Obama's Corporatism Strategy Might Advance Cap-and-Trade," Townhall.com, May 30, 2009; available at: http://townhall.com/columnists/TomBorelli/2009/05/30/obamas_ corporatism_strategy_might_advance_cap-and-trade?page=full&comments=true.

40. Economic Recovery Advisory Board, "Memorandum for the President," June 17, 2009; available at: http://www.whitehouse.gov/assets/documents/PERAB_Climate_Memo_with_Comments-Final.pdf.

41. Barack Obama, in a January 8, 2008, meeting with the editorial board of the *San Francisco Chronicle*, stated that "Under my plan of a cap-and-trade system ... if somebody wants to build a coal-powered plant, they can; it's just that it will bankrupt them." See video, "Obama on cap and trade: 'electricity rates would necessarily skyrocket,'" op cit.

42. Ibid. See also Borelli comments and link at Press Release, "President Obama's Cap-and-Trade Policy Takes Another Hit: BP, Caterpillar and ConocoPhillips Exit USCAP Global Warming Lobbying Group," National Center for Public Policy Research, February 17, 2010; available at: http://www.nationalcenter.org/PR-Caterpillar_USCAP_021710.html.

43. Press Release, "President Obama's Cap-and-Trade Policy Takes Another Hit: BP, Caterpillar and ConocoPhillips Exit USCAP Global Warming Lobbying Group," op cit.

44. Jim Tankersley, "Industry leaders join Obama on emissions limits," op cit.

45. Ibid.

46. See e.g.: "Statement of the U.S. Chamber of Commerce on Regulation of Greenhouse Gases Under the Clean Air Act," William L. Kovacs, U.S. Senate Environment and Public Works Committee, September 23, 2008; available at: http://www.uschamber.com/NR/rdonlyres/eaf66mxsezcul2vb2cuvpfooon cyhpyshcxpc7zzbsvgreuv4uh5zc2p6csnbnom6aw7qszmg5axla43722hyxeshfe/ 080923_epa_kovacs_testimony.pdf.

47. See, e.g.: "The Johnson & Johnson businesses worldwide have adopted a climate-friendly energy policy to reduce their operating costs, meet their emerging legal and societal obligations, and improve the environment for future generations. Johnson & Johnson strives to be a corporate environmental leader in the efforts to prevent climate change and partners with organizations working to improve GHG management. Joining EPA's Climate Leaders program has also provided Johnson & Johnson with useful guidance in developing a comprehensive system to measure and track its GHG emissions," Partner Profile, USEPA; available at: http://www.epa.gov/ climateleaders/partners/partners/johnsonjohnson.html.

48. R. Bruce Josten, "Letter to United States Senate on Climate Change," U.S. Chamber of Commerce, November 3, 2009; available at: http://www. uschamber.com/issues/letters/2009/091103climate.htm.

49. Tom Borelli, "Obama's Corporatism Strategy Might Advance Cap-and-Trade," op cit.

50. Roy Childs Jr., "Big Business and the Rise of American Statism," in *The Libertarian Alternative*, ed. Tibor Machan (Chicago: Nelson Hall, 1974), 226.

51. Associated Press, "White House releases Visitor Records," *MSN Money*, December 30, 2009; available at: http://news.moneycentral.msn.com/ticker/ article.aspx?Feed=AP&Date=20091230&ID= 10951885&Symbol=GE.

52. See, e.g.: "Era of meanness, greed drawing to end: GE's Immelt," Reuters, December 9, 2009; available at: http://www.reuters.com/article/idUS-TRE5B83PL20091209.

53. Press Release, "President Obama's Cap-and-Trade Policy Takes Another Hit: BP, Caterpillar and ConocoPhillips Exit USCAP Global Warming Lobbying Group," National Center for Public Policy Research, February 17, 2010.

54. Paul Vieira, "Big Government is Watching: Immelt," *Financial Post*, June 9, 2009; available at: http://www.financialpost.com/news-sectors/economy/story.html?id=1678384.

55. John Doerr and Jeff Immelt, "Falling Behind on Green Tech," *Washington Post*, August 3, 2209; available at: http://www.washingtonpost.com/wp-dyn/content/article/2009/08/02/AR2009080201563_pf.html.

56. Ibid.

57. Timothy P. Carney, "Government Electric: jet engines and smart meters," *Washington Examiner*, October 1, 2009; available at: http://www.washingtonexaminer.com/opinion/blogs/beltway-confidential/Government-Electric-update-jet-engines-and-smart-meters-63141777.html.

58. "GE AES Greenhouse Gas Services," General Electric website; available at: http://ge.ecomagination.com/site/water/products/aesg.html.

59. See, e.g.: Ben Shapiro, "NBC's ObamaVision: GE Uses Network To Push Obama's Green Agenda—And Rakes In the Dough," BigHollywood.com, November 16, 2009; available at: http://bighollywood.breitbart.com/bshapiro/2009/11/16/propaganda-ge-uses-nbc-to-push-obamas-green-agenda-and-rakes-in-the-dough/.

60. Timothy P. Carney, *Obamanomics: How Barack Obama Bankrupts You and Enriches His Wall Street Friends, Corporate Lobbyists, and Union Bosses* (Washington, D.C.: Regnery, 2009).

61. See, e.g.: Rachel Layne, "GE's Immelt Accepts Responsibility as Shares Fall (Update1)," Bloomberg News, March 3, 2009; available at: http://www.bloomberg.com/apps/news?pid=20601109&refer=home&sid=ajYCLEW617S4.

62. Russ Mitchell, "Behind the Green Doerr," *Portfolio*, April 16, 2007; available at: http://www.portfolio.com/executives/features/2007/03/29/Behind-the-Green-Doerr/.

63. Ibid.

64. Statement by John Doerr, Partner, Kleiner Perkins Caufield & Byers, Thursday, July 16, 2009, Submitted to U.S. Senate Committee on Environment & Public Works, Hearing Regarding "Ensuring and Enhancing U.S. Competitiveness while Moving toward a Clean Energy Economy"; available at: http://epw.senate.gov/public/index.cfm?FuseAction=Files.View&FileStore_id=475d0524-1b1d-4a26-9e7f-b3f5eb9b9dc7.

65. "EPW Policy Beat: China and the 'Clean Energy Race,'" U.S. Senate Environment and Public Works Committee Minority blog, July 20, 200; available at: http://epw.senate.gov/public/index.cfm?Fuse Action=Minority.Blogs& ContentRecord_id=995fdfb4-802a-23ad-48d9-1155d5a77bda.

66. Russ Mitchell, "Behind the Green Doerr," op cit.

67. Ibid.

68. Ibid.

69. Ibid.

70. Claire Cain Miller, "Expecting New Tax, Firm Prepares to Track Carbon," *New York Times*, May 31, 2009; available at: http://www.nytimes.com/2009/06/01/technology/start-ups/01carbon.html?_r=1&partner=rss&emc=rss.

71. "Al Gore could become world's first carbon billionaire," *Telegraph* (UK), November 3, 2009; available at: http://www.telegraph.co.uk/earth/energy/6491195/Al-Gore-could-become-worlds-first-carbon-billionaire.html.

72. Josh Mitchell and Stephen Power, "Gore-Backed Car Firm Gets Large U.S. Loan," *Wall Street Journal*, September 25, 2009; available at: http://online.wsj.com/article/SB125383160812639013.html?mod=WSJ_hpp_MIDDLTopStories.

73. Steve Mufson, "High Stakes Quest for Permission to Pollute," *Washington Post*, June 5, 2009; available at: http://www.washingtonpost.com/wp-dyn/content/article/2009/06/04/AR2009060404435.html.

74. See, e.g.: Chris Horner, "It's Fair to Say they Don't Think Much of You," *National Review Online*, June 3, 2009; available at: http://planetgore.national-review.com/post/?q=ZWYyMjE1ZDYwNzJjNDI5NDUzYmEwYmQ2ZDYxNDQxMmY=; citing Duke rate filing and Bruce Henderson, "Duke Energy asks to raise rates," *Charlotte Observer*, June 3, 2009 (accessed June 15, 2009); available at: http://www.newsobserver.com/business/local_state/story/33129.html. *Forbes* wrote that the scheme for awarding the "allowances" to retailers was created by Exelon, a retailer itself. Jonathan Fahey, "Exelon's Carbon Advantage," *Forbes*, January 18, 2010.

75. Christa Marshall, "Climate and Energy Issues Send Hordes to K Street," Greenwire, *New York Times*, February 10, 2010.

76. Coral Davenport, "Natural Gas Producers Lobby for Place in Green Energy Regime," *Congressional Quarterly*, September 4, 2009.

77. "A unit of London-based Man Group Plc, the world's largest hedge-fund company, called the emissions market 'a new playground' in the April edition of the Retirement Mutual Fund Quarterly Review." Mathew Carr and Saijel Kishan, "Europe Fails Kyoto Standards as Trading Scheme Helps Polluters," Bloomberg News, July 17, 2006; available at: http://www.bloomberg.com/apps/news?pid=20601087&sid=awS1xfKpVRs8&refer=home.

78. Liam Denning, "Sunny Forecast for Climate Exchange Stock," *Wall Street Journal*, July 17, 2009; available at: http://online.wsj.c; see also: Liam Denning, "Sunny Forecast for Climate Exchange Stock," *Wall Street Journal*, July 17, 2009; available at: http://online.wsj.com/article/SB12477675529145 2751.html om/article/SB124776755291452751.html.

79. Michelle Chan, "Subprime Carbon?: Rethinking the world's largest new derivatives market," Friends of the Earth, Washington, D.C., 2009; available at: http://www.foe.org/pdf/SubprimeCarbonReport.pdf.

80. Nathanial Gronewold, "Wall Street sees 'bucks to be made' in House climate plan," *E&E News*, April 4, 2009; available at: http://www.eenews.net/public/Greenwire/2009/04/02/2.

81. Brendan O'Neill, "Green-industrial complex gets rich from carbon laws," *The Australian*, July 3, 2009; available at: http://www.theaustralian.com.au/news/green-industrial-complex-gets-rich-from-carbon-laws/story-0-1225745383987.

82. Joanne Nova, "Climate Money: The Climate Industry: $79 Billion So Far—Trillions to Come," Science and Public Policy Institute, July 21, 2009; available at: http://scienceandpublicpolicy.org/images/stories/papers/originals/climate_money.pdf.

83. Ibid., 2.

84. Rachel Morris, "Could Cap and Trade Cause Another Market Melt down?" *Mother Jones*, June 8, 2009; available at: http://motherjones.com/politics/2009/06/could-cap-and-trade-cause-another-market-meltdown.

85. Ibid.

86. Amanda DeBard, "FERC nominee says agency might need to add 1,400 works (sic) to police carbon trading," *Washington Times*, August 7, 2009.

87. Hans Kudnani, "Making Profits for a Cleaner Cause," *Financial Times*, July 30, 2009; available at: http://www.ft.com/cms/s/0/444867fe-7ca1-11de-a7bf-00144feabdc0.html?nclick_check=1.

88. "Change is coming: A framework for climate change—a defining issue of the 21st century," *GS Sustain* (Goldman Sachs, New York, NY, May 2009); available at: http://www.unglobalcompact.org/docs/issues_doc/Environment/Change_is_Coming_Framework_for_Climate_Change.pdf.

89. Matt Taibbi, "The Great American Bubble," *Rolling Stone*, July 13, 2009; available at: http://www.rollingstone.com/politics/story/29127316/the_great_american_bubble_machine/7.

90. Joe Hagan, "Tenacious G: Is Goldman Sachs Evil, or Just Too Good?" *New York* magazine, July 26, 2009; available at: http://nymag.com/news/business/58094/.

91. "Denmark rife with CO_2 Fraud," *Copenhagen Post*, December 1, 2009; available at: http://www.cphpost.dk/news/national/88-national/47643-denmark-rife-with-co2-fraud.html.

92. "Forest-CO_2 scheme will draw organized crime: Interpol," Reuters, May 29, 2009; available at: http://www.reuters.com/article/idUSTRE54S1DS20090529.

93. Rowena Mason, "'Carousel' frauds plague European carbon trading markets," *Telegraph* (UK), December 30, 2009; available at: http://www.telegraph.co.uk/finance/newsbysector/energy/6912667/Carousel-frauds-plague-European-carbon-trading-markets.html.

94. "EU Carbon Market Fraud?" *Carbon Control News*, August 3, 2009, Vol. 3 No. 31.

95. Marlo Lewis, "A Skeptic's Guide to 'An Inconvenient Truth,'" Chapter XVII, "Consensus, Science, and Special Interests," Competitive Enterprise Institute, January 22, 2007; available at: http://cei.org/pdf/ait/chXVII.pdf (citations omitted).

96. Jim Efstathiou Jr., "Sandor Got Obama's Nod for Chicago-Style Climate Law," Bloomberg News, June 16, 2009; available at: http://www.bloomberg.com/apps/news?pid=20601103&sid=aFlkGZGxrOEQ.

97. Ibid.

98. Ibid.

Chapter 6

1. Berkeley Energy & Resources Collaborative (BERC) in Berkeley, CA, February 11, 2009; video available at: http://defendglenn.com/van-jones-takes-berkeley.html (accessed February 8, 2010).

2. Ben Geman, "Can Push for Climate Bill Forge a Lasting Labor-Enviro Alliance?" Climate Wire, *New York Times*, August 28, 2009; available at: http://www.nytimes.com/cwire/2009/08/28/28climatewire-can-push-for-climate-bill-forge-a-lasting-la-70854.html?pagewanted=2.

3. Posted by Ed Morrissey, "Van Jones and 'Revolution,'" September 3, 2009; video available at: http://hotair.com/archives/2009/09/03/video-van-jones-and-revolution/ (accessed February 11, 2010).

4. Samuel Gompers, quote from an article originally published in *Louisville Courier Journal*, Vol. 2, May 2, 1890; excerpt available at: http://www.history.umd.edu/Gompers/quotes.htm.

5. Phil Kerpen, "How Van Jones Happened and What We Need to Do Next," FOX Forum, September 6, 2009; available at: http://www.foxnews.com/opinion/2009/09/06/phil-kerpen-van-jones-resign/?loomia_ow=t0:s0:a16:g2:r3:c0.098474:b27570234:z0.

6. Al Gore, *Earth in the Balance: Ecology and the Human Spirit* (Boston: Houghton Mifflin, 1992), 274.

7. James Pethokoukis, "Pelosi, a vision in white—but not green," Reuters, June 30, 2009; available at: http://blogs.reuters.com/james-pethokoukis/2009/06/30/pelosi-a-vision-in-white-but-not-green/.

8. Edward Felker and Stephen Dinan, "Democrats urged to play down 'global warming,'" *Washington Times*, June 19, 2009; available at: http://www.washingtontimes.com/news/2009/jun/19/party-memo-urges-democrats-to-fix-pitch-on-climate/.

9. "Italy defies EU summit deal on climate change," December 9, 2008, EurActiv.com; available at: http://www.euractiv.com/en/climate-change/italy-defies-eu-summit-deal-climate-change/article-177876.

10. Press Release, "EU climate package to cost UK £9bn pa," October 9, 2008; available at: http://www.openeurope.org.uk/media-centre/pressrelease.aspx?pressreleaseid=85.

11. Michael Economides, "Green Jobs, Fast-tracking Economic Suicide," *Energy Tribune*, July 31, 2009; available at: http://www.energytribune.com/articles.cfm?aid=2140.

12. "Consequences of Alternative U.S. Cap-and-Trade Policies: Controlling Both Emissions and Costs," Brookings Institute, July 24, 2009; available at: http://www.brookings.edu/~/media/Files/rc/reports/2009/07_cap_and_trade/0727_cost_containment.pdf.

13. Testimony of Frances Beinecke, President, Natural Resources Defense Council, Before the Committee on Energy and Commerce and the Subcommittee on Energy and Environment, U.S. House of Representatives, hearing on "The American Clean Energy and Security Act of 2009," April 22, 2009; available at: http://epw.senate.gov/public/index.cfm?FuseAction=Files.View&FileStore_id=bc2b4ad1-5e19-4e53-aa12-bd3a7777d06f.

14. Ibid.

15. Matt Apuzzo and Brett Blackledge, "Stimulus Watch: Unemployment unchanged by projects," Associated Press, January 11, 2010; available at: http://www.roadrunner.com/news/topic/article/rr/9001/9994598/AP_IMPACT_Road_projects_dont_help_unemployment.

16. "RECOVERY ACT: Status of States' and Localities' Use of Funds and Efforts to Ensure Accountability," Government Accountability Office, December 2009; available at: http://www.gao.gov/new.items/d10231.pdf.

17. Peter Nicholas, "Some projects raise question: Where's the stimulus?" *Los Angeles Times*, June 14, 2009; available at: http://articles.latimes.com/2009/jun/14/nation/na-stimulus14.

18. "Stimulus saved or created 640,239 jobs: White House," Reuters, October 30, 2009; available at: http://www.reuters.com/article/idUSTRE59T2QP20091030.

19. Even the Obama administration claimed a per-job cost for stimulus "green jobs" at more than $135,000. Sean Higgins, "Obama's Green Jobs Program: $135,294 Per Job," *Investors Business Daily*, January 8, 2010; available at: http://blogs.investors.com/capitalhill/index.php/home/35-politics/1136-obamas-green-jobs-program-135294-per-job.

20. Joel Kotkin, "Nurturing Employment Recovery," *Forbes*, December 15, 2009; available at: http://www. forbes.com/2009/12/14/unemployment-jobs-creative-class-opinions-columnists-joel-kotkin.html.

21. Ibid.

22. See, e.g.: Chris Barret, "R.I., neighbors to do 'green jobs' study," *Providence Business News*, November 24, 2009; available at: http://www.pbn.com/detail/46357.html.

23. Ben Genham and Michael Burnham, "Labor Department plans to track 'green jobs,'" *Greenwire*, July 13, 2009; citing "Green Jobs: A Pathway to a Strong Middle Class"; available at: http://www.whitehouse.gov/assets/documents/mctf_one_staff_report_final.pdf.

24. Chris Horner, "Camelot, meet the New Deal," *National Review Online*, February 13, 2008; available at: http://planetgore.nationalreview.com/post/?q=OWQ5YzVmYTcwNzBmYTRmNWE2ZWMz NjMxNjgxYzIwOTA; citing *Baltimore Sun* blog at: http://weblogs.baltimoresun.com/features/green/chesapeake_bay/ (entry no longer available).

25. Andrew P. Morriss, William T. Bogart, Andrew Dorchak, and Roger E. Meiners, "7 Myths About Green Jobs" (March 11, 2009), U Illinois Law & Economics Research Paper No. LE09-007; Case Legal Studies Research Paper No. 09-14. Available at SSRN: http://ssrn.com/abstract=1357440.

26. "Economic impacts from the promotion of renewable energies: The German experience," RWI-
Essen, October 2009; available at: http://www.instituteforenergyresearch.org/germany/Germany_Study_-_FINAL.pdf.

27. Michael Economides, "Green Jobs, Fast-tracking Economic Suicide," *Energy Tribune*, July 31, 2009.

28. Andrew P. Morriss, William T. Bogart, Andrew Dorchak, and Roger E. Meiners, "7 Myths About Green Jobs" (March 11, 2009), U Illinois Law & Economics Research Paper No. LE09-007; Case Legal Studies Research Paper No. 09-14; available at SSRN: http://ssrn.com/abstract=1357440.

29. Ibid.

30. Samuel Sherraden, "Green Trade Balance," New America Foundation, June 22, 2009; available at: http://www.newamerica.net/publications/policy/green_trade_balance.

31. Ibid.

32. Andrew Light from the Center for American Progress on FOX Special Report with Bret Baier, November 13, 2009.

33. Chris Horner, "Camelot, meet the New Deal," *National Review Online*, February 13, 2008; available at: http://planetgore.nationalreview.com/post/?q=OWQ5YzVmYTcwNzBmYTRmNWE2ZWMzNjMxNjgxYzIwOTA=.

34. Ibid.

35. This is my figure calculating subsidies in the appropriated budget since 1970; see also discussion at: http://www.washingtonpost.com/wp-dyn/content/article/2008/04/13/AR2008041301752.html.

36. "BP – 'New Sources of Energy,'" commercial; video available at: http://www.youtube.com/watch?v=p9m7jo5I1GQ&feature=related.

37. See Chris Horner, "Camelot, meet the New Deal," *National Review Online*, February 13, 2008; available at: http://planetgore.nationalreview.com/post/?q=OWQ5YzVmYTcwNzBmYTRmNWE2ZWMzNjMxNjgxYzIwOTA=.

38. Jonah Goldberg, "Fossil future: new supplies of oil and coal must be part of any rational energy policy," *National Review Online*, July 6, 2009; available at: http://www.mywire.com/a/NationalReview/Fossil-future-new-supplies-oil/11442693/.

39. Mark Whitehouse, "Reinhart and Rogoff: Higher Debt May Stunt Economic Growth," *Wall Street Journal*, January 4, 2010; available at: http://blogs.wsj.com/economics/2010/01/04/reinhart-and-rogoff-higher-debt-may-stunt-economic-growth/.

40. See, e.g.: Calzada, et al., "Study of the effects on employment of public aid to renewable energy sources," op cit.

41. See, e.g.: "HAPPENING NOW: Obama speaks about the economy," CNN, January 16, 2009; available at: http://politicalticker.blogs.cnn.com/2009/01/16/happening-now-obama-speaks-about-the-economy/?fbid=yZ0gx9mu6Wk.

42. "Economic impacts from the promotion of renewable energies: The German experience," RWI-Essen, October 2009, p. 25.

43. "Study of the effects on employment of public aid to renewable energy sources," op cit; This quote is from the House testimony of the research team's leader, "Testimony of Gabriel Calzada álvarez, PhD before the House Select Committee on Energy Independence and Global Warming," op cit.

44. Ibid.

45. See, e.g.: claims made by Van Jones on WYOO, Burnie Thompson Show, May 8, 2009 (audio file sent to and transcribed by this author by Mr. Thompson).

46. Eric Lantz and Suzanne Tegen, "NREL Response to the Report 'Study of the Effects on Employment of Public Aid to Renewable Energy Sources from King Juan Carlos University,'" p. 1; available at: http://www.nrel.gov/docs/fy09osti/46261.pdf.

47. Keith Johnson, "Green Jobs, Ole: Is the Spanish Clean-Energy Push a Cautionary Tale?" *Wall Street Journal*, March 30, 2009; available at: http://blogs.wsj.com/environmentalcapital/2009/03/30/green-jobs-ole-is-the-spanish-clean-energy-push-a-cautionary-tale/tab/article/.

48. "Economic impacts from the promotion of renewable energies: The German experience," RWI-Essen, October 2009, p. 6.

49. "Testimony of Gabriel Calzada álvarez, PhD before the House Select Committee on Energy Independence and Global Warming," op cit.

50. Dominic Lawson, "When wind power blows, jobs will fall," *The Sunday Times* (UK), July 19, 2009; available at: http://www.timesonline.co.uk/tol/comment/columnists/dominic_lawson/article6719142.ece.

51. "Cap and trade in practice," *Wall Street Journal*, December 17, 2009; available at: http://online.wsj.com/article/SB100014240527487043983045745 98173402205330.html.

52. Calzada, et al., "Study of the effects on employment of public aid to renewable energy sources," op cit.

53. Andrew Light from the Center for American Progress on FOX Special Report with Bret Baier, November 13, 2009.

54. "Economic impacts from the promotion of renewable energies: The German experience," RWI-Essen, October 2009, p. 7.

55. David G. Tuerck, Benjamin Powell, and Paul Bachman, "'Green Collar' Job Creation: A Critical Analysis," MSIE, The Beacon Hill Institute at Suffolk University, Boston, MA, June 2009.

56. Jim Tankersley, "Wind energy job growth isn't blowing anyone away," op cit.

57. Jake Tapper, "What Did Bill Clinton Mean By 'We Just Have to Slow Down Our Economy' to Fight Global Warming?" ABC News, January 31, 2008; available at: http://blogs.abcnews.com/politicalpunch/2008/01/bill-we-just-ha.html.

58. Calzada et al., "Study of the effects on employment of public aid to renewable energy sources," op cit.

59. This author listened to this interview live on WINA 1070-AM in Charlottesville, Virginia, July 6, 2009, and contemporaneously posted at, "I rise to recognize the gentleman from Illiteristan," *American Spectator* blog, July 6, 2009; available at: http://spectator.org/blog/2009/07/06/i-rise-to-recognize-the-gentle.

60. Roger Pielke Jr., "Someone Please Explain This: UPDATED With an Explanation," *Prometheus*, February 18, 2009; available at: http://sciencepolicy.colorado.edu/prometheus/someone-please-explain-this-4972.

61. Alex Kaplun, "Senate Dems seek expansion of solar tax credits in jobs bill," *E&E News*, November 30, 2009.

62. Eoin O'Carroll, "Does wind power really provide more jobs than coal," *Christian Science Monitor*, January 31, 2009; available at: http://www.csmonitor.com/Environment/Bright-Green/2009/0131/does-wind-power-really-provide-more-jobs-than-coal.

63. "Wind jobs outpace coal," *Fortune*, January 28, 2009; available at: http://greenwombat.blogs.fortune.cnn.com/2009/01/28/wind-jobs-outstrip-the-coal-industry/.

64. Chris Horner, "Next to Be Dropped: the Rest of the 'Story'?" Planet Gore, *National Review Online*, February 23, 2009; available at: http://planet-gore.nationalreview.com/post/?q=YTllZWY3YjUxZjA1NGI5N2JjN2I2ZTYyMjZhNjlhMjI=.

65. Eoin O'Carroll, "Does wind power really provide more jobs than coal," *Christian Science Monitor*, January 31, 2009.

66. Data available at The National Mining Association, Fast Facts: http://www.nma.org/statistics/fast_facts.asp.

67. Data available at: http://www.eia.doe.gov/cneaf/electricity/epm/table1_1.html. EIA doesn't break it down beyond "other renewables" which means the entire suite of sources other than dams (wood, black liquor, other wood waste, biogenic municipal solid waste, landfill gas, sludge waste, agriculture byproducts, other biomass, geothermal, solar thermal, photovoltaic energy, and wind), which combine for a total of 2.3 percent. From "nameplate capacity," which is about four to five times what you should expect as actual production, wind could account for 2.2 percent, if the wind blew 100 percent of the time on all turbines; see: http://www.eia.doe.gov/cneaf/electricity/epa/epat1p2.html. However, the Pew Center on Global Climate Change, "Wind Power," available at: http://www.pewclimate.org/technology/factsheet/wind (accessed February 8, 2010), says that wind contributes 1.25 percent.

68. Testimony of Mike Carey, President, Ohio Coal Association, Hearing on Moving to a Clean Energy Economy, Senate Committee on Environment & Public Works, October 29, 2009; available at: http://epw.senate .gov/public/index.cfm?FuseAction=Files.View&FileStore_id=dec0a8cc-d350-4ade-9c5a-b22a591f0836.

69. Data available at The National Mining Association, "Annual Mining Wages vs. All Industries, 2008," spreadsheet: http://www.nma.org/pdf/m_wages.pdf.

70. David Roland_Holst Fredrich Kahrl, "Clean Energy and Climate Policy for U.S. Growth and Job Creation," November 2009; available at: http://are.berkeley.edu/~dwrh/CERES_Web/Docs/ES_DRHFK091024.pdf, p. 2.

71. Data available at "Energy Market and Economic Impacts of H.R. 2454, the American Clean Energy and Security Act of 2009," available at: http://www.eia.doe.gov/oiaf/servicerpt/hr2454/pdf/sroiaf(2009)05.pdf; see even the assessment by the often ideological FactCheck.Org, "Cap-and-trade: 'Green Jobs' or Job Killer?" October 27, 2009; available at: http://www.factcheck.org/2009/10/cap-and-trade-green-jobs-or-job-killer/ (accessed February 8, 2010), citing that EIA's conclusions: "These contradict Waxman and Markey's earlier claim (made June 28, two days after the bill passed) that "[t]his landmark bill will revitalize our economy by creating millions of new jobs. EIA projected that over time, the bill would likely become a drag on the economy and reduce job creation by hundreds of thousands of jobs under any of the 11 different sets of assumptions that it analyzed."

72. "Economic impacts from the promotion of renewable energies: The German experience," RWI-Essen, October 2009, p. 8.

73. Mcmorandum of Decision, Assistant Secretary of Energy Efficiency and Renewable Energy, U.S. Department of Energy, February 11, 2010; available at: http://www.nema.org/media/pr/upload/EERE_Buy_American_Categorical_Waivers.pdf.

74. Hugh Sharman and Henrik Meyer, "Wind Energy—the Case of Denmark," op cit.

75. "Press release from Vestas Wind Systems A/S, Randers," August 12, 2009; available at: www.vestas.com/Default.aspx?ID=470&NewsID=1321.

76. Erin Ailworth, "Evergreen shifts work to China," *The Boston Globe,* November 5, 2009; available at· http://www.boston.com/business/articles/2009/11/05/evergreen_shifts_work_to_china/.

77. "Highlights of Obama's Elyria Visit," WCPN Ohio Public Radio, January 22, 2010, http://www.wcpn.org/WCPN/news/29430/.

78. Steven Greenhouse December 2, 2009, "Elusive Goal of Greening U.S. Energy," *New York Times*; available at: http://www.nytimes.com/2009/12/03/business/energy-environment/03greenjobs.html?_r=1&hpw.

79. Ibid.

80. Thomas J. Pyle, "Green jobs America can't afford," *Washington Times*, December 2, 2009; available at: http://www.washingtonexaminer.com/opinion/columns/OpEd-Contributor/Green-jobs-America-cant-afford-78364867.html.

81. Russell Gold, "U.S. doles out grants for energy projects," *Wall Street Journal*, September 2, 2009; available at: http://online.wsj.com/article/SB125182848772276871.html.

82. Editorial, "Stimulus creates jobs in China," *Washington Times*, November 13, 2009; available at: http://www.washingtontimes.com/news/2009/nov/13/stimulus-creates-jobs-in-china/.

83. "Wind turbine jobs blow in China's direction," *Dallas Morning News*, November 17, 2009; available at: http://www.dallasnews.com/sharedcontent/dws/bus/columnists/jlanders/stories/DN-landers_17bus.1.ART0.State.Edition1.3f095e8.html.

84. Joel Kirkland, "Debate over climate bill's impact on jobs sharpens," *E&E News*, November 16, 2009.

85. Christopher Martin and Jim Efstathiou Jr., "China's labor edge overpowers Obama's 'green' jobs initiatives," Bloomberg, February 4, 2010; available at: http://www.bloomberg.com/apps/news?pid=20601103&sid=adIdrmtTtyw8.

86. Russ Choma, "Renewable energy money still going abroad, despite criticism from Congress," American University School of Communication, February 8, 2010; available at: http://investigativereportingworkshop.org/investigations/wind-energy-funds-going-overseas/story/renewable-energy-money-still-going-abroad/.

87. Howard Rich, "The 'Green Jobs' Scam Unmasked," Townhall.com, February 12, 2010; available at: http://townhall.com/columnists/HowardRich/2010/02/12/the_green_jobs_scam_unmasked?page=full.

88. "Economic impacts from the promotion of renewable energies: The German experience," RWI-Essen, October 2009, p. 7.

89. "Solar Power: Finally, A Reason to Invest Says HSBC," *Wall Street Journal*, September 24, 2009; available at: http://blogs.wsj.com/environmentalcapital/2009/09/24/solar-power-finally-a-reason-to-invest-says-hsbc/tab/article/.

90. Press Release, "REMARKS BY THE PRESIDENT AT UNITED NATIONS SECRETARY GENERAL BAN KI-MOON'S CLIMATE CHANGE SUMMIT," September 22, 2009; available at: http://www.whitehouse.gov/the_press_office/Remarks-by-the-President-at-UN-Secretary-General-Ban-Ki-moons-Climate-Change-Summit/.

91. "Transcript: Obama's First State of the Union Speech," January 28, 2010; available at: http://www.cnn.com/2010/POLITICS/01/27/sotu.transcript/index.html; see also Press Release, "Remarks of President Barack Obama—As Prepared for Delivery Address to Joint Session of Congress," February 24, 2009; available at: http://www.whitehouse.gov/the_press_office/remarks-of-president-barack-obama-address-to-joint-session-of-congress/.

92. Andrew Light from the Center for American Progress on FOX Special Report with Bret Baier, November 13, 2009.

Chapter 7

1. Kit Bond, "Yellow Light on Green Jobs: A Report by the Senate Subcommittee on Green Jobs and the New Economy: A Report by U.S. Senate Subcommittee on Green Jobs and the New Economy," Spring 2009; available at: http://bond.senate.gov/public/_files/BondGreenJobsReport.pdf.

2. Senator Christopher Bond, Opening Statement, EPW Committee Hearing on State and Local Green Jobs Efforts , July 21, 2009; available at: http://bond.senate.gov/public/index.cfm?FuseAction=PressRoom.FloorStatements&ContentRecord_id=9dd8bab2-f819-8596-586a-68950daad861&Region_id=&Issue_id=13c95e7a-f67c-6735-6ed1-97aea41597dc, citing *High Road or Low Road? Job Quality in the New Economy*, A Report by Good Jobs First, February 3, 2009; available at: http://www.goodjobsfirst.org/pdf/gjfgreenjobsrpt.pdf.

3. Phil Kerpen, "Obama's Green Groups Eye Lots of Greenbacks," FOX Forum, FoxNews.com, September 2, 2009; available at: http://www.foxnews.com/opinion/2009/09/02/phil-kerpen-unions-van-jones-apollo/.

4. Phil Kerpen, "How Van Jones Happened and What We Need to Do Next," op cit.

5. Christa Marshall, "Climate and Energy Issues Send Hordes to K Street," op cit.

6. "Alliance for Climate Protection, Blue Green Alliance Hit Road for Made in America Tour," BlueGreen Alliance, August 19, 2009; available at: http://www.bluegreenalliance.org/press_room/press_releases?id=0042.

7. Ibid., citing R. J. Smith in Joseph A. D'Agostino, "Conservative Spotlight: R. J. Smith," *Human Events*, October 29, 2001.

8. See, e.g.: Chris Horner, "The Truth About the Treasury Trove," *National Review Online*, September 17, 2009; available at: http://planet-gore.nationalreview.com/post/?q=ZDg1MWQxMDVlYzRkNz k0YjRlMDQzNGNjMzc5MTYwNDA=.

9. Michael O'Brien, "Biden to Labor Group: 'We Owe You,'" *The Hill*, May 12, 2009; available at: http://thehill.com/blogs/blog-briefing-room/news/cam-paigns/labor/35803-biden-to-labor-group-we-owe-you.

10. Michelle Malkin, "Labor's Big Foot at the White House," *New York Post*, May 13, 2009; available at: http://www.nypost.com/p/news/opinion/oped-columnists/item_cnW7XbCa9yS3ONgARv9gJL.

11. "Obama Makes Picks for Debt Commission," *Wall Street Journal*, February 26, 2010; available at: http://online.wsj.com/article/SB10001424052 7487046250045750892332331966378.html.

12. David Cote is CEO of USCAP rent-seeker Honeywell. Available at: http://www.us-cap.org/.

13. "Over His Political Career, President Obama Has Received At Least $818,968 From Labor," The Center for Responsive Politics Website, http://www.opensecrets.org/politicians/industries.php?cycle=Career&type=I&cid=N00009638&newMem=N&recs=20 (accessed July 10, 2009); "Since 1989, Vice President Biden Has Received At Least $345,249 From Labor," The Center for Responsive Politics Website, http://www.opensecrets.org/politicians/indus-tries.php?cycle=Career&type=I&cid=N00001669&newMem=N&recs=20 (accessed July 10, 2009); RNC Research, "The Bill Comes Due...Unions to Meet at the White House Today," Republican National Committee, July 13, 2009; available at: http://www.wisgop.org/news/NewsBack.aspx?guid=26b8b56f-4033-40d0-a6ba-d0a0a6ba483c.

14. Lisa Lerer, "Labor, greens team up," *Politico*, April 14, 2009; available at: http://www.politico.com/news/stories/0409/21188.html.

15. The claim that Calzada et al. were in essence unpatriotic, by acting against their country's interests in exposing the reality of Spain's scheme, emerged in many places, though Dr. Calzada writes that "the clearest of all was made by a leftist newspaper (it writes of the works of Marx, Engels, Lenin), on its front page and the three next pages with headline 'The neoliberal lobby of the Popular Party boycotts Spain in USA'" (*Publico*, July 19, 2009; available at: http://www.publico.es/internacional/239598/lobby/neoliberal/pp/boicotea/ espana/eeuu?pagCom=5). In the comments of the readers you can find people asking for a treason process or taking away my passport, and it includes a remarkable chart where I appear as the godfather of the neoliberal conspiracy pulling the strings." Also, the wind energy association, Asociación Empresario Eolica, published several articles against concluding that what might destroy jobs is the study. An example is this piece signed by about twenty authors in *Expansión* against the study. The title, translated by Google Translate, reads: "The report which will destroy renewable jobs," *Expansión*, May 28, 2009. The president of the wind association has a piece in *El Mundo* making the unpatriotic, anti-Spain line of argument. Finally, regarding the Communist-affiliated trade union Comisiones Obreras, it published an article "Verdades y mentiras de las renovables por ISTAS," May 8, 2009, ISTAS; available at http:// www.aperca.org/temppdf/a_noticia_prensa_istas.pdf.

16. Andrew P. Morriss, William T. Bogart, Andrew Dorchak, and Roger E. Meiners, "7 Myths About Green Jobs," March 11, 2009, U Illinois Law & Economics Research Paper No. LE09-007; Case Legal Studies Research Paper No. 09-14. Available at SSRN: http://ssrn.com/abstract=1357440, 15.

17. Ibid. 4; see also 43.

18. Max Schulz, "Big Labor, Green Jobs," *American Spectator*, October 13, 2009; available at: http://www.manhattan-institute.org/html/miarticle.htm?id=5493.

19. Ibid.

20. Ibid.

21. See, e.g.: David Bernstein, "The Davis-Bacon Act: Let's Bring Jim Crow to an End," CATO Briefing Paper No. 17, CATO Institute, January 18, 1993; available at: http://www.cato.org/pubs/briefs/bp-017.html.

22. Government Printing Office; data available at: http://www.gpo.gov/ davisbacon/.

23. This statement was issued on several occasions, including in U.S. Chamber of Commerce, "Letter Opposing the Manager's Amendment to S. 3036, the 'Lieberman-Warner Climate Security Act of 2008,'" June 4, 2008; available at: http://www.uschamber.com/NR/rdonlyres/eoawe6zqnyo5vgp2dswjrc5t4lr4 we765kgcgwuuke57zvnemz33udyjkdqdk36smeyj34kblfwnivhblrr7b4hl4ug/ 090730_capandtrade_testimony.pdf.

24. Report, "Statistical Programs of the United States Government: Fiscal Year 2010," September 30, 2009; available at: http://www.whitehouse.gov/omb/ assets/information_and_regulatory_affairs/10statprog.pdf, p. 81.

25. Max Schulz, "Big Labor, Green Jobs," op cit.

26. See, e.g.: "The Employee Free Choice Act"—better known as the "Card Check bill"—is a proposed law that would change how unions are allowed to organize workers in the United States. Big labor unions like the AFL-CIO, SEIU, and the Change to Win Coalition spent heavily during the 2009 election, and are pushing Congress to approve this law. Union membership has been declining—currently about 7.5 percent in the private sector—and they hope this law will change the rules and reverse that trend. "The Employee Free Choice Act"—the "Card Check" Bill. "Union Recognition—Secret Ballot Elections and Card Check Schemes," U.S. Chamber of Commerce; available at: http://www.uschamber.com/issues/index/labor/cardchecksecrbal.htm (accessed February 9, 2010).

27. See, e.g.: "Britain: Vestas workers call on Labour to nationalise plant," League for the 5th International, July 28, 2009; available at: http://www.fifthinternational.org/content/britain-vestas-workers-call-labour-nationalise-plant.

28. Paul Glader and Kris Maher, "Steelworkers Fault GE Stance on American Manufacturing," *Wall Street Journal*, July 16, 2009; available at: http://online.wsj.com/article/SB124770142774048435.html.

29. Jake Tapper, "What Did Bill Clinton Mean By 'We Just Have to Slow Down Our Economy' to Fight Global Warming?" ABC News, January 31, 2008; available at: http://blogs.abcnews.com/politicalpunch/2008/01/bill-we-just-ha.html.

30. Peter Behr, "Growing 'green' jobs is a long-term task, advocates say," *Climate Wire*, August 14, 2009; available at: http://www.eenews.net/public/climatewire/2009/08/14/1.

31. Data available at: http://apolloalliance.org/about/endorsers/ (accessed February 10, 2010).

32. Calzada, et al.. "Study of the effects on employment of public aid to renewable energy sources," op cit.

33. "Economic impacts from the promotion of renewable energies: The German experience," RWI-Essen, October 2009; available at: http://www.instituteforenergyresearch.org/germany/Germany_Study_-_FINAL.pdf.

34. Hugh Sharman and Henrik Meyer, "Wind Energy—the Case of Denmark," op cit.

35. "Yellow Light on Green Jobs: A Report by the Senate Subcommittee on Green Jobs and the New Economy," Spring 2009; available at: http://bond.senate.gov/public/_files/BondGreenJobsReport.pdf, at p. 17.

36. Sean Higgins, "Obama's Green Jobs Program: $135,294 Per Job," Investors Business Daily, January 8, 2010.

37. Kate Galbraith, "Paying extra for green power, and getting ads instead," *New York Times*, November 17, 2009; available at: http://www.nytimes.com/2009/11/17/business/energy-environment/17power.html.

38. Andrew P. Morriss, William T. Bogart, Andrew Dorchak, and Roger E. Meiners, "7 Myths About Green Jobs," U Illinois Law & Economics Research Paper No. LE09-007, March 11, 2009; Case Legal Studies Research Paper No. 09-14; available at SSRN: http://ssrn.com/abstract=1357440, p. 2.

39. Ibid., 96–97.

40. Jonah Goldberg, "Fossil future: new supplies of oil and coal must be part of any rational energy policy," op cit.

41. Ibid.

42. See, e.g.: "Project Labor Agreement Activity," Associated Builders and Contractors of Southern California; available at: http://www.abcsocal.org/Government_Affairs/06_07_Govt_Affairs_Report.aspx (accessed February 10, 2010).

43. Todd Woody, "A Move to Put the Union Label on Solar Power Plants," *New York Times*, June 19, 2009; available at: http://www.nytimes.com/2009/06/19/business/energy-environment/19unions.html.

44. Ibid.

45. Ibid.

46. Kevin Dayton, "FOX News Report Exposes Union Greenmail"; available at: http://www.thetruthaboutplas.com/2009/08/07/fox-news-report-exposes-union-greenmail/ (accessed February 10, 2010), citing August 7, 2009, report on FOX News by William La Jeunesse.

47. Ibid.

48. See, e.g.: Congressional Budget Office, "An Evaluation of Cap and Trade Programs for Reducing US GHG Emissions," June 200; available at: http://www.cbo.gov/doc.cfm?index=2876&type=0&sequence=2; see also Congressional Budget Office Economic and Budget Issue Brief, "Tradeoffs for Allocating Allowances in CO_2 Emissions," April 25, 2007; available at: http://www.cbo.gov/ftpdocs/80xx/doc8027/04-25-Cap_Trade.pdf.

49. Morrissey, "Greenpeace: Yeah, we misled, but we needed the emotionalism," HotAir.com, August 20, 2009; video and transcript available at: http://hotair.com/archives/2009/08/20/greenpeace-yeah-we-lied-but-we-needed-the-emotionalism/.

50. Joe Bast, "What Climate Change Can Do For the Left," *American Thinker*, June 17, 2009; available at: http://www.americanthinker.com/2009/07/what_climate_change_can_do_for.html.

51. Ibid.

52. Jonah Goldberg, "Global Warming as a Political Tool," Tribune Media, December 11, 2009; available at: http://article.nationalreview.com/417683/global-warming-as-a-political-tool/jonah-goldberg.

53. See, e.g.: Louise Gray, "Copenhagen climate summit: Tony Blair calls on world leaders to 'get moving,'" *Telegraph* (UK), December 13, 2009; available at: http://www.telegraph.co.uk/earth/copenhagen-climate-change-confe/6803921/Copenhagen-climate-summit-Tony-Blair-calls-on-world-leaders-to-get-moving.html.

54. Comments at a meeting with the editorial board of the *Calgary Herald*, quoted in *Financial Post* (Canada), December 26, 1998.

55. "State of the Union 2010 Full Text," *Huffington Post*, January 27; available at: http://www.huffingtonpost.com/2010/01/27/state-of-the-union-2010-full-text-transcript_n_439459.html.

56. See, e.g.: Chris Horner, "The Truth About the Treasury Trove," *National Review Online*, September 17, 2009; available at: http://planetgore.nationalreview.com/post/?q=ZDg1MWQxMDVlYzRkNzk0YjRlMDQzNGNjMzc5MTYwNDA=.

57. See, e.g.: Jack Turner, "Earth Day Green Jobs Message From Van Jones, Community Organizer In The Federal Family," April 22, 2009; available at: http://www.jackandjillpolitics.com/2009/04/earth-day-green-jobs-message-from-van-jones-community-organizer-in-the-federal-family/ (accessed February 10, 2010); see also: "Van Jones Takes Berkeley: New Video of Obama Jobs Czar," September 1, 2009; video available at: http://defendglenn.com/van-jones-takes-berkeley.html (accessed February 10, 2010).

58. Jacob Gershman, "The gang that can't insulate straight," *New York Post*, August 18, 2009; available at: http://www.nypost.com/p/news/opinion/oped-columnists/item_O0xf7NZdCrKRZr4OhGI4KL;jsessionid=8F3BABBA8E9B0 530DEA8A1434568DA16.

59. Deroy Murdock, "The prospects for revolt in 2010," *Washington Times*, January 1, 2010; available at: http://www.washingtontimes.com/news/2010/jan/01/the-prospects-for-revolt-in-2010/.

60. Andrew Malcom, "Obama's federal government can weatherize your home for only $57,362 *each*," *Los Angeles Times*, February 18, 2010; available at: http://latimesblogs.latimes.com/washington/2010/02/obama-stimulus-weatherization.html.

61. Jonathan Karl, "Report: Stimulus Weatherization Program Bogged Down by Red Tape," ABC News, February 17, 2010; available at: http://abc-news.go.com/WN/Politics/stimulus-weatherization-jobs-president-obama-congress-recovery-act/story?id=9780935.

62. "Green Jobs Czar Says 'White Polluters' Steered Poison Into Minority Communities," Breitbart TV; video available at: http://www.breitbart.tv/green-jobs-czar-says-white-polluters-steered-poison-into-minority-communities/ (accessed February 10, 2010).

63. Data available at: http://www.nam.org/~/media/Files/s_nam/docs/239500/239417.pdf.ashx (accessed February 10, 2010).

64. Administrator Lisa P. Jackson, Remarks to the National Association of Black Journalists, as Prepared, August 7, 2009; available at: http://yosemite.epa.gov/opa/admpress.nsf/8d49f7ad4bbcf4ef852573590040b7f6/1b7b0b968c43a7c58525760e005916b7!OpenDocument.

65. No longer available on Green the Block, but cited at, "Green For All, asthma, cockroaches and children of color," The Daily Kos; available at: http://www.dailykos.com/story/2009/8/26/772446/-Green-For-All,-asthma,-cock-roaches-and-children-of-color.

66. Administrator Lisa P. Jackson, Remarks to the National Association of Black Journalists, op cit.

67. See, e.g.: Matthew Vadum, "Greenwashing 9/11," *The American Spectator*, September 1, 2009; available at: http://spectator.org/archives/2009/09/01/greenwashing-911.

68. Lisa P. Jackson, Remarks to the National Association of Black Journalists, op cit.

69. Ibid.

70. Ibid.

71. *Hardball*, MSNBC, June 19, 2009; video and transcript available at Mark Finkelstein, "Matthews: 'Reparations Make Sense'"; available at: http://newsbusters.org/blogs/mark-finkelstein/2009/06/19/matthews-reparations-make-sense.

72. "Van Jones Takes Berkeley: New Video of Obama Jobs Czar," September 1, 2009; video available at; http://defendglenn.com/van-jones-takes-berkeley.html (accessed February 10, 2010).

73. Elena Foshay and Keith Schneider, "Congress Approves Clean Energy Provisions of Stimulus; Consistent With Apollo Economic Recovery Act," Apollo News Service, February 13, 2009; available at: http://apolloalliance.org/feature-articles/clean-energy-provisions-of-stimulus-are-consistent-with-apollo-economic-recovery-act/.

74. Ibid.

75. Phil Kerpen, "Obama's Green Groups Eye Lots of Greenbacks," op cit.

76. Tom Doggett, "U.S. Energy's Chu hails companies that left Chamber," Reuters, October 8, 2009; available at: http://www.reuters.com/article/idUSTRE5975AI20091008.

77. Aaron Klein, "Obama's 'green jobs czar' worked with terror founder," *World Net Daily*, August 13, 2009; available at: http://www.wnd.com/index.php?pageId=106653.

78. Matthew Vadum, "ACORN Getting Involved in Global Warming Hysteria," Capital Research Center, June 8, 2009; available at: http://www.capitalresearch.org/blog/2009/06/08/acorn-involved-in-global-warming-hysteria/.

79. Ibid., citing Ben Block, "Expanded coalitions support U.S. climate bill," Worldwatch Institute, June 8, 2009; available at: http://www.worldwatch.org/node/6146.

Chapter 8

1. Barack Obama, in a January 8, 2008, meeting with the editorial board of the *San Francisco Chronicle*, "Obama on cap and trade: 'electricity rates would necessarily skyrocket,'" op cit.

2. David Deming, "Death of a civilization," Lew Rockwell, May 13, 2009; available at: http://www.lewrockwell.com/orig9/deming2.html.

3. Fred Barnes, "No Energy from this Executive," *Weekly Standard*, June 15, 2009; available at: http://www.weeklystandard.com/Content/Public/Articles/000/000/016/588tpmuu.asp.

4. Press Release, "NATIONAL STRIPPER WELL ASSOCIATION (NSWA) CONFIRMS COST OF OBAMA ADMINISTRATION'S TAX POLICIES TO SMALL OIL AND GAS PRODUCERS AND FEDERAL GOVERNMENT," NSWA; available at: http://nswa.us/page_images/1250280813.pdf.

5. "U.S. wants G20 to axe fuel subsidies," Reuters, September 4, 2009; available at: http://www.reuters.com/article/idUSTRE58326U20090904; see also "U.S. budget drops fossil fuel subsidies," Energy Risk, February 2, 2010; available at: http://www.risk.net/energy-risk/news/1589833/us-budget-drops-fossil-fuel-subsidies.

6. Editorial, "Running on Empty," *Washington Times*, August 9, 2009; available at: http://www.washingtontimes.com/news/2009/aug/09/running-on-empty-34923454/.

7. Data available at: http://ostseis.anl.gov/documents/docs/Section369ExtractEnergyPolicyAct.pdf.

8. See, e.g.: "China's push for oil in Gulf of Mexico puts U.S. in tight spot," *Los Angeles Times*, October 22, 2009; available at: http://articles.latimes.com/2009/oct/22/business/fi-china-oil22.

9. Editorial, "Running on Empty," op cit.

10. "Oil shale proponents cite obstacles in tapping vast reserves," Land Letter, *E&E News*, February 11, 2010; available at: http://www.eenews.net/Landletter/2010/02/11/2.

11. Ibid.

12. See, e g.: Chris Good, "No Yucca in Obama's budget; Reid rejoices," *The Atlantic*, February 1, 2010; available at: http://politics.theatlantic.com/2010/02/no_yucca_in_obamas_budget_reid_rejoices.php.

13. See, e.g.: "Obama camp spies endgame in Oregon," AFP, May 16, 2008; available at: http://afp.google.com/article/ALeqM5h-wpxs1Re-8vx2Zk5xnYyg W1W67w.

14. Juliet Eilperin, "Salazar voids drilling leases on public lands in Utah," *Washington Post*, February 5, 2009; available at: http://www.washingtonpost. com/wp-dyn/content/article/2009/02/04/AR2009020401785.html.

15. Noelle Straub, "Utah lease report first step in larger oil and gas reforms, Salazar says," *E&E News*, October 8, 2009; available at: http://www.eenews.net/ public/eenewspm/2009/10/08/3.

16. Order No. 3289, "Addressing the Impacts of Climate Change on America's Water, Land and Other Natural and Cultural Resources," Department of the Interior, September 14, 2009.

17. "A clearer look at drilling," *New York Times*, October 13, 2009; available at: http://www.nytimes.com/2009/10/14/opinion/14wed2.html.

18. See, e.g.: Noelle Straub, "House lawmakers push to restore Utah protections," Land Letter, *E&E News*, November 12, 2009.

19. A document styled "NOT FOR RELEASE" found its way public, affirming that "[t]he Obama administration is looking into bypassing Congress to designate millions of Western acres as national monuments.... The document mentions 14 potential monument designations or expansions in 9 states: Arizona, California, Colorado, Montana, New Mexico, Nevada, Oregon, Utah, and Washington. Republicans estimated the new designations could cover up to 13 million acres.... The draft also mentions three tracts of land in Alaska and Wyoming—states where the president's Antiquities Act authority is limited— for potential non-monument conservation designations. It includes Alaska's Bristol Bay region, where environmental groups and salmon fishers have battled proposed energy and mineral development." Patrick Reis, "Document shows Obama admin exploring 14 new monuments," *E&E News*, February 18, 2010.

"Nearly every one of these proposed designations involves areas with energy potential. National monument designations of this scope could have significant impact on many western-based businesses, ranchers, HOV enthusiasts, property rights activists, and rural citizens. Sadly, this effort to lock up millions of acres of land is just one more example of a renewed War on the West undertaken by an Administration determined to limit public access, reduce domestic energy production, ignore basic property rights, and impede real job creation." February 16, 2010, email from Cody Stewart, Executive Director of the Congressional Western Caucus.

20. See, e.g.: Jim Tankersley, "Obama to Require Climate Impact Studies for New Federal Actions," *Los Angeles Times*, December 31, 2009.

21. Press Release, "Inhofe Responds to White House Press Release on NEPA," Senate Environment and Public Works Committee Minority, February 18, 2010.

22. Thomas J. Pyle, "Ninth Circuit ends drilling in federal oil fields," *San Francisco Chronicle*, December 12, 2008; available at: http://www.sfgate.com/ cgi-bin/article.cgi?f=/c/a/2008/12/12/EDEU14MI8P.DTL.

23. See, e.g.: Press Release, "Ban on Outer Continental Shelf Lifted One Year Ago ... Yet Still No Action, Unemployment Rate and Energy Costs Soar As OCS Remains Unutilized," Congressman Don Young, July 14, 2009; available at: http://donyoung.house.gov/News/DocumentSingle.aspx?DocumentID=138137.

24. Representative Doc Hastings, "Obama blocks new energy exploration," Townhall.com, July 14, 2009; available at: http://townhall.com/columnists/ DocHastings/2009/07/14/obama_blocks_new_energy_exploration.

25. See, e.g.: "Timber Trouble," FOX News, December 11, 2009; video available at: http://www.foxnews.com/search-results/m/27876595/timber-trouble. htm; see also Andre Meunier, "Environmentalists hope Obama policy derails Oregon logging," OregonLive.com, March 3, 2009; available at: http://www. oregonlive.com/environment/index.ssf/2009/03/environmentalists_hope_ obama_p.html.

26. See, e.g.: Jessica Leber, "Obama Admin Scraps Logging Plan in Ore. Carbon Sinks," Climate Wire, *New York Times*, July 17, 2009; available at: http:// www.nytimes.com/cwire/2009/07/17/17climatewire-obama-admin-scraps- logging-plan-in-ore-carbo-10938.html.

27. See, e.g.: Josh Timmer, "Have we started to fill our carbon sinks?" ARS Technica, November 18, 2009; available at: http://arstechnica.com/science/ news/2009/11/have-we-started-to-fill-our-carbon-sinks.ars?utm_source= rss&utm_medium=rss&utm_campaign=rss.

28. See, e.g.: Devin Nunes, "It's fish vs. farmers in the San Joaquin Valley," *Wall Street Journal*, August 14, 2009; available at: http://online.wsj.com/arti- cle/SB10001424052970204619004574318621482123090.html.

29. See, e.g.: Erin Kelly, "McCain blasts Obama administration over copper mine," AZcentral.com, June 17, 2009; available at: http://www.azcentral.com/news/articles/2009/06/17/20090617—McCainMine.html.

30. See, e.g.: "Federal judge halts gravel mine expansion," *Greenwire*, August 14, 2009.

31. See, e.g.: Press Release, "Center for Biological Diversity Announces Climate Law Institute, Dedicates $17 Million to Combat Global Warming," Center for Biological Diversity, February 12, 2009; available at: http://www.biologicaldiversity.org/news/press_releases/2009/climate-law-institute-02-12-2009.html.

32. See, e.g.: Marlo Lewis PhD, "Kempthorne: Whistling past the graveyard," *National Review Online*, May 17, 2008; available at: http://planetgore.nationalreview.com/post/?q=MThhNjc2NjUxZDZiNTQxNDhmZWQ1Y2Y3NmVkZjU5MGU=.

33. See, e.g.: Marlo Lewis, "Center for Biological Diversity Declares war on U.S. economy, self-governance," *National Review Online*, February 24, 2009; available at: http://planetgore.nationalreview. com/post/?q=MGM5OTVjZ-TUzN2ZmYTE3NTc1ZGZiNjc3ZTA1ODI2ZWI=.

34. "Obama and the 'South Park' gnomes," *Wall Street Journal*, May 26, 2009; available at: http://online.wsj.com/article/SB124329131991652291.html.

35. Gerard Jackson, "Why a cap and trade carbon taxes will savage living standards," *Brookes News*, May 11, 2009; available at: http://brookesnews.com/091105obamaenergy.html.

36. Email to the author from Matthew Vadum, Capital Research Center.

37. Email to the author from a staffer for Congressman Todd Aiken.

38. "Read my lips...No new coal plants!" *Washington Post*, September 24, 2008; available at: http://voices.washingtonpost.com/fact-checker/2008/09/read_my_lipsno_new_coal_plants.html.

39. Nancy Pelosi on *Meet the Press*, NBC News, August 24, 2008; transcript available at: http://www.msnbc.msn.com/ id/26377338/page/3/; see also: Jeffrey Ball, "Fuel for Debate: Pelosi Suggests Natural Gas Isn't a Fossil Fuel," *Wall Street Journal*, August 24, 2008; available at: http://blogs.wsj.com/environmentalcapital/2008/08/25/fuel-for-debate-pelosi-suggests-natural-gas-isnt-a-fossil-fuel/.

40. See, e.g.: John D. McKinnon, "Pelosi on Natural Gas: Fossil Fuel or Not?" *Wall Street Journal*, August 24, 2008; available at: http://blogs.wsj.com/washwire/2008/08/24/pelosi-on-natural-gas-fossil-fuel-or-not/tab/article/.

41. Nancy Pelosi on *Meet the Press*, NBC News, August 24, 2008.

42. Ibid.

43. See e.g.: Ed Morrissey, "Video: Harry Reid says energy makes him sick," HotAir.com, July 1, 2008; video available at: http://hotair.com/archives/2008/07/01/video-harry-reid-says-energy-makes-him-sick/.

44. Michael O'Brien, "Reid: 'Men, when they're out of work, tend to become abusive'," *The Hill*, February 22, 2010; available at: http://thehill.com/blogs/blog-briefing-room/news/82803-reid-men-when-theyre-out-of-work-tend-to-become-abusive.

45. *Meet the Press*, NBC News, August 2, 2009; transcript available at: http://www.msnbc.msn.com/id/32241917/ns/meet_the_press/page/2/.

46. This was a drop from about 1.5 percent in 2007, almost identical to wind and solar's combined contribution to U.S. electricity supply; data available at: http://www.eia.doe.gov/cneaf/electricity/epa/epa_sum.html.

47. See, e.g.: Stephen Power, "As OPEC Prepares to Meet, Chu Focuses on U.S. Energy," *Wall Street Journal*, February 20, 2009; available at: http://online.wsj.com/article/SB123508025907226643.html.

48. Energy Perspectives, http://www.eia.doe.gov/emeu/aer/ep/ep_frame.html.

49. Noelle Straub, "Sweeping Rahall bill draws criticism, qualified support," *E&E News*, September 10, 2009.

50. Michael Riley, "Interior chief Salazar's first year a gusher of controversy," *Denver Post*, 1/24/10; available at: http://www.denverpost.com/commented/ci_14256364.

51. Eryn Gable, "Interior agencies showing marked shift in leasing policies," Land Letter, *E&E News*, November 19, 2009.

52. See, e.g.: Paul Foy, "Feds hold back $40 million in Utah drill leases," *Salt Lake Tribune*, August 9, 2009; available at: http://www.sltrib.com/news/ci_13026590.

53. Eryn Gable, "Interior agencies showing marked shift in leasing policies," Land Letter, *E&E News*, November 19, 2009; available at: http://www.eenews.net/public/Landletter/2009/11/19/3.

54. Bonner Cohen, "Utah counties sue U.S. over cancelled Utah leases," *Environment & Climate News*, Heartland Institute, August 2009.

55. See, e.g.: Bonner Cohen, "Utah counties sue U.S. over cancelled Utah leases," *Environment & Climate News*, Heartland Institute, August 2009; available at: http://www.heartland.org/full/25662/Utah_Counties_Sue_US_Over_Cancelled_Leases.html.

56. Paul Foy, "Feds hold back $40 million in Utah drill leases," *Salt Lake Tribune*, August 9, 2009.

57. See, e.g.: "Salazar to keep Colo. Leases," Greenwire, August 14, 2009.

58. Phil Taylor, "BLM yanks 71,000 acres in Ala. from lease sale," Land Letter, *E&E News*, December 10, 2009.

59. Scott Streater, "BLM Director Abbey sets decisive tone with Nev. land withdrawal," Land Letter, *E&E News*, November 5, 2009.

60. "BLM yanks Wyo. lease parcels, requests agency review," Land Letter, *E&E News*, November 5, 2009.

61. "U.S. rejects Alaska refuge land swap deal," Greenwire, July 20, 2009.

62. Ibid.

63. Edward Felker, "Lawmaker joins push to up cost of drilling," *Washington Times*, June 1, 2009; available at: http://www.washingtontimes.com/news/2009/jun/01/powerful-lawmaker-joins-push-to-up-cost-of-drillin//print/.

64. See, e.g.: Statement of Alan B. Krueger, Assistant Secretary for Economic Policy and Chief Economist, US Department of Treasury, to the Subcommittee on Energy, Natural Resources, and Infrastructure, September 10, 2009 (Department of the Treasury, Fiscal Year 2010 Budget Justification).

65. http://blog.energytomorrow.org/2010/02/2011-budget-no-new-taxes-on-oil-and-gas.html, reported at Noelle Straub, "Proposal raises oil and gas fees, launches climate centers," Greenwire, February 1, 2010.

66. Edward Felker, "Lawmaker joins push to up cost of drilling," *Washington Times*, June 1, 2009.

67. "ANALYSIS OF THE SOCIAL, ECONOMIC AND ENVIRONMENTAL EFFECTS OF MAINTAINING OIL AND GAS EXPLORATION AND PRODUCTION MORATORIA ON AND BENEATH FEDERAL LANDS: Assessment of the Combined Relative Impacts of Maintaining Moratoria and Increased Domestic Onshore and Offshore Oil and Gas Resource Estimates," Science Applications International Corporation (SAIC), Gas Technology Institute (GTI), February 15, 2010; see: http://www.naruc.org/resources.cfm?p= 353.

68. Bonner Cohen, "Utah counties sue U.S. over cancelled Utah leases," *Environment & Climate News*, Heartland Institute, August 2009.

Chapter 9

1. James Delingpole, "'Global warming': time to get angry," *The Telegraph* (UK), February 23, 2010; available at: http://blogs.telegraph.co.uk/news/james-delingpole/100027173/global-warming-time-to-get-angry/.

2. Neil King and Stephen Power, "Times tough for energy overhaul," *Wall Street Journal,* December 12, 2008; available at: http://online.wsj.com/article/SB122904040307499791.html.

3. See, e.g.: Daniel Mitchell, "America vs. Europe," CATO Institute, January 15, 2010; available at: http://www.cato-at-liberty.org/2010/01/15/america-vs-europe/.

4. "Greens' real target: U.S. economy," *Investors Business Daily*, December 7, 2009; available at: http://www.investors.com/NewsAndAnalysis/Article.aspx?id=514619.

5. Ibid.

6. Glenn Thrush, "DeFazio: Tax oil futures," *Politico*, July 6, 2009; available at: http://www.politico.com/blogs/glennthrush/0709/DeFazio_Tax_oil_futures_.html.

7. "Countries rated on oil security," *Washington Times*, May 19, 2009; available at: http://washingtontimes.com/news/2009/may/19/countries-rated-on-oil-security/.

8. Ibid.

9. See, e.g.: Jasmina Kelemen, "Mexico's Pemex seeks to stem the decline in oil production," ICB, September 4, 2009; available at: http://www.icis.com/Articles/2009/09/07/9243874/mexicos-pemex-seeks-to-stem-the-decline-in-oil-production.html.

10. Press Release, "FACT SHEET: U.S.-China Shale Gas Resource Initiative," The White House, November 17, 2009; available at: http://energy.gov/news2009/documents2009/US-China_Fact_Sheet_Shale_Gas.pdf.

11. "Shale gas is U.S. energy 'game changer' says BP CEO," Reuters, January 20, 2010; available at: http://www.reuters.com/article/idUSTRE6OR4XQ20100128.

12. Ed Crooks, "China and Russia lead oil deals," *Financial Times*, June 12, 2009.

13. Ibid.

14. See, e.g.: Press Release, "Retired Brass: Developing Domestic Energy Resources Key to National Security," Senate Environment and Public Works Committee Minority, October 28, 2009; available at: http://epw.senate.gov/public/index.cfm?FuseAction=PressRoom.PressReleases&ContentRecord_id=9D25BE3A-802A-23AD-4D66-ADEC75F32D84; referencing Congressional Research Service, "Memorandum to Senate Committee on Environment and Public Works: Terminology, Reporting, and Summary of U.S. Fossil Fuel Resources," October 20, 2009; available at: http://epw.senate.gov/public/index.cfm?FuseAction=Files.View &FileStore_id=01feb68b-ef57-4748-8f5c-d88c0e7d6bd5; see also "McCain: Lift Offshore Drilling Moratorium," CBS News, June 16, 2008; available at: http://www.cbsnews.com/stories/2008/06/16/politics/main4184958.shtml.

15. Congressional Research Service, "U.S. Fossil Fuel Resources: Terminology, Reporting, and Summary," October 28, 2009; available at: http://epw.senate.gov/public/index.cfm?FuseAction=Files.View&FileStore_id=f7bd7b77-ba50-48c2-a635-220d7cf8c519.

16. Ibid.

17. Ibid.

18. See, e.g.: Henry Lamb, "Wilderness V. Development: Take Care of America First," Arctic National Wildlife Refuge, December 17, 2001; available at: http://www.anwr.org/features/issues/wilderness-dev.htm.

19. See, e.g.: U.S. Geological Survey World Petroleum Assessment 2000; data available at: http://energy.cr.usgs.gov/WEcont/chaps/ES.pdf; see also: "Immediately Expand Domestic Oil and Gas Exploration and Production," Institute for 21st Century Energy, U.S. Chamber of Commerce; available at: http://www.energyxxi.org/issues/Expand_Production.aspx.

20. "BP Statistical Review of World Energy"; data available at: http://www.usaee.org/usaee2009/submissions/presentations/Finley.pdf; see also: http://www.bp.com/genericarticle.do?categoryId=9003467&contentId=7053792.

21. Data available at: http://www.bp.com/liveassets/bp_internet/globalbp/globalbp_uk_english/reports_and_publications/statistical_energy_review_2008/STAGING/local_assets/2009_downloads/statistical_review_of_world_energy_full_report_2009.pdf.

22. Michael Lynch, "U.S. Gas Resources: Julian Simon Lives! (Malthus, Hotelling, Hubbert are wrong again)," Master Resource, June 22, 2009; available at: http://www.masterresource.org/2009/06/us-gas-reserves-an-expanding-resource-malthus-hotelling-hubbert-are-wrong-again/.

23. "But are proven reserves all that's left? Several analyses put ultimate reserves at much higher levels. . . . The USGS calculates that humanity has already consumed about 1 trillion barrels of oil equivalent, which means 82 percent of the world's endowment of oil and gas resources remains to be used." Ronald L. Bailey, "Peak Oil Panic," *Reason* Magazine, May 2006; available at: http://reason.com/archives/2006/05/05/peak-oil-panic.

24. Jonah Goldberg, "Fossil future: new supplies of oil and coal must be part of any rational energy policy," *National Review*, July 6, 2009.

25. Michael Lynch , "U.S. Gas Resources: Julian Simon Lives! (Malthus, Hotelling, Hubbert are wrong again)," op cit.

26. See, e.g.: "Iran falling short of oil refining ambitions," Reuters, June 19, 2007; available at: http://www.reuters.com/article/idUSL1490018620070619; for a more recent affirmation in the Obama context, see Edgar M. Bronfman, "Realism and leverage for engaging Iran," *Huffington Post*, March 20, 2009; available at: http://www.huffingtonpost.com/edgar-m-bronfman/realism-and-leverage-for_b_177456.html.

27. See, e.g.: Tom Fowler, "Why refiners got the shaft in Waxman-Markey," *Houston Chronicle*, August 20, 2009; available at: http://blogs.chron.com/newswatchenergy/archives/2009/08/why_refiners_go_1.html. It is possible, though hard to imagine, as the author implies, that such a sensitive sector received such disproportionately negative treatment under a bill largely because of their political representation.

28. Data available at: http://www.globalclimatelaw.com/2009/11/articles/climate-change-litigation/epa-rejects-permit-for-bp-whiting-refinery/.

29. See, e.g.: "BP Whiting Refinery Permit Sent Back to the Drawing Board," *Environment News Service*, October 21, 2009; available at: http://www.ens-newswire.com/ens/oct2009/2009-10-21-092.asp.

30. "U.S. refiners say climate laws are biggest challenge," Reuters, October 29, 2009; available at: http://www.reuters.com/article/idUSN2914081720091029.

31. Angel Gonzalez, "Oil Industry details costs of climate bill," *Wall Street Journal*, April 24, 2009; available at: http://online.wsj.com/article/SB125108183527152913.html.

32. Press Release, "Obama administration: no documented cases of hydraulic fracturing contamination," Senate Environment and Public Works Committee Minority, December 8, 2009; available at: http://epw.senate.gov/ public/index.cfm?FuseAction=Minority.PressReleases&ContentRecord_id= 70289be8-802a-23ad-479d-ca2d6f6b36cd&Region_id=&Issue_id=87c0818b-7e9c-9af9-7e75-f5bfde0fc3dd.

33. Ibid.

34. Ibid.

35. See, e.g.: Rick Stouffer, "Marcellus Shale estimated natural gas yield rises to nearly 500 trillion cubic feet," *Pittsburgh Tribune-Review*, July 28, 2009; available at: http://www.pittsburghlive.com/x/pittsburghtrib/business/s_ 635579.html.

36. H.R. 2766 (11th Congress); "DeGette, Polis introduce FRAC Act aimed at closing hydraulic fracturing 'loophole,'" *Colorado Independent*, June 9, 2009; available at: http://coloradoindependent.com/ 30784/degette-polis-introduce-frac-act-aimed-at-closing-hydraulic-fracturing-loophole; see also: S. 1215 (11th Congress).

37. Cathy Landry, "Duplicative hydraulic fracturing rules could imperil U.S. economy," API; available at: http://www.api.org/Newsroom/hf-rules-usecon.cfm.

38. Ibid.

39. Ibid.

40. Energy in Depth; available at: http://www.energyindepth.org/tag/ byron-dorgan/ (accessed February 9, 2010).

41. "Power play: Fracturing plan wrong, indefensible," *The Oklahoman*, June 15, 2009; available at: http://newsok.com/power-play-fracturing-plan-wrong-indefensible/article/3377851?custom_click=headlines_widget.

42. Data available at: http://www.whitehouse.gov/issues/energy-and-environment (accessed February 9, 2010).

43. Louis Gray, "'Planned recession' could avoid catastrophic climate change," *Telegraph* (UK), September 30, 2009; available at: http://www.telegraph.co.uk/earth/earthnews/6248257/Planned-recession-could-avoid-catastrophic-climate-change.html.

44. See, e.g.: "Mafia link to Sicily wind farms probed," *Financial Times*, May 4, 2009; and "Top executives arrested in Italy wind farm probe," *Financial Times*, November 12, 2009.

45. See, e.g.: Robert Schlesinger, "New York Terrorism Trial Will Show U.S. at Its Best," *U.S. News & World Report*, November 24, 2009; available at: http://www.usnews.com/articles/opinion/2009/11/24/new-york-terrorism-trial-will-show-us-at-its-best.html.

46. James Morrison, "Bridge to Somewhere," *Washington Times*, December 17, 2008; available at: http://www.washingtontimes.com/news/2008/dec/17/embassy-row-78132610/.

47. Sometimes they are, sometimes they aren't; data available at: http://www.semiconductor-today.com/news_items/2008/AUGUST/FIRSTSOLAR_190808.htm.

48. Data available at: http://www.fact-index.com/m/mi/minitel.html.

49. Gregg Easterbrook, "The Dirty War Against Clean Coal," *New York Times*, June 28, 2009; available at: http://www.nytimes.com/2009/06/29/opinion/29easterbrook.html.

50. Steven F. Hayward, "Behold, Everything Old is New Again: The Great Energy Society," American Enterprise Institute, June 8, 2009; available at: http://blog.american.com/?p=1684.

51. See, e.g.: Calzada, et al., "Study of the effects on employment of public aid to renewable energy sources," op cit.

Chapter 10

1. See, e.g.: "Obama camp spies endgame in Oregon" AFP, May 16, 2008; available at: http://afp.google.com/article/ALeqM5h-wpxs1Re-8vx2Zk5xnYyg W1W67w.

2. Kenneth Walsh, "Carol Browner on Climate Change: 'The Science Has Just Become Incredibly Clear,'" op cit.

3. See, e.g.: Dave Burdick, "Obama Cranks Up White House Thermostat: 'You Could Grow Orchids In There,'" *Huffington Post*, January 29, 2009; available at: http://www.huffingtonpost.com/2009/01/29/obama-cranks-up-white-hou_n_162127.html.

4. See, e.g.: Peter Fairley, "Speed Bumps Ahead for Electric Vehicle Charging," *IEEE Spectrum*, January 2010, on how the prospect of recharging a relatively miniscule number of electric cars even at night threatens to bring the grid down; available at: http://spectrum.ieee.org/green-tech/advanced-cars/speed-bumps-ahead-for-electricvehicle-charging.

5. Floor Speech, Senator James Inhofe, "Nuclear Energy: Regulatory Challenges," June 3, 2009; available at: http://epw.senate.gov/public/index. cfm?FuseAction=Minority.Speeches&ContentRecord_id=abe5fcff-802a-23ad-45d6-040f2ac4ac9a&IsPrint=true.

6. See, e.g.: American Coal Foundation, "FAQs About Coal"; available at: http://www.teachcoal.org/aboutcoal/articles/faqs.html#howmuch (accessed February 6, 2010).

7. U.S. Energy Information Administration, "Net Generation by Energy Source: Total (All Sectors), Electric Power Monthly with data for October 2009, Table 1.1. Net Generation by Energy Source: Total (All Sectors), 1995 through October 2009," January 15, 2010; available at: http://www.eia.doe.gov/cneaf/electricity/epm/table1_1.html.

8. Ibid.

9. See, e.g.: Jeff St. John, "Obama calls for doubling renewable energy in three years," GreenTechMedia, January 8, 2009; available at: http://www.greentechmedia.com/articles/read/obama-calls-for-doubling-renewable-energy-in-three-years-5479/.

10. See, e.g.: Jeffrey Stinson, "Europe warms to nuclear energy," *USA Today*, June 4, 2007; available at: http://www.usatoday.com/news/world/environment/2007-06-03-euronukes_N.htm.

11. "Electricity prices for second semester 2008," Eurostat, Report 25/2009, published July 14, 2009; available at: http://epp.eurostat.ec.europa.eu/cache/ITY_OFFPUB/KS-QA-09-025/EN/KS-QA-09-025-EN.PDF; and "Average Retail Price of Electricity to Ultimate Customers by End-Use Sector, by State," U.S. Energy Information Administration, Electric Power Monthly with data for August 2009, November 13, 2009.

12. Per *NUS Consulting Group's International Electricity Report and Cost Survey 2006-2007*, cited in Power Engineering International, "Global Electricity Pricing: Ups and Downs of Global Electricity Prices," accessed at "Ups and downs of global electricity prices: the main conclusions of NUS Consulting Group's International Electricity Report and Cost Survey 2006-2007, are that the cost of electricity across the globe is at its most volatile for several decades, and this volatility is set to continue for the foreseeable future," July 1, 2007; available at: http://www.accessmylibrary.com/coms2/summary_0286-32775026_ITM.

13. See, e.g.: Gabriel Calzada álvarez, Raquel Merino Jara, Juan Ramón Rallo Julián, and José Ignacio García Bielsa, "Study of the effects on employment of public aid to renewable energy sources," King Juan Carlos University (Madrid, Spain), March 2009; available at: http://www.juandemariana.org/pdf/090327-employment-public-aid-renewable.pdf.

14. Louise Gray, "'Planned recession' could avoid catastrophic climate change," *The Telegraph* (UK), September 30, 2009; available at: http://www.telegraph.co.uk/earth/earthnews/6248257/Planned-recession-could-avoid-catastrophic-climate-change.html.

15. "Government's green energy plan may cost 17 times more than its benefits," *The Telegraph* (UK), August 10, 2009; available at: http://www.telegraph.co.uk/finance/newsbysector/energy/6001259/Governments-green-energy-plan-may-cost-17-times-more-than-its-benefits.html.

16. Elizabeth Rosenthal, "Europe Turns Back to Coal, Raising Climate Fears," *New York Times*, April 23, 2008; available at: http://www.nytimes.com/2008/04/23/world/europe/23coal.html?pagewanted=print.

17. See, e.g.: "Air Permit for Coal Power Plant on Navajo Land Sent Back to EPA," Environment News Service, September 25, 2009; available at: http://www.ens-newswire.com/ens/sep2009/2009-09-25-091.asp; see also analysis at "EPA Appeals Board Determines PSD Permit Applicant Must Consider IGCC in Coal Plant BACT Analysis," Troutman Sanders LLP, Washington D.C.; available at: http://www.troutmansandersenergyreport.com/2009/10/epa-appeals-board-determines-psd-permit-applicant-must-consider-igcc-in-coal-plant-bact-analysis/ .

18. Joel Kirkland, "Exxon-Xto Deal Forces Congress to Reconsider Natural Gas," Climate Wire, *New York Times*, January 25, 2010; available at: http://www.nytimes.com/cwire/2010/01/25/25climatewire-exxon-xto-deal-forces-congress-to-reconsider-94843.html.

19. James Taylor, "Ohio Dam Project Blocked By Activists and State EPA," *Environment & Climate News*, September 2009, Heartland Institute Chicago IL; available at: http://www.heartland.org/full/25800/Ohio_Dam_Project_Blocked_By_Activists_and_State_EPA.html.

20. "Italy recovering from big blackout," CNN, September 28, 2003; available at: http://www.cnn.com/2003/WORLD/europe/09/28/italy.blackout/index.html.

21. Christa Marshall, "Plant cancellations rise as decade ends," Climate Wire, December 24, 2009.

22. Ibid.

23. "100 Coal Plants Unplugged: 400 Million Tons of CO_2 Prevented!" Sierra Club; available at: http://www.sierraclub.org/coal/100plants/.

24. Margaret Kriz Hobson, "The Sierra Club's Burning Desire: Attorney Bruce Nilles discusses the group's efforts to block new coal-fired power plants," *National Journal*, September 5, 2009.

25. See, e.g.: "'The Clunkers of the Power Plant World': Old Coal-Fired Plants May Escape Climate Bill's Regulations," *Washington Post*, August 17, 2009; available at: http://www.washingtonpost.com/wp-dyn/content/article/2009/08/16/AR2009081601806.html.

26. Siobhan Hughes, "ACLU, Sierra Club Donor to Cut Funding," *Wall Street Journal*, December 10, 2009; article available at: http://newsits.com/?oFiZBiib.

27. See, e.g.: Bill Gertz, "China blocks U.S. from Cyber-warfare," *Washington Times*, May 12, 2009; available at: http://www.washingtontimes.com/news/2009/may/12/china-bolsters-for-cyber-arms-race-with-us//print/.

28. See, e.g.: "Air Permit for Coal Power Plant on Navajo Land Sent Back to EPA," Environment News Service, September 25, 2009; available at: http://www.ens-newswire.com/ens/sep2009/2009-09-25-091.asp.

29. See Nevada Clean Energy Campaign website, http://www.nevada-cleanenergy.com/about-us/; and "Coalition launches no new Blackstone coal campaign"; available at: http://www.nevadacleanenergy.com/go/news/coalition-launches-new-no-blackstone-coal-campaign/.

30. Data available at: http://www.noblackstonecoal.com/.

31. Dennis Wagner, "Tribe's environmental fight," *Arizona Republic*, November 2, 2009; available at: http://www.azcentral.com/arizonarepublic/news/articles/2009/11/02/20091102navajo1102.html.

32. Ibid.

33. See, e.g.: Gabriel Calzada álvarez, Raquel Merino Jara, Juan Ramón Rallo Julián, and José Ignacio García Bielsa, "Study of the effects on employment of public aid to renewable energy sources," op cit.

34. Data available at: http://www.sanjuancitizens.org/air/desertrock.shtml (accessed February 6, 2010).

35. These two Columbia University sociologists laid this out in a 1966 article in *The Nation*: Richard Cloward and Frances Piven, "The Weight of the Poor: A Strategy to End Poverty," *The Nation*, May 2, 1966.

36. Jeff Zeleny, "Obama Weighs Quick Undoing of Bush Policy," *New York Times*, November 9, 2008; available at: http://www.nytimes.com/2008/11/10/us/politics/10obama.html.

37. See, e.g.: Mike Lillis, "Bank of America to Cease Lending to Mountaintop Mining," *Washington Independent*, December 5, 2008; available at: http://washingtonindependent.com/21145/bank-of-america-to-cease-lending-for-mountaintop-mining. See also BofA's preening about pressure group awards for its capitulation and posturing at: http://environment.bankofamerica.com/press.jsp.

38. Amanda Carpenter, "Coal company cuts 500 jobs, blames environmentalists," Hot Button column, *Washington Times*, December 9, 2009; available at: http://www.washingtontimes.com/weblogs/back-story/2009/dec/09/coal-company-cuts-500-jobs-blames-environmentalist/?cpage=10.

39. Ibid.

40. *National Parks Conservation Association v. Ken Salazar, Secretary of the United States Department of the Interior, et al.*, United States District Court for the District of Columbia, Civil Action No. 09-00115, August 12, 2009. See analysis at Gwen Pinson, "Federal Judge Denies Obama Administration's Motion to Vacate the Stream Buffer Zone Rule," September 16, 2009; available at: http://www.martindale.com/environmental-law/article_Dinsmore-Shohl-LLP_797528.htm.

41. September 3, 2009, letter from EPA to U.S. Army Corps of Engineers; available at: http://www.epa.gov/region03/mtntop/pdf/Mining_COE_Spruce1_Ltr_3Sep09.pdf.

42. Amanda Carpenter, "Coal company cuts 500 jobs, blames environmentalists," op cit.

43. "United States Senate Report: THE MINGO LOGAN SPRUCE NO. 1 MINE – EPA IGNORES TRANSPARENCY, CONCERNS OF WEST VIRGINIA OFFICIALS. *EPA Permit Veto Stops 253 New Jobs, Threatens Energy Security*," January 14, 2010; available at: http://www.epw.senate.gov/public/index.cfm?FuseAction=Files.View&FileStore_id=ec6c3919-4949-457d-b0d3-6ca95e441494.

44. "Coal can use Oklahoma Senator's help," WBOY-TV, January 21, 2010; available at: http://wboy.com/story.cfm?func=viewstory&storyid=73795.

45. Patrick Reis, "RFK Jr., Massey CEO debate mountaintop mining before W.Va. audience," *E&E News*, January 22, 2010; available at: http://www.eenews.net/public/Greenwire/2010/01/22/3.

46. William Yeatman, "Obama's EPA delivers a lump of coal to Appalachia," *Richmond Times-Dispatch*, December 20, 2009; available at: http://www2.timesdispatch.com/rtd/news/opinion/commentary/article/ED-YEAT20_20091218-205207/312436/.

47. Patrick Reis, "Byrd's swipe at industry stirs strong reactions in W.Va.," Greenwire, December 7, 2009.

48. Patrick Reis, "Senators slam EPA over mountaintop removal," *E&E News*, October 21, 2009.

49. Darren Samuelsohn, "Sen. Rockefeller criticizes Obama proposals on tax breaks, regulation," Greenwire, February 4, 2010.

50. Ibid.

51. See EPA Letter to the Honorable Jo-Ellen Darcy, Assistant Secretary of the Army (Civil Works); available at: http://wvgazette.com/static/coal%20tattoo/epamtrlettersept2009.pdf. The National Mining Association repeated the 10 percent-plus figure in a statement submitted to a June 25 hearing of the U.S. Senate Environment Committee hearing of the Water and Wildlife Committee.

52. Ken Ward Jr., "EPA: All 79 mining permits need more review," *Charleston Gazette*, September 30, 2009; available at: http://blogs.wvgazette.com/coaltattoo/2009/09/30/epa-all-79-mining-permits-need-more-review/.

53. "Energy Facts Weekly," Week of January 18, 2010; available at: http://us1.campaign-archive.com/?u=29bc7d5d85828d574f86c157a&id=70e99ef407.

54. Editorial, "A Clearer Clean Water Act," *New York Times*, June 1, 2009.

55. "Obama Regulations Put Jobs, Energy Security, and Local Communities at Risk," June 11, 2009; available at: http://epw.senate.gov/public/index.cfm?FuseAction=Minority.PressReleases&ContentRecord_id=d0da9e19-802a-23ad-4a2a-f9841145b64c&Region_id=&Issue_id.

56. "Enviro groups tread lightly with Endangered Species Act in Appalachia," Greenwire, August 10, 2009.

57. Data available at: http://www.epa.gov/NSR/. See also "Making Sense of the New Source Review," *EHS Today*, May 13, 2004; available at: http://ehstoday.com/environment/ehs_imp_36991/.

58. "The New Climate Litigation," *Wall Street Journal*, December 28, 2009; available at: http://online.wsj.com/article/SB1000142405274870347870457461215062125742.html.

59. *Massachusetts v. EPA*, Scalia, J, Dissenting, N.2; available at: http://www.supremecourtus.gov/oral_arguments/argument_transcripts/05-1120.pdf.

60. Ibid.

61. "Too Hot to Handle: Fuel Temperatures, Global Warming, and the Political Question Doctrine," Professor Laurence H. Tribe, Joshua D. Branson, Tristan L. Duncan, Washington Legal Foundation, Critical Legal Issues Working Paper Series, Number 169, January 2010; available at: http://www.wlf.org/Upload/legalstudies/workingpaper/012910Tribe_WP.pdf.

62. William Tucker, "Going Nuclear," op cit.

63. U.S. Nuclear Statistics, Energy Information Administration, December 2009; available at: http://www.eia.doe.gov/cneaf/nuclear/page/operation/stat-operation.html.

64. See, e.g.: "US Eyes Nuclear Rebirth After Three Mile Island," AFP, March 27, 2009.

65. See, e.g.: Program Description, American Experience, "Meltdown at Three Mile Island," PBS; available at: http://www.pbs.org/wgbh/amex/three/filmmore/description.html.

66. See, e.g.: Jack Spencer, "Time to Fast-Track New Nuclear Reactors," Heritage Foundation, Web Memo # 2062, September 15, 2008; available at: http://www.heritage.org/Research/energyandenvironment/wm2062.cfm.   This remains true as of this writing.

67. See, e.g.: Ian Talley, "Congressional Budget Chief Says Climate Bill Would Cost Jobs," *Wall Street Journal*, October 14, 2009; available at: http://online.wsj.com/article/SB125555070414585571.html.

68. Media Release, "European Household Electricity Price Index for Europe (HEPI)," E-Control and VaasaETT, June 16, 2009; available at: http://www.e-control.at/portal/page/portal/medienbibliothek/presse/dokumente/pdfs/HEPI_Juni_englisch_final.pdf.

69. "Nuclear Power in France," World Nuclear Association; available at: http://www.world-nuclear.org/info/inf40.html.

70. See, e.g.: World Nuclear Association, "Plans For New Reactors World-wide," January 2010; available at: http://www.world-nuclear.org/info/inf17.html.

71. Anthony Faiola, "Nuclear power gains support," *Washington Post*, November 24, 2009; available at: http://www.washingtonpost.com/wp-dyn/content/article/2009/11/23/AR2009112303966.html?hpid=topnews.

72. "Open letter to the President's science advisor," February 1, 2010; available at: http://docs.google.com/fileview?id=0BzIU3Bd_MTpFN2ZjMjU3NDktNDNhNS00ZjM0LTk3Y2MtZjBkMmQyMWMxYTUx&hl=en (accessed February 6, 2010).

73. Testimony before the U.S. House Committee on Government Reform, March 21, 2007, a line also telegraphed in a *Rolling Stone* interview with Jann Wenner, "40th Anniversary Issue: Al Gore," November 15, 2007; available at: http://www.jannswenner.com/Archives/Anniversary_Issue.aspx.

74. Prepared Statement of Marvin S. Fertel, President and Chief Executive Officer, Nuclear Energy Institute, Hearing before the Committee on energy and Natural Resources, U.S. Senate, 111th Congress, March 18, 2009; available at: http://www.docstoc.com/docs/19441025/NUCLEAR-ENERGY-DEVEL-OPMENT——Senate-Congressional-Report-111th-Congress-2009.

75. Fred Barnes, "No Energy from this Executive," *The Weekly Standard*, June 15, 2009; available at: http://www.weeklystandard.com/Content/Public/Articles/000/000/016/588tpmuu.asp?page=2.

76. Remarks by President Barack Obama, Hradcany Square, Prague, Czech Republic, April 5, 2009; available at: http://www.whitehouse.gov/the_press_office/Remarks-By-President-Barack-Obama-In-Prague-As-Delivered/.

77. See, e.g.: "$13 billion later, nuclear waste site at dead end," Associated Press, March 5, 2009; available at: http://www.msnbc.msn.com/id/29534497/.

78. See, e.g.: "Obama Pushes Nuclear Energy to Boost Climate Bill," Associated Press, January 31, 2010; available at http://abcnews.go.com/Business/wireStory?id=9709897.

79. "President Obama Announces Money for Nuclear Power Plant," FOX news, February 16, 2010; available at: http://whitehouse.blogs.foxnews.com/2010/02/16/president-obama-announces-loan-for-nuclear-power-plant/.

80. "Obama's nuclear balancing act," Living on Earth, week of October 17, 2008; available at: http://www.loe.org/shows/segments.htm?programID=08-P13-00042&segmentID=2.

81. See, e.g.: "Steven Chu Energy Secretary Confirmation Hearing," January 13, 2009; available at: http://neinuclearnotes.blogspot.com/2009/01/steven-chu-energy-secretary.html.

82. William Tucker, "France is Completely Nuclear," *Terrestrial Energy* May 16, 2009; available at: http://www.terrestrialenergy.org/blog/?p=11.

83. Senator James Inhofe, "Nuclear Energy: Regulatory Challenges," Washington, D.C., June 3, 2009; available at: http://epw.senate.gov/public/index.cfm?FuseAction=Minority.Speeches&ContentRecord_id=abe5fcff-802a-23ad-45d6-040f2ac4ac9a&IsPrint=true.

84. See Press Release, "Inhofe, Vitter Request GAO Oversight of New Nuclear License Applications," U.S. Senate Committee on Environment and Public Works, July 7, 2009; available at: http://epw.senate.gov/public/index.cfm?FuseAction=Minority.PressReleases&ContentRecord_id=5599d04b-802a-23ad-40c6-24966681ef5d&Region_id=&Issue_id=.

85. Senator James Inhofe, "Nuclear Energy: Regulatory Challenges," Washington, D.C., June 3, 2009.

86. See, e.g.: "'Nuclear Pork' Cut Out of Final Recovery and Reinvestment Package," Environment News Service, February 12, 2009; available at: http://www.ens-newswire.com/ens/feb2009/2009-02-12-094.asp. See also Department of Energy: http://www.lgprogram.energy.gov/.

87. Mark Clayton, "Nuclear power's new debate: cost," *Christian Science Monitor*, August 13, 2009; available at: http://lists.econ.utah.edu/pipermail/energy/2009-August/000957.html.

88. Fueling Nuclear's Future; available at: http://www.usec.com/ (accessed February 6, 2010).

89. Katherine Ling, "U.S. denies loan guarantee for Ohio fuel-production plant," Greenwire, July 28, 2009.

90. Ibid.

91. Jonathan Riskind, "U.S. offers new cleanup jobs at ex-nuclear plant in Piketon," *Columbus Dispatch*, July 28, 2009; available at: http://www.dispatch.com/live/content/local_news/stories/2009/07/28/piketon?9.html?sid=101.

92. "American Centrifuge Manufacturers," USEC; available at: http://www.usec.com/americancentrifuge_manufacturing_rebuilding.htm.

93. See "Levy County Nuclear Plant, Levy County, FL," Project, No Project; available at: http://pnp.uschamber.com/2009/03/levy-county-nuclear-power-plant-levy-county-fl.html.

94. See, e.g.: Katherine Ling, "Industry lobbying fails to topple state moratoria, anti-nuke groups say," *E&E News*, August 27, 2009.

95. See, e.g.: "TVA scales back plans for Ala. plant," Greenwire, August 10, 2009.

96. See, e.g.: Greenwire, "Enviro groups petition to block TVA reactor," July 16, 2009.

97. See, e.g.: Katherine Ling, "Low-level waste emerges as hurdle for new reactors," Greenwire, March 16, 2009.

98. See, e.g.: Dave Flessner, "Tennessee: Estimates rise for nuclear plant," *Chattanooga Times Free Press*, December 12, 2008; available at: http://www.timesfreepress.com/news/2008/dec/12/tennessee-estimates-rise-nuclear-plant/.

99. Peter Behr, "Political Headwinds Hit a Reactor Project on the Chesapeake," ClimateWire, *New York Times*, September 18, 2009; available at: http://www.nytimes.com/cwire/2009/09/18/18climatewire-political-headwinds-hit-a-reactor-project-on-84809.html.

100. Senator James Inhofe, "Nuclear Energy: Regulatory Challenges," June 3, 2009.

101. See, e.g.: Matthew L. Wald, "Wind energy bumps into power grid's limits," *New York Times*, August 26, 2008; available at: http://www.nytimes.com/2008/08/27/business/27grid.html.

102. Ibid.

103. See, e.g.: Peter Behr, "Green groups want in on transmission planning for renewable power," Climate Wire, *New York Times*, September 9, 2009.

Conclusion

1. George F. Will, "Awash in Fossil Fuels," *Washington Post*, November 22, 2009; available at: http://www.washingtonpost.com/wp-dyn/content/article/2009/11/20/AR2009112002619.html.

INDEX

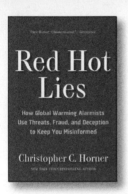